For Reference

Not to be taken

from this library

LIKE THE WIND

MAKES 4 SERVINGS

1½ pounds whiting

3 cups bread crumbs

½ cup olive oil

½ cup pignoli (pine nuts)

¼ cup chopped fresh parsley

2 cloves garlic, minced

1 box yellow, 1 box red fresh
  cherry tomatoes, cut in half

2¼ teaspoons kosher salt

1½ teaspoons freshly ground
  black pepper

Sea salt

1 pound orecchiette

The affordable Ford Model T motorcar was several years into production and pouring onto rudimentary new road systems in droves, while planes flew high above. The ease and wonder of these new modes of transport were reason enough to get up and go. The American impulse toward bigger, better, and faster inspired sport and utility in these endeavors as well, with the inaugural Indianapolis 500 car race and advent of air mail covering as-yet uncharted territory.

ORECCHIETTE WITH WHITING
MASSIMILIANO NANNI

Clean the whiting of bones, heads, and tails. Cut into 1-inch pieces and set aside. Toast the bread crumbs in a frying pan with ¼ cup of the oil over medium heat. Add the pignoli, parsley, and half of the garlic and sauté a few minutes until aromatic.

Start heating a large pot of water to boil. In a second frying pan, heat the remaining ¼ cup oil and cook the whiting with the cherry tomatoes, the remaining garlic, the kosher salt, and pepper.

When the pot of water boils, add a pinch of sea salt with the orecchiette. Cook 12 to 13 minutes to desired tenderness. Drain. Add the orecchiette to the frying pan containing the whiting and sauté 1 to 2 minutes. Toss with half of the toasted bread crumb mixture in a warmed casserole. Add the remaining bread crumb mixture atop each serving as it is plated.

Massimiliano Nanni *learned to cook in the seaside town of Rimini, Italy, where his mother was a restaurant manager. He brought his native food to New York with Piadina in Greenwich Village and the pizzeria Saraghina in Brooklyn's Bed-Stuy, a venture that allowed him to buy his dream truck: a 1965 Ford Econoline pickup. His latest venture, Celestino, draws inspiration from the cuisines of the seaside regions of Spain and Italy. The notion of staging an authentic Mediterranean seafood bistro in one of the borough's most landlocked areas is as quirky and inspiring as Massimiliano's signature smile.*

SHIPS IN THE NIGHT

1 pound sole fillets, skinned, cut in
   large chunks, and thoroughly chilled

Whites of 2 large eggs, plus more
   if needed

2½ cups heavy cream, chilled, plus
   ¼ cup more if needed

Kosher salt and freshly ground
   white pepper

1½ cups fresh white bread crumbs,
   lightly toasted

8 tablespoons unsalted butter, melted

The Titanic's spectacular end on her maiden voyage across the Atlantic needs no introduction. Rather than focus on her demise, we imagined a formidable final evening, with an elaborate menu and impeccable service. Chef Tower helped us set the scene by conjuring the spirit of his grandfather, a passenger on the ship, who might have chronicled that last meal with something like this:

"When the White Star liner RMS Titanic struck the iceberg at 11:30 p.m., we had finished the Crème Glacée and someone was ordering more Punch Romaine. I was halfway through my first cognac. Four hours after our great ship sank, the Carpathia picked up the ten people in our lifeboat and hustled us off in blankets to some available staterooms. The next day my valet discovered this menu folded in the breast pocket of my evening clothes, the same ones I was wearing in the lifeboat. The menu was titled: Banquet Offert par M. Bruce Ismay aux Passagers de 1ère Classe, R.M.S. Titanic."

Ismay was the president and director of the White Star line, which owned the *Titanic*, and his was the most important table in the dining room that night.

QUENELLES À LA LYONNAISE
JEREMIAH TOWER

Put the sole and egg whites in a food processor and puree, scraping the fish down into the center every few seconds to create a fine puree. Put the puree in a bowl in an ice water bath and beat in 2 cups of the cream in a steady stream. Beat for 2 minutes or until thoroughly incorporated, but do not overbeat. (This can be done in the food processor, but only quickly and with a sure hand so that the cream does not turn to butter.) Add ½ teaspoon each salt and pepper and mix again briefly. Cover the bowl and refrigerate for a couple of hours.

Fill a large wide saucepan or frying pan with at least 2 inches of water and bring to just below a simmer (180°F). Do not boil.

BANQUET OFFERT
– par –
M. Bruce Ismay
aux Passagers
de 1ère Classe,
RMS Titanic

Hors d'oeuvre variés

Huitres

**Pâté de saumon,
sauce Gribiche**

Filet mignon à la Lili

Quenelles à la Lyonnaise

**Rôti de mouton,
sauce menthe**

Rognons avec pommes paille

**Carottes nouvelles à la crème
et pommes nouvelles**

Punch Romaine

Pigeons rôtis, salade cresson

Asperges, sauce blanche

Pâté de foie gras

Salade de celeri

Pudding Waldorf

**Gelée de pêche à la
Chartreuse**

**Gâteau au chocolat
et à la vanille**

Crème glacée française

Poach a tablespoon of the quenelle mixture for 3 to 4 minutes and taste for seasoning. Add more salt and/or pepper if necessary. If the quenelle falls apart, add half an egg white and mix again. If it is too tight, mix in ¼ cup cream.

Scoop some of the quenelle mixture into a large soupspoon up along the edge of the bowl to get an oval shape and smooth surface. Dip a second spoon the same size into the hot water and slide it under the mixture, rolling it out into the water. Keep doing this to make 4 quenelles, keeping track of which the first one is. Poach for 8 minutes each, turning them over halfway through. When the first 4 quenelles are cooked, take them out, drain on paper towels, cover with wet paper towels, and refrigerate. Repeat with the rest of the mixture.

Meanwhile, preheat the oven to 350°F.

Mix the bread crumbs with almost all the butter and season lightly. Brush the bottom of a gratin dish with the remaining butter, and put the quenelles in the dish ¼ inch apart. Pour ½ cup cream over the quenelles and cover them with the buttered bread crumbs. Bake for 25 minutes or until the quenelles are puffed up and hot all the way through and the bread crumbs golden. Serve immediately. ✤

Jeremiah Tower *began his culinary career in 1972 as co-owner and executive chef of Chez Panisse in Berkeley, California. He opened and owned several other successful and highly acclaimed restaurants in San Francisco, Hong Kong, Singapore, and Seattle, and has written several award-winning and best-selling cookbooks. Jeremiah is the winner of the 1996 Outstanding Chef of the Year award from the James Beard Foundation, and he is one of a handful of keystone personalities who together shaped and defined food, farming, and dining as we know it today.*

LIVING ON BORROWED WATER

The Los Angeles–Owens River Aqueduct was completed in 1913, under fire from detractors who preferred the river choose its own course. Using only the force of gravity, the aqueduct conveyed water 238 miles from the Sierra Nevada, to provide developers with the resources to develop the San Fernando Valley and Los Angeles through World War II. An unimaginable bounty of fresh produce, livestock, and fowl was sustained by this industrious, though contentious, borrowed water source.

CHICKEN AU RIESLING WITH TANGERINE SALAD

DANIEL MATTERN & ROXANA JULLAPAT

Prepare the chicken: Rinse the chicken thoroughly under cold running water and pat dry with paper towels. Season liberally with about 1 tablespoon of the salt and the pepper, going somewhat heavier on the meatier parts such as the breast and the thighs. Let the chicken sit at room temperature for 30 minutes.

Set an oven rack in the middle position and preheat the oven to 400°F. Cut each onion into 8 thick wedges and place on the bottom of a 12-inch skillet or a roasting pan slightly bigger than the chicken. (The onions will impart flavor and act as a roasting rack.) Place the chicken on top of the cut onions. Tuck the wing tips behind the back and truss the legs with butcher's twine.

Melt the butter in a small nonreactive saucepan. Whisk in the Riesling and ¼ cup tangerine juice. Stir in the garlic, rosemary, thyme, and remaining teaspoon of salt. Pour all over the chicken.

Put the chicken in the oven and set a 15-minute timer. Once the timer goes off, pull the chicken from the oven and generously spoon the butter mixture at the bottom of the pan all over the chicken. Place the chicken back in the oven and set another 15-minute timer. Repeat this basting process at least two more

MAKES 4 SERVINGS

For the chicken

One 4- to 4½-pound chicken
1 tablespoon plus 1 teaspoon kosher salt
½ teaspoon freshly ground black pepper
2 small onions, peeled
8 tablespoons unsalted butter
½ cup Riesling (on the dry side)
¼ cup freshly squeezed tangerine juice
8 garlic cloves, peeled and mashed with the back of a chef's knife
½ cup loosely packed fresh rosemary leaves
¼ cup loosely packed fresh thyme leaves

For the tangerine salad

6 cups watercress, loosely packed
1 tablespoon minced shallot
½ cup freshly squeezed tangerine juice
¼ cup extra virgin olive oil
Kosher salt and freshly ground black pepper
6 seedless tangerines, peeled and sectioned

Special equipment

Instant-read thermometer

times. Depending on the size of your chicken and performance of your oven, the chicken will be ready in 45 minutes to 1 hour. The butter and the sugar content in the wine will encourage the chicken skin to brown beautifully. The chicken is properly cooked when an instant-read thermometer inserted between the thigh and the breast reads 165°F. Remove the chicken from the oven. Let sit for 10 minutes before carving.

Prepare the salad: Place the watercress in a large bowl. In a smaller bowl, whisk together the shallot, ½ cup tangerine juice, and olive oil to form an emulsified vinaigrette. Toss the watercress gently with the vinaigrette, season with salt and pepper to taste, and transfer to a serving dish. Garnish the salad with the tangerine slices. Serve alongside the chicken while it is still warm, although it will be just as delicious at room temperature. Enjoy! 🦋

In a land renowned for its dependable sunshine and bursting with fresh produce, husband-and-wife team **Daniel Mattern** *and* **Roxana Jullapat** *are taking full advantage at Cooks County in Los Angeles. Steps from the famed West Hollywood farmers' market, the duo serves up some of the most inventive, elegantly prepared, market-driven fare in town. With a common past at AOC, Campanile, Lucques, AMMO, and Portland's Clarklewis, Daniel and Roxana have honed their symbiotic crafts and forged a bold vision of farm-fresh ingenuity softened by rustic charm.*

STEP HIGH, STOOP LOW, AND LEAVE YOUR DIGNITY OUTSIDE

MAKES 1 COCKTAIL

1¾ ounces Ransom WhipperSnapper whiskey
1 ounce Kronan Swedish Punsch
¼ ounce Byrrh
Cracked ice
1 lemon peel for mixing
1 long lemon peel twist to garnish

"These ingredients are not an obvious combination, but the juxtaposition of such disparate elements that somehow form a very harmonious whole seemed to me to be the very essence of what that counterinstitution the Dil Pickle Club was all about—the same way it brought such disparate types of people together and somehow got them to commune under one roof."

Former Wobblies organizer John "Jack" Jones turned a hole-in-the wall in Chicago's Tooker Alley into a laborers' meeting place—the Dil Pickle Club—that soon became the epicenter of a convergent arts and countercultural movement at the height of the Chicago Renaissance. A sign by the door reading ELEVATE YOUR MIND TO A LOWER LEVEL OF THINKING beckoned the era's radical activists, artists, and bohemian authors inside.

"HIFALUTIN" COCKTAIL
DEL PEDRO

Combine the first 3 ingredients in a mixing glass filled with cracked ice and stir. Apply lemon essence by squeezing the peel of 1 lemon directly into the mixing glass as you add the liquid, drop it in, and leave it in there while you stir the drink. Strain into a chilled cocktail glass, garnished with the long peel of other lemon.

"The drink was conceived with 1914 America in mind as well as the 'nobrow' nature of the Dil Pickle Club, which, as far as we know, was founded that year," Del says. "I chose the WhipperSnapper whiskey as a stand-in for the spirit of the country itself at that time—young, rawboned, exciting, and full of personality. I also felt that it fairly represented the irreverent but high-quality nature of the Dil Pickle Club. I added two very 'old world' products— the Swedish Punsch and the Byrrh."

*A walking encyclopedia on the Dil Pickle Club and a myriad historical subjects, **Del Pedro** has been behind bars in New York City for almost twenty-five years, from a Harlem dive to an iconoclastic Greenwich Village bar and restaurant, a world-famous SoHo cocktail palace, and now his own joint, Tooker Alley in Brooklyn.*

OVER THE CHERRY TREE

Decades ahead of the space age, physicist and inventor Robert Goddard envisioned rocket travel to the moon. As a boy reading H. G. Wells's *The War of the Worlds*, he became transfixed with the sky and built a ladder up the side of a cherry tree, from the top of which he dreamed of impossible feats of flight. He later recounted, "I was a different boy when I descended the tree from when I ascended. Existence at last seemed very purposive."

When he filed a pair of patents laying the groundwork for spaceflight in 1914—one for a multistage rocket design, and another for the first liquid-fueled rocket—his impossible dream seemed close enough to touch.

CHERRY TREE DREAM CAKE
ALLISON KAVE & KEAVY BLUEHER

Prepare the cake: Preheat the oven to 350°F. Butter and flour a 9 by 13-inch glass baking dish.

In a stand mixer or large bowl, whisk together the flour, sugar, baking powder, and salt. Beat in the butter until it takes on a sandy texture. Beat in the egg whites one at a time, blending fully after each addition, and scrape down the sides of the bowl each time. Finish with the whole egg and beat well to incorporate. In a small bowl, whisk together the sour cream, vanilla, and amaretto. Drizzle into the batter in three additions, beating well and scraping down the sides of the bowl after each addition. Beat until the batter is light and fluffy. Fold in the cherries. Pour the batter into the prepared baking dish.

Bake in the center of the oven, rotating once halfway through, for 30 to 40 minutes. Prick the center of the cake with a toothpick or cake tester to ensure that it comes out dry. Remove from the oven to cool. Prick the surface all over with a fork.

Prepare the jelly layer: In a medium saucepan, heat the cherry juice with the gelatin over medium heat, until the gelatin is

MAKES 12 TO 16 SERVINGS

For the cake

12 tablespoons unsalted butter, softened, plus more for the pan

12 ounces (3 cups) cake flour, plus more for the pan

12 ounces (1¾ cups) granulated sugar

1 tablespoon baking powder

½ teaspoon fine sea salt

4 large egg whites

1 large egg

1 cup sour cream

1 teaspoon vanilla extract

¼ cup amaretto liqueur or 1 teaspoon almond extract

1 cup fresh cherries, pitted and halved

For the jelly layer

2 cups cherry juice or water

Four ¼-ounce envelopes unflavored gelatin

1½ cups Cherry Heering liqueur or kirsch

For the topping

2 cups heavy cream

½ cup confectioners' sugar

¼ cup bourbon

½ cup blanched almonds, toasted and chopped

¼ cup brandied cherries (optional)

"It's loosely inspired by Lane cakes, which were very popular in the South. It's also baked in a Pyrex dish, a nod to another major invention of the time."

dissolved, about 5 minutes. Remove from the heat and stir in the liqueur until fully blended. Pour the jelly mixture over the surface of the cake, and refrigerate until set, at least 2 hours. The jelly will seep into the cake and set inside the crumb.

Prepare the topping: When the cake is ready, whip the heavy cream with the confectioners' sugar and bourbon until stiff. Spread the whipped cream over the surface of the cake, and top with chopped almonds and brandied cherries, if desired. Slice and serve.

> *"Keavy and I wanted to pay homage to [Goddard's beloved tree] by incorporating cherry flavors into our dessert," Allison says. "And of course, we've got to make it boozy!"*

Who says cake and pie can't get along? **Keavy Blueher** *of Kumquat Cupcakery and* **Allison Kave** *of First Prize Pies teamed up in 2012 to bridge the gap between the spirituous and the sweet. Under the moniker Butter & Scotch, Keavy and Allison have devised Brooklyn's first dessert and craft cocktail bar, with a focus on seasonal ingredients and fun, nostalgic creations blurring the line between bar glass and bakeware.*

SHANGHAI SURPRISE

Fashion in the early 1910s was highly influenced by the style and colors of the Orient. From Coco Chanel to Charles Worth, Erté to Poiret, designers inspired escapism from an impending war that would mark the end of innocence. Taking a cue from the costume of the Ottoman Empire and Asia, the binding corsets of the previous decade gave way to looser, more playful shapes, hemlines, and patterns, fueling a craze for vividly colored fabrics, fluid silhouettes, and mysterious fragrances that transformed the chaste, feminine palette of the Western woman into something flowing, vibrant, and free spirited. This transformation dovetailed with the exotic kaleidoscope of spices and flavors that had been making its way to American shores from the East for centuries. Some of these worldly treasures are found in *zongzi*, often referred to as "Chinese tamales": traditional glutinous rice bundles stuffed with cured pork belly, juicy Chinese sausage, orbs of salted duck egg yolks, or dried delectables such as baby shrimp and scallops, beautifully wrapped in aromatic bamboo leaves.

GRANDMA HSIANG'S SHANGHAINESE ZONGZI
DANIELLE CHANG

🌾 ***Prepare the meat filling:*** Cut the pork belly into 1 by 1 by 2-inch pieces. Combine the soy sauces, rice wine, cinnamon, star anise, and five-spice powder. Stir, add the pork belly, cover, and marinate overnight or for at least 4 hours.

Prepare the rice: Rinse and drain. Add the soy sauce, stir, and let stand at room temperature overnight or for at least 2 hours.

Prepare the leaves: Rinse and soak in water at room temperature overnight or in hot water for 30 minutes.

Assemble and cook the zongzi: Place two leaves on a work surface and overlap to make a 5-inch piece. Fold 2 to 3 inches of the

MAKES 12 ZONGZI

For the meat filling
2 pounds pork belly
3 tablespoons soy sauce
2 tablespoons dark soy sauce
2 tablespoons rice wine
One 1-inch cinnamon stick
2 pieces star anise
1 teaspoon five-spice powder

For the rice
3 cups sweet rice
2 tablespoons soy sauce

For the leaves
24 bamboo leaves (dried, available in Asian markets)
Twelve 3-foot lengths cotton string

stem inward to form a straight edge. Ultimately, you want to create a pyramid-shaped dumpling. Cup the rectangular end, place 1 tablespoon of rice in the "cup," and spread the rice about 3 inches toward the leaf tip. Place 2 pieces of meat over the rice. Add 2 tablespoons rice to cover the meat so that the meat is completely enveloped. Bring the other part of the leaf over the rice-filled cup. Tie a string lightly around the zongzi, so that the rice can expand during the cooking process.

Place the zongzi in a large pot. Add water to cover. Cover the pot, bring to a boil, then simmer for about 1 hour. Turn the heat down to low and cook for 3 hours more. Make sure there is enough water to cover the zongzi at all times. As the zongzi cook, the luscious fillings meld with the sticky rice, forge with the bamboo leaves, and fill your kitchen with anticipation—moist with the scent of the bamboo leaves blended with equal parts savory and sweetness.

When the zongzi are ready, cut off the string, unfold, and dig in! The zongzi can be kept refrigerated for a week or frozen for months. ✺

"When I was growing up," Danielle says, "my home was always stocked with zongzi, as they keep an eternity in the freezer and are always appreciated on a rainy Sunday.

"The Shanghainese version, which is what my grandmother fed us as children, is a streamlined—and what I consider to be a perfected—version of this popular Chinese treat. There are at least 1,001 recipes for zongzi, but to my mind, my grandmother's is the most delicious. Even at ninety-six years of age, she is still blessed with the good health to make these little gifts for her five children, along with her myriad grandchildren and ever-expanding tribe of great-grandchildren."

Danielle Chang *is the founder of Luckyrice, a culinary agency based in New York, and creator of the Luckyrice Festival, a national celebration of Asian cultures and cuisines. Prior to starting Luckyrice, Danielle was the CEO of fashion and lifestyle company Vivienne Tam.*

"A FINE INSTITUTION"

Jesse Lynch Williams's comedic play *Why Marry?* introduced the radical notion that a couple could live together happily outside the binding contract of marriage. The production, which opened at the Astor Theatre in New York City, was awarded the first Pulitzer Prize for drama.

We asked Kelly Hogan for a main course that echoes the sentiment of the play, featuring two prominent, distinct flavors or ingredients with harmonious interplay that complement one another without being fully integrated or obscured by blending together. Her delicious marriage of flavors might have changed the minds of Williams's protagonists, sending them racing for the altar, but only if it were set with two platters, a pair of good knives, and a wine decanter.

BREADED PORK CHOPS WITH TART CHERRY CARAWAY PORT WINE SAUCE

KELLY HOGAN

Prepare and brine the meat: Put all the ingredients (except the meat and bacon grease and oil) into a heavy-duty gallon plastic freezer bag, seal it, and shake well to blend the ingredients and dissolve the salt. Put your meat into the brine and seal the bag, removing as much air as possible, then shake it up and get everything acquainted in there. Leave it to sit for about 45 minutes, flipping the bag and shaking it a couple of times during the brining. I leave my brining bag out on the counter, because I want my meat to be room temperature when I fry it.

Prepare the breading: Put the caraway and poppy seeds into a large, deep dry frying pan over medium heat. Toast the seeds for 5 to 7 minutes, until aromatic, stirring and watching constantly.

SERVES 4 HUNGRY PEOPLE, OR 6 SAD DIETERS

For the brine and meat
2 cups water

3 tablespoons kosher or coarse sea salt

1 tablespoon whole cloves

2 teaspoons freshly ground black pepper

1 teaspoon onion powder

One 6-inch sprig rosemary, plus
  ½ teaspoon dried rosemary leaves,
  crushed to release flavor

4 bay leaves

6 to 8 bone-in pork chops,
  about ¾ inch thick (see Notes)

Bacon grease and vegetable oil, for frying
  (see Notes)

For the breading
2 tablespoons caraway seeds

1 teaspoon poppy seeds

3 cups day-old seedless rye bread crumbs,
  coarsely ground in a food processor

2 cups all-purpose flour

3 tablespoons kosher or course sea salt

1 tablespoon freshly ground black pepper

1 tablespoon ground white pepper

1½ tablespoons onion powder

For the cherry sauce

2 or 3 shallots, chopped fine

1 cup tawny port wine

Juice and grated zest of
  1 medium orange

2 cups tart cherries in unsweetened
  juice, drained and gently mashed
  just a bit (reserve juice)

1 or 2 dashes red wine vinegar

1 teaspoon caraway seeds

1 medium apple, peeled and diced small

½ cup golden raisins (soaked in hot
  water to plump, then drained)

½ cup low-sodium chicken broth

Kosher salt and fresh ground
  black pepper

Special equipment

Brown paper bag

Grind with a spice grinder or mortar and pestle until very fine, like flour.

Put your ground seeds into a brown paper grocery bag with the remaining breading ingredients, and shake everything up to blend. Since toasting and grinding the caraway and poppy seeds can be labor intensive, save any leftover breading flour in a plastic freezer bag for making this recipe another time.

Prepare the pork chops: After 45 minutes, remove your pork chops from the brine, pat dry with paper towels, and set aside on a plate to air-dry for about 15 minutes.

Preheat your oven to 200°F and set up an ovenproof platter covered in paper towels or, even better, a wire rack on a rimmed baking sheet to place inside the oven. This will be for keeping your fried chops warm while you make the sauce.

After your pork chops have air-dried, place them one at a time into the breading bag, roll the bag closed, and shake it around to coat each chop. Keep adding chops one at a time to the bag and shaking. Check to make sure the chops are not sticking together and that all are coated, and leave 'em in the bag.

Now . . . let's fry!

Disclaimer: I'm not trying to insult anybody by going into such minute frying detail here, but I want you to avoid eating greasy pork chops. And because I can't stand doing dishes, I just use the same pan that I used to toast my caraway and poppy seeds. This whole deal is gonna be a one-pan affair, so get your splatter shield ready and here we go . . .

Into your large deep frying pan, put 1 heaping tablespoon bacon grease for a nice smoky flavor. Melt the bacon grease over medium heat, then add enough vegetable oil to cover the bottom of your frying pan to about ¼ inch deep. Don't use olive oil for this—it smokes when you try to fry with it over high heat.

Increase heat to medium-high and get your oil very hot but not smoking—you gotta watch it like a hawk! Now, grab a pork chop out of the breading bag, shaking gently to remove excess flour. Carefully lay it into the grease to see if the oil is hot enough. It should make a big "fsssssh!" sizzling sound and start bubbling around your chop right away. If you're getting the proper sizzle, add a few more chops, leaving at least an inch between them in the pan. If not, increase the heat (you can keep cooking what is now the sacrificial first chop), wait another minute, and then add more chops when the grease is hot enough. Cook in batches of 3 or 4 chops, always letting the oil get back up to cooking temp before putting in the next batch.

Cook each chop until nicely browned, about 3 minutes a side, adjusting for thicker or thinner chops. Move each one onto your prepared rack or platter to keep warm in the oven.

Some folks like to test the cooked temperature of pork to make sure it's up to 165°F, but I hate overdone pork and I'm still alive. I usually cut into one of the thicker chops to peek and make sure it's cooked all the way through.

When all your chops are fried up nice and brown and are in the oven, you can start your cherry sauce.

Prepare the cherry sauce: In your frying pan, pour out all but about 3 tablespoons of your frying oil, making sure to leave the browned pork bits in the pan. Over medium heat, sauté your shallots in the oil until softened and aromatic, about a minute or so.

Increase the heat to medium-high and add the port wine, orange juice (about ⅓ cup), ¼ cup of the cherry juice, and a couple of dashes of red wine vinegar, to taste, whisking and scraping up the browned bits to incorporate them into the liquid. Cook 3 or 4 minutes.

Add the cherries, caraway seeds, orange zest, diced apple, golden raisins, and chicken broth and bring to a boil. Reduce the heat and while whisking, simmer the sauce down until it is thickened and reduced by about a third in volume and coats a wooden spoon (about 10 minutes), all the while adjusting to taste with salt and pepper and/or more vinegar, more wine, or more juices.

After the cherry sauce is thickened and swerved to your taste druthers, serve it spooned generously over your fried pork chops, with spaetzle, buttered egg noodles, or savory pierogi on the side.

NOTE: I was thinking about 1917 WWI wartime conservation and went with a cheap-but-decent pack of assorted pork chops,

"Pork and cherries, cookin' in a pan

Two different tastes, goin' hand-in-hand

Fry chops early, simmer sauce late

They'll meet and marry on your dinner plate!"

> "If you're not 'country' enough to have a bacon grease can in your fridge, then fry up a few pieces of bacon for the grease . . . and sneak-eat the bacon all by yourself as a 'cook's reward.'"

❈

but you can go hog wild with any sort of pork chop, cutlet, or pork steak—just keep in mind that these will be breaded and pan-fried, so try not to choose anything too thick.

NOTE: I used a jar of Door County cherries, but you can use fresh or unsweetened canned or frozen cherries. If frozen, soak them in a little hot water to make juice.

> *"It may sound weird coming from a dedicated 'and then there's Maude!' feminist like myself,"* Kelly says, *"but I was greatly inspired for this recipe by the economical tips and humor and illustrations in the 1917 book* A Thousand Ways to Please a Husband with Bettina's Best Recipes: The Romance of Cookery and Housekeeping.*"*

Kelly Hogan *is the singer from Atlanta with pipes of gold who, having built her musician muscles singing with Andrew Bird and M. Ward, and touring with Robyn Hitchcock, migrated to Chicago in the late nineties and joined the band of acclaimed singer-songwriter Neko Case. Her catalog of solo recordings will stand the test of time beside those of some of music's greatest heartbreaking crooners.*

ALFRED & GEORGIA & DIEGO & FRIDA

Alfred Stieglitz did much to canonize photography as a legitimate art form. He is perhaps best known for his sensual, erotic, and deeply personal photographs of artist Georgia O'Keeffe, who was twenty-three years his junior. Shot during their early affair and subsequent marriage, the photos portray her in black-and-white, as a beautiful, relaxed, dreamlike, voluptuous form. The couple traveled from New York and New Mexico with famous friends like Frida Kahlo, Diego Rivera, and Tina Modotti. Sex, drugs, and art all had a place in the decadent scene populated by artists, intellectuals, and revolutionaries. Theirs was a dreamy, placid existence—which seemed far away from the world war that was raging across Europe—colored by the Southwest's hazy, desert sun setting somewhere between reality and fantasy.

CALDO DE OSTIONES DEL 1918
BARBARA SIBLEY

Prepare the stock: In a large stockpot, heat the oil over medium heat. Add the onion and garlic and sauté until the onion is translucent. Add the wine and cook to reduce by one-half. Add the fish bones and sauté until the meat on them begins to become opaque. Add the carrots, bay leaves, epazote, thyme, peppercorns, cloves, and jalapeño. Cover with water, about 6 cups, and add the salt. Turn the heat to high and bring to a boil. As soon as the stock boils, reduce the heat to low and simmer for half an hour. Skim the foam off the stock as needed.

Remove from the heat and cool until the oil floats to the top. Skim off and discard the oil. Strain the stock through a colander lined with wet cheesecloth and reserve.

Prepare the puree sofrito: In a blender, combine the onion, garlic, chipotles, adobo, and olive oil. Blend until smooth. Add the tomatoes and continue to blend until liquefied. Strain through cheesecloth and set aside.

MAKES 6 SERVINGS

For the fish stock (see note)
2 tablespoons extra virgin olive oil
½ cup coarsely chopped onion
4 cloves garlic, chopped
1 cup white wine, such as verdejo
2 pounds red snapper bones and heads
2 carrots, chopped
2 bay leaves
1 sprig epazote
1 teaspoon fresh thyme leaves
1 teaspoon whole black peppercorns
4 whole cloves
1 jalapeño, sliced
Water to cover (about 6 cups)
2 tablespoons kosher salt

For the puree sofrito
½ cup chopped onion
2 cloves garlic
2 chipotle chilies in adobo
2 tablespoons adobo from chipotles
3 tablespoons extra virgin olive oil
5 ripe plum tomatoes, cut up

For the sopa de ostiones
3 tablespoons olive oil
1 cup diced peeled russet potatoes (½-inch dice)
½ cup diced onion (½-inch dice)
½ cup diced carrot (½-inch dice)
1 cup diced fennel (½-inch dice)
2½ cups fish stock
1 teaspoon fresh thyme leaves
½ teaspoon fresh oregano leaves
⅛ teaspoon ground white pepper
½ teaspoon saffron threads
1 teaspoon kosher salt
½ cup chopped fresh parsley
16 ounces shucked oysters, with their liquor (about 5 oysters per serving)

Prepare the sopa de ostiones: In a large stockpot over medium heat, add the olive oil and vegetables in this order, sautéing each lightly for a few minutes before adding the others: potatoes, onions, carrots, and fennel. Stir constantly and make sure the vegetables do not brown at all. Be careful not to overcook; they must be firm and slightly crunchy.

Pour in all the puree sofrito and fry until the tomato becomes a deep red and is cooked through. Lower the heat to low and continue to cook until the puree is reduced by about a third. Whisk in the fish stock and bring to a low boil. Reduce the heat and cook for about 5 minutes.

When the vegetables are tender but not overcooked, stir in the thyme, oregano, white pepper, and saffron. Allow them to flavor the soup. Taste and adjust salt as needed. Keep in mind that some oysters are more salty than others. Stir in chopped parsley.

Increase the heat to medium and add the oysters to the soup one at a time. Drop them gently into the soup to poach until they are opaque and slightly firm to the touch. Do not overcook.

Ladle into bowls and garnish as desired with sliced avocado and parsley, fennel fronds, or epazote. In my house, it was traditional to drop a pearl from the oyster into each bowl of soup. Serve with lime wedges. 🪰

NOTE: You will have fish stock left over. Cover well and refrigerate for a week or freeze for up to 3 months. The soup base may be made the day ahead and reheated before dinner, when the oysters are added at the last minute and poached. In this case, care must be made not to overcook the vegetables.

Barbara Sibley *was born and raised in Mexico City, where she collected traditional, rare, and ancient Mexican recipes. Her New York restaurant career began at La Tulipe, a* New York Times *three-star French restaurant. In 2000, she opened La Palapa Cocina Mexicana, which has been awarded the "Distintivo" by Sabores Autenticos de Mexico Foundation. In 2009, she cowrote a cookbook of Mexican small plates, titled* Antojitos.

For the garnish
Sliced avocado
Parsley sprigs
Fennel fronds
Epazote leaves
Pearls
Lime wedges

Special equipment
Cheesecloth

BETTER THAN SLICED BREAD

The still-indispensable automatic pop-up toaster was patented by Charles Strite in 1919. A modified version of his design would become the Model A-1-A Toastmaster, capable of browning bread on both sides simultaneously with a heating element set on a timer and ejecting the toast when finished. The wonder that was machine-sliced, machine-wrapped bread would not follow for a decade more. But Chef Corey Cova has a use for the revolutionary automated toasting device that is "better than sliced bread."

SLICED FOIE GRAS WITH BUTTERED TOAST SOUBISE, BLACKBERRY-PORT MOSTARDA, CRISPY PORK, AND SOFT BLUE CHEESE

COREY COVA

Prepare the pickled mustard seeds: Cook all the ingredients in a narrow pot on medium heat, stirring occasionally, until the seeds have plumped and there is little liquid left. Cool. Store in a nonreactive container.

Prepare the mostarda: Cook the blackberries, sugar, and water over medium-high heat until reduced to a syrup. Add the port and reduce to a syrup again. Finish by adding the lime juice and mustard seeds. Cool to room temperature. The final mostarda, cooled, should resemble a nice jam.

Prepare the buttered toast soubise: Melt the butter in a pot. Add the onion and salt and cook slowly, not allowing the onion to brown, for 45 minutes to 1 hour. Transfer the cooked onion and butter to a blender, add the toast, and blend on high speed for 2 minutes. Before stopping the blender, check to see if the sauce

MAKES 4 SERVINGS

For the pickled mustard seeds
1 cup yellow mustard seeds
1 cup cider vinegar
2 cups water
1 cup sugar

For the blackberry-port mostarda
6 ounces (1 cup) blackberries
2 ounces (¼ cup plus 1 tablespoon) sugar
1 cup water
1 cup fine tawny port
Juice of 1 lime
2 tablespoons pickled mustard seeds

For the buttered toast soubise
10 tablespoons unsalted butter
1 large onion, diced small
1 tablespoon kosher salt
1½ pieces white, sliced bread, toasted

For the braised pork and foie gras
1 quart beer
1 tablespoon chili flakes
2 tablespoons kosher salt, plus more for seasoning
1 tablespoon fennel seeds
4 cloves garlic, chopped
½ onion, chopped
1 sprig thyme
1 sprig rosemary
3 tablespoons cider vinegar
8 ounces pork belly
Eight 1-ounce portions foie gras
Salt
Vegetable oil

For serving

Four ¾-ounce portions soft blue cheese, such as Gorgonzola

1 bunch tart sorrel or cress

has broken; if so, slowly add some water until the mixture is smooth. Strain through a fine-mesh sieve. Refrigerate.

Prepare the braised pork and foie gras: Preheat the oven to 375°F.

In a small lidded roasting pan, combine the beer, chili flakes, salt, fennel seeds, garlic, onion, thyme, rosemary, and vinegar. Add the pork. Cover tightly with a lid, and braise in the oven for 2 hours or until exceptionally tender. Once cooked, remove the pork and chill it for 8 hours or longer. Slice the pork in ½-inch pieces. (Reserve the liquid for another use, such as another braising liquid or a soup.)

Season the foie gras and pork with salt. In a very hot pan, sear both sides of the foie gras for 10 to 15 seconds per side, until brown. In another hot pan with a little oil, brown both sides of the pork slices until crispy. Once the meats are cooked, rest them for a couple of minutes on a paper towel.

To plate: Gently heat the soubise. Smear the soubise on four plates, and begin to layer: 1 slice foie gras, topped by a slice of pork, then a portion of cheese, then a good spoonful of the mostarda on the cheese as well as a few drops on the plate. Finish the dish by topping the stack with a slice of foie gras, and garnishing with whatever greens you might have. 🌿

Northern California native **Corey Cova** *got his start serving as a culinary specialist in the US Navy. He landed in East Harlem after a stint with Michael Symon and schooling at the Culinary Institute of America. His neighborhood hot spots Earl's Beer & Cheese, ABV, and Dough Loco catch diners off guard with uncommon ingredient pairings. Corey effortlessly conflates a century of culinary tastes, trends, and techniques with his delightful sense of humor and affinity for nostalgia, and his belief that all food should comfort.*

HOW DRY I AIN'T . . .

Prohibition began on January 17, 1920, when the Eighteenth Amendment to the Constitution of the United States went into effect, giving rise to bathtub gin, speakeasies, Pink Ladies, rum running, brass knuckles, and the Roaring Twenties. A sprawling subculture of cavalier sex and illicit drugs developed, and organized crime came to power to provide illegal potables to a clandestine market of hard men and fast women. The spit curls of the Chicago jazz baby, the roar of the tommy gun, and the bottomless thirst for more are all served straight up, and cold as ice.

MAKES 1 COCKTAIL

2 ounces Tito's vodka
1 ounce Dolin Blanc vermouth
2 dashes Peychaud's bitters
Pernod absinthe rinse
Lemon twist

"BYE-BYE, ALBATROSS" COCKTAIL

TIFFANY SHORT

Stir the first three ingredients together with ice. Strain into a chilled cocktail glass rinsed with absinthe. Garnish with a large lemon twist.

Texas native **Tiffany Short***'s career in cocktails and comestibles took off in Washington, Virginia, at the James Beard Award–winning Inn at Little Washington. In 2011, Tiffany found herself in New York, shaking drinks at Joe's Pub, one of the city's most loved music and performance venues, where she opened a cocktail lounge upstairs in the newly constructed mezzanine of the Public Theater. Short has caught nothing but raves: the* New York Times *wrote, "Her bubbly enthusiasm and deep knowledge of all things alcoholic make for some fun suggestions. You know you're in good hands."*

Keedick Coulter
Joe Dobias
Fany Gerson
Justin Warner
Evelyn De Luna
Steve Dustin
Jasper White
Marc Forgione
Peter Endriss & Chris Piz
Jenn Louis

20

zulli

For the pickle dressing

1 cup extra virgin olive oil

½ cup red wine vinegar

½ cup tarragon vinegar

8 bay leaves

One 3-ounce bottle capers, drained and mostly mashed

1 to 2 tablespoons sugar (depending on preference for sweetness)

½ teaspoon dry mustard (optional)

1 tablespoon Worcestershire sauce

1½ teaspoons Tabasco sauce

Salt

Other fresh ingredients you may add at your discretion: basil (a lot); thyme (a little); oregano (some)

For the pickled shrimp

2½ pounds shrimp, peeled, deveined, and cooked

3 to 5 onions, thinly sliced

½ to 1 lemon, sliced (optional)

For the tomato aspic

1 quart tomato juice, canned or fresh when in season

1 large onion, sliced

6 whole black peppercorns

2 bay leaves

3 stalks celery, preferably with leaves

4 whole cloves

1 to 2 teaspoons salt

About 1 tablespoon sugar

About 2 teaspoons tarragon vinegar or cider vinegar

About 1 tablespoon freshly squeezed lemon juice

About 1 teaspoon Worcestershire sauce (optional)

PUT WHEELS ON IT

In 1921, the Union Pacific Railroad debuted its dining car, and the first drive-in restaurant opened in Dallas, Texas. Americans were on the go, and their meals had to catch up with them. What might the home cook of 1921's version of fast food look like? A picnic at a table that could be anywhere, for those catching their meals where they could or taking a moment to stop and enjoy the scenery.

PICKLED SHRIMP AND TOMATO ASPIC PICNIC
KEEDICK COULTER

Prepare the pickle dressing: Combine all the ingredients.

Prepare the pickled shrimp: Alternate layers of shrimp and onions in glass jars. If desired, put a couple of lemon slices in the jar. Pour the pickle dressing unstrained into jars until nearly full, secure the lids, and refrigerate to marinate for 1 to 3 days. Shake the jars occasionally to give them a good mix. Good for about a week.

Prepare the tomato aspic: Gently simmer the tomato juice along with the onion, peppercorns, bay leaves, celery, and cloves for 15 minutes to add flavor to the juice. Season the juice to taste with salt, sugar, vinegar, lemon juice, Worcestershire, and Tabasco. Once you approve the flavor, strain the liquid and return to a simmer on the stove.

Mix the gelatin with ¼ cup cold water until soft, then whisk into the simmering juice until completely dissolved. Remove from the heat and continue whisking (it will help to do so in an ice water bath) until the gelatin begins to thicken. Lightly grease the molds with oil. Pour the mixture into the molds, cover, and refrigerate for several hours or overnight. Serve in the molds.

About 1 teaspoon Tabasco sauce
  (optional)
Two ¼-ounce envelopes gelatin
  (2 tablespoons)
¼ cup cold water
Salad oil, for greasing the molds

Special equipment
Glass canning jars and lids
  (16-ounce jars)
6 to 8 4-ounce ramekins for the aspic

"These recipes are a great example of how my mother and grandmother appreciate food. Pickled shrimp and tomato aspic both have delicate flavors that show off the main characters without overpowering them. Both also look and feel elegant without requiring years of culinary training or expensive ingredients (at least not if you happen to be in Wilmington during shrimp season)."

Armed with a refurbished military pressure fryer and heaps of southern wisdom imparted by his Virginian mother and North Carolinian grandmother, **Keedick Coulter** *serves New York City the best fried chicken this side of the Mason-Dixon at Bobwhite Lunch & Supper Counter. Keedick's modest menu is inspired by the thrifty and resourceful cooks of his lineage. Nothing goes to waste, so be sure to grab a seat at the counter when surplus chicken and biscuit dough turn into irresistible potpies. His matron saints taught Keedick to treat food with gratitude and serve it with graciousness, a rare combination in modern urban dining that keeps his customers coming back for more.*

POT OF GOLD

The majestic Gold Coast of Long Island's North Shore in the 1920s is the setting for F. Scott Fitzgerald's signature novel *The Great Gatsby*. Unlike Jay Gatsby's fictional West Egg manor, the Gold Coast was a real place, where palatial mansions offered a glittering seaside escape from the cramped quarters of Manhattan. The Vanderbilts, Whitneys, Roosevelts, and Guggenheims all claimed sprawling seasonal estates in this playground of the rich and powerful. They spared no expense on magnificent, delirious soirées complete with such local delicacies as lobster, shrimp, oysters, and enough Champagne to fuel the seductive orgy of fame, money, and beauty long into the humid August nights.

THE LONG ISLAND "SOUND OFF"
JOE DOBIAS

Prepare the broth: Separate the lobsters into bodies, claws plus knuckles, and tails. Shell the shrimp and remove the heads. Combine the lobster bodies, shrimp shells and heads, water, paprika, turmeric, and cayenne in a heavy-bottomed pot.

Bring to a boil and simmer for 1 to 2 hours, until the liquid is reduced to about 3 quarts. Strain the broth into a clean pot, return to the heat, and bring to a boil.

Poach the lobster claw/knuckles for 13 to 15 minutes in the broth, then shock in an ice water bath; set the claws and knuckles aside. Bring the broth to a boil again and poach the lobster tails for 10 minutes, then shock in an ice water bath; set the tails aside. Shell all the lobster meat, discard the shells, and reserve the broth.

Prepare the soup base: In a large pot, over medium heat, melt the butter. Whisk in the flour and cook for 3 to 4 minutes, whisking the whole time, to make a light roux. Gradually whisk broth into the roux. Add cream, cayenne, and 1 teaspoon of the salt; taste and add additional salt if desired.

MAKES 4 TO 6 SERVINGS

For the lobster broth
Two 1¼-pound lobsters
24 head-on, shell-on pink shrimp
1 gallon water
2 tablespoons paprika
1 teaspoon ground turmeric
1 teaspoon cayenne pepper

For the soup base
5 tablespoons unsalted butter
5 tablespoons all-purpose flour
3 quarts broth (from above)
½ cup heavy cream
½ teaspoon cayenne pepper
2 teaspoons kosher salt

For the soup
2 quarts soup base (from above)
Lobster meat (from above)
24 oysters, shucked, liquor reserved
Shrimp (from above)
1 pound bay scallops, abductor muscle removed
1 tablespoon chopped fresh dill
1 tablespoon chopped fresh parsley
Fresh bread or croutons

Bring to a high simmer and cook uncovered for 5 minutes.

Reduce the heat to low and, whisking frequently, slowly simmer uncovered for 20 to 30 minutes, until the base thickens.

Prepare the soup: Over low heat, bring the base to a low simmer. Add the lobster meat and cook for 4 minutes, stirring occasionally. Add the oysters and their liquor and cook for 2 minutes, stirring occasionally. Add the shrimp and scallops and cook for 2 minutes, stirring occasionally.

Serve in warmed bowls, garnished with dill and parsley and topped with fresh bread or croutons.

Joe Dobias *was born and raised on the North Shore of Long Island, in Port Jefferson Station, where he landed his first job in hospitality as a busboy at a local seafood place. Joe, along with his partner and fellow Long Island native Jill Schuster, presides over the self-described "aggressive American" restaurant Joe Doe in Manhattan. Joe's hometown flavors, superior skill, and infectious charm all make their way into this elegant first course that warrants dressing for dinner.*

DUNK YOUR WHISKERS

Ice cream desserts date back centuries, to when the methods of their manufacture were guarded royal secrets. Salt-insulated hand-cranked churns and other labor-intensive preparations followed, but they weren't for the faint of forearm. The invention of the first alcohol-cooled electric ice cream machine introduced an exciting and easy process for bringing what was once the province of kings into reach of wagging tongues, swiveling hips, and shimmying fringe hems across the dance floors of the Jazz Age.

PRALINE ICE CREAM WITH BOURBON CARAMEL SAUCE
FANY GERSON

Prepare the pecan praline: Line a sheet pan with parchment paper.

Mix the brown sugar, granulated sugar, cream, butter, salt, ground cinnamon, and water in a heavy-bottomed saucepan and place over medium-high heat. Stirring constantly to prevent burning, cook until the caramel reaches the soft ball stage, 238° to 240°F. Remove the pan from the heat and add the pecans, stirring vigorously and carefully with a wooden spoon or heat-proof spatula until cool and the pecans remain suspended in the candy, about 2 minutes. Pour the praline onto the prepared sheet pan and allow to cool. Once cool, break into pieces by coarsely chopping with a knife or banging lightly with a rolling pin. Store in an airtight container until ready to use.

Prepare the ice cream: Put 1 cup of the cream in a medium saucepan with the cinnamon, sugar, and salt and cook over medium heat until the sugar dissolves. Remove from the heat and stir in the remaining cream, the milk, and vanilla extract. Cover and chill the ice cream base in the refrigerator until you are ready to use it.

MAKES ABOUT 1 QUART ICE CREAM

For the pecan praline
1 packed cup light brown sugar
½ cup granulated sugar
½ cup heavy cream
4 tablespoons unsalted butter
¼ teaspoon kosher salt
1 teaspoon freshly ground cinnamon, (preferably Mexican canela)
2 tablespoons water
1 cup pecan halves

For the ice cream
2 cups heavy cream
One 3-inch piece cinnamon (preferably Mexican canela)
¾ cup granulated sugar
Pinch salt
1 cup whole milk
¾ teaspoon pure vanilla extract

MAKES ABOUT 2 CUPS SAUCE

For the bourbon caramel sauce
2 cups granulated sugar
⅓ cup water
2 tablespoons light corn syrup
½ teaspoon freshly squeezed lemon juice
1¼ cups heavy cream
4 tablespoons unsalted butter
3 tablespoons bourbon
¾ teaspoon pure vanilla extract

Special equipment
Ice cream maker

Remove the cinnamon stick and freeze the ice cream in your ice cream maker according to the manufacturer's instructions. If you had this device in the twenties, it made you quite popular indeed!

Once the ice cream is frozen, stir in the broken pieces of praline; store the ice cream in the freezer until ready to scoop.

Prepare the caramel sauce: In a medium saucepan, combine the sugar, water, and corn syrup. Stir over medium heat until the sugar is dissolved. Turn up the heat and continue to cook, without stirring, until the liquid begins to turn golden. Swirl the pan lightly and continue to cook, without stirring, until it reaches a dark amber color. Remove from the heat and add the heavy cream, being very careful to avoid the splattering that may burn you. Once the bubbling subsides, stir until the caramel is dissolved. Add the butter, bourbon, and vanilla extract, stirring gently until it all comes together. Allow to cool slightly. Serve warm over the ice cream.

NOTE: Praline and sauce can be prepared in advance.

> *Fany got to thinking about where she might be found enjoying an ice cream in 1923. Inspired by jazz music and her two cats, Charles and Mingus, she conjured glimpses of a decadent party in New Orleans full of beautiful, playfully dressed revelers dancing the night away, sneaking bites of a popular flavor of ice cream called Mexican Praline that once swept the bayou region and beyond. Her boozy caramel sauce is a nod to the dissenters of Prohibition, who might consider omitting the caramel and plunking scoops of the ice cream right into a glass of brandy or bourbon to be served as a float. She calls this "indulgence to the max!"*

Inspired by the beloved dessert of her youth, **Fany Gerson** *took to the streets of New York, pushing carts full of colorful, refreshing, and sweet frozen* paletas *to street fairs around the city all summer long. When she started her business, La Newyorkina, the Mexican-born chef and author of* My Sweet Mexico *had trouble deciding whether to freeze, bake, or fry her way into people's hearts . . . so she's decided to have it all!*

COLD CUTZ

When Clarence Birdseye developed a "quick freeze" method that allowed many types of food (some rapidly perishable) to be preserved by cold, he ushered in an age of flavor and imagination that allowed many Americans to experience out-of-season foods as well as those that had probably traveled a great distance from their point of origin. Lacking the imparted flavors of pickled or preserved goods, frozen foods were a boon to flavor, economy, and variety for the home cook.

"I CAN'T BELIEVE IT'S THE MIDDLE OF WINTER" PEA SOUP

JUSTIN WARNER

Combine the peas, water, salt, vanilla, and lime juice in a blender, and blend until smooth. (Work in batches if need be.) Pour into a large pot over medium heat.

While the soup heats, wash out the blender pitcher and blend the sour cream and mint. Ladle the soup into bowls. Garnish with the sour cream mixture. Celebrate spring in winter.

Justin may be best known as the insanely popular and widely loved winner of the eighth season of the television program Food Network Star.

Justin Warner *is a gifted storyteller who grew up in western Maryland. A fine example of this talent is his explanation for how he got his chops in the food and dining universe: "I started working in restaurants when I was thirteen or fourteen and since I have no other marketable skills, I haven't stopped. I opened Do or Dine in 2011, and since we were too broke to hire a chef, I put the apron on myself."*

MAKES ABOUT 6 SERVINGS

2 pounds frozen peas
1 quart water
1 tablespoon kosher salt
1 teaspoon pure vanilla extract
Juice of 1 lime, strained
1 cup sour cream
2 tablespoons fresh mint leaves

In regard to this fabulous and satisfying pea soup, he says, "I like this dish because it's incredibly easy and is vegan (without the garnish), gluten-free, allium free."

DON'T TOUCH THAT DIAL

MAKES 6 SERVINGS

3 medium-to-large russet potatoes
(see Note)

1 large egg (see Note)

¾ cup all-purpose flour, plus more
for shaping

Chopped parsley

Salt and freshly ground black pepper

3 to 4 tablespoons butter

½ onion, chopped

3 slices bacon, chopped (optional)

Radio was coming into its own in 1925. In March, Calvin Coolidge would be the first president to nationally broadcast his inaugural address. Radio news brought the ends of the earth closer to the center, and a radio set became necessary equipment for almost every home. Popular music flourished, consecrating the great Jazz Age and establishing "country" as a uniquely American genre with the debut of Nashville's *Grand Ole Opry* program. Rather than simply spreading content like music and news, radio became a form of entertainment all its own, and many families in 1925 were eating their suppers by the glow of the radio dial, to the tune of serial programs like *National Radio Homemakers Club*, *The Happiness Boys*, and *The Gold Dust Twins*. The couch potato, as it were, may well have been born in 1925.

NANA'S SKINNY PINNIES
EVELYN DE LUNA

Boil the potatoes in their skin for 20 to 30 minutes, until fork-tender. Rinse with cold water and chill overnight in the refrigerator.

Peel and mash the potatoes. Add the egg, flour, parsley, and salt and pepper to taste and blend well in a food processor or a stand mixer with the dough hook attachment. Turn the dough onto a floured board and knead a few times with your hands. The mixture will be sticky but should not fall apart. Break off a piece and roll with your hands into a long, thin strip (a skinny pinny!). Cut the strip into pieces and sprinkle with flour. Take another chunk off the big piece and roll. Repeat until all the dough is used. Sprinkle with flour and let sit for 10 minutes while you put on a pot of water to boil.

Drop the pieces into the boiling water. Stir gently with a wooden spoon so you don't break them up. Watch carefully until the water comes back to a boil. The dumplings will rise to the

> "Meat, potatoes, and vegetables were what almost every meal was made of. Homemade dumplings were about the most exotic of the foods we ate, exotic for me anyway."

top when the water boils. Let them bubble gently for a few minutes, no more than 5.

While they're cooking, melt the butter in a pan. Sauté the onion in the butter until golden. You can also sauté bacon with the onion instead of using plain onion.

Drain the dumplings and pour the onion and butter over them. Add a little salt if needed. 🌾

NOTE: You can start with cold leftover mashed potatoes if you have them. If you're using leftover mashed potatoes, skip the egg; the dough will be too moist.

Evelyn imagines a Sunday night meal her grandmother would have prepared for her mother, while listening to the newfangled sound box. "My mother, Martha, was born in 1918 in Corona, Queens, and was the youngest of fifteen children," Evelyn says. "She said she always did her homework to the radio." When she was growing up, she recalls, "For Sunday dinners, we would have mashed potatoes and a roast, and we always ate at one o'clock. We didn't have dessert during the week, but we almost always did on Sundays. On Sunday night, everyone ate whatever they wanted: leftovers, a sandwich, scrambled eggs. We used to watch Your Hit Parade *on TV, which was the hit songs of the day, but on TV instead of the radio."*

Evelyn De Luna *is a talented cook, a confident artist, and a crossword puzzle's worst nightmare. In the kitchen, she has a miraculous ability to prepare an entire multicourse dinner that's extraordinarily (and inexplicably) all hot and ready at the same time. Evelyn is also Noah's mother.*

RUN WITH THE HARE, HUNT WITH THE HOUNDS

Game hunting was a beloved pastime of the outdoorsman in the 1920s. *Field and Stream* was as well known as Abercrombie and Fitch, both of which were indispensable guides and outfitters to the American hunter, respectively. Meats like deer, duck, and quail were not only part of the hunter's diet but also on highbrow menus in restaurants across the country. Prized for their meat and pelts, the frequently hunted and ever-multiplying population of rabbits were a reliable, flavorful, and abundant source of meat and an integral part of the American food chain.

BRAISED RABBIT, GNOCCHI, BLACK TRUMPET MUSHROOMS, ESCAROLE, AND AMERICAN GRANA

STEVE DUSTIN

Prepare the rabbit: Preheat the oven to 350°F.

Cut the rabbit into 5 pieces: 2 hind legs, 2 front legs, and the center portion of the body. Season the rabbit with sea salt and pepper. Heat the canola oil in a heavy-bottomed roasting pan over medium heat. Add the rabbit and cook until golden brown on all sides, approximately 10 minutes. Do not crowd the pan; if needed, sear the rabbit in two batches. Once the rabbit is golden brown, remove and set aside.

In the same roasting pan, combine the carrots, onion, celery, and garlic and cook until golden brown, approximately 7 minutes. Add the tomato paste and cook for an additional 3 minutes. Add the thyme, bay leaf, peppercorns, vinegar, and wine. Reduce until the alcohol is cooked out of the wine. Add the chicken stock and bring to a boil. Remove from the heat and add back the rabbit. Cover the roasting pan with aluminum foil.

MAKES 6 SERVINGS

For the rabbit
1 rabbit (whole)
Sea salt and freshly ground black pepper
2 tablespoons canola oil
2 carrots, chopped
1 white onion, chopped
3 stalks celery, chopped
4 cloves garlic, chopped
¼ cup tomato paste
5 sprigs thyme
1 bay leaf
1 tablespoon whole black peppercorns
½ cup sherry vinegar
2 cups white wine
2 quarts chicken stock or low-sodium chicken broth

For the gnocchi
2 medium russet potatoes
1 whole egg
1 egg yolk
1 tablespoon ricotta cheese
Sea salt and freshly ground black pepper
1 cup all-purpose flour, plus more for kneading
½ cup olive oil

For the garnish
2 heads escarole
½ pound black trumpet mushrooms
2 tablespoons canola oil
2 tablespoons unsalted butter
¼ pound American grana cheese, for grating

Place the roasting pan in the oven and cook for 1½ hours. Check to make sure that the rabbit is tender and falling off the bone. If it is not, cook for an additional 30 minutes.

Carefully remove the rabbit from the roasting pan and set it aside on a plate to cool until you can handle it by hand. Strain the braising liquid and discard the vegetables and herbs.

Reduce the braising liquid until it reaches a thick, sauce-like consistency. While the braising liquid is reducing, pick all of the rabbit meat off the bones. Discard the bones. Once the liquid is reduced, add the rabbit meat. Reserve under refrigeration if not serving soon.

Prepare the gnocchi: Peel the potatoes, dice them coarsely, and cook in salted water until tender, but not falling apart. Drain the potatoes and let them air-dry for 5 minutes.

Use a potato ricer or food mill to grind the potatoes into very fine pieces. Put them in a large bowl.

Add the whole egg, egg yolk, ricotta, salt, and pepper and combine. Incorporate the flour with the potato mixture by running your hands from the bottom of the bowl through the mixture, keeping the mixture very light and fluffy. When almost fully mixed, move the dough to a lightly floured surface and knead for 3 minutes until everything comes together. Cover the dough with plastic wrap and let it rest for 20 minutes.

Bring a large pot of salted water to a boil.

Cut pieces of dough and roll them beneath your hands on a lightly floured surface to form a log about 1 inch in diameter. Cut the logs into pieces 1 inch wide. Now you should have light, fluffy pieces of gnocchi that are 1 inch by 1 inch. Continue until all of the gnocchi are rolled out and cut.

Add the gnocchi to the boiling water and cook until they float to the surface, approximately 3 minutes. Transfer the gnocchi with a slotted spoon into an ice water bath to rapidly cool them. Once cool, drain the gnocchi and gently toss them with the olive oil. Store in the refrigerator. Everything to this point can be done up to 2 days before serving and refrigerated until needed.

Put it all together: On the day of serving, chop the escarole and clean with cold water. Drain thoroughly. Clean the black trumpet mushrooms by soaking them in bowl of cold water. (Sometimes black trumpets have pine needles stuck to them; be sure to clean thoroughly.) Drain well.

In a large, heavy-bottomed sauté pan, heat the canola oil. Add approximately 6 gnocchi per person served to the oil; this might need to be done in two batches if the pan is not large enough. Crisp the gnocchi on both sides until golden brown. Once the gnocchi are crisp, add the black trumpet mushrooms and escarole, and cook for 1 minute. Add the braised rabbit and reduced braising liquid. Cook until everything is hot. Remove from the heat, add the butter, and stir until all of the butter has melted.

Plate everything together in warmed large bowls and top with grated American grana.

Steve Dustin *is the executive chef at Monument Lane in New York City. Growing up in rural Michigan, he developed an appreciation for quiet outdoor activities: fishing for wide-mouth bass on nearby lakes and tending to the strawberries, beets, and rhubarb in his family's garden. "My father grew up fishing and hunting with his father in Michigan and Canada," he says. "One of my first memories of my father hunting was him coming home after an afternoon trip with two rabbits that he had shot. I watched and was amazed as he skinned, gutted, and cleaned the rabbits. Then I asked 'What are we going to do now?' 'Now we're going to eat them,' he replied."*

SWEDISH EXOTICA

The history of salt cod extends far beyond New England. Preserving food with salt came into fashion in the seventeenth century, as inexpensive salt from Mediterranean Europe was produced on a large scale and imported to sustain the people of Sweden and Norway during their long winters. Later, during the American Revolution, salt cod played a role in the "triangular trade" to sustain the colonies, well-to-do Europeans, and Caribbean plantation workers. Although the shipping lines remain the same, the products have certainly changed. The Scandinavians eventually returned the favor by introducing their own exotic product to America in 1927, when, during Ford's production of the new Model A, Swedes rolled out the Volvo.

OLD-FASHIONED SALT COD CAKES
JASPER WHITE

MAKES 8 CAKES

1 pound boneless salt cod
2 medium russet potatoes, peeled
7 tablespoons butter
½ small yellow onion, minced
1 teaspoon dry mustard
2 to 4 dashes Worcestershire sauce
1 whole egg
3 egg yolks
Freshly ground black pepper
3 tablespoons olive oil
Flour

Soak the cod in a large bowl of cold water for 6 to 8 hours, changing the water 2 or 3 times. Drain. Put the potatoes in a pot of cold water and cook over medium-high heat until tender, about 40 minutes. Drain, then mash with a potato ricer or masher; set aside.

Put the cod in a medium pot of water, bring to a boil over high heat, and boil for 5 minutes. Drain well, then break the fish into flakes.

Melt 4 tablespoons of the butter in a small pan over medium heat. Add the onion and cook until soft, 3 to 5 minutes. Combine the onion, potatoes, cod, mustard, Worcestershire sauce, egg, and egg yolks in a medium bowl. Season to taste with pepper, shape into 8 cakes, and chill.

Melt the remaining 3 tablespoons butter with the oil in a large skillet over medium heat. Dredge the cod cakes in flour, shaking off the excess, and fry until golden, about 5 minutes per side.

Jasper White *was born in 1954 in New Jersey, and spent much of his childhood on a farm near the Jersey shore. He credits his love of good food to his Italian grandmother. Jasper began his cooking career in 1973, and after graduating from the Culinary Institute of America he spent several years working and traveling around the United States before settling in Boston in 1979. In 1990, Jasper received the James Beard Award for Best Chef, Northeast. He is also the author of four cookbooks,* Cooking from New England, Lobster at Home, Fifty Chowders, *and* The Summer Shack Cookbook, *all of which are regarded as seminal texts on seafood and northeastern cuisine.*

SURREALISTIC PILLOWS

MAKES 4 SERVINGS

For the pasta dough

1¾ cups type 00 flour, plus additional
  for the work surface

1¼ cups semolina flour

9 large egg yolks (preferably farm fresh)

½ cup water

For the gelée

1 head black garlic

1 quart lobster stock

2 teaspoons fresh squid ink

3 sheets gelatin, soaked in cold water,
  excess squeezed out

For the sweet corn ravioli

3 cups fresh corn kernels
  (from about 4 ears corn)

4¾ cups chicken stock

3 leaves fresh lemon verbena,
  bound together

½ cup finely ground polenta

½ cup cream cheese, softened

½ cup finely grated Parmigiano-
  Reggiano cheese

1 tablespoon finely shredded fresh basil

1 tablespoon finely shredded fresh mint

¼ teaspoon chili flakes

Kosher salt and freshly ground
  black pepper

Olive oil

¼ Vidalia onion, cut in ⅛-inch dice

½ cup arborio rice

½ cup dry white wine

1 sprig thyme

1 fresh or ½ dried bay leaf

Pasta dough (from above)

3 large egg yolks, lightly beaten

Expanding on the earlier themes that had infiltrated fine art before them (Impressionism, abstractionism, Dada), the surrealists set out to find a reality beyond the physical, a place that was exposed in dreams and the subconscious or the even deeper unconscious mind. From the terrifying and nightmarish depictions of dreams by Salvador Dalí and Max Ernst to the vivid hue and energy of Joan Miró and the erotic and anxiety-inducing photographs of Man Ray and Hans Bellmer, the artists of the era explored the contrast of the fantastical and shocking against the backdrop of the normal and the serene. Their legacy is one of color, surprise, grandeur, and hallucination against a calm, placid setting, even if only deceptively veiled in normalcy.

SWEET CORN "SUNRISE" RAVIOLI, DAY BOAT MAINE LOBSTER

MARC FORGIONE

Prepare the pasta dough: In a large bowl, whisk both flours until combined. Make a well in the flour blend and add the egg yolks and water.

Using a fork, whisk together the yolks and water and gradually start to incorporate the flour, starting with the inner rim of the well. As you expand the well, keep pushing up the flour from the base of the mound to keep the well shape. The dough will come together when about half of the flour is incorporated. Once this happens, knead the dough with your hands, using your palms and the heel of your hands to flatten out the dough. Once the dough has come together, dump the dough onto a lightly floured work surface and knead it for 5 minutes more. Wrap the dough in plastic wrap and let sit for 1 hour at room temperature before rolling out.

For the lobster and assembly

Two 1¼-pound day boat Maine lobsters

Canola oil

1 cup verbena stock (from above)

Kosher salt

1 teaspoon chopped fresh parsley

¼ cup finely shredded fresh basil

2 tablespoons finely shredded fresh lemon verbena

Corn shoots

8 tablespoons unsalted butter, softened

Special equipment

Handheld or stand blender

Juicer (optional)

Hand-cranked meat grinder

Pastry bag fitted with ½-inch plain tip

Pasta machine or pasta roller attachment

2-inch and 2½-inch ring cutters or ravioli mold

Prepare the gelée: Fill a small bowl with hot water and soak the black garlic for about 10 minutes. Peel the garlic (the skins should pop right off) and set aside. In a saucepot, heat the lobster stock over medium-high heat until reduced by half. Add the black garlic and use a handheld blender or stand blender to puree until smooth. Strain through a fine-mash strainer. Whisk in the squid ink. Add the gelatin and whisk until well mixed and dissolved. Pour into an 11 by 17-inch rimmed baking sheet (liquid should come up about ⅛ inch high). Place the pan in the fridge and let the gelée set.

Prepare the sweet corn ravioli: Using a juicer, press 1¼ cups of the corn kernels; you should get about ½ cup corn juice. If you don't own a juicer, puree 1¼ cups of corn kernels in a blender, transfer the pureed corn to a kitchen towel or cheesecloth, and squeeze out the juice so that you get ½ cup. Set aside the remaining whole kernels—you will need them for the ravioli as well as at the end when assembling the dish.

In a 4-quart pot set over high heat, bring 3 cups of the chicken stock to a boil. Add the lemon verbena, cover, and remove from the heat. Let the broth infuse for 10 minutes. Discard the verbena, set aside 1 cup for later use, and return the pot to the stove top. Over low heat, slowly whisk in the polenta. Cook, whisking constantly, for 5 minutes. Remove from the heat, cover, and let sit in a warm place for 10 minutes. Transfer to a bowl. Whisk in the cream cheese, Parmigiano-Reggiano, corn juice, ¾ cup of the remaining corn kernels, the basil, mint, chili flakes, and salt and pepper to taste. Cover and set aside.

In a small pot over high heat, bring the remaining 1¾ cups stock to a boil. Remove from the heat and keep hot.

In a large sauté pan over high heat, heat enough olive oil to cover the bottom of the pan until just before it starts to smoke. Add the onion, reduce the heat to medium, and cook until soft, about 5 minutes. Do not let the onion pick up any color. Add the rice and cook, stirring, for 1 minute. Add the wine and cook, stirring, until it gets absorbed. Add the thyme and bay leaf and ladle in the hot stock, 1 ladle at a time, allowing the stock to become absorbed before adding another. Taste and adjust seasonings.

Transfer the risotto to a meat grinder set to the medium die and grind into the bowl with the polenta mixture. Mix to combine. Set the risotto-polenta batter over an ice water bath and let cool completely. Once cool, transfer the mixture to the pastry bag and set aside.

Lightly dust the surface of the counter with some flour. Using a pasta machine or a pasta roller attachment for your stand mixer, roll the pasta on the #1 setting of the machine (about 2.5 mm). Cut the dough into 12 by 5-inch strips. Divide the strips into two parts: tops and bottoms. Brush the bottom strips with beaten egg yolks and pipe 2 tablespoons of risotto-polenta filling every 2 inches or so—the diameter of filling should be about 1½ inches.

Place the top sheets on the bottom ones, and, using the back end of a 2½-inch ring cutter, press down to shape the ravioli. Using a 2-inch ring cutter, cut out the ravioli. You can do this using a ravioli mold—you won't need the ring cutters. Transfer the cutout ravioli to a lightly floured, parchment paper–lined baking sheet—you may need more than 1 sheet. Set aside 4 ravioli. (If making ravioli ahead of time, freeze the ravioli on a baking sheet for 20 minutes before placing in a tightly sealed container and freezing until needed.)

Prepare the lobster: Position a rack in the middle of the oven and preheat the oven to 350°F. Kill the lobsters by stabbing them through the head with a chef's knife. Remove the claws/knuckles and set aside. Cut the tails off the lobster bodies; cut the tails into 1-inch pieces still in their shells. Place the lobster claws in a shallow baking dish and bake for 5 minutes. Transfer the claws to a cooling rack and allow them to cool to room temperature. Once cool, remove the meat from the claws and knuckles and set the meat aside. In a wok or a sauté pan over high heat, heat just enough canola oil to cover the bottom of the pan until just before it starts to smoke. Add the lobster tails and cook for 1 to 2 minutes. Add the reserved lemon verbena stock. Transfer the pieces to a tray and poke the meat out of the shells with your fingers or a fork. Reserve the verbena stock in the pan.

Assemble the dish: When ready to serve, bring a large pot of salted water to a boil; reduce the heat to medium and keep on a simmer while you prepare the rest of the dish.

Using the same ring cutter as for the ravioli, press down into the gelée to cut out 4 disks. Set aside.

In a medium skillet over high heat, heat enough canola oil to cover the bottom of the dish until just before it starts to smoke. Add the reserved lobster meat and cook for 1 minute. Add the remaining 1 cup corn kernels, season with a pinch of salt, and cook for 30 seconds. Add the parsley, basil, verbena, and corn shoots; toss in the pan; and immediately remove from the heat. Swirl in the butter and set aside.

When ready to serve, heat the verbena stock until warmed through. Increase the heat on the pot of salted water to high, making sure it is at a rolling boil, and add the ravioli. Cook for 20 seconds and, using a slotted spoon, immediately transfer to warm plates. Scatter the lobster meat and corn kernels around the ravioli. Place one round of the gelée on top of the ravioli. Just before serving, in front of the diner, spoon a ladleful of the hot stock over the gelée disk so that it "melts" over the ravioli.

If the phrase "gifted and talented" seems clichéd, then you've probably never applied it to a person as deserving of that description as **Marc Forgione**. *Confident, cocky, and a damn good chef, Marc holds royal court with New American cuisine at the highly starred, repeatedly awarded, and phenomenally well reviewed restaurant that bears his (family) name in New York City.*

A CRASH HEARD 'ROUND THE TABLE

The decadence and luxury that characterized the Roaring Twenties came to a grinding halt when the calamity of Black Tuesday on Wall Street plummeted the nation into an uncertain future. An era in stark contrast to the illusory comforts of the '20s, the forthcoming Great Depression was a time for abrupt adjustment of lifestyle, starting with the kitchen cupboard. Even the most indulgent palates reeled in their expectation of grandeur, and once-decadent dishes were revised with more modest ingredients.

CHICKEN WITH BUCKWHEAT DUMPLINGS IN A MUSHROOM BROTH

PETER ENDRISS & CHRIS PIZZULLI

Brine the chicken: One day in advance, bring all ingredients except the chickens and oil to a boil in a large pot. Turn off the heat, let cool completely, and strain into a large container. Submerge the chickens in the brine, cover, and refrigerate for 12 to 18 hours.

Prepare the dumplings: Bring a large pot of salted water to a boil, and reduce to a simmer to cook the dumplings. Soak the buckwheat bread in the milk to soften. Once all the milk has been absorbed, squeeze the bread until a paste-like consistency forms. Add the egg, scallions, salt, and pepper, and mix well. Fold in the flour, mixing gently until it holds together. Using two teaspoons, form the dough into small football shapes and drop into the simmering water. If the dough fails to hold shape, add more flour until it retains shape and holds together when dropped into the water. Once the desired consistency is achieved, form the rest of the dumplings, and cook them for 5 minutes in the simmering water. Remove the dumplings from the water and set aside

MAKES 6 TO 8 SERVINGS

For the brined chicken

2 quarts water

¼ cup kosher salt

⅛ cup plus 1 tablespoon sugar

1 teaspoon coriander seeds

2 whole cloves

1 bay leaf

3 cloves garlic, crushed

¼ onion, sliced

1 teaspoon whole white peppercorns

4 sage leaves

Two 4- to 5-pound chickens, halved

1 teaspoon olive oil

For the dumpling dough

4 cups diced buckwheat bread

1 cup milk

1 egg

½ cup diced scallions

1 teaspoon kosher salt

1 teaspoon freshly ground black pepper

1 cup all-purpose flour, plus more if needed

For the mushroom broth

2 tablespoons extra virgin olive oil

1 pound cremini mushrooms, coarsely chopped

1 shallot, sliced

1 tablespoon chopped fresh thyme

1 bay leaf

1½ quarts chicken stock

Pinch grated lemon zest

Salt and freshly ground black pepper

Chopped chives, for garnish

1929

in a warm place on a piece of parchment or wax paper until the mushroom broth is prepared.

Prepare the chicken: Preheat the oven to 400°F. Remove the chicken from the brine and pat dry. Heat 1 teaspoon olive oil in an oven-safe pan over medium-high heat and sear the chicken, skin side down, until the skin is nicely browned. Leaving the chicken in the same pan, place in the oven, uncovered and skin side down, until cooked through. Remove from the oven, transfer to a plate, turn skin side up, and allow to rest 5 minutes.

Prepare the mushroom broth: Discard any excess fat from the chicken pan and reheat with 2 tablespoons of the olive oil. Once the pan is hot, add the mushrooms, shallot, thyme, and bay leaf, stirring occasionally until caramelized, making sure not to burn the mushrooms. Add the chicken stock, and simmer until reduced by one-third.

Add the dumplings, lemon zest, and salt and pepper to taste and simmer for 1 minute. Remove the bay leaf. Once the broth is ready and the dumplings are thoroughly cooked, place the chicken in bowls, adding broth and dumplings. Garnish with chives and serve immediately. 🪶

At their Brooklyn-based restaurant and bakery Runner & Stone, Blue Ribbon Brasserie alum **Chris Pizzulli** *and* **Peter Endriss** *(formerly of Per Se, Bouchon, and Amy's Bread) pair house-made bread and pastries with a market-driven menu resplendent with homemade pastas. Having forged meaningful connections with local farmers, purveyors, and artisans during their tenures at Smorgasburg and the New Amsterdam Market, Peter and Chris offer an intriguing and well-conceived neighborhood dining experience, not for the faint of carb.*

HIDE AND SEEK

1 pound cottage cheese
3 large eggs
1 cup all-purpose flour, plus more
  for shaping
1 teaspoon baking powder
Butter and sour cream, for serving

In the 1930s, "making do" was an art honed by necessity. The cheaper the ingredients and plainer the packaging, the better. The introduction of the Twinkie, with its simple sponge cake encasing a sweet creme-filling surprise, brought a welcome, simple pleasure. These treats soon became a favorite after-school snack, and their popularity endures today. Jenn Louis's family favorite lidnivikis might be considered an old-world prototype of the popular, uniquely American treat, one that would please the cost-conscious cook as well as those wary of cavities.

LIDNIVIKIS
JENN LOUIS

Preheat oven to 350°F and line a large baking sheet with a silicone baking mat or nonstick foil.

In a large bowl, mix the cottage cheese, eggs, flour, and baking powder until just combined. Sprinkle a long sheet of wax paper or parchment paper generously with flour, and pour half of the batter on top of the flour in a line. Lifting one side of the paper toward the opposite edge, form the batter into a soft cylinder. Unwrap the paper and cut the cylinder into 1½-inch slices; they will be very soft. Place the slices on the baking sheet. Repeat with the second half of the batter.

Bake the slices until lightly golden brown. Place in a casserole dotted with butter and serve warm, topped with sour cream.

Time on a dairy kibbutz and an Outward Bound excursion inspired **Jenn Louis** *to found the full-service catering company Culinary Artistry before going on to open Lincoln Restaurant and Sunshine Tavern with her husband, David Welch. The Portland, Oregon, chef brings her own history to the table here, immortalizing her grandmother's lidnivikis, which Jenn's mother taught her to make. The simple dough is made fluffy with its own creamy surprise, and takes a roll form reminiscent of the Twinkie.*

Ivy Stark
Belinda Chang
Gabriella Gershenson
Nathan Hazard
José Andrés
Aldo Maiorana
Chad Robertson
Elaine Learnard & Ann-
Hong Thaimee
Nicole Taylor

30

Marie Scheidt

HARDEST-WORKING WOMAN IN GLENDALE

In 1931, James M. Cain was a decade away from introducing his fictional heroine Mildred Pierce to America, but the 1941 novel is set in the 1930s. Chef Ivy Stark envisioned "a fancy pot roast that Mildred Pierce (the ultimate Depression-era middle-class striver) might make, with hints from her Mexican cooks at the chicken and waffle joint."

POT ROAST ESPECIAL A LA GRINGA
IVY STARK

Prepare the marinade: Whisk together the olive oil, beer, and cider vinegar. Add the garlic, salt, pepper, ground chipotle, bay leaves, mustard, basil, oregano, and thyme. Mix well.

Prepare the roast: Trim the beef chuck and place in a large glass bowl or casserole. Pour the marinade over, cover, and refrigerate at least 2 hours or overnight.

Preheat the oven to 300°F.

Remove the meat from the marinade and pat dry. Reserve the marinade. Over medium-high heat, melt the lard in a heavy braising pan. Brown the roast 3 minutes on each side. Add the onions and cook until the onions are tender, about 5 minutes. Add the garlic; cook until it's just soft and golden, about 2 minutes; and add the beef broth, tomatoes, salt, bay leaves, beer, water, and the reserved marinade. Add the chilies and simmer until soft, about 10 minutes. Transfer the chilies and 1 cup of the braising liquid to a blender. Puree the chilies until smooth and return to the pot.

Cover and roast for 3 to 4 hours at a very slow simmer, until the meat is tender. While the meat is roasting, prepare the guacamole, pico de gallo, and rice.

MAKES 6 TO 8 SERVINGS

For the marinade
½ cup olive oil
1 cup dark beer (preferably Mexican)
¼ cup cider vinegar
4 cloves garlic, smashed
2 teaspoons fine sea salt
1 teaspoon freshly ground black pepper
1 teaspoon ground chipotle chili
2 bay leaves
1 teaspoon dry mustard
1 teaspoon dried basil
1 teaspoon dried Mexican oregano
1 teaspoon dried thyme

For the roast
One 4-pound beef chuck roast
3 tablespoons lard
2 medium onions, sliced
4 cloves garlic, minced
1 cup beef broth
6 plum tomatoes, peeled, seeded, and chopped
1 teaspoon fine sea salt
2 bay leaves
3 cups dark beer
3 cups water
2 ancho chilies, seeded
2 pasilla chilies, seeded

For the guacamole

2 tablespoons finely chopped
    cilantro leaves
2 teaspoons finely chopped white onion
2 teaspoons minced jalapeño or
    serrano chilies (seeds and membranes
    removed, if desired)
½ teaspoon kosher salt
2 large ripe avocados, preferably
    California Hass, pitted and peeled
2 tablespoons cored, seeded,
    finely chopped plum tomatoes
    (1 small tomato)
2 teaspoons freshly squeezed lime juice

For the pico de gallo

5 plum tomatoes, finely diced
1 white onion, finely diced
1 bunch cilantro, chopped
1 jalapeño chili, minced
1 serrano chili, minced
Juice of 1 lime
Salt and freshly ground black pepper

For the lemon-poblano rice

4 teaspoons extra virgin olive oil
2 large shallots, minced
1 poblano chili, roasted, peeled,
    seeded, and diced
1½ cups long-grain white rice
2 tablespoons unsalted shelled
    sunflower seeds
2 cups chicken stock
½ cup freshly squeezed lemon juice
½ teaspoon kosher salt
2½ tablespoons grated lemon zest
Cilantro leaves, for garnish

Prepare the guacamole: In a medium bowl, use the back of a spoon to mash 1 tablespoon of the cilantro, 1 teaspoon of the onion, 1 teaspoon of the chili, and the salt together against the bottom of the bowl.

Add the avocados and gently mash them with a fork until chunky-smooth. Fold the remaining cilantro, onion, and chili into the mixture. Stir in the tomatoes and lime juice, taste, and adjust the seasonings. Cover with plastic wrap directly on the surface of the guacamole.

Prepare the pico de gallo: Combine the tomatoes, onion, cilantro, chilies, and lime juice in a nonreactive bowl; season to taste with salt and pepper. Refrigerate for at least 1 hour before serving to allow the flavors to combine.

Prepare the lemon-poblano rice: Heat the oil in large heavy saucepan over medium heat. Add the shallots and poblano and sauté 3 minutes. Add the rice and sunflower seeds; stir for 2 minutes. Stir in the chicken stock, lemon juice, and salt; bring to boil. Reduce the heat to low; cover and cook until the liquid is absorbed and the rice is tender, about 20 minutes. Stir in 2 tablespoons of the lemon zest. Season with salt and pepper. Keep warm.

When ready to serve, mound the rice on a large serving platter and sprinkle with the remaining lemon zest and cilantro, for garnish.

To assemble the dish: When the meat is very tender, remove from the braising liquid and allow to rest for 30 minutes. Slice very thin across the grain. Fan the meat over the rice on the platter. Mound the guacamole and the pico de gallo in the center of the platter and serve. 🌿

Ivy Stark *is the corporate executive chef for acclaimed modern Mexican outfit Dos Caminos. She caught the culinary bug as a child in Colorado, and would eventually attend what became ICE in New York. Mentored by Mary Sue Milliken and Susan Feniger at the award-winning Border Grill, Ivy has worked coast to coast, leaving her mark on Sign of the Dove, Cena, Ciudad, Rosa Mexicano, Zocalo, Brasserie 8½, and Match Uptown. She's mom to two dachshunds, Frida and Diego, and enjoys running all over Brooklyn.*

THE GLAMOROUS LIFE

With the Great Depression in full swing, America turned to the silver screen for distraction and escape. The impractical excesses of the Roaring Twenties, now a distant memory for most, were lived out by a select set of larger-than-life personalities like Garbo, Dietrich, Crawford, and Harlow, sequestered in the Hollywood Hills, avatars of the dream life, for whom the decadent party of years past never ended.

"THE SUN ALSO RISES" PUNCH
BELINDA CHANG

Combine the ice, liquid ingredients, and lemon slices in a large punch bowl, and stir. Garnish with edible flowers, if desired.

VARIATION: This punch can also be made a bit tamer with the addition of lemon juice and/or lemonade.

James Beard Award–winning sommelier and hospitality powerhouse **Belinda Chang** *has overseen the cellars for some of the top restaurants from San Francisco to Chicago to New York City. She appreciated the chance to create a cocktail for us. "While wine will always have a most important place in my life, it is with spirits that I have been able to indulge my inner chef," she says. "It is in my home kitchen/cocktail bar that I'm able to shake, stir, and concoct to my heart's delight!"*

MAKES 1 (STRONG!) STANDARD PUNCH BOWL

1 large ice block (molded to fit the punch bowl)

Four 750-ml bottles rosé Champagne (The more decadent the label, the more delicious the punch, but if you do not like your invitees so much, rosé Prosecco or cava will also work)

1½ bottles (750 ml) absinthe, plus more for dipping (optional)

3 cups thyme simple syrup (equal parts water and sugar steeped with fresh or dried thyme, and strained)

6 lemons, sliced

Edible flowers, for garnish (optional)

Sugar cubes (optional)

Special equipment

Punch bowl

Absinthe spoons, for lighting cubes of sugar dipped in absinthe over individual punch cups, bohemian-style, (optional)

"Nothing says glamour like rosé Champagne, and nothing says intrigue, decadence, and hedonism like absinthe."

TOP BANANA

Special effects were expensive and rare in 1930s cinema, but a big gamble on a big ape paid off handsomely when *King Kong* premiered after nearly a year of production. Americans flocked to the movies in droves to see this high-tech adventure film, which followed the simian superstar from his jungle capture to his publicity tour as the so-called "eighth wonder of the world." In a spectacular finale, King Kong bravely scales the breathtaking (and only recently completed) Empire State Building, then the tallest man-made structure on Earth, only to crash to his inevitable death. Opening the cinematic door to countless epics, dramas, and big-budget long shots, *King Kong* cemented America's obsession with animation, camera tricks, and movie magic.

ROASTED BANANAS, THREE WAYS
GABRIELLA GERSHENSON

Roast the bananas: Preheat the oven to 400°F. Line a baking sheet with foil.

Place the banana halves skin side down on the baking sheet. Bake for 10 to 15 minutes, until the bananas give off a rich scent and liquid starts to seep from the fruit. The peel should be black and the fruit tender.

Brûlée style: Spread 1 teaspoon sugar evenly over the cut side of each banana half. Use a torch to evenly apply fire to the sugar until it's dark brown and bubbly. Let the sugar shell harden, and serve with vanilla ice cream.

If you don't have a torch, place the sugared bananas under your broiler for 3 minutes or so, until the sugar has melted and browned.

With maple-rum sauce: Combine the cream, brown sugar, and maple syrup in a small saucepan and cook over medium-high

SERVES 4 TO 6

For the roasted bananas
3 yellow, unblemished bananas,
  split in half lengthwise,
  still in their peels

Brûlée style
6 teaspoons granulated sugar
Vanilla ice cream, for serving

Special equipment
Kitchen torch (optional)

With maple-rum sauce
¾ cup heavy cream
½ cup packed light brown sugar
¼ cup maple syrup
1 tablespoon dark rum
Pinch salt

With whipped coconut cream
One 14-ounce can full-fat coconut milk
½ teaspoon vanilla extract

"This very simple preparation takes almost no time to make, and is easy, healthy, and infinitely customizable— brûléed with sugar, bathed in maple-rum sauce, topped with a diabolically rich whipped coconut cream, or any idea that strikes your fancy. I think Kong would approve."

heat, whisking, until combined. Let the mixture come to a boil, then adjust the temperature to low. Cook, stirring occasionally, until the sauce thickens to coat the back of a spoon, about 25 minutes. Take off heat, pour in the rum, and add the salt. Stir to combine and serve immediately, drizzled over the banana halves.

With whipped coconut cream: Place the can of coconut milk in the refrigerator for several hours or overnight. When sufficiently chilled, open the can and separate the liquid (reserve for other use) from the creamy solids. Place the cream in a stand mixer and whip the cream for 3 minutes or until the texture is that of ultra-thick whipped cream. (You could use a hand mixer.) Fold in the vanilla. Serve on top of the banana halves.

"Bananas are already irresistible to King Kong, but I discovered that roasting the fruit coaxes out a ripe brown-sugar flavor and custardy texture that takes them to a whole other level," Gabriella says.

If anyone knows how to soothe a savage beast, it's the graceful and ravishing **Gabriella Gershenson**, who is a senior editor at Saveur magazine and previously edited Time Out New York's dining section.

KEEP YOUR GIN UP

On the morning of February 9, 1934, New York City awoke to a surprise in the form of a bone-chilling –15°F temperature. To the present, that day has stood as the coldest the city has ever recorded. Several people from Brooklyn to the Bronx lost their lives, and dozens were treated for frostbite or exposure. Despite the chill and risk to life and limb, there was also reason to celebrate. Prohibition had been repealed a scant two months earlier, and importers of Scotch and gin from the British Isles had been stockpiling for months in advance. New Yorkers might have warmed up by sipping "slings," a very popular American style of drink that predated the cocktail, whose name was probably derived from the German *schlingen*, meaning to gulp or swallow hastily.

MAKES 1 COCKTAIL

2 ounces London dry gin
1 tablespoon superfine sugar
1 lemon wedge
Near-boiling water
Peel of 1 lemon
Freshly grated nutmeg

HOT GIN SLING
NATHAN HAZARD

Combine the gin, sugar, and a squeeze of lemon juice in an 8-ounce heatproof mug.

Top with water and stir until the sugar is dissolved. Express oil from the lemon peel over the surface of the drink and garnish with nutmeg. Serve immediately.

Nathan Hazard *was raised on the Sonoran Mexican cuisine of the Southwest but came of age working in the dining rooms of some of the Northwest's finest slow food institutions. Now a Los Angeleno, he documents gastronomical pleasures and spirituous libations on his blog,* The Chocolate of Meats. *A gin lover himself, Nathan admits that hot gin might be a hard sell to the modern drinker, but he proclaims, "I'm a gambling man!"*

POWER STRIP

When Rudolph Haas patented a mutation from his orchard, he turned a botanical anomaly into a household staple: the Haas avocado. This same year, the Hoover Dam generated electricity to someday power the glitzy future of a sleepy town called Las Vegas. We turned to Chef José Andrés of Las Vegas's China Poblano to celebrate the Haas (now Hass) avocado in a manner befitting Sin City.

BEIJING GLASS NOODLES
JOSÉ ANDRÉS

MAKES 2 SERVINGS

For the sesame dressing

5½ tablespoons sesame paste

2½ tablespoons fermented soy paste

1 tablespoon plus 1 teaspoon aged soy sauce

1 tablespoon plus 1 teaspoon Chinkiang black vinegar

1 teaspoon sesame oil

½ teaspoon kosher salt

1 teaspoon sugar

1⅓ cups canola oil

5½ tablespoons rice vinegar

For the noodles

1 cup cooked cellophane noodles

1 teaspoon kosher salt

¼ cup sesame dressing (from above)

¼ avocado, thinly sliced

¼ cup bean sprouts

¼ cup julienned carrot

¼ cup thinly sliced napa cabbage

¼ cup julienned jicama

1 tablespoon julienned red Fresno chili

1 teaspoon thinly sliced chives

½ teaspoon white sesame seeds

Prepare the sesame dressing: Blend all ingredients together until smooth.

Prepare the noodles: In a small bowl, toss together the cellophane noodles, salt, and 2 tablespoons of the sesame dressing. Place in the middle of a glass serving bowl. Arrange the avocado, bean sprouts, carrot, napa cabbage, jicama, chili, and chives around the bowl. Drizzle the remaining sesame dressing on top of the vegetables and noodles. Sprinkle with sesame seeds.

José Andrés *was named Outstanding Chef of the Year at the 2011 James Beard Foundation Awards, and in 2012,* Time *magazine called him one of its 100 Most Influential People in the World. He is dean of the Spanish studies program at the International Culinary Center.*

...AND EAT IT, TOO

Edith Bouvier Beale made her debut at the Pierre Hotel in New York City on New Year's Day, 1936. The papers gushed over her appearance, describing her dress as white net appliquéd in silver, accented by the wreath of gardenias she wore in her hair. This was Edie's coming out into society, and a far cry from the embattled and disillusioned woman she would later be immortalized as in *Grey Gardens*. The Albert and David Maysles documentary portrayed Little Edie as a tragic figure who, as a young girl, lamented, "You can't have your cake and eat it too in life." Aldo Maiorana imagined this pear tarte à la tatin as an elegant debutante's breakfast at the Pierre, although its decadent simplicity might be as well suited for the unlikely fashion icon and eccentric woman getting on in years.

PEAR TARTE À LA TATIN
ALDO MAIORANA

Prepare the dough: In a bowl, whisk together the flour and salt. Empty the flour mixture onto a work surface, preferably marble, and make a well in the mixture. Crack the egg into it and with your fingers mix the white and yolk of the egg together, then start incorporating some flour into the mixed egg. When the mixture is pasty (not dry), squeeze the lemon into it. Cut the butter into this, using a pastry blender or chef's knife. Knead with your fingers to form a smooth ball. Wrap in plastic wrap and let rest in the refrigerator for at least 1 hour.

Prepare the pears: Peel, halve, and core the pears. Dot the frying pan with the butter and melt over medium-low heat. On top of the butter, arrange the pears as tightly as possible, cut side up. Continue cooking at medium-low heat until a little color appears on the pears. Sprinkle the sugar on the open faces of the pear halves to sweat some of the juices that begin the caramelization. Do not turn the pears. Cook until the caramel is golden blond but the pears are still firm.

MAKES 8 TO 10 SERVINGS

For the dough
1 cup plus 2 tablespoons unbleached
all-purpose flour, plus more for rolling
Pinch salt
1 large egg
A good squeeze fresh lemon juice
4 tablespoons unsalted butter, chilled

For the pears
8 to 10 Bosc pears, fat and round at the
bottom, brownish but not bruised
4 tablespoons unsalted butter, diced
½ cup sugar

Special equipment
Pastry blender or chef's knife
9-inch cast-iron or stainless-steel
frying pan
Rolling pin
12-inch ceramic plate

Finish the tarte: Preheat the oven to 375°F. Lightly dust the work surface with flour. Remove the dough from the refrigerator and roll out with a rolling pin on the work surface until the dough is very thin and round. With a paring knife, trace a perfect circle the same size as the frying pan opening; set this circle of dough on top of the pears. Tuck the dough into the sides of the pan around the pears. Make an incision in the center of the dough, a chimney for the steam to escape. Put the pan into the heated oven and bake until the pastry top is golden brown.

To remove the finished tarte from the frying pan, cover the opening with the ceramic plate and invert until the tarte comes away from the pan, landing downside up on the plate. Tip: Hold the handle of the pan with a pot holder and the plate with the other hand while inverting. 🌿

Little Edie might have changed her mind about having her cake and eating it too if she'd tried **Aldo Maiorana**'s *pear tarte à la tatin, a dish that brings new life to the breakfast ritual for the precious while Bosc pears are in season. Aldo was born in Sicily and raised in France, and the coffee he roasts at his café in Greenport, New York, tastes of both influences. Having served as majordomo to a French navy commander in the South Pacific and toured Paris, Caracas, and Provence, Aldo settled on Long Island's North Fork, where his pastries and biscotti are legendary and his buttery scones a well-guarded secret (believe us, we tried to get the recipe!).*

BY THE DARK OF THE KNIGHT

Twenty-seven issues into publication, *Detective Comics* introduced Batman. The magazine went on to become the longest continually published comic book in American history, and it is still in circulation today.

Chad Robertson conjured this edible tribute to the city of Gotham and its long-standing guardian, dark as the night sky, with a fruit filling underneath its cowl as sweet as the Dark Knight's mild alter ego, Bruce Wayne.

GOTHAM BUCKWHEAT APPLE TART

CHAD ROBERTSON

Prepare the dough: Measure the flour onto your work surface. Spread the flour out into a rectangle about ⅓ inch deep. Scatter the butter cubes over the flour. Toss a little of the flour over the butter so that your rolling pin won't stick, then begin rolling. When the butter starts flattening out into long, thin pieces, use a bench scraper to scoop up the sides of the rectangle so that it is again the size you started with. Repeat the rolling and scraping 3 or 4 times—the dough will be a shaggy pile with visible long ribbons of butter throughout.

In a medium bowl, whisk together the salt, Sucanat, and cornstarch. Beat in the yolks one at a time. Whisk in the crème fraîche and continue whisking until thoroughly combined. Scrape the flour-butter mixture together into a mound, make a well in the center, and pour the egg yolk mixture into the well. Using the bench scraper, scoop the sides of the dough onto the center, cutting the wet ingredients into the dough.

Keep scraping and cutting until the dough is a shaggy mass. Shape the dough into a rectangle about 10 by 14 inches. Lightly dust the top with flour. Roll out the rectangle until it is half again as large. Scrape the top, bottom, and sides together and

MAKES 1 DOUBLE-CRUST 9-INCH TART, 4 TO 6 SERVINGS

For the buckwheat tart dough

2⅓ cups buckwheat flour, plus more for shaping

21 tablespoons unsalted butter, cut in 1-inch cubes and frozen

2 teaspoons fine sea salt or kosher salt

1 cup Sucanat

1 teaspoon cornstarch

4 large egg yolks

1 tablespoon plus 1 teaspoon crème fraîche or kefir

For the apple filling

7 to 8 firm apples (such as Gravenstein, Jonathan, or Granny Smith), peeled, cored, and coarsely grated

1 tablespoon freshly squeezed lemon juice

⅓ cup walnuts, toasted and finely ground

1 tablespoon buckwheat flour

2 teaspoons cornstarch

3 tablespoons plus 1 teaspoon unsalted butter, melted

⅓ cup granulated sugar

½ vanilla bean, split lengthwise, seeds scraped

¼ cup packed golden raisins, soaked in hot water for 10 minutes, drained

For the tart

Yolk of 1 large egg

2 tablespoons heavy cream

Raw sugar

Special equipment

Rolling pin

Bench scraper

9-inch tart pan with removable bottom

reroll. Repeat 3 or 4 times until you have a smooth and cohesive dough. You should have a neat rectangle measuring about 10 by 14 inches. Transfer the dough to a large baking sheet, cover with plastic wrap, and chill well, about 1 hour.

Prepare the apple filling: While the dough is chilling, in a large bowl, toss together the grated apples and lemon juice. Stir in the walnuts, flour, cornstarch, butter, sugar, vanilla bean seeds, and golden raisins until well combined.

Prepare the tart: Divide the dough into two equal portions. To roll a circle from what is roughly a square, start out with the dough positioned as a diamond in front of you, with the handles of the rolling pin at two points of the square. Roll from the center toward each end, flattening only the center, not the two points that are nearest to and farthest from you (at top and bottom); leave those two points thick. Now turn the dough so that the flattened-out corners are at the top and bottom. Again roll from the center toward the points nearest to and farthest from you, again stopping short of both the top and the bottom. Now you should have a square that has little humps in between the pointy corners. Roll out the thicker areas and you will begin to see a circle forming. Keep rolling until the dough is a little more than ⅛ inch thick (each circle should be about 14 inches in diameter). Repeat with the remaining portion of dough. Transfer the circles to a baking sheet using your rolling pin, placing parchment in between the layers. Chill the dough until firm, about 10 minutes.

Fit one circle of dough into the bottom of your tart pan, folding in the sides to ensure that the dough is not stretched to fit the tart pan but instead meets all the curves of the pan. Place the apple filling in the center of the dough, evening it out so the pan is full to the brim but the filling is not mounded. Lay the second dough circle on top of the base, pressing from the center out to expel excess air and pinching down on the edges to adhere the top dough to the bottom. Chill until firm, about 10 minutes.

While the tart is chilling, preheat the oven to 400°F.

In a small bowl, whisk together the egg yolk and cream. Brush the egg wash over the tart, then sprinkle with raw sugar. You can

bake the tart immediately or hold it, unwrapped, for a couple of hours in the refrigerator. (Or you can skip the egg wash and sugar at this point, wrap the tart airtight, and freeze it for up to 2 weeks. When ready to bake, remove it from the freezer, brush with egg wash and sprinkle with sugar, and bake immediately, increasing the baking time by 10 minutes.)

Bake the tart until the crust has visibly puffed and baked to dark blue-brown, about 30 minutes, rotating the tart at the halfway point to ensure even browning. If the pastry is browning too quickly, reduce the oven temperature to 375°F or tent the tart loosely with aluminum foil. Remove from the oven and let cool to room temperature on a wire rack; serve warm or at room temperature. ⚜

Chad Robertson *is one-half of the husband-and-wife team at Tartine Bakery in San Francisco, continually regarded as the best bakery and breakfast in the city. He and his partner, Elisabeth Prueitt, won the James Beard Foundation's award for Outstanding Pastry Chefs in 2008.*

THE LAST THANKSGIVING

Ever since President Lincoln's 1863 Thanksgiving Proclamation, the government and people of the United States have agreed "to set apart and observe the last Thursday of November next, as a day of Thanksgiving and Praise." This tradition endured until 1939, when Franklin Roosevelt decreed that the annual holiday would be celebrated a week earlier. The reason was economic: there were five Thursdays in November that year, which meant that Thanksgiving would fall on the thirtieth, leaving just twenty shopping days until Christmas. By moving the holiday up a week, the president hoped to give the depressed economy a lift by allowing shoppers more time to make their purchases and spend more money.

Protesting citizens and angry letters made their way to the White House in droves. Split almost across party lines, the country celebrated separately, with Democratic states observing the newly designated "Franksgiving," and so-called red states staying true to the final Thursday in the month as a "Republican Thanksgiving." Franksgiving wreaked holiday havoc between families and calendar printing presses alike. The year 1938 was the calm before the storm, when Americans were able to enjoy the most comforting classic of them all, a roast turkey with chestnut stuffing, hold the drama.

THANKSGIVING TURKEY WITH SAUSAGE AND CHESTNUT STUFFING

ELAINE LEARNARD & ANN—MARIE SCHEIDT

ON THANKSGIVING EVE

🦃 **Prepare the stuffing:** Experience has shown that the best way to prepare the chestnuts for the stuffing is to have a friend who peels them at his or her house and brings them over

MAKES 16 TO 20 SERVINGS, PLUS LEFTOVERS IF YOU'RE LUCKY

For the stuffing

4 cups peeled chestnuts, broken into pieces (see directions; we usually leave a handful as whole chestnuts)

16 tablespoons unsalted butter (approximately)

4 to 6 large yellow onions, diced

1 bunch celery, diced

2 heaping tablespoons whole or rubbed dried sage (it is light and puffy, so you need more of it than of the other herbs)

1 tablespoon dried thyme

1 tablespoon dried summer savory

4 large bay leaves

Freshly ground black pepper

2 pounds firm supermarket white bread (Pepperidge Farm or Arnold—anything fancier does not seem to improve the outcome; Wonder and the like don't hold up well), dried to be crisp but not toasted on very low heat in the oven right on the racks, torn in pieces, and allowed to cool

Two 16-ounce packages Jones Sausage (the short, fat cylinder, not the individual links), separated into smallish bits while being cooked in a frying pan, drained

Salt

in time to add to the stuffing before it is chilled for the night. (If the friend also irons the table linens, so much the better.) If you must peel them yourself, make X's on the round side of the chestnuts with a sharp knife, roast or boil 8 or 10 at a time, and shell and peel each batch while it is still hot. Your fingers may get a little burned, brown, tired, and sticky. Make sure to leave enough time for this task; it can take a while.

Once the chestnuts are ready, in a very large pot, melt half the butter, add the onions and celery, and cook on medium-low heat until the vegetables are tender. Add the sage, thyme, savory, and bay leaves. Put each of the herbs in your palm and crush it up between your hands before adding, to make it smaller and to freshen the flavor, except for the bay leaves—those can go in whole. (I beg you not to use prepared seasoning; it ruins the whole stuffing.) Grind a generous amount of black pepper into the pan and stir the seasonings into the vegetables. Mix in the bread pieces.

When the bread is fully combined with the buttery vegetables, add the drained sausage and mix well. This takes some physical effort. Finally, add the chestnuts and mix again. Add salt if needed. When you are mixing the main ingredients together, add melted butter as needed to get things mixed and blended.

Be sure to taste this stuffing. It should taste and smell like Thanksgiving. Adjust the seasonings if necessary, putting any additional herbs into some melted butter to blend into the mix.

Cool the stuffing, cover, and chill well overnight.

NOTE: There is controversy about making stuffing in advance, about what temperature is safe to store it at, and whether to cook it inside the bird. We have found that it is fine made ahead of time as long as it is kept chilled and separate from the bird overnight, and the roasting temperature for the turkey is never at less than 350°F.

ON THANKSGIVING DAY

Prepare the turkey: About 6 hours before you plan to serve dinner, preheat the oven to 450°F. Take the bird from the refrigerator or the trunk of your car or wherever else you stored it.

For the turkey and broth

One 24- to 26-pound turkey
  (A big turkey is easier to cook right than a small one, and it is a very forgiving dish. We have always gotten our turkey from Raleigh Farms—one of Long Island's last operating poultry farms—in Kings Park, Suffolk County, New York.)
8 to 12 tablespoons unsalted butter
1 handful whole black peppercorns
1 peeled onion stuck with
  3 or 4 whole cloves
1 teaspoon or so dried thyme
2 or 3 bay leaves
Freshly ground black pepper

For the gravy

Turkey drippings, still in the roasting pan
Broth (from above)
Salt
2 heaping tablespoons cornstarch
1½ cups cold water

Remove the giblets and neck from the bird and wash the cavity. Remove any stray large feather quills that may still be present around the neck opening.

Prepare the broth for the gravy: Set the heart, liver, and kidneys to cook in about 2 tablespoons of the butter in a frying pan on medium to low heat. Place the neck and any meat juices in the giblet bag in a pot with about 1 quart water, and add the peppercorns, onion, thyme, and bay leaves. Cover the pan, bring the water almost to a boil, lower the heat, and cook this broth for at least an hour. Feed the fried heart and liver to someone who loves them, and add the kidneys (cut in 2 or 3 pieces) to the broth in the pot. Pour boiling water into the frying pan in which you cooked the giblets, stir around to get the browned buttery bits, and then add that water to the broth. Cook a little longer and then strain and set aside.

Stuff the bird: Once you've started making the broth, use your hands to get as much stuffing as deep into the cavity from both ends as you can. Allow the stuffing to overflow a little from the main cavity (the one that will be facing up, on top, when the bird is in the pan) and then just pull the skin up around it; no need to lace or sew. At the other end of the bird, tuck the extra skin under the stuffing. We have read advice about stuffing birds loosely but do not do that with a big turkey. People prefer the stuffing that has been in the bird, so you want to get as much in as possible; both bird and stuffing benefit from the close encounter. So stuff the bird as much as you can and place in the roasting pan with the legs sticking up. The extra stuffing can be cooked in two greased casseroles—put in the oven when you take the turkey out to wait for carving—because not enough fits in the bird to feed the twenty-odd who have come for dinner.

Roast the bird: Heat about 1½ cups water with 4 tablespoons of the butter and a generous grinding of black pepper in a small pot. This will be used when the bird is first in and there is not yet enough juice for basting.

An ordinary large roasting pan and a very large bird are a good combination. The bird just fits in the pan and the juices (necessary for basting and good gravy) do not evaporate. So much of the bird is above the pan that it will not steam the meat, which would make the bird tough.

Put the stuffed bird in the pan and rub a little butter over the skin of the bird on the breast and legs. Put it in the oven and set the timer for 20 minutes. After 20 minutes, lower the heat to 350°F, baste the bird with the water-butter in the pot, and close up the oven as quickly as possible. Baste faithfully every 20 minutes for the first hour and three-quarters; after that, you can slack off a little. Begin using the pan juices for basting when you have some, but be careful not to spill the juices over the side or spray the contents of the baster around the oven (don't laugh—this happens very easily and wastes precious flavorful liquid). Spray a little of the water-butter from the baster into the stuffed cavity a few times to keep the inside moist, but don't waste the pan juices on this.

Conventional wisdom says 20 minutes to the pound for fowl. Our bird is always ahead of this schedule, more like 12 minutes to the pound. We've learned that larger birds cook at a faster rate. Birds (even the organic ones!) will usually have a pop-up timer and you can trust this little device. The test by wiggling the legs is also accurate: a cooked bird wiggles freely.

Prepare the gravy: When the bird has been removed from the pan to a platter or carving board (a two-person job, and it's worthwhile to use actual turkey lifter tools if you can), put the entire roasting pan on the stove over low heat. One person makes gravy while the other scoops out the stuffing and carves, because both tasks take attention and time (the gravy maker is usually overseeing vegetable preparation at the same time and the carver is protecting the meat on the platters from kitchen thieves). Add some of the broth you made from the giblets and neck to the roasting pan and keep stirring, scraping up the skin and other bits from the bottom and sides of the pan. Salt to taste.

Add the cornstarch to the cold water and stir well with a fork. You will use the cornstarch to thicken and the broth to extend the gravy as needed; it is important to be slow and incremental about both these additions, since you are balancing opposites.

"We are both incredibly grateful to the girls and their daughter, Emily, for sharing this incredible recipe, and welcoming us at their annual November gathering, which is indeed a blessing."

—Noah + Paul

Add the dissolved cornstarch mix to the roasting pan a tablespoon or two at a time and stir it while it heats, giving it a chance to thicken. Don't add more until you are sure that the thickening of the previous addition is complete. Add broth as you taste; you want to keep the turkey flavor strong but you want enough gravy for the whole meal (and, with luck, for the leftovers). Strain the gravy from the roasting pan into a separate pot and continue heating. By this point, the consistency should be as thick or thin as you want it. Discard the unused cornstarch mixture, but save the broth and the contents of the strainer to add to the turkey bones and skin when you make soup the next day. Adjust the salt before serving.

Now here's the best part. Sit down with your guests, breathe deeply, and look at every person around the table. It is a joy and a blessing to have these dear ones with you. Give thanks.

NOTE: The complaints about turkey are that it is dry and/or tasteless. To avoid these problems, start with a good bird, stuff it with something flavorful and moist, baste it, and take it out of the oven and let it rest when it is done.

At the risk of alienating friends and gaining enemies, Noah and Paul are willing to go out on a limb and boldly proclaim the following: There is no other turkey, in this dimension or any other, that could possibly top this one. This recipe is truly the meaning of family, food, and giving thanks. Without hyperbole, it is the juiciest, most succulent, most hedonistic turkey you will ever have in all of your days. Make no mistake, accept no substitutions, and pray they invite you sometime.

Notwithstanding their preference for vegetarian cooking, **Elaine Learnard** *and* **Ann-Marie Scheidt** *(family friends of Noah's for over twenty-five years) have made a traditional Thanksgiving dinner together since 1978. Side dishes change, the stuffing has gotten richer, but the turkey is always fresh and organic, and once included, a guest—it has been pointed out—is ever after expected back.*

MAKING LOVE

Struck by a wave of nationalism, Siam attempted to modernize itself by changing the name of the nation to Thailand, which literally translates to "land of the free." This new era for Southeast Asia promoted the export of its unique culture and cuisine to the United States. In the coming decades, Thai dishes would dramatically gain popularity and undergo several American makeovers and hybridizations—in some cases, with disappointing results. In this case, Hong Thaimee provides a recipe, inspired by that original excitement of the Thai people of 1939 who were eager to share their culture, history, and exotic flavors with the world, in its original, flavorful form.

GRILLED SHRIMP PAD THAI FOR TWO

HONG THAIMEE

Prepare the sauce: Combine all of the ingredients in a bowl and stir until well combined. Set aside.

Prepare the pad thai: Heat a grill over medium heat until hot and coat the surface with vegetable oil. Cook the shrimp until no longer translucent, about 4 minutes. Brush lightly with the sauce. Remove from the heat and set aside.

Heat the 2 tablespoons oil in a wok over medium heat and cook the garlic and shallot until the garlic is fragrant, about 1 minute (do not brown). Increase the heat to high and add the eggs. Break the yolks and stir gently, but do not scramble. Cook for 1 to 2 minutes.

Once the eggs are fully cooked, add the noodles and about ½ cup of sauce. Stir until the noodles are soft. Add the tofu and turnip. Mix well. Stir in the chives, bean sprouts, and peanuts, reserving some as condiments. Serve with the grilled shrimp and

MAKES 2 SERVINGS

For the sauce
¼ cup tamarind puree or paste
¼ cup palm sugar
¼ cup fish sauce

For the pad thai
2 tablespoons vegetable oil, plus more for grilling
1 pound shrimp, deveined, heads removed, shells left on (6 to 8 large shrimp)
2 teaspoons finely chopped garlic
2 teaspoons finely chopped shallot
2 large eggs (preferably organic)
6 ounces rice stick noodles, hydrated in room-temperature water
¼ cup extra-firm tofu, finely diced
1 tablespoon pickled turnip (available at Asian specialty stores)
2 ounces chives, cut into 1-inch lengths (¼ cup)
4 ounces (½ cup) bean sprouts
2 tablespoons peanuts, crushed

For the garnish
Ground red chilies
A couple of lime wedges
Fresh banana blossom, cored (optional)

garnish with a sprinkling of ground chilies, a wedge of lime, and fresh banana blossom, if desired. ✺

Hong has explained that pad thai was introduced by Prime Minister Phibunsongkhram as the nation's national dish, after the change in Siam's name. "The prime minister produced pad thai to promote nationalism and to reduce the domestic rice consumption during its tough economy in the midst of World War II," she says. "The stir-fry technique derives from Chinese immigrants. Instead of using a curved wok like the Chinese would, flat iron woks known as kra ta pad *thai were created. The best pad thai I ever had was back in the day when it was cooked on a flat wok on a real charcoal stove—a steady heat that crisps a crusty egg, caramelizes the sauce over the noodles without making them mushy, and adds a hint of a smoky flavor."*

The word "love" is a constant in **Hong Thaimee***'s vocabulary, whether it's an expressed devotion for the cuisine of her native Thailand; the love she feels when immersed in the kitchen; or the atmosphere of love she strives to create at Ngam, the Manhattan restaurant where she serves modern Thai comfort food. This powerful and genuine attitude is all part of Chef Hong's approach to introducing New Yorkers and the world to authentic, updated Thai flavors as she works to become the female face of the popular Southeast Asian cooking style in the United States.*

"Trust me, this is the kind of pad thai that will declare a Thai in you!"

MY HEART BELONGS TO HATTIE

For the mascarpone icing

2 cups mascarpone cheese

2 cups confectioners' sugar

¼ teaspoon pure vanilla extract

½ cup unsweetened dried coconut chips

For the lemon curd filling

4 large egg yolks

Pinch salt

1 cup granulated sugar

½ cup freshly squeezed lemon juice
  (3 to 4 lemons)

8 tablespoons unsalted butter

Grated zest of 1 lemon

For the cake

1 pound plus 4 tablespoons
  unsalted butter, plus 1 tablespoon
  for the cake pans

4½ cups all-purpose sifted flour,
  plus 4 tablespoons for the cake pans

1½ cups cream cheese

4½ cups granulated sugar

9 large eggs

½ cup unsweetened coconut milk

1 teaspoon pure vanilla extract

For garnish

Fresh unsprayed gardenia buds

Special equipment

Three 9-inch round cake pans

At the twelfth annual Academy Awards, a tearful Hattie McDaniel, looking every inch a Hollywood star in a demure floor-length blue gown and with gardenias in her hair, exclaimed, "My heart is too full to tell you just how I feel." She had just received one of the highest honors any actor can attain, the Oscar for Best Performance by an Actress in a Supporting Role. The irony of this victorious moment was that the role she was honored for was that of a maid in the film *Gone with the Wind*. The same limiting and stereotypical role was offered to her time and again by the writers and directors who failed to recognize her talent, depth, and charisma. Before she gave her acceptance speech she and her companion were sitting at a special segregated table just for the two of them, while her white unnominated costars populated the best seats at the front of the house as the film swept most of the award categories. Thankfully, Ms. McDaniel's personal life was anything but segregated. Locally, she was perhaps even more famous for her hospitality than her acting talent. Ms. McDaniel counted Bette Davis and Clark Gable as close friends who would never miss one of her large-scale soirées complete with larger-than-life spreads of sumptuous food and free-flowing cocktails. She truly was a Hollywood A-lister who gained the respect and admiration of her peers, with or without an Oscar.

LEMON COCONUT STACK CAKE
NICOLE TAYLOR

Prepare the mascarpone icing: Using an electric mixer, combine the cheese, sugar, vanilla, and coconut chips. Cover and chill in the fridge.

Prepare the lemon curd filling: In a bowl, whisk the yolks, salt, sugar, and lemon juice. Cut the butter into pats and add. Place the mixture in a saucepan over low to medium heat. Whisk until the curd is thick, around 15 minutes. Take off the stove and

whisk in the lemon zest. When cool, put in a container and store in the fridge.

Prepare the cake: Preheat oven to 325°F. Butter and flour three 9-inch cake pans.

Using an electric mixer, cream the butter and cream cheese. Gradually add the sugar and beat until fluffy. Add the eggs one at a time, beating well after each addition. Add the coconut milk. In stages, incorporate the flour, but do not overbeat. Stir in the vanilla. The batter will be thick. Transfer equally into the 3 cake pans. Bake for 1 hour. Use the toothpick method to test doneness. Let the layers cool a few minutes in the pan, then invert onto cooling racks. Let cool completely before assembling the cake. If the icing has hardened, let it come to room temperature to soften.

Assemble the cake: Cut each layer in half horizontally with a serrated knife to separate each layer into 2 disks. Lay the first half-layer down on a plate or cake pedestal and spoon on lemon curd; spread it to cover almost to the edge. Stack the next half-layer on top, and cover it with mascarpone icing. Stack the next layers, alternating curd and icing. Be generous with the icing on the top of the final layer and add a circle of curd in the center.

Dress the top of the cake with fresh gardenias. Cut with a fancy cake cutter and serve on elegant dessert plates. 🌿

> *Nicole tells us her cake is "an ode to Hattie's elegance on the screen and at home . . . As the first African American person to win an Oscar, Ms. McDaniel was best known for her talent, gorgeous hats, and love for flowers (she delayed one of her weddings because the bridal bouquet was stuck on a plane), and she loved celebrating and entertaining."*

Georgia native **Nicole Taylor** *has been an artisanal candy maker, an activist, and a social media maven, and is currently the host of* Hot Grease, *a progressive food culture radio program on Heritage Radio Network. Nicole worked as a community outreach consultant for the Brooklyn Food Coalition, raised funds for the Urban Justice Center through the Vendy Awards, and now is an instructor for a GED and internship program that weaves in urban farming. She is featured in* America I Am: Pass It Down Cookbook *and is a principal at NAT Media.*

Marcus Samuelsson

Michael Harlan Turkell

Kenneth McCoy

Gail Zweigenthal

Shuna Lydon

Noel Cruz, Nicole Ponsec

Beatrice Ojakangas

Joshua Marcus

Alex Raij

Jason Denton

40

a, & Miguel Trinidad

TALK OF THE TOWN

Earle MacAusland's Gourmet *magazine* heralded an era of good living through good cooking. The timing wasn't ideal for such a publication: the United States would enter World War II, and rationing would go into effect, soon thereafter. The magazine became an instant collectible, as subscribers were urged to save their issues until rationing was over. Enjoying a sixty-seven-year run, *Gourmet* saw America's evolution through the decades. A huge fan of the magazine himself, Marcus Samuelsson offers up an elegant snack that says "good living," suitable for getting a party started or curling up and enjoying by yourself.

GRAVLAX WITH CAVIAR AND CRÈME FRAÎCHE
MARCUS SAMUELSSON

Combine the sugar, salt, and peppercorns in a small bowl and mix well. Place the salmon in a shallow dish and rub a handful of the salt mixture into both sides of the fish. Sprinkle the salmon with the remaining mixture and cover with the dill.

Cover the dish with plastic wrap and let stand for 6 hours in a cool spot, then transfer the salmon to the refrigerator to cure for 36 hours.

Scrape the seasonings off the gravlax. Slice it on the bias into thin pieces. Serve on pumpernickel toast points or blini, with a dollop of crème fraîche and caviar.

NOTE: Buy only the freshest salmon for gravlax; ask the fish market for sushi-quality fish. If wild salmon from the Pacific Northwest or Alaska is in season, so much the better; wild salmon has more flavor and a better texture than the farm-raised fish.

Marcus Samuelsson *is the Ethiopian-born, Swedish-raised chef behind Harlem's Red Rooster, Marc Burger, Ginny's Supper Club, and*

MAKES 12 TO 14 SERVINGS

1 cup sugar
½ cup kosher salt
2 tablespoons cracked white pepper
2½ to 3 pounds skin-on salmon fillet, in one piece, pin bones removed
2 or 3 large bunches fresh dill, coarsely chopped (including stems)

For serving
Pumpernickel bread or blini
Crème fraîche or sour cream
Caviar

1941

others. He became the youngest chef to be honored with a three-star review from the New York Times *as executive chef at Aquavit, where he was also awarded Best Chef: New York City by the James Beard Foundation in 2003. Marcus has brought his worldly perspective to several acclaimed cookbooks, and plays host to presidents and dignitaries between stints serving the best fried yard bird in Harlem.*

SNOW JOB

In 1942, America was at war. By year's end, with rationing in full effect, many Americans were looking forward to the much-needed distraction of a simple holiday at home. The silver screen came to the rescue with the feature-length fluff piece *Holiday Inn*. In its most memorable scene, audiences were treated to "White Christmas," an Irving Berlin–Bing Crosby song about a soldier's longing to engage in a holiday that's simple, honest, and spent with family. The lighthearted tune instantly became a holiday classic, and has since sold over fifty million copies.

BLINTZ-KRIEG DUCK
CHINESE FIVE-SPICE DUCK BLINTZES WITH TART CHERRY SAUCE
MICHAEL HARLAN TURKELL

Prepare the blintz skins: Combine the flour, eggs, milk, sugar, and salt in a food processor and blend until smooth, scraping down the sides of the container intermittently. Transfer the batter to a pitcher, cover with plastic wrap, and let rest in the fridge for at least 1 hour or up to 3 days.

Place a nonstick crepe pan over medium heat. Brush the surface with butter and pour in 2 to 3 tablespoons of batter, lifting the pan from the heat as soon as the batter hits it and tilting so the batter forms a thin, even layer. Cook the batter for 1½ to 2 minutes, until tiny bubbles appear on the surface and the top looks dull. Transfer to a sheet of wax paper, uncooked side up. Cover with another sheet of wax paper and a paper towel. Continue making the rest of the batch, stacking the finished skins between sheets of waxed paper and paper towels.

Blintzes can be used immediately or cooled, wrapped airtight, and stored in the freezer for up to 1 month.

MAKES 8 BLINTZES, 4 SERVINGS

For the blintzes
(adapted from Dorie Greenspan)

1 cup all-purpose flour
4 large eggs, at room temperature
1 cup milk, at room temperature
½ teaspoon sugar
Pinch salt
Unsalted butter, melted, for cooking
8 ounces cream cheese, softened

For the cherry sauce

2 cup thawed frozen, pitted tart or dark cherries
1 piece star anise
1 tablespoon cornstarch
1 cup cold water
Confectioners' sugar
Lemon juice

For the duck

One 12- to 16-ounce duck breast half
Salt
1 teaspoon Chinese five-spice powder
1 tablespoon unsalted butter

Special equipment

Nonstick crepe pan
Wax paper
Cast-iron (or oven-safe nonstick) skillet

Prepare the cherry sauce: In saucepan, warm the cherries and star anise on medium-low heat. In a small bowl, combine the cornstarch and water and mix until well blended. Slowly add the cornstarch slurry to the cherries. Heat until thickened, 10 to 15 minutes. Remove the star anise. Stir in confectioners' sugar to sweeten and add lemon juice to adjust acidity.

Prepare the duck: Preheat the oven to 250°F. Score the skin of the duck breast in a crosshatch or diamond pattern, but do not cut into the flesh. Rub in salt and the five-spice powder. Heat a cast-iron skillet to medium-high heat. Add the butter and duck breast, skin side down. Cook about 5 minutes, without burning the skin. If it smells and/or looks like the skin is burning, turn the heat down to medium. Flip the duck over and cook for about 5 minutes more.

Add 2 tablespoons of the cherry sauce to the rendered fat and glaze the duck. Finish it in the oven for approximately 5 minutes, or to your desired doneness.

Remove from the oven, let rest, and slice on an angle into 8 pieces.

Assemble the blintzes: Place 2 tablespoons cream cheese in the center of a blintz skin, and top with a slice of duck. Roll up the blintz. Repeat with 7 more blintz skins. Put 2 filled blintzes on each plate and spoon warm cherry sauce on top.

> *"I'm engaged to a shiksa," Michael says. "I often cook for her family during the holidays but leave one tradition untouched (until now). After all the presents are open on Christmas morning, her mother makes blintzes filled with softened cream cheese, topped with a cherry sauce all Michiganders have in their blood, and dusted with a snowflake shake of powdered sugar. I'm usually halfway done before grace, not out of disrespect but due to my unbridled enthusiasm."*

Michael Harlan Turkell *is a photographer, host of the Heritage Radio Network's* The Food Seen, *and former photo editor of* Edible Manhattan *and* Edible Brooklyn. *He's also a pretty good cook and an all-around incredible guy. For all of those reasons and more, he's a valued friend.*

"With every year that passes, we're hungry for more of the same, and thankful, for all that we've gained."

RIVETED

MAKES 1 COCKTAIL

2 ounces W. L. Weller bourbon
½ ounce Gran Classico Bitter
¼ ounce allspice dram
½ ounce Aperol
¼ ounce Combier Original triple sec
Brandied cherry and orange twist

Wartime brought her into existence, a popular song gave her a household name, and Norman Rockwell painted her for the cover of the *Saturday Evening Post*. When women entered the workforce to replace the men who had gone off to war, they were fulfilling a duty to their country. J. Howard Miller gave a face to their effort with his iconic "We can do it!" employee morale poster, depicting a female factory worker rolling up her sleeve. Decades later, Rosie the Riveter's image still endures as a symbol of empowerment.

"THE AMÉRICAIN" COCKTAIL
KENNETH McCOY

Combine the first 5 ingredients in a mixing glass, add ice, and stir. Strain and serve up in a chilled coupe with a brandy-soaked cherry and orange essence added (from an orange twist, discarded).

For "The Américain," Kenneth envisioned a scene in which the shift bell has just rung and Rosie puts down her wrench to grab a seat at a bar and enjoy a much-deserved after-work whistle whetter. Having recently taken in a screening of the year's favorite film, *Casablanca*, she lets her imagination run to Morocco.

Adding the brandied cherry garnish, Kenneth seems to have fallen under the same spell as Rosie. "There is something smoldering, sexy, and seductive about this cocktail."

Kenneth McCoy *was raised in the New York City bars owned by his father and frequented by musicians and actors of the '70s and '80s. An accomplished actor himself, he says one of his favorite roles is running one of the coolest downtown haunts, TriBeCa's Ward III.*

" 'The Américain' is a worldly affair, starting with a bourbon that was available at the time, adding Combier for a hint of Paris, bitter orange peel and allspice for a taste of the Mediterranean, and Aperol to recall Italy."

DOING MORE WITH LESS

From tires to typewriters, sugar to shoes, distribution of almost every staple of American life in the 1940s became tightly rationed. Home cooks and culinary professionals alike were forced to come up with new ways to "do more with less" and to create interesting substitutes for otherwise familiar products and ingredients such as cream or butter. While some would turn to canned milk, instant coffee, or dehydrated eggs, a resourceful mind would have looked to more local, readily available foods that could sustain the body and soul during lean times.

SEAFOOD STEW WITH TOMATOES AND BASIL

GAIL ZWEIGENTHAL

Prepare the quick rouille: Stir all the ingredients together in a bowl and chill, covered. Can be made a few days ahead.

Prepare the stew: In large skillet, heat the oil and sauté the onion and fennel over moderate heat for about 10 minutes. Add the garlic and cook, stirring, for a few minutes more, without burning the garlic. Stir in the oregano, thyme, saffron, tomatoes, clam juice, and wine, and simmer about 30 minutes. Store up to 2 days ahead, reheating on the day of serving.

Preheat the oven to 400°F. On a large baking sheet, combine the shrimp with a tablespoon or so of olive oil and salt and pepper to taste and roast for 6 to 7 minutes, until just done. Remove from the baking sheet and chill.

In a kettle, steam the clams in a little water with Old Bay seasoning added, if desired. As they open, transfer them to a bowl. Cook down the liquid until the flavor is intensified. Strain through cheesecloth or a coffee filter into another bowl. Chill the clams and broth separately.

MAKES 6 TO 8 SERVINGS

For the quick rouille

1 cup Hellman's mayonnaise

1 tablespoon lemon juice

2 teaspoons paprika (I use Spanish smoked sweet paprika)

1 teaspoon (or less) cayenne pepper

1 clove garlic, minced

For the stew

¼ cup olive oil, plus more for cooking the seafood

1 large onion, chopped

1 bulb fennel, trimmed and sliced thin on a mandoline

2 tablespoons chopped garlic

2 teaspoons dried oregano

2 teaspoons chopped fresh thyme

¼ teaspoon saffron threads, or more to taste (optional)

One 28-ounce can Muir Glen fire-roasted crushed tomatoes

3 cups bottled clam juice (three 8-ounce bottles of Cento will do)

1 cup dry white wine

1 pound large shrimp (about 18), shelled and deveined

Salt and freshly ground pepper

18 littleneck clams

½ teaspoon Old Bay seasoning (optional)

8 large sea scallops

Cayenne pepper

½ cup chopped fresh basil leaves

For the ciabatta toast

1 loaf ciabatta bread (can be day-old)

1 tablespoon extra virgin olive oil

1 clove garlic, cut in half

"Substituting chopped fresh tomatoes for canned would be more appropriate for the era, as would substituting whatever fish or shellfish was available. I don't know if bottled clam juice was available in 1945, but a homemade shrimp or clam broth would certainly work."

In a skillet, sauté the scallops in oil for 3 to 4 minutes, turning once, until just opaque. Cut one in half to test for doneness. Quarter the scallops and chill.

Prepare the ciabatta toast: Preheat the oven to 350°F. Slice the ciabatta on a diagonal, brush with olive oil, and rub with a cut garlic clove. Bake on a baking sheet about 20 minutes.

At serving time, add the seafood to the stew and reheat, adding as much strained clam broth as needed to thin to desired consistency. Taste for seasoning and adjust with cayenne, salt, and pepper. Stir in some of the rouille and add the basil. Serve the toast on the side.

"When trying to come up with a recipe that would have been appropriate to 1945, when such things as meat and eggs were severely rationed, my mind went to those things that could be foraged—like clams, scallops, and other seafood if one was lucky enough to live near a bay and the ocean, and vegetables that one could grow," Gail says. "This seafood stew fits the bill, and aside from being delicious, most of the work can be done a day or more ahead."

Gail Zweigenthal *has loved food for as long as she can remember. Her earliest memory is of going to the local Chinese restaurant with her family at age four and claiming an entire order of barbecued spareribs for herself. She learned to cook in her seventh-grade home economics class; and later in high school, when a "very sophisticated friend" introduced her to* Gourmet, *she was hooked. At age twenty-one, when Gail landed a position as an editorial assistant at the magazine, she was over the moon. She spent thirty-four years on staff at* Gourmet, *serving as editor in chief for the last ten. At a time when only a handful of women held the same title at any publication, Gail was at the helm of one of the twentieth century's most opulent and adored magazines. Not too shabby for the blue-eyed charmer from the home economics class. Since then she has earned a master's degree in psychoanalysis, but her most gratifying times are when she is entertaining friends and eating barbecued spareribs.*

IT'S MORE FUN TO COMPUTE

In 1945, an amazing advance in technology was completed. The first general-purpose electric computer, the Electronic Numerical Integrator and Computer (ENIAC), emerged from the veil of secrecy under which it was constructed during the final years of the Second World War and was heralded in the press as a "Giant Brain," a tool that would change the course of America's scientific affairs and expand the capacity of reason. The device, which filled a large room and weighed thirty tons, was a precursor to the modern desktop computer.

ORIGINAL BRAIN TAPIOCA AMBROSIA
SHUNA LYDON

Prepare the tapioca: Bring the water to a boil in a large saucepan. When the water is at an active boil, pour in the tapioca, stirring with a wooden spoon to break it up. Do not turn down the heat. Stir aggressively but intermittently for 8 to 10 minutes, until the liquid looks less like the Milky Way and more like a cloudy day. Shut off the heat, cover, and set a timer for 20 minutes.

After 20 minutes, the tapioca should appear clear and thick. Stir to break up the mass and pour through a sieve to drain off the liquid. Meanwhile, heat the coconut milk with the milk, raw sugar, and salt. When the coconut milk mixture comes to a boil, tilt the drained tapioca in. Turn the heat down to a simmer and set a timer for 10 minutes. Stir every couple of minutes.

Crack the eggs into a bowl and whisk to break up, like you're making scrambled eggs. Add the granulated sugar and whisk to combine. After about 10 minutes, the tapioca should be thickening. Pour in the egg mixture and stir continuously for about 5 minutes. Shut off the heat and stir in the vanilla. Place a small amount in a bowl and set in the refrigerator.

MAKES 6 TALL PARFAIT GLASSES

For the tapioca
6½ cups cold water
1½ cups small pearl tapioca
One 14-ounce can organic coconut milk
1¾ cups milk
½ cup raw or turbinado sugar
Pinch kosher salt
4 large eggs
5 tablespoons granulated sugar
Dash vanilla extract

For the topping
1 cup unsweetened dried coconut
A combination of 3 or 4 tangerines, blood oranges, and/or navel oranges
½ cup dried sour cherries, or 1 cup pitted fresh cherries

In a few minutes, taste the tapioca. Sprinkle in a bit more vanilla, sugar, or salt to your specific taste. Portion into six parfait glasses and set in the refrigerator. Make sure there are no strong smells in your fridge like onions, garlic, or fish; dairy-based desserts will always absorb smells.

Prepare the topping: Toast the coconut gently over low heat in a small saucepan; set aside to cool. Cut the skins off the citrus and cut inverted triangles into the fruit, removing only the segments but no white pith. Carefully reserve in a bowl in the refrigerator.

When ready to serve, sprinkle the parfait tops with cherries and assorted citrus segments, and top generously with toasted coconut.

NOTE: Extra tapioca will keep in a tightly covered container for 7 to 10 days, refrigerated.

> *"Tapioca, the weird, mysterious, and exotic faraway ingredient, somehow slipped past officials looking out for Communist infiltrators. Together with coconut, oranges, and all-American cherries, this dessert represents nicer, prettier thoughts after a ravaging war with devastating consequences and secrets about the future revealed."*

Shuna Lydon *identifies herself as a fruit-inspired pastry chef. She has worked in such notable kitchens as the French Laundry, Gramercy Tavern, and Anna Hansen's Modern Pantry in London. Shuna is also the author of* Eggbeater, *an irresistible read of a blog with an insider perspective not often covered in mainstream food media. When she isn't baking in basement kitchens, Shuna can be found scouring farmers' markets and New York's Chinatown for peak-season fruit and new ingredients.*

"Ambrosia:
food of the gods,
of utopia,
of the future!"

MAKES 4 TO 6 SERVINGS

3 bay leaves

6 cloves garlic, peeled

4 whole fresh finger chilies, plus ¼ cup chopped or diced fresh finger chilies

¼ cup whole black peppercorns

2 pounds pork belly, in 1 piece

2 pig ears, cleaned

2 pork snouts, cleaned and deboned

Vegetable oil

1 tablespoon minced garlic

2 ounces minced fresh ginger (¼ cup)

¼ cup chicken livers, pureed

¼ cup kalamansi juice

¼ cup sugarcane vinegar

Salt and freshly ground black pepper

4 to 6 large eggs

2 ounces red onions, diced (½ cup)

Special equipment

Dutch oven

Grill pan or barbecue

Deep-fry thermometer

Small cast-iron skillets or sizzle plates (1 for each serving)

THOUSAND ISLANDS

Although the Philippines originally declared their independence from Spain's colonial rule in 1898, it wasn't until July 4, 1946, that the United States recognized this nation made up of thousands of islands. Filipino cuisine draws on the vestiges of Chinese trade routes and the cultures of Spanish settlers and Malay travelers; frequently, all of these influences are recognizable in a single dish. It often goes a step further, riffing and mashing up touchstones of American comfort food and Western culture like Spam or hot dogs, all while retaining a unique island flavor. An excellent example of this balancing act is sisig, the tasty pork pileup and unofficial national dish whose interpretations and preparations also number well into the thousands.

SISIG

NOEL CRUZ, NICOLE PONSECA & MIGUEL TRINIDAD

Preheat the oven to 350°F. In a large Dutch oven, combine the bay leaves, garlic cloves, whole chilies, peppercorns, pork belly, ears, and snouts and add enough water to come 1 or 2 inches up the side of the pot. Bring to a boil, then transfer to the oven and braise for 2½ to 3 hours, until the snout and ears are tender. Baste the meats with the braising liquid occasionally, adding more water if necessary. Remove the pork parts from the braising liquid and allow them to cool. Discard the braising liquid and clean and dry the Dutch oven.

In a hot grill pan brushed lightly with oil, or oven an open flame, grill the pig ears and snouts until slightly charred. Remove from the heat and cool slightly. Slice the ears and snouts into thin strips and set aside.

Heat 1 to 2 quarts oil to 350°F in the Dutch oven. Dice the pork belly and deep-fry until lightly crispy; set aside.

In a large frying pan, heat 2 tablespoons vegetable oil over medium-high heat until shimmering.

Add the minced garlic, chopped chilies, and ginger and cook for 1 minute. Add the pureed liver and stir until cooked through. Add the sliced pork parts, the diced pork belly, kalamansi juice, and vinegar. Incorporate all the ingredients well and cook until heated through. Season with salt and pepper; set aside.

To assemble each serving: Heat a small cast-iron skillet or cast-iron sizzle plate over a high flame. Carefully pour in 1 teaspoon oil and add 5 ounces (¾ cup) of the pork mixture.

Top each serving with a raw egg and garnish with the diced red onion. Serve in the skillet or sizzle plate.

Formerly an advertising executive by day and dishwasher-hostess-server-bartender by night, **Nicole Ponseca** *is now a restaurateur. Her goal was simple: put Filipino food on the culinary map and make pinoys proud. Chef* **Miguel Trinidad** *combines his Dominican heritage and New York City upbringing in the kitchen. He keeps honesty, simplicity, and quality as cornerstones of his cooking philosophy. "I like to keep the energy positive in the kitchen," he says. "It has an impact on the food."* **Noel Cruz** *is a graduate of the Culinary Institute of America and the French Culinary Institute, with certification from the American Sommelier Association. He likes long walks on the beach and finger painting. This talented trio can be found at Maharlika and Jeepney in Manhattan's East Village.*

"COOKING LIGHT"

While at work building magnetrons for the radar tube division of Raytheon, to be utilized by the navy during WWII, Percy Spencer noticed that the candy bar he had in his pocket had melted. Through more focused experimentation, with a variety of foods and limiting radar exposure to the inside of a metal box, Spencer somewhat inadvertently invented the Radarange, the precursor of the modern microwave oven. The first commercially produced oven was six feet tall, weighed over seven hundred pounds, and was available at a cost of $5,000. Though the first household countertop model was still twenty years ahead, Spencer's candy-soiled pocket laid the groundwork for a machine that would eventually save cooks much more time than that, collectively, in kitchens around the world.

KONVOLUTE
DANISH FRUIT-FILLED ENVELOPES
BEATRICE OJAKANGAS

Prepare the pastry: Note that pastry dough must be refrigerated for at least 4 hours, up to 3 days in advance, for the easiest handling.

Measure 3½ cups flour into a bowl or work bowl of a food processor fitted with a steel blade. Cut the butter into ¼-inch slices and add to the flour. Process or cut the butter into the flour until the butter is about the size of kidney beans.

In a large bowl, dissolve the yeast in the warm water. Let stand 5 minutes. Stir in the cream, salt, eggs, and sugar. Add the cardamom, if desired.

Add the flour-butter mixture to the liquid ingredients, and with a rubber spatula mix carefully just until the flour is moistened. Place in a clean bowl, cover tightly with plastic wrap, and refrigerate 4 hours, overnight, or up to 3 days before use.

MAKES 25 PASTRIES

For the quick-method Danish pastry
3½ to 4 cups all-purpose flour
¾ pound unsalted butter, chilled
Two ¼-ounce envelopes active dry yeast (4½ teaspoons)
½ cup warm water
½ cup heavy cream or undiluted evaporated milk
½ teaspoon fine salt
2 large eggs, at room temperature
¼ cup sugar
½ teaspoon freshly crushed cardamom seeds (optional)

For the apricot or prune preserves
1 cup dried apricots or pitted prunes
1 cup sugar
1 cup water
1 to 2 tablespoons freshly squeezed lemon juice

For the fresh berry preserves
2 cups fresh strawberries, raspberries, or other seasonal berries, crushed
1 cup sugar

For the filling and decoration
½ cup almond paste
1 egg, slightly beaten
Swedish pearl sugar

Turn the dough out onto a lightly floured board, and dust the dough with flour. Pound, flatten, and roll the dough with a floured rolling pin to make a 16 by 20-inch rectangle. Fold the rectangle into thirds, making three layers. Turn the dough 90 degrees and roll it out into a rectangle again. Fold from the short sides into thirds. This should result in a perfect square. Repeat folding and rolling again if you wish. Wrap and chill the dough 30 minutes, or as long as overnight.

Prepare the apricot or prune preserves: In a large glass bowl or microwave-safe bowl, combine the apricots or prunes with the sugar and water. Microwave at high power for 10 minutes, stirring once or twice, until the fruit has absorbed most of the liquid. Turn into a food processor or blender and process until smooth. Add lemon juice to taste. Cool completely before filling the pastries.

Prepare the fresh berry preserves: In a large glass bowl or a microwave-safe bowl, combine the berries and sugar. Microwave at high power for 10 minutes. Stir. Return to the microwave oven and cook at high power for another 5 to 8 minutes, until the mixture is thick and jam-like and most of the juices have been absorbed. The mixture will appear glossy. Cool completely before filling the pastries.

Assemble the pastries: Cover 2 large baking sheets with parchment paper. Roll out the chilled pastry on a lightly floured surface to make a 20-inch square. The pastry may "pull back" during rolling, so let it rest between rolling efforts until you get it to the 20-inch goal size. Using a pizza cutter or a straight-edged knife, cut the pastry into 4-inch squares, making a total of 25 squares.

Mix your choice of fruit preserve together with the almond paste (easiest to do in a food processor fitted with a steel blade). Dot each of the pastry squares with this mixture.

Fold two opposite corners of a square to overlap slightly and partially cover the filling. Repeat with each pastry square, placing them on the parchment-covered baking sheets 2 inches apart. Set aside and allow to rise in a cool place for 30 to 45 minutes, or wrap and refrigerate until ready to bake, as long as overnight.

Preheat oven to 375°F.

Before baking, brush the pastries with the beaten egg and sprinkle with pearl sugar. Bake the pastries for 8 to 10 minutes, until golden. Serve warm. Store any leftovers at room temperature. ✦

Beatrice Ojakangas *stepped into the spotlight at the Pillsbury Bake-Off in 1957, ten years before the microwave would make its way onto American countertops, when her Chunk O' Cheese Bread took second prize. Beatrice elevated America's esteem for the appliance with her innovative techniques for accelerating myriad preparations, famously demonstrated on Julia Child's cooking show. She is the author of multiple cookbooks, including the first Finnish cookbook published in America and* The Great Scandinavian Baking Book, *which was inducted into the James Beard Cookbook Hall of Fame in 2005.*

WELCOME HOME

The eastern shores of the Mediterranean can be lush and tropical but are also dry and harsh. This dichotomy resulted in a complex, original, and multifaceted style of cooking and eating. The culinary history of this part of the world is possibly one of the oldest, But on May 14, 1948, when the United Nations and the United States recognized Israel, a modern twentieth-century nation was born. A new population migrated to the Near East, bringing more northern or central European traditions with them. Old and new merged and a unique blend of people, cultures, and identities fused, modernizing almost every aspect of their lives.

ROASTED GOOSE WITH MATZO BALL GNOCCHI AND MORELS IN SHERRY CREAM SAUCE

JOSHUA MARCUS

Prepare the goose: Bring the goose to room temperature and preheat the oven to 325°F. Cut excess fat from the goose and render this fat in a medium cast-iron skillet over high heat. Reserve the rendered schmaltz.

Meanwhile, remove the wing tips and giblets. Using a large needle, gently prick holes in the skin of the goose to help render the fat while cooking, taking care not to go too deep and damage the flesh. This will help make the skin crispy.

Liberally season the goose with salt and pepper; place on a rack in a roasting pan, breast side up; and put into the oven. When the goose reaches 135°F internal temperature, remove the bird from the oven but do not turn the oven off. Carefully cut the breasts from the goose. (This will prevent overcooking.) Place the remaining bird back in the oven.

In a large sauté pan, place one or both breast halves (depending on the number of people enjoying dinner with you and/or your

MAKES 8 TO 10 SERVINGS

For the roasted goose
One 10- to 12-pound goose
Salt and freshly ground black pepper

For the matzo ball dough
½ cup rendered goose schmaltz
  (can substitute or add duck or chicken
  schmaltz, if need be)
½ medium red onion, diced
2 squares unsalted matzo, broken
  into smaller pieces
6 tablespoons chicken stock
½ cup ginger beer
¼ bunch parsley, coarsely chopped
1 sprig dill, coarsely chopped
1 teaspoon baking powder
4 eggs, lightly beaten
Salt and freshly ground black pepper
2 cups matzo meal

For the matzo ball gnocchi
3 ounces (½ cup) matzo ball dough (from above)
½ cup all-purpose flour
1 clove garlic, minced

For the sherry cream sauce
1 pound morel mushrooms, cleaned
  (or sliced cremini mushrooms if need be)
2 tablespoons dry sherry
2 tablespoons chicken stock
¼ cup heavy cream
1 ounce Parmesan cheese, freshly grated
  (¼ cup), plus more if need be
Salt and freshly ground black pepper
1 sprig oregano, finely chopped
2 or 3 basil leaves, finely shredded

Special equipment
Instant-read thermometer
Knitting or trussing needle
Gnocchi paddle

level of gluttony), skin side down. There is no need to oil the pan, as the fat that renders from the goose will be sufficient. Crisp the skin. Remove the breast, slice thinly, arrange on a heatproof serving platter, cover, and reserve. Do not clean the pan.

Check the remaining bird in the oven and once the leg/thigh reaches 170°F, remove from the oven. Turn down the oven as low as it will go. Cut off the legs and thighs from the goose the same way you would cut up a duck. Pan-sear the legs and thighs until crispy, as you did with the breasts, in the same pan. Remove from the pan. Do not clean the pan; leave any rendered fat in it. Add the legs and thighs to the breasts on the serving platter, cover loosely with foil, and keep in a warm oven.

Prepare the matzo ball dough: In a sauté pan, combine the goose fat and onion, and sauté until the onion is soft.

In a large bowl, combine the broken matzo, chicken stock, ginger beer, sautéed onion, parsley, dill, and baking powder. Stir in the eggs and salt and pepper. Let this mixture sit until the liquid has been absorbed by the matzo.

Mix thoroughly. Stir in your matzo meal, letting the meal get incorporated slowly. The dough should not be too firm. Otherwise you will get really, really dense balls. Cover this mixture and place in the refrigerator.

Prepare the gnocchi: To form the gnocchi, roll out about 3 ounces (½ cup) of the dough on a lightly floured surface. (Reserve the remaining dough.) Cut the roll every inch, then roll the pieces on a gnocchi paddle, keeping your hands, the paddle, and the work surface all lightly floured.

Heat the reserved pan with the goose fat and add the minced garlic clove. Add the gnocchi and brown lightly on one side and then on the other.

Prepare the morels and sauce: Toss the morels in with the gnocchi and sauté together until the morels are golden. Hit the pan with the sherry (watch out for flames, but if someone from the opposite sex is around, it makes you look real cool!) and then the chicken stock. Let the gnocchi absorb both liquids, then hit with the cream and the cheese. Season to taste with salt and pepper.

"Geese were an easy way to gather enough fat for cooking while following kosher laws that dictate that pork fat is not to be used. The breasts were cured, then smoked and spiced to make pastrami, and a fantastic tradition was born."

Finish with the oregano, basil, and a little more cheese. Pour the gnocchi, morels, and sauce over the goose meat and serve.

"Jews in Eastern Europe at the turn of the last century were very poor," Josh says. "Their cuisine reflects that. They made stews and cured meat as a way to prolong the shelf life of products. Curing was one of the great European traditions, but beef was very expensive, while goose was plentiful."

Joshua Marcus grew up in New Rochelle, New York, and is the Pied Piper of all things smoked, cured, and schmaltzed at Josh's Deli in South Florida.

ACROSS A CROWDED ROOM

Rodgers and Hammerstein's "Some Enchanted Evening," from their 1949 musical *South Pacific*, was the duo's biggest hit. Amid lush orchestration and soaring melody, the protagonist observes his love interest and croons of seizing the moment: "Once you have found her, never let her go." To commemorate the resonant show tune, and pay homage to the love of a French expat living in Polynesia for a nurse from the American South, we turned to a chef with an evident wanderlust, Alex Raij.

POISSON CRU WITH SWEET POTATO AND PEANUT
ALEX RAIJ

In a large bowl, season the fish with salt to taste. Add citrus zest and juices and let stand 10 minutes, tossing from time to time.

Gently stir in the coconut milk, ginger ale, shallot, scallions, sugar, ginger, fish sauce, and Scotch bonnet. Chill until you are serving, no more than 3 hours.

To Serve: Fold in the cilantro, yam, and avocados. Adjust the seasoning by adding more salt or brown sugar if needed. Divide among 6 plates or bowls. Finish with a thread of peanut-vanilla oil and sprinkle with chopped peanuts.

Alex Raij is chef-owner of La Vara, Txikito, and El Quinto Pino. Known for her tapas and regional Spanish cuisine, she was voted Chef of the Year in the 2012 Eater Awards. Her worldly curiosity made her a natural for considering how the star-crossed lovers in South Pacific would translate to the table. Poisson cru is a revered Polynesian favorite with hints of French influence.

MAKES 6 SERVINGS

2 pounds sashimi-quality dry-pack scallops, tuna, fluke, or snapper, cut in ½-inch cubes

Salt

Grated zest of one lime, calamansi, or yuzu

5 tablespoons freshly squeezed lime, calamansi, or yuzu juice

1 tablespoon freshly squeezed lemon juice

One 14-ounce can unsweetened coconut milk with no stabilizers, shaken

¼ cup ginger ale

¼ cup minced shallot

3 scallions, thinly sliced, white and light green parts only

1 tablespoon brown sugar, plus more if needed

1 teaspoon grated ginger

½ teaspoon Thai fish sauce

⅛ teaspoon very finely minced Scotch bonnet or habanero pepper flesh, no seeds

3 tablespoons finely shredded fresh cilantro

1 large yam, boiled in salted water with skin on until tender, peeled, and diced in ½-inch cubes, at room temperature

3 Hass avocados, firm but ripe, diced just before serving, at room temperature

For the garnish

¼ cup toasted peanut oil, mixed with the seeds of 1 Madagascar vanilla bean

½ cup chopped roasted salted peanuts

MAKES 4 SERVINGS

For the steaks

Four 1½-inch-thick-cut 10-ounce shell
steaks (also known as minute steaks)
2 garlic cloves, coarsely chopped
¼ cup extra virgin olive oil
1 tablespoon cracked black pepper
3 to 4 sprigs thyme
Kosher salt

For the potatoes

1½ pounds Yukon gold potatoes
2 cups kosher salt
8 tablespoons unsalted butter, melted
Handful Italian parsley

For the beans

1 pound green beans, trimmed
1 tablespoon extra virgin olive oil
Kosher salt
1 cup heavy cream
1 shallot, minced
Freshly ground black pepper
2 pats salted butter
Grated zest of 1 lemon

MAKES 1 COCKTAIL

For the whiskey sour

2 ounces bourbon
½ ounce simple syrup
Juice of 1 lemon
Soda water
1 bourbon-soaked cherry

Special equipment

Outdoor charcoal barbecue
Chemical-free wood charcoal

PUT IT ON PLASTIC

On an evening in 1949, entrepreneur Frank McNamara was folding his napkin at the end of a posh business meal and realized that he had left his wallet in his other suit. Ashamed, he telephoned his wife to ask if she could bring cash to the restaurant. Vowing never to suffer the humiliation again, McNamara and a partner created Diners Club in 1950, to enable travel and dining sans cash. Frank's embarrassing evening was the start of an inseparable link between elegant dining in the moment and paying for it later.

WOOD CHARCOAL—BROILED MINUTE STEAK WITH CREAMED BEANS, ROASTED POTATOES, AND A CLASSIC WHISKEY SOUR

JASON DENTON

Prepare the steaks: Buy the steaks the night before you want to serve, and ask your butcher for the precise cut requirements listed. "Minute steak cuts" were classic in the late '40s and '50s. Since they are only 1½ inches thick, the meat really takes on the marinade.

Combine the garlic, olive oil, and pepper (no salt!) with a few sprigs of thyme. Lay out the steaks in a glass baking dish. Pour the marinade over the steaks and refrigerate.

Two hours before cooking, pull the steaks out of the fridge so the temperature can level off. Brush the excess marinade off the steaks.

Ignite the grill and let it get hot. (Use chemical-free wood charcoal for a great smoky taste.)

Generously salt the steaks on each side. Cook for 1 minute on each side.

Prepare the potatoes: Preheat the oven to 400°F.

Rinse the potatoes and leave in the colander.

Pour 2 cups kosher salt onto a baking sheet. Roll the potatoes in the salt while they are still damp, so the salt sticks to the outside of each potato. Lay the potatoes on the baking sheet. Put the potatoes in the oven 1 hour before you want to serve.

Cook for 45 minutes, or until fork-tender. Pull them out, rub off the salt, and give them a little smash. Put all the potatoes in a mixing bowl with melted butter and chopped parsley. Mix until the potatoes are coated. Serve hot!

Prepare the beans: Preheat the oven to 350°F.

Lay the green beans on a baking sheet and top with the olive oil and 1 teaspoon salt. Roast for 12 to 15 minutes.

Remove from the oven and let cool slightly.

Combine the heavy cream and shallot in a sauté pan over medium heat, and reduce the mixture by half. Add salt and pepper to taste. Add the butter.

Transfer the beans to a serving dish, top them with the cream, and garnish with the lemon zest. Serve hot!

Prepare the whiskey sour: Combine the bourbon, simple syrup, and lemon juice in a cocktail shaker and give 12 rounded shakes.

Strain over crushed ice in a rocks or Collins glass, add a splash of soda, and garnish with a bourbon-soaked cherry. 🌿

> *In regard to the manly menu he's created, Jason explains that "the 1950s were known as America's placid decade. It was calm, somewhat carefree, and hopeful. Dining out very much echoed that sentiment. Excess was not frowned upon but embraced."*

Jason Denton's *first taste of hospitality came from working in restaurants in Seattle when he was a teenager. In 1998, armed with a simple panini press and only four hundred square feet of space, Jason opened the diminutive but highly successful 'ino in New York City's West Village. Known for its robust Italian wine list and delicious menu, the award-winning restaurant built a loyal following and is often credited with creating both the Italian specialty sandwich and the wine bar craze in the United States. Having presided over multiple restaurants in Manhattan and Brooklyn, and coauthored two cookbooks, Jason has earned the right to relax with his wife, Jennifer, and sons Jack and Finn in Battery Park City, New York.*

"An overall hearty and delicious dining experience was the norm—hence the beginning of Diners Club."

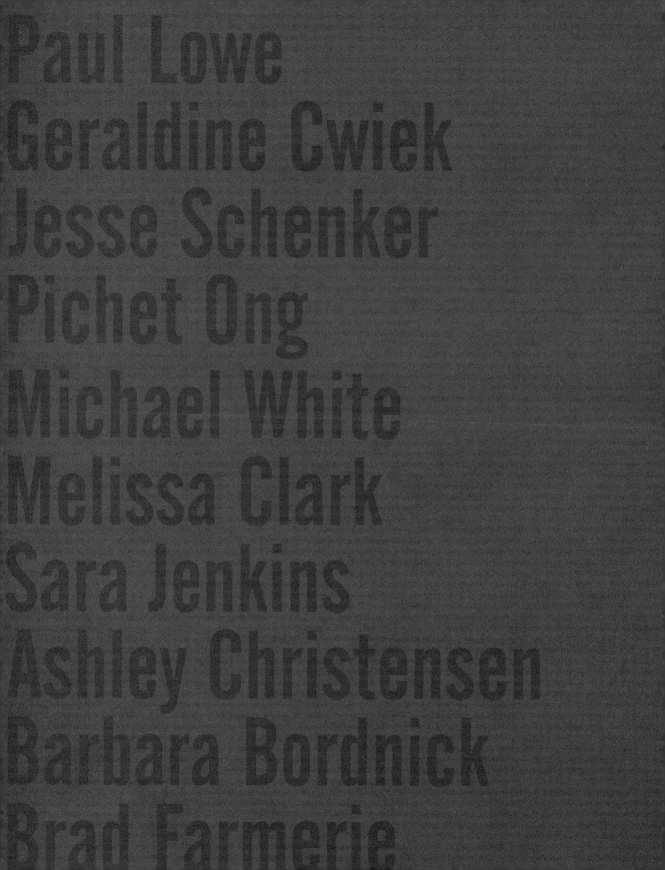

Paul Lowe

Geraldine Cwiek

Jesse Schenker

Pichet Ong

Michael White

Melissa Clark

Sara Jenkins

Ashley Christensen

Barbara Bordnick

Brad Farmerie

50

A SIDE WITH A SEAT BELT

Ever since Joseph L. Mankiewicz's All About Eve *won Best Picture at the twenty-third Academy Awards, the tale of its precocious namesake's fierce, ruthless ambition has become a modern parable for one-upsmanship. Watch out for Eve! Food stylist, photographer, journalist, and founder of* Sweet Paul Magazine *Paul Lowe got into the role to bring us a side dish that could utterly usurp your entrée. "Fasten your seat belts, darlings," says Paul. "This is going to be one spicy evening."*

MARGO'S FIERY ROASTED CHILI AND FETA DIP

PAUL LOWE

MAKES 8 SERVINGS

1 long red chili
Olive oil
8 ounces feta cheese (2 cups crumbled)
2 tablespoons freshly squeezed
  lemon juice
1 clove garlic, chopped
Fresh thyme
Melba toast, for serving

Special equipment
Blender

Preheat the oven to 375°F.

Cut the chili in half and remove the seeds. Place in a small ovenproof pan, drizzle with olive oil, and roast until the edges start to blacken.

In a blender, combine the chili with the feta, lemon juice, garlic, and 6 tablespoons olive oil. Whiz until you have a smooth dip. Transfer to a bowl and drizzle with a little olive oil. Add some fresh thyme and melba toast, and it's ready to serve.

A native of Norway who got his love for cooking from his aunt and grandmother, **Paul Lowe** *curates recipes, craft, and lifestyle in a whimsical, winsome, and approachable manner in his quarterly magazine,* Sweet Paul.

6 or more leftover steamed and
 seasoned blue crabs

½ pound dried lima beans

4 to 6 slices bacon

1 medium onion, diced

4 carrots, sliced

4 stalks celery, sliced

6 quarts water

Two 10.75-ounce cans condensed
 tomato soup

½ cup pearled barley

4 white potatoes, peeled and
 cut in ½-inch cubes

2 cups chopped cabbage

1 pound fresh string beans, trimmed

One 10-ounce package frozen corn

3 to 4 tablespoons Old Bay Seasoning

Coarse sea salt

BEYOND THE BLUE

The Chesapeake Bay Bridge—a project that had been on Maryland state's to-do list since 1938 but was shelved during wartime—was opened to traffic in 1952. Spanning 4.2 miles across the nation's largest estuary, the bridge was then the world's longest continuous over-water steel structure. The beautiful body of water below it, long teeming with the iconic blue crab, had sustained the fishing and crabbing industries and nourished the populations on the Eastern and Western Shores through the ages. Steamed with beer, vinegar, and copious amounts of Old Bay Seasoning, blue crab is served unfussily by the bushel on newspaper-lined tabletops, with shell-cracking wooden mallets as utensils and rolls of paper towels for the vain effort of keeping tidy. Leftovers from a crab feast reappear in dishes for days—in crab cakes, salads, quiches, and simple soups.

GERALDINE'S MARYLAND CRAB SOUP
GERALDINE CWIEK

Refrigerate at least 6 steamed crabs after a crab feast to make this soup the next day. Well-seasoned crabs, caked with Old Bay Seasoning, are the key to the flavor of the soup.

Soak the beans in a bowl of water overnight until they soften. Discard any skins that float to the top.

Remove and discard the top shells of the crabs. Clean their insides and crack the bodies in half with claws and legs still attached. Reserve 8 halved bodies, and pick and reserve the meat from the remaining couple of crabs.

In a large, heavy-bottomed soup pot, cook the bacon until crisp and brown. Set the cooked bacon aside to use as a garnish later on. Add the onion to the hot bacon grease and sauté until translucent. Add the carrots and celery and continue to sauté

5 minutes more. Remove the vegetables from the pot and set aside. Add the water, tomato soup, and barley to the fat in the pot and simmer for 30 minutes.

Add the 8 halved crabs along with the picked crab meat, potatoes, and cabbage. Stir, then simmer 20 minutes.

Add the string beans, corn, and the sautéed vegetables, and simmer 15 minutes, until all ingredients are cooked through. Use Old Bay Seasoning and sea salt to adjust the flavor. Ladle into bowls with one half crab in each serving, and garnish with crumbled bacon. ❧

Geraldine Cwiek *(1943–1997) was a bookkeeper and single mother of four, of whom Paul is the youngest and only son. She grew up in Baltimore, Maryland, in a Highlandtown row home with a soda shop-turned-dry-goods-store downstairs that was owned and operated by her Polish immigrant mother, Bertha. As a young girl, Gerrie learned to cook Polish favorites like sour beef and dumplings, golabki, and kruschiki, and passed these recipes on to her children along with her own takes on frugal regional fare like Maryland fried chicken, potato pancakes, and this crab soup. She was not a gourmet and cooked not for perfection but out of love and necessity. At Christmas, the house was filled with the scent of her butter press cookies and trademark red velvet cake, a tradition Paul and his sisters continue each year, the next best thing to having Geraldine's own.*

OUTSIDE THE BOX

America was glued to the television as an escape from the threat of the nuclear arms race that defined the early years of the Cold War. TV sets burst into full color for households that could afford one, the first *TV Guide* was published, and 68 percent of all televisions were tuned in as Lucy Ricardo gave birth to little Ricky. Carl Swanson ensured that there was no need to abandon the riveting developments on the small screen for even a moment when he introduced the first TV dinner in 1953, named for the shape of the tray it was served on, which resembled the front panels of a 1950s television set. Here, chef Jesse Schenker reverse-engineers Swanson's TV dinner, turning its identifying ingredients into an elegant Wellington.

MAKES 2 SERVINGS

1 large russet potato
¼ cup heavy cream
1 tablespoon unsalted butter
1 tablespoon chopped flat-leaf parsley
Salt and freshly ground black pepper
8 ounces beef tenderloin, cleaned
1 sheet puff pastry
1 cup frozen peas, thawed
1 large egg, beaten

BEEF WELLINGTON
JESSE SCHENKER

Preheat the oven to 375°F.

Wrap the potato in foil and bake for 45 minutes. While it's still warm, peel the potato and place the flesh in a bowl with the cream, butter, and parsley and beat until fully incorporated and smooth; add salt and pepper to taste. Set aside to cool.

Sear the tenderloin on all sides and set aside.

On a clean cutting board, lay the puff pastry sheet flat. Spread the cooled potato mixture evenly in the center; sprinkle with the frozen peas. Place the tenderloin on top, adding salt and pepper to taste. Cut down the puff pastry, leaving about a 2½-inch border, or just enough to fold over the beef; discard the excess. Fold the pastry over the meat and seal together, crimping with a fork. Lightly brush the beaten egg over the puff pastry and place in the refrigerator for 30 minutes. While the Wellington is chilling, preheat the oven to 350°F. Bake the Wellington for 15 to 18 minutes, until golden brown.

Jesse Schenker *is the classically trained French chef with an armful of tattoos who made the daring move of opening a private dining club in Harlem after working under Gordon Ramsay. In 2010, he made it public, moving his contemporary American concept Recette to Greenwich Village. Just months after its opening, Recette received glowing two-star reviews from both the* New York Times *and* New York *magazine.*

**MAKES ONE 8-INCH CAKE,
10 TO 12 SERVINGS**

**For the mint and
mascarpone mousses**

1 pound cold mascarpone cheese

1½ cups heavy cream

⅓ cup sugar

2 teaspoons vanilla extract

1 tablespoon mint extract

Green food coloring

For the wafers

6½ ounces unsweetened chocolate,
  chopped

2 tablespoons heavy cream

3 large eggs

3 cups all-purpose flour

¼ cup black cocoa powder

4 teaspoons baking powder

1 teaspoon baking soda

14 tablespoons butter

1½ cups sugar

1 teaspoon fine salt

1 tablespoon vanilla extract

For assembly

2 tablespoons milk chocolate
  crunchy pearls

Special equipment

2 large pastry bags

2 star pastry tips

Stand mixer with a paddle attachment

Double boiler

2½-inch ring cutter

Wire cooling rack

8-inch decorative cardboard round

POP!

The postwar era of Great Britain was a slow, gray effort to rebuild and return to normalcy. The young artists of early 1950s Britain looked to America's reconstruction and materialism, inspired by the characteristic bright colors, loud noises, and screaming typefaces. Their aesthetic became pop, a movement that blurred the lines between art, media, and commerce, later anointing Warhol as its king. The devotees of this new form embraced a loud, garish departure from the suffering of the previous decade and a glimpse into a bright future.

GRASSHOPPER ICEBOX CAKE
PICHET ONG

Prepare the mousses: Combine the mascarpone, cream, sugar, and vanilla in a bowl. Whisk slowly until combined, then at higher speed until the mixture is fluffy and holds soft peaks. Set aside a little more than half of the mixture. Whip the remaining mixture to stiff peaks.

Add the mint extract and food coloring to the mixture with soft peaks, and whip to firm peaks. Fill separate piping bags with one mousse each and leave them at room temperature so they stay soft for assembly. If preparing a day ahead, refrigerate and then leave outside the fridge to temper for an hour so they are soft enough to pipe. You will have two pastry bags: one with green mousse and one with white.

Prepare the wafers: Melt the chocolate in a double boiler and reserve. Whisk together the cream and eggs and reserve. Sift together the flour, cocoa powder, baking powder, and baking soda; reserve.

Using a stand mixer fitted with a paddle attachment, cream the butter with the sugar, salt, and vanilla, until light and fluffy. Add the melted chocolate and mix well. Pour the cream and the egg mixture into the chocolate-butter mixture in a slow stream while

mixing. Stop the machine, scrape the bottom of the bowl, and mix again until thoroughly combined. Add the sifted dry ingredients and mix until well incorporated. Divide the dough into four disks, each 1 inch thick; wrap with plastic wrap; and refrigerate the dough for at least 4 hours to rest. (This recipe makes enough dough for two 8-inch cakes. You may choose to store two disks of dough in the refrigerator or freezer until your next use, or bake them all and use the leftover cookies for delicious ice cream sandwiches!)

Preheat the oven to 350°F. Line rimmed baking sheets with parchment paper. Roll each disk of dough ⅛ inch thick and cut with a 2½-inch ring cutter. Place the cookies on the baking sheets, about an inch apart. For each cake you will need 80 cookies: approximately 2 disks of dough.

Place the scraps from the cutouts on a separate baking sheet in a single layer. Working in batches, bake the cookies for 9 to 10 minutes, until they are dry to touch on top but not well done. Bake the sheet of scraps for a little bit longer, about 12 minutes total.

Let the cookies and scraps cool completely on wire racks.

Assemble the cake: Using one piping bag, place a small amount of white mousse on a decorative cardboard round for cookies to stick to. Using the other bag, swirl green mousse on the bottom, about ½ inch thick. Place cookies on top in a neat arrangement. Repeat the process with white cream and cookies. There should be 7 layers total, starting and ending with the green cream. Top with crushed cookie from the scrap tray and milk chocolate pearls. Refrigerate for at least 4 hours or overnight. Serve straight from the refrigerator and enjoy! ⚘

Eating and cooking are **Pichet Ong**'*s hobby and heartbeat. Pichet combines the fond flavors of his childhood with modern cooking techniques to create whimsical sweet and savory offerings that are seasonal, delightfully experimental, and nostalgic. Pichet's creations can be found worldwide, from Sydney to Beijing, Istanbul to Dubai, and Tokyo to New Orleans.*

FOOTLOOSE AND COLLAR FREE

When two characters from disparate castes found commonality and romance over a shared meal of spaghetti and meatballs in a darkened alley, American viewers' hearts melted. Considered one of the most iconic moments in American animated film, Lady and the Tramp's accidental kiss as they swallow the same strand of pasta meant major success for Disney. We asked prince of pasta Michael White to create a romantic meal that could be enjoyed in a similar manner, fostering a sense of puppy love.

POLENTA CON RAGÙ DI SALSICCIA

MICHAEL WHITE

For the polenta: In a heavy-bottomed saucepot, combine the milk, water, and salt over medium-high heat. Just before it reaches a rolling boil, whisk in the polenta in a steady stream. When it starts to thicken, change to a wooden spoon and continue stirring. It may seem loose but will cook down and thicken naturally. Lower the heat, cover, and cook for 2½ to 3 hours, stirring every 5 to 10 minutes. Whisk in the butter and Parmigiano.

For the ragù: Heat extra virgin olive oil in a medium sauté pan over medium heat. Add the garlic and onion and sauté until translucent. Add the sausage and cook for about 6 minutes, breaking up clumps, until slightly browned. Add the wine to deglaze and continue to cook for about 3 minutes until dry. Add the tomatoes. Cook over low heat for 30 to 45 minutes, until the flavors have combined. Season with salt and pepper.

To assemble: Heat the broiler. Place the polenta in a terra-cotta dish. Top with the sausage ragù. Stud with mascarpone cheese, bread crumbs, and Parmigiano. Place under the broiler for 2 minutes to melt and brown the cheese.

MAKES 2 SERVINGS

For the polenta
2 cups milk
2 cups water
1 teaspoon kosher salt
⅔ cup polenta (coarse cornmeal)
3 tablespoons unsalted butter
½ cup shredded Parmigiano

For the ragù
Extra virgin olive oil
1 clove garlic, minced
1 small onion, chopped
1 pound sausage meat (no fennel)
3 tablespoons dry white wine
One 28-ounce can crushed tomatoes
Salt and freshly cracked black pepper

For serving
Mascarpone cheese
Bread crumbs
Freshly grated Parmigiano

Special equipment
Terra-cotta dish

*Although **Michael White**'s soulful interpretation of Italian cuisine might suggest that he's a boot-country native, the Wisconsin-raised chef is just an ardent (and expert) convert. Michael's culinary career began at Chicago's Spiaggia and at Ristorante San Domenico in Imola (near Bologna). Midwestern pride hasn't diminished his global ambitions: as the co-owner of Altamarea Group, White has opened seven restaurants worldwide, including Al Molo in Hong Kong. The flagship, Marea, boasts two Michelin stars and won the 2009 James Beard Award for Best New Restaurant in America. Additional projects include the Michelin-starred Ai Fiori, Osteria Morini (locations in SoHo and New Jersey), Nicoletta, and Due Mari, with new properties on the horizon; and Michael is no stranger at the White House.*

WOULDN'T IT BE LOVERLY?

The hottest ticket on Broadway in 1956 was to *My Fair Lady* with Rex Harrison and Julie Andrews. It would go on to sweep the Tony Awards the following year, and was later adapted to film. Americans have long been fascinated by the charms and mysteries of class, society, manners, and all things British. We asked the loverly Melissa Clark to whip up a cheeky, elegant British dish that would surely please the newly refined Ms. Doolittle and appeal to us American Anglophiles as well.

ROASTED LEG OF LAMB WITH MINT SALSA VERDE
MELISSA CLARK

MAKES 6 TO 8 SERVINGS, PLUS LEFTOVERS

1 bone-in leg of lamb (6 to 7½ pounds), rinsed and patted dry
6 cloves garlic, chopped
2 tablespoons fresh thyme leaves
¾ cup extra virgin olive oil
1 tablespoon plus ½ teaspoon kosher salt
2¼ teaspoons freshly ground black pepper
½ cup finely chopped fresh parsley
½ cup finely chopped fresh mint
4 teaspoons finely chopped drained capers
Lemon wedges, for serving

Rub the lamb with two-thirds of the garlic, the thyme, and ¼ cup olive oil. Season the meat with 1 tablespoon salt and 2 teaspoons pepper. Cover with plastic wrap and refrigerate for at least 2 hours or overnight. Remove the meat from the refrigerator at least 30 minutes before cooking. Preheat the oven to 400°F. Place the lamb in a large roasting pan. Roast 30 minutes; reduce the heat to 350°F and roast until medium-rare (140° to 145°F on an instant-read thermometer), 60 to 90 minutes more. Remove the lamb from the pan and rest for 10 to 15 minutes before carving.

While the lamb cooks, in a small bowl combine the parsley, mint, capers, and the remaining garlic, salt, and pepper. Stir in the remaining ½ cup oil.

To serve, transfer the sliced lamb to a large serving platter. Spoon the salsa verde over the meat; serve with lemon wedges.

"The idea of serving lamb with mint is a good one," Melissa Clark says. "After all, they are ready at the same time, with fresh mint sprouting in spring, just when lambs, born in winter, are ready to be . . . um . . . let's say culled. This said,

that glob of mint jelly served next to the usual roasted lamb leg or saddle is usually a fake green, vile thing, shimmering and unappetizing. Instead, I made the herb the star of a bright salsa verde, full of vim and zest, a bracing tonic for any season."

Redheaded, button-nosed food writer **Melissa Clark** *is beloved by all who are privy to a flash of her megawatt smile. She earned an MFA in writing from Columbia University, and began a freelance food writing career in 1994. Since then, her work has garnered awards from the James Beard Foundation and the International Association of Culinary Professionals. She is a staff member of the* New York Times, *where she writes the popular Dining Section column "A Good Appetite." In addition, Melissa has written thirty-three cookbooks, many in collaboration with some of New York's most celebrated chefs.*

FORTUITOUS MEATING

Claiborne helms the food desk at the *New York Times*, premiering his oft-imitated star system for restaurant criticism. Ginsberg's "Howl" is slammed for indecency, and Kerouac is on the road, while Lennon meets McCartney.

The year 1957 calls for a four-star, man-size main course that conjures Allen's animal, Jack's wanderlust, John and Paul's harmony—a tall order, for which Sara Jenkins has the perfect fix.

BISTECCA CHIANINA
SARA JENKINS

Set up the fire with a lot more coals than you think you need. Have a spray bottle with water handy. Ideally you will have two areas in your grill, hot and medium. Let the coals begin to gray. Score the fat on the side of steak so it does not warp while cooking. Do not salt the steak! When the coals are ready, begin cooking the steak, laying it down over the hottest part of the grill and moving it frequently. You are trying to get an even char all over, not grill marks. After about 10 minutes, flip the steak and immediately sprinkle a heavy quantity of salt (1 to 2 tablespoons) over the just cooked side. Apply a nice amount of cracked black pepper from the mill. Keep moving the steak around to cook the other side for 8 to 10 minutes. Remove from the grill to a wooden grooved cutting board and sprinkle the same amounts of salt and pepper on the second side. Let rest for 10 minutes.

Slice steakhouse-style, down the bone and into ½-inch slices on either side. Drizzle olive oil over the cut slices. Serve with lemon on the side; more oil, salt, and pepper; and a basket of freshly picked arugula. Eat with your hands for the purest expression of animal passion!

MAKES 2 SERVINGS

One 3-inch-thick porterhouse steak (about 3 pounds)

Sea salt (Sicilian medium coarse is good)

Freshly ground black pepper

¼ cup estate-produced and -bottled Tuscan or Umbrian olive oil, preferably from the most recent harvest

Lemon wedges (some say this is sacrilege!)

A bunch of arugula (picked fresh from the garden is nice)

Special equipment

Charcoal grill

Sara Jenkins's *memories of her Tuscan and Roman childhood inspired her artisanal, pasta-centric menu at Porsena in New York City's East Village. A few blocks away at Porchetta she hawks her version of Italy's street food, a richly seasoned pork roast. "This is the steak I long for," she says. "Drizzled with Tuscan olive oil, served with a chilled bottle of Grechetto (the local white wine), eaten on a long, hot summer afternoon under the shade of a massive chestnut tree as the cicadas hum and a cooling breeze wafts up from the valley below."*

"Steak in Tuscany traditionally comes from the white Chianina cow, the Etruscans' ancient beast of burden, said to be the oxen used by Romulus to till the fields where he built Rome."

IF YOU CAN'T STAND THE HEAT, GET OUT OF THE KITCHEN...

Born in one of the poorest parts of eastern Louisiana, the wild, flamboyant Jerry Lee Lewis exploded onto the Southern music scene in the 1950s, soon joining the ranks of Elvis, Johnny Cash, and Chuck Berry. Ironically, the bat-out-of-hell bad boy of rock was also a devout Christian and nephew to televangelist Jimmy Swaggart. His uncle's influence couldn't stop him from kicking, screaming, and shouting his way through electrifying performances that drove teenagers wild and made their parents hysterical. Recorded and released in 1957, Lewis's signature hit "Great Balls of Fire" shot to number one on the country charts, and went on to become one of the largest-selling singles of all time. By 1958, probably having revealed too much about his personal life to a reporter in London, Lewis returned to the United States to find himself banned from radio stations and record stores.

Undeterred, he has been writing, recording, and courting controversy ever since and was inducted into the Country Music Hall of Fame in 1986. Lewis's explosive spectacle performances have made him emblematic of Nashville's music scene and the theatrical South of the late '50s.

CRISPY CHICKEN LIVER TOAST WITH CAYENNE AÏOLI AND PICKLE RELISH

ASHLEY CHRISTENSEN

Prepare the aïoli: Marinate the cayenne in the vinegar for 20 minutes to open up the spice in the pepper. In a mixing bowl, whisk the egg yolks until airy and slightly more pale in color. Add the cayenne vinegar and the salt and whisk again until frothy. While whisking continuously, slowly drizzle in the canola oil until it is emulsified in, creating the aïoli. The aïoli will be slightly thick and coating to the palate. You may refrigerate this aïoli for up to 3 days, but it is best served fresh.

MAKES 6 TO 8 SERVINGS

For the aïoli
2 teaspoons cayenne pepper
2 tablespoons red wine vinegar
2 egg yolks
½ teaspoon fine sea salt
1 cup canola oil

For the pickle relish
1 cup small-diced pickles
 (use your favorites)
2 shallots, minced
¼ cup olive oil
Salt and freshly ground black pepper

For the liver
1 pound chicken livers
 (trimmed of any sinew)
2 cups whole milk
1 cup buttermilk
½ pound (5½ cups) all-purpose flour
1 tablespoon cayenne pepper
2 teaspoons fine sea salt
Canola oil, for frying
A crusty baguette, for serving

Special equipment
Brown paper bag

Prepare the pickle relish: In a bowl, mix the pickles, shallots, and olive oil. Season to your preference with salt and pepper, keeping in mind that some pickles may be vibrant enough not to need additional seasoning. Keep at room temperature for immediate use, or refrigerate if preparing in advance. If you do prepare this in advance, allow it to come up to room temperature before serving it.

Prepare the livers: Cover the livers with the whole milk and soak in the fridge overnight to pull excess blood and impurities out of the livers. Remove the livers from the milk and pat dry. Place them in a shallow bowl and cover them with buttermilk. In a brown paper bag, mix the flour, cayenne, and sea salt.

Heat ½ inch of canola oil in a cast-iron skillet over medium heat, to around 325°F. Line a baking sheet with three layers of paper towels.

While the oil is heating, transfer the livers to the flour in the paper bag. As you lift the livers from the buttermilk to transfer them to the flour, shake off excess buttermilk. They should just be lightly coated. Try to coat the livers with flour as you drop each one into the bag, preventing them from sticking together.

Once all of the livers are in the bag, grasp the top of the bag and shake vigorously to ensure that all of the nooks and crannies of the livers are coated with the flour. Transfer them one by one to the hot oil, spacing them out so that they are not touching one another. If this requires frying in two rounds, do so. As you see the edges of the livers browning, flip them with a pair of tongs. Once both sides are golden brown and crisp, remove the livers from the pan and place them on the paper towels, to absorb excess grease.

Be cautious! The livers tend to release a bit of liquid while cooking, which makes the oil pop a bit. Be sure to have a dry kitchen towel in hand to protect yourself while maneuvering the livers around the pan.

To serve: Slice and toast the baguette. Coat the toasted face of the bread with the spicy aïoli. Stack high with the crispy chicken livers and spoon the pickle relish over the top of the livers. Boom! ⚘

Ashley's spirited recipe is a play on Nashville hot chicken. "It ties into the boudin backbone of Louisiana by way of the chicken livers," she says.

Ashley Christensen *is master and commander of a Raleigh, North Carolina, empire of four bars and eateries. At Poole's Diner, her inventive, retro-styled menu and decor have made it a local favorite and a necessary destination for out-of-towners. Ashley is a three-time semifinalist for the coveted James Beard Award for Best Chef: Southeast.*

LADY SYNCS THE BLUES

½ pound margarine or butter
(the original recipe calls for margarine,
but I use butter), plus more for
greasing the pan

1 cup sugar

4 large eggs, separated

1½ cups all-purpose flour

1 teaspoon baking powder

2 ounces sweet almonds, blanched
and finely grated or pulverized in
a spice grinder

Miles Davis's incomparable musical style vaulted him to fame and acclaim. His 1959 album *Kind of Blue* created new directions and multiple tangents for jazz, modernizing an already dynamic and varied art form. *Kind of Blue* is Miles Davis's most popular and best-selling album, and is also one of the best-selling jazz albums of all time. Widely regarded by professional reviewers and armchair aficionados as incredibly influential, it also has the honor of having been inducted into the Library of Congress's National Recording Registry.

SANDKAGE

DANISH POUND CAKE

BARBARA BORDNICK

Preheat the oven to 325°F. Thoroughly grease a 9 by 5-inch loaf pan.

Stir the margarine or butter and sugar until the mixture goes frothy. Stir in the egg yolks one at a time, then the flour, baking powder, and almonds. Beat the egg whites until very stiff, then fold them carefully into the batter.

Gently transfer the batter to the pan. Bake the cake for 1 hour.

Test with a toothpick and let cool before serving.

"Kind of Blue *and* Ascenseur pour l'Échafaud (Elevator to the Gallows) *were ever present in my studio in the '70s and '80s, especially when I was working on a calendar of great women in jazz," Barbara says. The calendar, commissioned by Polaroid and titled* A Song I Can See, *was a series of 8-by-10 photographs of the legendary women who contributed to the genre in the twentieth century. Using large-format Polaroid film, Barbara created iconic*

likenesses of women who, in some cases, were never photo-graphed before and would never be shot again, preserved just once for the annals of history.

After stints in Copenhagen and Paris, **Barbara Bordnick** *made a name for herself in New York as a photographer. Her landmark career and contributions to fashion, advertising, and fine art photography are all the more remarkable considering that Barbara rose to fame at a time when the industry was truly a boys' club.*

UNDER THE KNIFE

Revered as a benchmark of American cinema, Psycho *was poorly reviewed at its premiere but went on to become the film that made half of the country terrified to take a shower. From Saul Bass to Alfred Hitchcock, almost everyone involved has come to be honored as a master of his craft. But it is perhaps the performances of Janet Leigh (as the ironically named Marion Crane) and the ultimate scenery chewer himself, Anthony Perkins as the taxidermy-obsessed serial killer, Norman Bates, that end up stealing the show. As a nod to Norman, and his less-than-typical tastes, we asked Brad Farmerie to create a "stuffed bird" that would please even the most demanding mother, steal the scene in every close-up, and even look great in black-and-white.*

"STUFFED BIRD"
BRAD FARMERIE

Prepare the brined bird: Combine all ingredients except the wine and chicken and bring to a boil.

Cool to room temperature and add the wine. Place the chicken in a plastic tub with a tight-fitting lid. Add the brine and cover with the lid.

Brine in the refrigerator for 12 hours, flipping the container every few hours to evenly coat the bird.

Prepare the chorizo-corn stuffing: Brown the chorizo in a little duck fat, then remove the meat, reserving the fat in the pan. Add the celery, carrot, onion, sage, and thyme to the fat and sweat over low heat until the vegetables are translucent. Add the corn and cook for 1 to 2 minutes, until the corn is cooked. Remove the vegetables from the heat and let cool.

In a large bowl, whisk together the egg, chicken stock, and cream. Add the cooked meat and vegetables, and stir to combine.

MAKES 6 TO 8 SERVINGS

For the brined bird
2½ cups chicken stock
1 cup water
¼ cup kosher salt
⅓ cup light brown sugar
¼ cup Chinese black vinegar
2 tablespoons cider vinegar
2 tablespoons soy sauce
1 bay leaf
5 sprigs thyme
2 sprigs tarragon
1 clove garlic, smashed
1 shallot, sliced
1 teaspoon fennel seeds
¼ teaspoon smoked paprika
½ teaspoon coriander seeds
¼ teaspoon Aleppo pepper
¼ teaspoon mustard seeds
¼ teaspoon herbes de Provence
¼ cup dry white wine
One 4-pound air-chilled chicken, head and feet on

For the chorizo-corn stuffing
10 ounces fresh chorizo, removed from casing and finely chopped
Duck fat or extra virgin olive oil
⅔ cup diced celery
2 tablespoons grated carrot
⅔ cup chopped onion
1½ teaspoons chopped fresh sage
½ teaspoon finely chopped fresh thyme
⅔ cup corn kernels
1 egg, beaten
2 tablespoons chicken stock
2 tablespoons heavy cream
5 cups white bread cubes, crust removed
⅓ cup chopped fresh chives
Salt and freshly ground black pepper

Place the bread cubes and chives in a separate large bowl and slowly pour in the meat-vegetable-egg mixture, stirring all the time to combine. Season with salt and pepper.

Cook the bird: Preheat the oven to 325°F.

Remove the bird from the brine, thoroughly drain, and pat dry. Stuff the stuffing into the cavity of the chicken, loosely packing it in. Truss the bird with a needle and kitchen string to help contain the stuffing. Roast until a thermometer inserted into the thigh reaches 160°F, about 1 hour 30 minutes. It will continue to cook even when removed from the oven. Allow the chicken to rest at room temperature for 30 minutes; this will offer a much more moist, delicious bird.

Prepare the serving dish: Place the stuffed chicken on a serving platter and cut it free from the ties that bind (aka the string you used to truss it). Garnish the plate with blistered tomatoes, tomatillo, fresh cilantro, fried sage, and oregano. Enjoy! ✳

> Brad's Psycho-*inspired stuffed bird "is dressed to impress—whether for a classic horror movie, a luxe dinner party, or an anxiety-inducing Thanksgiving, the bird is center stage and has to play the part."*

When **Brad Farmerie** *was a kid in Pittsburgh, his mother, an avid home cook, exposed him to a variety of cuisines and insisted on home-baked bread and vegetables straight from the family garden. That influence is present in Brad's contributions to New York restaurants, Public, Madam Geneva, and Saxon + Parole.*

For serving
Blistered tomatoes
Tomatillo
Fresh cilantro
Fried sage
Oregano

Special equipment
Trussing needle
Kitchen string
Instant-read thermometer

"Source a farm-fresh chicken, preferably with the head and feet attached— a centerpiece that can make any night a celebration. Next, erase any lead belly bomb memories of stuffing with my recipe full of knockout punches— salty/spicy chorizo, sweet corn, moisture-rich veggies, an abundance of fresh herbs, and just enough cheap white bread to keep you grounded in '60s and '70s Americana. A memorable meal in the making."

❧

Jacques Pépin

Hooni Kim

Jeff "Beachbum" Berry

Jim Botsacos

Troy Sidle

David Schuttenberg

Ghaya Oliveira

Brian Konopka & Salva

Steve Schul & Paul Zab

Claudia Gonson

FRANCO-AMERICANS

After several rewrites, edits, and extreme pare downs, Julia Child leaped into the hearts and homes of Americans with *Mastering the Art of French Cooking.* The book aimed to present classic (and sometimes difficult or fussy) French cooking techniques, with their possibly obscure ingredients, to the home cook. The book became an instant classic and a runaway success, with James Beard proclaiming, "I only wish I had written it myself." But Child was only one part of the wave of Francophilia that was sweeping the whole country. The recently installed First Lady Jacqueline Kennedy redecorated the White House, restoring the interiors to their original grandeur, and insisted on entertaining on the same grand scale, hiring a chef named René Verdon, whom she interviewed in French. Many families attempted to emulate the First Lady's worldly sensibilities both in decorating and in dining. Meanwhile, a young French chef named Jacques Pépin, who had relocated to the United States in 1959, was working his way up at New York's historic Pavillon restaurant. Later, Howard Johnson, a regular Pavillon customer, hired Jacques to develop recipes for the quintessentially American restaurant chain, where he served as director of research and new development for ten years.

STUFFED QUAIL WITH GRAPE SAUCE
JACQUES PÉPIN

Prepare the stuffing: Coarsely chop the leek, carrots, and celery in a food processor. You should have about 3 cups total. Melt 1 tablespoon of the butter in a large skillet. Add the vegetables, garlic, and ¼ cup water and cook, covered, over medium heat for 10 minutes or until the vegetables are soft and the water has evaporated. Add the salt and pepper, mix well, and set aside to cool.

MAKES 4 SERVINGS

1 leek, trimmed (leaving some green), split, washed, and cut into 1-inch pieces (about 2 cups)

2 carrots, cut into 1-inch pieces (about ¾ cup)

2 stalks celery, cut into 1-inch pieces (about ¾ cup)

2 tablespoons unsalted butter

2 cloves garlic, crushed and finely chopped (about 1 teaspoon)

1 teaspoon kosher salt

¼ teaspoon freshly ground black pepper

4 large quail (about 7 ounces each) or semiboneless quail (about 5 ounces each)

1 pound chicken bones (if using semiboneless quail)

2 teaspoons vegetable oil

1 quart water

1½ tablespoons dark soy sauce

1 teaspoon honey

1 cup seedless white grapes

½ teaspoon cornstarch, dissolved in 1 teaspoon water

1 tablespoon minced fresh parsley or chives

Special equipment
Food processor

Pastry bag fitted with a plain tip (optional)

Steamer

Prepare the quail: Cut through the shoulder joints of each quail and, using your fingers and thumbs, separate the meat from the central carcass and pull the carcass out without cutting the skin open. Cut off the ends of the drumsticks and remove the wing tips, leaving the first and second joint of the wings attached to the shoulder. Remove the thighbones. (All the removed bones should weigh about 8 ounces.) The only bones remaining in the quail will be the ones in the drumsticks and attached wings. Put the quail bones or chicken bones in a skillet in one layer with the remaining 1 tablespoon butter and the oil and brown over low heat, covered, turning them occasionally, for 20 minutes.

Add the 1 quart water and 1 tablespoon of the soy sauce to the skillet and bring to a boil. Reduce the heat, cover, and boil gently for 30 minutes. Strain the stock through a fine-mesh sieve set over a saucepan; discard the bones. Boil the stock to reduce it to 1 cup. Set aside in the pan.

Preheat the oven to 425°F.

Using a pastry bag with a tip, or a spoon, stuff the quail with the cooled vegetable mixture. Arrange the quail on a heatproof plate, place them in a steamer, and steam, covered, over boiling water for 5 minutes.

Meanwhile, mix the remaining ½ tablespoon soy sauce with the honey in a small bowl.

Transfer the quail to a small ovenproof skillet and brush them with the soy mixture. Roast them in the oven for 10 minutes, then baste them with the liquid that has accumulated in the skillet.

Heat the broiler and broil the quail 6 to 8 inches from the heat for 5 minutes, until nicely browned.

Meanwhile, add the grapes to the reserved stock, bring to a boil, and boil for 1 minute. Add the dissolved cornstarch and stir until the sauce thickens. When the quail are cooked, arrange them on a serving platter. Strain the accumulated juices in the skillet into the sauce, then pour the sauce over the quail. Sprinkle with parsley or chives and serve. 🪶

NOTE: This recipe was originally published in *Essential Pépin* (Houghton Mifflin Harcourt, 2011).

Jacques Pépin *was born in Bourg-en-Bresse, near Lyon. He was first exposed to cooking as a child in his parents' restaurant, Le Pelican. At age thirteen, he began his formal apprenticeship at the distinguished Grand Hotel de l'Europe in his hometown. He subsequently worked in Paris, training under Lucien Diat at the Hôtel Plaza Athénée. From 1956 to 1958, Jacques was the personal chef to three French heads of state, including Charles de Gaulle. Jacques is not only an accomplished chef and culinary hero to millions but also an extremely talented artist, illustrator, and painter who resides in Connecticut.*

DOCTOR'S ORDER

MAKES 4 SERVINGS

1 tablespoon sesame oil

1 tablespoon vegetable oil

1 pound pork belly,
cut into 1 by 1 by ¼-inch cubes

3 tablespoons minced garlic

1 tablespoon minced ginger

1 pound napa cabbage kimchi,
cut into 1- to 2-inch strips

3 quarts dashi, chicken stock,
water (whatever is available)

2 tablespoons *gochujang*
(Korean red pepper paste)

2 to 4 tablespoons *gochugaru*
(Korean chili flakes), depending
how spicy you want it

2 packs instant ramen (preferably
Nongshim Shin Ramyun)

4 hot dogs, cut on the bias into
½-inch pieces

One 12-ounce can Spam,
cut into 1 by 1 by ¼-inch cubes

1 pound silken tofu, cut into
1-inch cubes

1 bunch scallions, trimmed and
roughly chopped

2 to 3 tablespoons soy sauce

Capitalizing on the already popular series of James Bond novels by Ian Fleming, the film *Dr. No* (the debut of the Bond series) attempted to capture the glamour, mystery, and international appeal of James Bond himself, portrayed by the dashing Scotsman Sean Connery. In the film, Bond travels to Jamaica, tailed by the incredibly beautiful Honey Rider (played by the superhuman Ursula Andress). While reviews were tepid, the low-budget film was quite profitable and went on to spawn not only a multitude of Bond adventures but also a multitude of imitators, defining the very spy genre itself. *Dr. No* remains one of the most popular and referenced film of the sixties. For this year, we wanted a dish that would combine glamour, sex appeal, the mystery of international espionage, and a distinct heat.

BOODAE JJIGAE

SPICY DMZ STEW

HOONI KIM

Heat the sesame oil and vegetable oil in a pot over medium-high heat. Sear the pork belly on one side, then add the garlic and ginger and stir-fry for 3 minutes. Remove and reserve the pork, leaving the fat in the pan. Stir-fry the kimchi for 5 minutes. Stir in the dashi, *gochujang*, *gochugaru*, and 1 packet of the ramen soup base, if desired. Add the hot dogs, Spam, and the stir-fried pork belly and cook for 5 minutes. Add the ramen noodles and tofu and cook for 2 minutes. Add the scallions and cook for 1 minute more. Season with soy sauce and serve quickly as the ramen noodles can easily overcook. It's best to eat the stew with the noodles first, and then any leftover stew with rice.

Hooni Kim *was born in Seoul, but since the age of ten, he's lived stateside in New York and we've been lucky to have him. As the chef and owner of Hanjan and Danji, where patrons line up well before opening, the dashing Hooni reinvents Korean cuisine in his own signature*

small-plates style. *The chef's spicy stew, he says, was originally invented in 1962 "in a small US army base town in Korea named Uijungbu. It was after the Korean War and proteins were scarce all over Korea. Fortunately the local Koreans in the town had access to US army meats such as Spam, hot dogs, and bacon and this dish was invented. So very Korean in flavor using US-based processed meats. Fusion out of necessity!" Mr. Bond would approve.*

TIKI BOOM

The Polynesian cocktail craze ignited in 1930s Hollywood by Don the Beachcomber seemed to have reached its saturation point in 1963, when Walt Disney unveiled the Enchanted Tiki Room at Disneyland. But the popularity of the Luau Restaurant in Beverly Hills, which served regulars like Liz Taylor, Warren Beatty, and Eartha Kitt, was evidence that the tiki boom was here to stay.

LUAU COCONUT COCKTAIL
JEFF "BEACHBUM" BERRY

MAKES 1 COCKTAIL

1 whole young coconut (see Note)

2 ounces fresh coconut water, drained from the young coconut

½ ounce freshly squeezed lime juice

½ ounce unsweetened pineapple juice

1 ounce simple syrup (1 part organic cane sugar dissolved in 1 part water)

1 ounce canned coconut milk (Thai Kitchen Organic preferred)

1 ounce light Virgin Islands rum

1 ounce gold Virgin Islands rum

Remove the top of the coconut with a large, very sharp chef's knife. Start by shaving the fibrous outer skin from the top of the coconut with light strokes, until you've exposed the crown of the inner shell. With a good whack, dig the heel of your knife into the side of the crown, taking care to keep your free hand well away from the strike zone. You should now easily be able to pry the coconut open. Drain the coconut water into a container and set aside. Save the empty coconut shell, too.

Pour 2 ounces of the fresh coconut water, the lime and pineapple juices, simple syrup, coconut milk, and both rums into a cocktail shaker filled with ice cubes. Shake vigorously. Pour unstrained into the coconut shell. Garnish with a long-handled spoon, for spooning out the soft, jelly-like young coconut meat—delicious after soaking in rum and lime!

NOTE: Young coconuts are much easier to deal with than the hard-shelled mature variety. Not only are they simpler to open, but they make a good drinking vessel, as the shell sits evenly on a tabletop. They are available in the produce section of many supermarkets and in Asian and Latin groceries.

This drink is his updated take on a classic served at the Luau Restaurant. "Its conversation-piece presentation typifies the theatrical 1960s tiki drink style, as does its

flavor profile," Jeff says. The drink harks back to the origins of tiki, "as Don the Beachcomber first started serving drinks in a young coconut back in the 1930s when he single-handedly invented the tiki bar and the tiki drink."

Jeff "Beachbum" Berry *is a learned scholar of tropical drinks, with a history-spanning site (beachbumberry.com), a comprehensive i-device app, and a growing library of retuned tiki recipes under his belt.*

MAKES APPROXIMATELY 24 SMALL DONUTS, 6 SERVINGS

For the loukomas (Greek donuts)

1 ounce fresh yeast

¾ cups whole milk

5 tablespoons water

4 cups all-purpose flour, sifted, plus more for kneading

3 tablespoons plus 1 cup sugar

½ teaspoon fine salt

½ cup full-fat plain yogurt (preferably Fage)

3 tablespoons butter, softened

1 large egg

Nonstick cooking spray

2 tablespoons ground cinnamon

1 quart canola oil, for frying

1 quart olive oil, for frying

For the mastic mix

1 teaspoon sugar

1 small piece mastic

MAKES 6 SERVINGS CHOCOLATE

For the hot chocolate

2 cups whole milk

2 cups heavy cream

Mastic mix (from above)

2 tablespoons sugar

Pinch salt

3 ounces semisweet chocolate, chopped

3 ounces bittersweet chocolate, chopped

Steamed milk foam, for serving

Ground cinnamon, for serving

FAIR GAME

With the world watching and America attending, the 1964 world's fair was a modern collision of technology, media, music, commerce, and cuisine, and the lavish Greek Pavilion was no exception. As quoted in the official guide, exhibit highlights were "Depictions of Greece's innumerable contributions to civilization" as well as portraits of "the Great Greeks who helped formulate Western thought." By night, the pavilion restaurant became a market with wandering minstrels, goods like Greek rugs and honey for sale, and samplings of Mediterranean and Aegean dishes to be eaten romantically "under the stars."

KAKAO ME MASTIHA KE LOUKOUMAS

MASTIC-SCENTED HOT CHOCOLATE AND CINNAMON-SUGAR GREEK DONUTS

JIM BOTSACOS

Prepare the loukoumas: Put the yeast in a large bowl. In a medium saucepan, combine the milk and water and bring to approximately 100°F. Remove from the heat and whisk into the yeast until fully dissolved.

Place the flour in a stand mixer fitted with a dough hook. Add 3 tablespoons of the sugar, the salt, yogurt, butter, and egg. Turn the mixer on at low speed and slowly begin adding the water-yeast mixture until the dough comes together. If it looks a little dry add a touch more water. Once it comes together, turn out onto a lightly floured work surface. Knead until the dough comes together, silky in texture like light, slightly tacky pizza dough. Line a rimmed baking sheet with parchment paper, coat with nonstick spray, and place the dough in the pan, pushing down lightly so the dough takes the form of the pan. Cover with

Instant-read thermometer
Stand mixer
1½- to 2-inch ring cutter
Deep-fry thermometer
Spice grinder
Double boiler

plastic wrap and put in a warm area to rest for about 20 minutes or until double in size; the dough will be more elastic.

Remove the plastic and turn out onto a lightly floured work surface; the dough will be in the shape of the sheet pan. Lightly dust the dough with a small amount of flour. Using a wooden rolling pin, roll over the dough gently end to end, pushing out the air until the dough is approximately ¼ inch thick and the size of the sheet pan. Cover and let rest about 5 minutes.

Line another baking sheet with parchment paper. Using a ring cutter, begin cutting the dough. Cut all the donuts as close together as possible so as not to waste much of the dough. Place the cut donuts on the sheet pan. Cover if not frying them immediately.

Line a baking sheet with several layers of paper towels. In a large bowl, combine the cinnamon and the remaining 1 cup sugar. Into a deep, heavy stainless-steel pot fitted with a deep-fry thermometer, pour the canola and olive oils. Slowly heat the oils to 325°F. Place 4 donuts in the oil; they will begin to puff and get lightly golden around the edges. Using a slotted spoon, gently turn each donut over to the other side, and cook for 1 minute until golden. Remove and place on the paper towels to drain the oil. Let the oil return to 325°F before frying the next 4 donuts. While the donuts are still warm, toss them in the cinnamon-sugar mixture.

Prepare the mastic mix: Grind the sugar and mastic together well in a spice grinder. Set aside.

Prepare the hot chocolate: In a medium stainless-steel saucepan, combine the milk, cream, mastic mix, 2 tablespoons sugar, and salt. Place over medium heat and whisk until well combined. As the mixture comes to a simmer, whisk occasionally so that the milk does not burn.

While the milk mixture is heating, place all the chopped chocolate in the top of a double boiler over low heat, allowing the chocolate to become soft while the milk is coming up to temperature.

Continue whisking the milk mixture until it comes to a bare simmer. Strain the milk mixture into the softened chocolate. The heat from the milk will melt the chocolate completely. Whisk to combine. Transfer the chocolate-milk mixture to the saucepan over medium heat, continuously mixing until it comes to the first sign of a simmer. Remove from the heat and whisk for 30 seconds more, until completely combined.

To serve: Place hot chocolate in mugs and top with steamed milk foam to create the look of a cappuccino. Sprinkle lightly with cinnamon. Serve with Greek donuts.

Jim Botsacos *has been serving the best in authentic, elevated Greek cuisine at beloved New York mainstay Molyvos since its opening in 1997. Over the last fifteen years, Jim has paid homage to time-honored recipes while infusing Greece's traditional cuisine with modern touches. Jim's talent and vision have elevated our perception of Greek food to the highest levels of taste and sophistication.*

LIVE WIRE

Bob Dylan had already achieved fame as the leading songwriter of the American folk music revival, accompanied by his signature acoustic guitar and harmonica. But he shocked audiences at the 1965 Newport Folk Festival with his first jarring, plugged-in, and entirely electrifying rock and roll performance.

"ELECTRIC GIN" COCKTAIL
TROY SIDLE

Grab some ice. Shake it up. Serve it in whatever you want. Don't have a glass? It'll be delicious in a paper cup.

Troy brings us this cocktail homage to Dylan, which he says would be just as irreverent on a modern menu. "It's highbrow enough to be insulted by its own components. It's throwback rock and roll in a glass."

After stops at Chicago's the Violet Hour, Brooklyn's the Counting Room, and elsewhere, Denver native and cunning spirits alchemist **Troy Sidle** *mans his own bar at Pouring Ribbons in New York City's East Village.*

MAKES 1 COCKTAIL

2 ounces Beefeater gin
½ ounce fresh lime juice
½ ounce simple syrup
1 teaspoon Tang powder
1 ounce Chartreuse

1965

"In 1965, there was an air of thoughtful rebellion. The moment Dylan goes electric, the rebel continues to rebel, even against his fans. He does what he wants. That's rock and roll."

MAKES 4 SERVINGS

2 whole pig ears
Kosher salt
2 cups Japanese plum wine
4 pork sirloin steaks
  (approximately 1½ pounds total)
½ cup sugar
¼ cup water
1½ tablespoons dry Chinese mustard
  or Colman's English mustard
One ½-pound Asian pear,
  cut in ¼-inch dice
1 Thai chili, thinly sliced crosswise
2 teaspoons toasted sesame seeds
Dash rice vinegar
3 sheets nori
½ cup all-purpose flour
1 large egg
1 cup panko bread crumbs
2 cups finely sliced napa cabbage
2 shiso leaves
½ lemon
Vegetable oil, for frying
¼ cup fresh flat-leaf parsley leaves
Sesame oil, for drizzling

Special equipment

Spice grinder
Gas or charcoal grill

THE BOLD AND THE BEAUTIFUL

In 1966 tensions were escalating all over the United States. Protests and violence related to the Vietnam War and civil rights were spreading anxiety across many parts of the nation. That same year, while the United States was embroiled in the space race with the USSR, NASA's Lunar Orbiter One produced photographs of a fragile, beautiful blue Earth hovering above a gray lunar landscape, making an excellent case for the people of the planet to unify. Dovetailing with this sentiment, NBC's fall lineup included a science fiction drama called *Star Trek* that portrayed a multinational crew, operating an exploratory vessel in the darkness of space, some three hundred years in the future. Fans of this program (and its future generations and incarnations) would cite its ability to combine science, fantasy, and an optimistic view of the future despite a turbulent present. In a particularly trailblazing move, *Star Trek* presented America's first televised interracial kiss, when the substantially sexy William Shatner planted his lips on those of the knock-out stunning, drop-dead gorgeous, legs-up-to-here Nichelle Nichols.

SIRLOIN À LA SULU
PORK SIRLOIN TEPPANYAKI WITH PIG EAR TONKATSU
DAVID SCHUTTENBERG

THE DAY BEFORE:

Clean pig ears thoroughly, ensuring there is no leftover hair. Place in a medium stockpot, cover with cold water, and bring to a simmer. Add ¼ cup kosher salt and continue to simmer for 1 to 1½ hours, until the ears offer no resistance when pierced with a small knife or cake tester. Remove from the water and allow to cool to room temperature on a wire rack. Cover and leave in fridge overnight.

While the ears are cooking, whisk together 1½ cups of the plum wine and 2 tablespoons salt. Place the steaks in a zippered plastic

bag and pour the seasoned wine over them. Seal the bag tightly and leave in fridge overnight, turning every few hours.

In a medium saucepot, combine the sugar, the water, mustard, and ¼ teaspoon salt and bring to a boil. Once the sugar has dissolved, add the pear and Thai chili. Reduce the heat to low and simmer until the liquid has thickened, and the pear is soft but not falling apart. Remove from the heat. Stir in the sesame seeds and rice vinegar. Check and adjust seasoning. Cool, cover, and leave in fridge overnight.

THE DAY OF SERVING:

Remove the pear mostarda from the fridge 2 hours before serving. Crumble 2 of the sheets of nori into small pieces. Place in a spice grinder and spin until powdered. Fold the third sheet into 2-inch squares, then thinly julienne. Set the julienned nori aside.

Place 3 bowls on a table. In the first, combine the powdered nori and the flour. In the second, whisk the egg. In the third, place the panko.

In a medium bowl, cover the napa cabbage with warm water and add a generous pinch of salt. Mix together and let sit while preparing the rest of the meal. Julienne the shiso leaves and set aside.

Heat a gas or charcoal grill to medium-high heat. Place a wire cooling rack over a baking sheet next to the grill. Line another baking sheet with paper towels and put near the stove.

While the grill is heating, cut the pig ears into 2-inch-long, ¼-inch-wide strips. Working with a few pieces at a time, toss the strips first in the nori/flour mixture, then in the egg wash, and finally in the panko until well covered in bread crumbs, but not clumped together. Let sit on a paper towel while grilling the pork steaks.

Remove the pork steaks from the bag and pat dry. Discard the marinade.

In a pint glass filled with ice, make a drink for the grillmaster: squeeze in the half lemon and top with the remaining ½ cup of plum wine.

Season the pork steaks generously with kosher salt. Grill over medium-high heat for 4 to 6 minutes per side, until just barely pink on the inside but nicely charred on the outside. Place on the cooling rack to rest.

While the steaks are resting, heat a cast-iron skillet over high heat. Add vegetable oil to 1 inch deep. Fry the pig ears until golden brown and crispy. Lift out with a slotted spoon or fry ladle and put on the paper towels to drain.

Drain the napa cabbage. In a large stainless-bowl, toss the warm pig ears, drained cabbage, parsley, and shiso julienne with a touch of kosher salt and a drizzle of sesame oil.

Serve the grilled pork steaks atop some of the pear mostarda with the crispy pig ear tonkatsu salad on the side. Top the salad with the nori julienne.

> *When we asked David for a recipe that called to mind expansion, the hope of the future, and an unexplored frontier that defined the late '60s, he said, "I immediately thought of the Time-Life series Foods of the World. I've been collecting it via a number of West Coast thrift store scores for several years now.*
>
> *"I also immediately conjured images of the Benihanas that started popping up all over the place in that era. I wanted to capture some of that classic Japanese steakhouse fare and add in a modern take on a classic tonkatsu."*

David Schuttenberg, *who called the kitchens of Craft and Fatty Crab home, currently presides over all things meaty at Dickson's Farmstand Meats in New York's Chelsea Market, where he spends his days honing his charcuterie-making skills; curing and smoking various cuts of beef, pork, and lamb; and stuffing more sausages than he cares to admit.*

LOVE IS ALL

When as many as one hundred thousand people peacefully converged on the Haight-Ashbury neighborhood of San Francisco in the summer of 1967, they ignited a major cultural shift known as the "Hippie Revolution." Peace, free love, and antiestablishmentarianism were on the agenda in one of the most fervent public discourses ever to shake up popular culture. Pastry chef Ghaya Oliveira has taken a flower from her hair and created a quiet moment away from the crowded streets with this free-flowing, creamy dessert in homage to the Summer of Love.

ROSE WATER SOUFFLÉ
GHAYA OLIVEIRA

Prepare the pistachio sponge cake: In a food processor, combine all the ingredients and pulse until smooth. Pass the batter through a fine-mesh sieve. Transfer to the canister of a whipped cream maker and charge with 4 nitrogen cartridges (leaving the fourth attached). Shake well, and squeeze the batter from the siphon to fill half of an 8-ounce paper cup. Microwave on high for 1 minute. Remove the cup from the microwave and invert onto a rack. Repeat to make 8 cups total. Let the cups sit out overnight to dry, then break each cake into small pieces.

Prepare the rose water soufflé: Position a rack in the lower third of the oven and preheat to 400°F. Coat the insides of eight 13-ounce soufflé dishes with the butter, then sprinkle with 3 tablespoons sugar, shaking out excess.

In a small bowl, whisk to combine ¼ cup of the milk with the cornstarch. Pour the remaining milk into a saucepan, bring to a simmer, and stream in the cornstarch mixture while whisking, until smooth. Continue cooking on low heat, whisking until thickened, about 3 minutes. Whisk in the rose water in three additions, and then pour into a heatproof bowl.

MAKES 8 SERVINGS

For the pistachio sponge cake (makes extra)
2½ cups pistachio flour

1 cup plus 3 tablespoons sugar

1½ cups pasteurized egg whites, or 12 fresh

9 tablespoons all-purpose flour

1 tablespoon pistachio paste

For the rose water soufflé
2 tablespoons unsalted butter, softened

¾ cup plus 3 tablespoons sugar

1¼ cups milk

7 tablespoons cornstarch

⅔ cup rose water

1¼ cups pasteurized egg whites, or 9 fresh

8 teaspoons organic rose petal jam

Special equipment
Food processor

Whipped cream maker (siphon and nitrogen cartridges)

Eight 13-ounce soufflé dishes

Stand mixer

In a stand mixer, whip the egg whites on medium speed to reach soft peaks, then stream in the remaining ¾ cup sugar while whipping, until they reach stiff peaks. Add ½ cup of the whipped whites to the rose water mixture and whisk until well incorporated and smooth. With a rubber spatula, fold in the rest of the whites in three additions, until no streaks remain but the mixture is still fluffy.

Fill each prepared ramekin one-third full with the soufflé mixture. Top with about ½ cup crumbled pistachio cake and then a teaspoon of rose petal jam. Fill ramekins to the rim with the remaining soufflé mixture.

Level off the top of each soufflé with a small knife, then run the tip of your thumb around the inner edge of each ramekin, creating a shallow indentation. Place the ramekins on a baking sheet, and bake for 8 to 10 minutes, until the soufflés rise and set (centers should be a bit jiggly). Serve immediately.

Tunisian-born pastry chef **Ghaya Oliveira** *learned to cook alongside her mother before gracing Daniel Boulud's kitchens with her Mediterranean-inspired sweets at Café Boulud, Bar Boulud, and Boulud Sud. She was a 2012 James Beard Award nominee for Outstanding Pastry Chef and is currently executive pastry chef at Boulud's flagship, Daniel.*

FLY GIRLS

American eyebrows rose higher than a miniskirt when *Coffee, Tea or Me?* was published in 1967, an alleged tell-all about what really happened in the sky and on the ground (and everywhere in between) for the glamorous women of international airline hostessing. By 1968, the golden age of air travel was upon us, and flying across the country or even around the world was no longer an extravagant fantasy but an affordable reality for many people in the United States. The journey was often more thrilling than the destination, as luxury, splendor, and service were all part of the package that came with an airline ticket. Brian and Sal's first course is an introduction to an exotic land that, for Americans in 1968, would have suddenly seemed almost within reach.

TUNA FEVER
BRIAN KONOPKA & SALVADOR BARRERA

Wrap the ahi and white tuna in plastic wrap and place in the freezer to firm up before slicing. Cut ⅛-inch-thick slices of each loin. Cut the slices into disks with a small ring cookie cutter. Dice the remaining scrap pieces of tuna and reserve in a bowl in the refrigerator for the tartare. In a small bowl, combine the mayonnaise, yuzu pepper sauce, minced jalapeño, masago, togarashi pepper, scallion, and water, and reserve for the sauce.

Take the diced tuna from the refrigerator and mix in 2 tablespoons of the masago sauce. Season with salt and pepper to taste.

Place the tartare on a chilled plate inside a large rectangular pastry cutter and press the tuna into the corner of the cutter to form the rectangular shape. Arrange alternating slices of ahi and white tuna on top of the tartare to form a checkerboard pattern. Spoon the masago sauce around the tuna. Garnish with the julienne of cucumber, radish, and kaiware and serve.

MAKES 4 SERVINGS AS AN APPETIZER OR FIRST COURSE

6 ounces ahi tuna loin (sushi grade)

6 ounces white tuna loin (sushi grade)

¼ cup Kewpie mayonnaise (Japanese style)

2½ tablespoons yuzu pepper sauce

¼ jalapeño chili, seeds removed, minced

1 tablespoon masago (orange) fish roe

¼ teaspoon togarashi pepper

1 scallion, thinly sliced

2 tablespoons cold water

Salt and freshly ground black pepper

¼ Japanese or Persian cucumber, peeled and julienned

1 baby red radish, julienned

¼ ounce kaiware (Japanese radish sprouts)

Special equipment

Small ring cutter

Large rectangular pastry cutter

Brian Konopka *began his professional career at age eighteen, during his externship from the Culinary Institute of America at Le Cirque restaurant. After graduation, Brian spent the next ten years working for the Maccioni family at Le Cirque. During that time, Brian opened three of the Maccionis' restaurants, including Le Cirque 2000 in the Palace Hotel, which received four stars from the* New York Times. *Today, Brian is the president and CEO of Kobeyaki Restaurants, which focus on healthy and artistic Japanese fare.*

Long before graduating from New York's Institute of Culinary Education, **Salvador Barrera** *often accompanied his chef grandmother to her restaurant in Veracruz, Mexico, and assisted her on catering jobs. After graduating from culinary school, Salvador went on to work in the kitchens of the thirty-unit Japanese concept Todai. Impressed by the young chef's work ethic, meticulous skill, and desire to learn, executive chef Eiko Takahashi took Salvador under her tutelage for five years, teaching him the ways of Japanese cooking and food preparation. Today, Salvador is a partner at Kobeyaki.*

A MANY-SPLENDORED THING

The nation's attention turned skyward when Apollo 11 made the first manned landing on the moon, while down below the Stonewall Riots erupted in New York's Greenwich Village, marking the beginning of the modern gay rights movement. The guys from Cocktail Buzz filled a tall order by creating a distinctive drink and appetizing accompaniment that raise a flag, make an incontrovertible statement and a giant leap for mankind.

THE '69 COCKTAIL WITH LAMB CHOPS AND STUFFED MUSHROOMS
STEVE SCHUL & PAUL ZABLOCKI

MAKES 1 COCKTAIL

For the '69 cocktail
1½ ounces rye
¾ ounce brandy or cognac
¾ ounce sweet vermouth
¼ ounce Galliano l'Autentico
¼ ounce quality grenadine
Orange peel, to express
Blueberry, raspberry, blackberry, orange peel, lime peel, and lemon peel, or other very colorful garnish, such as Gummi bears (skewer them on a garnish pick in a rainbow pattern, as if they were a part of an ursine chorus line)

MAKES 10 TO 12 SERVINGS EACH OF LAMB AND MUSHROOMS

For the lamb chops with mint gremolata
⅔ cup flat-leaf parsley
1⅓ cups fresh spearmint
1 tablespoon fresh oregano (optional)
1 clove garlic, finely minced
Zest of 1 lemon
1 teaspoon lemon juice
2 pinches salt, plus extra for seasoning
3 tablespoons extra virgin olive oil, plus more for coating the chops
12 rib lamb chops (preferably frenched)
Freshly ground pepper

Prepare the cocktail: Shake the first five ingredients in ice for 20 seconds. Strain into a chilled cocktail glass or coupe. Pinch the orange peel, peel side out, over the drink, allowing the oils to express into it, and rub it around the rim; discard. Garnish with berries and citrus peel, in an artistic fashion, skewered on a pick.

NOTE: For a fruitier cocktail, you can add a berry or two of your choice before shaking. If you do, make sure to double-strain so as not to get any seeds in the drink.

Prepare the mint gremolata: Separately chop the parsley, mint, and oregano uniformly. Combine them in a bowl. Add the garlic, lemon zest, lemon juice, salt, and olive oil. Mix well.

Prepare the lamb chops: Heat a grill pan until smoking hot. Meanwhile, drizzle olive oil over the chops, coating them entirely. Season both sides with salt and pepper. Place the chops on the grill pan, cooking 4 minutes per side for rare. Remove the chops and serve with a dollop of mint gremolata.

For the cheddar and caramelized onion–stuffed mushrooms

2 tablespoons olive oil

2 tablespoons unsalted butter

1 large yellow onion, sliced

1 pound button mushrooms (smaller ones are better)

2 teaspoons Worcestershire sauce

2 tablespoons brandy or cognac

4 ounces sharp cheddar cheese, cut into ¼-inch-thick 1-inch squares

¼ ounce Parmesan cheese, crumbled

Finishing salt, such as Maldon

Special equipment

Grill pan

Prepare the stuffed mushrooms: Preheat the oven to 350°F. Cover a baking pan with parchment paper, then place a wire cooling rack atop the paper.

Heat the 2 tablespoons oil and 2 tablespoons butter over medium heat in a large skillet. Add the onion and slowly cook until caramelized, stirring occasionally, about 40 minutes. Reduce the heat if the onion starts to brown too quickly.

Meanwhile, remove and discard the stems from the mushrooms. Wash the mushroom caps and set aside.

When the onion has caramelized, add the Worcestershire and brandy. Simmer for a minute, making sure to deglaze the pan. Transfer the onion to a plate or bowl, and set aside. Add the mushroom caps to the skillet, top with a lid, and heat on low for 2 to 3 minutes, flipping once, until the mushrooms soften slightly. Drain any excess water from the mushrooms, and place top down on the rack. Gently press 1 square of cheddar into each cap. (You may have to cut the cheese into smaller pieces, depending on the size of the caps.) Top the cheddar with a generous dollop of the onion mixture, then a little piece or two of Parmesan. Transfer to the oven and bake for 15 to 20 minutes. Remove and transfer the mushrooms to a serving plate. Sprinkle with finishing salt. Serve immediately.

PAIRING NOTE: Sharp cheddar cheese pairs splendidly with the '69 Cocktail, bringing out hints of cocoa. Put out a wedge after dinner and mix up a few more rounds.

> "This dish can be eaten year-round but is perfect for springtime, the season of rebirth and renewal, when lamb has historically been served," Paul and Steve note. "The mint and parsley add a freshness that pairs perfectly with the '69 Cocktail, highlighting the spices in the sweet vermouth and Galliano. The savoriness of the mushroom combination creates an explosion of umami on first bite. Pairing it with a '69 Cocktail coaxes out even more flavors."

Paul Zablocki, *a writer, and* **Steve Schul**, *a photographer, share a love for cocktail hour, the interplay of flavors, and getting busy in the kitchen. They mix drinks and pair them with hors d'oeuvres and document the pairings on their website, CocktailBuzz.com, and news-letter,* "Buzzings" from Cocktail Buzz.

HONOR THY MOTHER

In the late 1960s, the unintended side effects of the industrial revolution and its modern conveniences were causing air, water, and soil pollution, and they posed a threat to the Earth's ability to harbor life. Government scientist J. Murray Mitchell's grim prophecy warned that the growing pollution could warm the Earth enough to cause a "greenhouse effect" that would create catastrophic danger for every living thing on Earth. In 1970, Wisconsin Senator Gaylord Nelson's efforts would lead to the first Earth Day, when he proclaimed, "We only have one Earth, so we need to take care of her." By the year's end, even notorious opportunist Richard Nixon got on board by signing the Clean Air Act into law on New Year's Eve. His prophecy was more hopeful: "I think that 1970 will be known as the year of the beginning, in which we really began to move on the problems of clean air and clean water and open spaces for the future generations of America."

CLAUDIA'S CRUNCHY SALAD
CLAUDIA GONSON

Chop it all up, add dressing, and toss. Best after chilling!

Noah met Claudia on an assignment for Saveur *magazine, where she prepared this salad. It has become something of an obsession ever since; in fact, he believes that this dish could convince salad haters to change their foolish ways.*

Claudia Gonson *is a multitalented musician who manages, records, and performs with the Magnetic Fields as their pianist, percussionist, and occasional singer. She also sings with the band Future Bible Heroes, has played drums in the bands Tender Trap and Honeybunch, and has written and performed her own music with Shirley Simms and author Rick Moody. She is the manager of songwriter Stephin Merritt, whom Claudia met in high school.*

MAKES 4 TO 6 SERVINGS

2 large cukes (peeled if you want)
1 bulb fennel
2 stalks celery
2 carrots, peeled
Bit of sweet white onion, finely chopped
1 small green or colorful bell pepper
Cherry tomatoes (if you want;
  I don't usually add them, because
  they're not crunchy)
1 big handful unsalted sunflower seeds
Salt and pepper
1 scant tablespoon safflower oil
  or canola oil
Dash seasoned rice vinegar
3 to 5 drops sesame oil

Gael Greene

Ben Mims

Sally Darr

Liza Queen

Silvano Marchetto

Wade Burch

Eduard Frauneder & W

Rhonda Kave

Kemp Minifie

Anita Lo

70

BEHEAD EVERY GREAT WOMAN...

Gloria Steinem delivered her "Address to the Women of America" in the same year that stuntman Evel Knievel set a world record for jumping nineteen cars. In an era when testosterone-fueled feats made national headlines, Steinem sought to reform perceptions of sex and race and to revolutionize the foundation of human society.

We were looking for a recipe that shifts the focus from traditional home economics to nourishing the aspirations of a career-minded individual in its wholesomeness and ease of preparation. Culinary icon Gael Greene took the working woman home, where her memories of her mother's macaroni and cheese have sustained her through multiple decades of cultural relevance.

"ALMOST LIKE MOM'S" MACARONI AND CHEESE
GAEL GREENE

Preheat the oven to 350°F. Spray the bottom and sides of a shallow 6-cup metal baking dish with olive oil spray. (A flat baking pan gives more crispiness than a loaf pan. Use a pan that can go under the broiler later.) Bring several quarts of water to a rolling boil. Add the kosher salt. Boil the macaroni until just tender. Drain well. Immediately turn out the macaroni into the baking dish. Toss the macaroni with a tablespoon of olive oil. Then add the cheese, ham or bacon if you want, milk, salt, and pepper and mix well.

Bake for 10 minutes, then remove from the oven (close the oven door) and stir. Taste for seasoning. Sprinkle the fresh bread crumbs and Parmigiano-Reggiano on top. Bake for another 15 minutes. If there is still some milk in the bottom, return to the oven for another 5 to 10 minutes. If the topping has not browned and crisped like my mom's, stick the baking dish under the

MAKES 2 MAIN COURSE SERVINGS, 4 SIDE SERVINGS, OR FEEDS 1 BUSY WOMAN ALL WEEK LONG

Olive oil spray or 1½ tablespoons mild-flavored olive oil, plus 1 tablespoon olive oil for tossing

1 tablespoon kosher salt

½ pound small elbow macaroni

2½ cups shredded or chopped firm cheese (My mother used Velveeta, but I make this with sharp cheddar and Emmentaler, half and half. Once I threw in some leftover Brie, a triple crème from France, and a half-cup of crème fraîche and the result was celestial.)

½ cup chopped baked ham or crumbled crisp bacon (optional)

1 cup whole milk

1½ teaspoons fine salt

1 teaspoon freshly ground black pepper

¼ cup fresh bread crumbs

¼ cup grated Parmigiano-Reggiano

> "It isn't even close to good macaroni if it doesn't stick to the bottom and sides of the pan, and the top must be browned and crusty. Restaurants fail because they use too much cheese."

❁

broiler, 3 or 4 inches away from the heat, and brown, watching so the topping doesn't burn. ❁

> *"The goal is crisp, not creamy. Use half-and-half instead of milk if you like it creamier. I must confess I made this the other day with skim milk—since cholesterol was invented, I feel wanton using whole milk."*

Gael Greene *is the well-hatted restaurant critic and author who changed the way Americans think about food with her witty and insightful reviews during her thirty-plus years at New York magazine. She cofounded the organization Citymeals-on-Wheels with James Beard. Despite having experienced the pinnacle of dining and every food trend along the way, Gael reveres well-prepared macaroni and cheese above all. The dish, she says, is close to the memory of her Detroit-born mom's baked macaroni.*

BREW-MANCE

In the early 1970s, the popular method of percolating coffee—which involves cycling water through ground coffee and boiling it to the point of burning—was unseated by the introduction of a home brewing device named Mr. Coffee. This new automatic drip style of coffee revolutionized the home cup, and sold millions in the United States. The technique and technology completely changed the way Americans consumed caffeine, setting off a craze and a demand for better brews and beans.

BANOFFEE MOUSSE PIE
BEN MIMS

Prepare the mousse pie shell: Heat the oven to 350°F. Grease a 9-inch deep-dish glass pie plate with butter and coat evenly with sugar, or spray with nonstick spray; set aside.

Place the egg yolks and ¼ cup of the sugar, the vanilla, and salt in a large bowl and beat on medium-high speed with a hand mixer until pale and thickened, and the mixture falls in thick ribbons when the beaters are lifted. Add the chocolate and coffee and stir until smooth. In a separate bowl, with clean beaters, beat the egg whites and the remaining ¼ cup granulated sugar until stiff peaks form. Add half the whites to the chocolate mixture and fold with a rubber spatula until almost incorporated. Add the remaining whites and fold until just incorporated and mixture is homogeneous.

Pour into the pie plate and, using a small offset spatula or butter knife, spread the mousse so that it evenly covers the bottom and sides of the pie plate, without covering the rim. Bake for 25 minutes, and then turn off the oven and let the pie sit for 10 minutes in the cooling oven. Remove from the oven and let cool to room temperature. Press the mousse down slightly to fit into the shape of the pie plate.

MAKES 8 SERVINGS

For the mousse pie shell
Unsalted butter, softened, or nonstick baking spray
½ cup sugar, plus more for the pan (optional)
4 eggs, separated
1 teaspoon vanilla extract
½ teaspoon kosher salt
4 ounces semisweet chocolate, melted
2 tablespoons strongly brewed coffee

For the filling
1½ cups canned or homemade dulce de leche
6 bananas, sliced
¾ cup heavy cream
¼ cup strongly brewed coffee, chilled
2 tablespoons sugar
½ teaspoon kosher salt

To garnish (optional)
1 tablespoon ground coffee
Coarsely grated bittersweet chocolate

Special equipment
9-inch deep-dish glass pie plate

Prepare the filling and assemble the pie: Pour the dulce de leche over the cooled pie shell and, using an offset spatula or butter knife, spread it evenly over the bottom of the pie. Arrange banana slices evenly in concentric circles over the dulce de leche. In a large bowl, combine the cream, coffee, sugar, and salt, and beat on medium-high speed with a hand mixer until stiff peaks form. Pour over the bananas and spread evenly, sealing the cream to the edge of the mousse pie shell. Sprinkle the top with ground coffee and/or chocolate shavings and refrigerate for at least 1 hour to set the pie. Serve chilled.

The New York Times Dessert of the Year in 1972 was Maida Heatter's Chocolate Mousse Torte. That same year, Banoffee Pie was invented and served across the pond in the United Kingdom. Coincidentally, both recipes used instant coffee granules to accent the other flavors and add depth to chocolate or toffee.

"Intrigued by this, I decided to omit the instant coffee granules and use more fresh coffee in its place," Ben says. His original recipe combines the two desserts, bringing coffee to the foreground in the flavor of the pie.

Ben Mims *is currently the pastry chef at Bar Agricole restaurant in San Francisco. He was the associate food editor at* Saveur *magazine for over four years. Ben is also working on a southern desserts cookbook for Rizzoli International Publications.*

MAKES 10 BRIOCHES

For the sponge

One ¼-ounce envelope active dry yeast
  (2¼ teaspoons)
Pinch sugar
¼ cup lukewarm milk
1½ cups sifted all-purpose flour

For the brioches

Sponge (from above)
¼ cup sugar
3 large eggs, lightly beaten
¾ teaspoon fine salt
12 tablespoons unsalted butter, well
  softened, plus additional for greasing
  the bowl and molds
¾ cup all-purpose flour, plus more for
  kneading and shaping

For the egg wash

1 large egg
2 tablespoons heavy cream

Special equipment

Bench scraper
Food processor
10 small fluted brioche molds
Deep cake pans, to cover the molds

INDUSTRIOUS REVOLUTION

When the Cuisinart made its American debut in the early 1970s, culinarians hailed the product as nothing short of revolutionary. In the words of Craig Claiborne, the Cuisinart "performs tasks in seconds that formerly required long tedious minutes if not to say hours." The manufacturer of this magnificent device sent complimentary test models to icons like James Beard and Julia Child to encourage their kind words. However, it was the story by then–senior editor of *Gourmet* Sally Darr that lit up cash registers across the country, as chefs and homemakers alike discovered the miracles of creating complex dishes like salmon mousse, Salisbury steak, and pasta fresca in a fraction of the time.

FLUTED BRIOCHES
SALLY DARR

Prepare the sponge: In a bowl, proof the yeast and the pinch of sugar in the milk for 10 minutes.

Add ½ cup of the flour and stir just until combined. Cut a deep cross in the mixture and sift 1 cup more of the flour over the mixture, but do not combine it. Let the sponge rise, covered with a kitchen towel, in a warm place for 1 hour.

Prepare the brioches: In a food processor fitted with the steel blade, combine the sponge and sifted flour with the ¼ cup sugar, eggs, and salt and spin the machine for 2½ minutes. Spread the butter over the mixture and spin the machine for a few seconds more, just until the butter is incorporated. Turn out the dough onto a lightly floured surface and, using a bench scraper, incorporate about ¾ cup more flour. Transfer the dough to a lightly buttered large bowl and let it rise, covered, for 3 hours or until it is tripled in bulk. Punch down the dough, transfer it to another bowl, and chill it, covered with plastic wrap and a heavy towel, overnight.

Form the brioches: The next day, preheat oven to 375°F. Butter the brioche molds well.

Punch down the dough and with floured hands form most of the dough into 10 balls, each about the size of a table tennis ball and weighing 2 ounces. Put the balls in the brioche molds and make a deep indentation in the top of each ball. Divide the remaining dough into 10 tear-shaped pieces. Set 1 piece, point down, in each indentation. Let the dough rise, covered with inverted deep cake pans, in a warm place for 3 hours, or until it has filled the brioche molds completely. Make the egg wash by lightly beating the egg with the cream and brush on the dough. Bake the brioches on a baking sheet in the lower third of the oven for 15 to 20 minutes, until they are well browned. Turn out the brioches onto a wire cooling rack. Serve them warm. ✺

NOTE: This recipe originally appeared in the April 1975 issue of *Gourmet* magazine.

In 1969, **Sally Darr** *left a career in textiles to join the staff of the* Gourmet *test kitchen as food editor. Ten years later, she and her husband opened La Tulipe on West 13th Street in Manhattan. The French-inspired restaurant received three stars from Mimi Sheraton at the* New York Times, *and was a favorite of Julia Child's. Sally's famed eatery is responsible for advancing the career of Food Network star Sara Moulton, who started at La Tulipe as chef tournant, and it was the venue where future chef Barbara Sibley started out as a seventeen-year-old hatcheck girl.*

NUDE BY THE FIRE IN THE SEVENTIES

America was beginning to mellow out. The riotous young activists of the previous decade were growing up, falling in love, getting married, and starting families. Coming down from the acid rock of the '60s, the era's musical trend was identified by a light sound, what came to be known as "soft rock." The sound track of singer-songwriters like Janis Ian, Rupert Holmes, Bread, and Christopher Cross set the new mood of young America, who embraced long nights spent lounging with lovers by the fire with a bottle of Chianti and shared fondue. Stoke the flames, turn up the hi-fi, and make room on the shag carpet. This sensual and versatile dish can be portioned for two, three, four, or more, because tonight there is plenty of romance to go around.

SEVENTIES KEY PARTY ARTICHOKE CROCK
LIZA QUEEN

Braise the artichokes: Trim the artichokes by removing approximately 4 to 5 layers of the leaves. You can stop when the bottom 2 inches of the artichoke are light green. Cut the top portion of the artichoke so that only the light green remains. Trim and peel the stem. Cut the artichoke in half lengthwise and carefully remove all the choke with a small spoon. Rub with lemon. In a wide pan with tall sides, place the artichokes in a single layer. Add equal parts olive oil and water until the liquid just covers the artichokes. Add the oregano, thyme, bay leaves, garlic, sea salt, white pepper, and chili flakes. Bring up to a simmer and cover with a lid lined with parchment paper. Maintain a slow simmer; begin checking for doneness after 20 minutes. This will take 20 to 30 minutes, depending on the size of your artichokes. To see if they are done, insert a paring knife into the heart to check the texture. Remove from the liquid and let cool.

MAKES ABOUT 1 QUART

For the braised artichokes
4 medium-large artichokes
½ lemon
Olive oil
2 sprigs oregano
4 sprigs thyme
2 large fresh bay leaves
5 cloves garlic, smashed
2 tablespoons sea salt
2 teaspoons ground white pepper
1 teaspoon chili flakes
Freshly squeezed lemon juice

For the caper aïoli
4 egg yolks
3 tablespoons drained capers
4 large cloves garlic, peeled
Approximately 2 cups olive oil
Grated zest of 1 lemon
Juice of 1½ lemons
Salt

For the dip
Braised artichokes (from above), coarsely chopped
2 red bell peppers, diced medium
2 cups grated pecorino cheese (the higher quality, the better)
1½ to 2 cups caper aïoli (from above)
1 anchovy fillet, minced
1 teaspoon ground white pepper
Large pinch sugar
1 tablespoon distilled white vinegar
Sea salt

Prepare the caper aïoli: In a food processor, combine the egg yolks, capers, and garlic. Process until light and foamy. While the food processor is running, add olive oil in a thin stream until the aïoli is quite thick. Add the lemon zest and juice and salt to taste. Pulse to mix.

Prepare the dip: Throw everything into a bowl! Mix, taste, and adjust for aïoli, salt, sugar, and vinegar. At this point, you can keep this dip refrigerated in a sealed container for up to 4 days; in fact, the longer it sits, the better it tastes. You can cook off as much as you would like at a time.

Preheat the oven to 325°F. Boil about a quart of water.

Place the dip in 4- to 6-ounce ramekins and set these in a baking pan. Pour in boiling water to come one-third of the way up the sides of the ramekins. Bake for 30 to 35 minutes, until the dip is just barely starting to get a little bit golden on top.

Prepare the shishito peppers: Heat a cast-iron skillet or grill to medium-high.

Coat the peppers in olive oil and char until they are just barely blackened and beginning to wilt. Toss with sea salt.

To serve: On a cutting board, place your cooked artichoke dip ramekins, the peppers, and either crispy flatbread or very crusty, warmed peasant bread.

> *"I have always curated the menus at my restaurants with items from various points of my personal eating history,"* Liza says. *"The artichoke dip is one of the few that reaches all the way back to when I barely had all my teeth, as well as my late teens, when I was starting to take food and cooking seriously.*
>
> *"I was born in 1974. I am the daughter of a beautiful cook who was both frustrated and befuddled by the picky eater with whom she had somehow ended up. While I would fastidiously pick out any and all onions, no matter how minuscule, and absolutely, flat-out refuse to eat a lettuce leaf, I was oddly enamored of both artichokes and capers at a very young age.*

For the shishito peppers
(optional; can sub jarred pickled banana peppers)

2 to 4 shishito peppers per person
Olive oil
Sea salt
Crispy flatbread or warmed crusty peasant bread, for serving

"When I was at Oberlin College, the biggest eating-out thrill to be had was at the Great Lakes Brewery in Cleveland, Ohio. And my two very favorite things on its menu were cheddar-beer soup and an artichoke dip upon which my own recipe is based.

"Despite the fact that casseroles have long since gone out of fashion, and this particular one is so very easily mockable for its shaggy-avocado-carpetness, it remains a completely and utterly satisfying starter. Perfect for firelight and Chablis as well as my Williamsburg restaurant, where it proudly resides for the duration of California's artichoke season."

Liza Queen is the renegade chef-owner of Potlikker in Williamsburg, Brooklyn, where she serves up idiosyncratic, comforting food culled from a rich culinary history. After winning over a following at the former Queen's Hideaway in Greenpoint, Liza spent two years cooking her way across Vietnam. Liza describes her reverence for the culinary past that along with her market-driven menus keeps diners coming back in droves.

DOWNTOWN GIRLS

In the early 1970s, the part of Manhattan now known as SoHo was called "Hell's Hundred Acres," owing to the multitude of fires that broke out in dozens of abandoned loft buildings where prostitutes, drug dealers, and gangs made their homes. Things weren't much prettier on the west side of the city. The docks along the Hudson River were also deserted save for the hookers, pimps, and thieves who populated the rotting, collapsing structures along the river's edge. Before downtown began to gentrify, and before Italian restaurants in New York meant anything other than cheap red sauce joints that slung rubbery meatballs and sloppy spaghetti, a Florentine named Silvano Marchetto took a chance in opening a microscopic four-table restaurant in the former Bimbo's bar space. In 1975, his menu focused on the food of his childhood spent in Florence and Tuscany, and was a far cry from the gelatinous, bland dishes that defined Manhattan's version of "authentic" Italian. As the empty buildings nearby gentrified and reinvented themselves as galleries, artists' studios, and fashion houses, Da Silvano restaurant became a haunt for celebrities and fame seekers of an entirely new generation. Almost by accident, Silvano had nailed the famous real estate mantra: "Location, location, location."

MAKES 4 TO 6 SERVINGS

⅓ cup extra virgin olive oil

5 cloves garlic: 3 smashed and peeled, 2 minced

4 anchovy fillets

1 tablespoon capers, drained but not rinsed (do not use capers packed in salt, as they will be too salty)

2 tablespoons coarsely chopped pitted black Greek or Moroccan olives

One 28-ounce can high-quality Italian plum tomatoes, drained and coarsely chopped

Fine sea salt

1 pound spaghetti

¼ cup minced flat-leaf parsley

Freshly ground black pepper

SPAGHETTI PUTTANESCA

PASTA FROM THE PANTRY, AKA "WHORE-STYLE"

SILVANO MARCHETTO

Warm the olive oil over medium heat in a sauté pan wide and deep enough to hold all the ingredients (including the pasta, once cooked).

Add the 3 smashed garlic cloves and cook until golden brown, 2 to 3 minutes, being careful *not* to burn them. Remove the smashed garlic from the pan and discard. Add the 2 cloves minced garlic, anchovies, capers, olives, and tomatoes. Toss

together with a wooden spoon, lower the heat, and cook for 5 to 10 minutes.

While the sauce is cooking, bring a large pot of salted water to a boil over high heat. Add the spaghetti, cover the pot, return to a boil, and cook uncovered until the spaghetti is al dente, about 8 minutes, or whatever the packaging indicates. You may want to taste the pasta 1 to 2 minutes ahead of what the package recommends, to make sure you do not overcook it.

Drain the spaghetti and add it to the pan with the sauce. Toss. Add the parsley and season with black pepper. Toss again and sauté for about 30 seconds.

Serve immediately.

NOTE: Do not use kalamata olives—they are too tasteless. It may surprise you that I use Greek rather than Italian olives, but Greek olives have more flavor because they are soaked in seawater and then dried in the sun.

> *"Before I opened Da Silvano in 1975, my friends used to ask me a lot to cook at parties, and this was usually one of the dishes I would make . . . It takes very little time and effort, just enough for your appetite to build. Once I opened the restaurant on May 1, 1975, it was an instant hit with the customers, and it has been on the menu ever since."*

In 2015, Chef **Silvano Marchetto** *will be celebrating Da Silvano's fortieth anniversary.*

"The name of this dish actually means 'whore-style pasta,' so called because they say prostitutes prepared it for themselves in between visits from 'clients.'"

SPIRIT OF '76

For the ribs
2 slabs beef ribs

For the rub
2 tablespoons kosher salt
1½ tablespoons light brown sugar
1 tablespoon sweet paprika
1½ teaspoons cayenne pepper
½ teaspoon ground cumin
1 tablespoon granulated onion
2 teaspoons freshly ground black pepper

For the glaze
½ cup dark corn syrup
One 12-ounce can Coca-Cola
3 tablespoons light brown sugar
3 tablespoons prepared yellow mustard
1 teaspoon chili powder
Pinch cayenne pepper
Kosher salt and freshly ground
  black pepper

Special equipment
Charcoal grill
Hickory wood
Barbecue brush

July 4, 1976, was no ordinary Independence Day party. America was celebrating its two-hundredth birthday and the anniversary of the Declaration of Independence. Across the country, bicentennial festivities and fireworks memorialized the bloody battles that freed colonists from the tyranny of British rule, and the creation of an independent nation. Commemorative coins, Main Street parades, and a myriad of trinkets and tie-ins built up to a summertime frenzy, but the most popular way to celebrate was by engaging in that most transcendental of all American activities: the backyard barbecue.

FIRECRACKER FOURTH OF JULY BEEF RIBS
WADE BURCH

Prepare the ribs: Place the ribs on a clean cutting board and pull off the membrane, the thin fatty skin that lines the underside of the ribs. Trim the ribs of excess fat.

Prepare the rub: Whisk together all the ingredients. Rub the beef ribs with the rub and place on a large baking sheet, cover with plastic wrap, and, if time permits, let marinate in the refrigerator for 8 hours or overnight.

Prepare the glaze: Combine the ingredients in a medium saucepan and bring to a simmer. Cook until thickened, about 8 minutes, stirring with a wooden spoon to keep from burning. Set aside to cool.

Grill the ribs: Using hickory and charcoal, heat the grill to 250°F.

Place the charcoal and hickory to one side of the grill. (Make an indirect heat source.)

Remove the ribs from the refrigerator. Place the ribs meatier side down on the grill, away from the coals. Cook the beef for 3 hours, adding more coals as needed.

Flip the ribs and cook until the ribs bend and the meat easily separates from the bone, 30 to 45 minutes. Baste the ribs twice with the glaze using a barbecue brush, and cook for another 5 minutes. Allow the meat to rest 10 minutes before cutting into individual ribs. 🪶

"Both of my grandmothers were amazing cooks, as were my mom and dad," says Wade. "I guess I figured if I wanted to keep eating well, I'd better find a way to make some money." He did so by finding his own way into the kitchen, cooking across all three coasts with stops including the Plaza Hotel, a stint working under the "godfather of American cuisine" Larry Forgione, and the Pan Pacific Hotel in San Francisco. Wade is currently the executive chef at the posh Royal Oaks Country Club in Dallas.

Wade Burch *is a true southerner whose roots are tied to Texas City, Texas, located on the Gulf Coast near Galveston.*

THUNDER AND SMOKE

In 1977, Fleetwood Mac released their eleventh and most successful studio album, *Rumors*. The combination of a band at the height of their artistry and a song cycle charting the dramas in their personal lives made the record an unforgettable pop milestone. We turned to the duo Edi and the Wolf for a thundering dish with the harmony of multiple voices or flavors, and a prevailing smokiness reminiscent of Stevie Nicks's lead.

SCHLUTZKRAPFEN

AUSTRIAN RAVIOLI WITH BUTTERNUT SQUASH, SUGAR SNAP PEAS, AND PICKLED CORN

EDUARD FRAUNEDER & WOLFGANG BAN

Prepare the pasta dough: Make a well in the center of the flour and put the egg yolks and butter into it. Incorporate until a dough is formed. Knead for 10 minutes. Let rest for 30 minutes. Flatten into two long strips.

Prepare the filling: Mix all the ingredients until thoroughly combined. Place a tablespoon of filling on 1 strip of dough every 2 inches. Brush the edges with the beaten egg. Place the second strip of dough on top and press tightly so that there is no air in the filling. Use a 2-inch ring cutter and stamp out the ravioli. Cook in salted boiling water until al dente.

Prepare the pickled corn: Remove the husks from the corn and set aside. Cut the corn from the cob and set aside. Bring the remaining ingredients to a boil. Remove from the stove top and add the corn kernels. Let cool.

Prepare the sugar snap peas: Remove and discard the stem end and string from each sugar snap pod. Blanch the peas in salted boiling water. Cool in an ice water bath.

Prepare the butternut squash: Peel the squash and cut in half. Scoop out the seeds. Combine the salt, star anise, thyme, garlic,

MAKES 4 TO 6 SERVINGS

For the pasta dough
1 cup all-purpose flour
11 large egg yolks
4 tablespoons unsalted butter, softened
1 egg, beaten

For the filling
½ cup ricotta cheese
7 ounces soft goat cheese
½ bunch parsley, finely chopped
1 clove garlic, minced
Salt and freshly ground black pepper

For the pickled corn
2 ears corn, with husks
2 cups vegetable broth
⅓ cup white balsamic vinegar
2 heaping tablespoons sugar
3 teaspoons kosher salt
½ teaspoon pickling spice

For the sugar snap peas
4 ounces sugar snap peas
Salt

For the butternut squash
1 medium butternut squash
1 tablespoon sea salt
3 pieces star anise
15 sprigs thyme
4 cloves garlic, mashed
6 tablespoons brown sugar
Butter, softened

For the smoked husk oil
Husks from 2 ears corn
2 cups grape-seed oil
Parmesan cheese, for serving

brown sugar, and butter and spread out on a baking dish. Bake the squash on the spice bed at 375°F for 45 minutes. Let cool. Cut into ¼-inch-thick slices. When ready to plate, sauté the squash, sugar snap peas, and pickled corn in butter until hot.

Prepare the smoked husk oil: Broil the husks until a nice char forms. Blend the charred husks in a blender with the grape-seed oil. Strain.

To plate: Place 5 ravioli in each bowl. Garnish with squash, peas, and pickled corn. Drizzle smoked corn husk oil and shave fresh Parmesan over the ravioli and serve. 🌿

> *"Schlutzkrapfen is one of the most popular starter dishes in Austria,"* says Edi. *"With time, this peasant's dish became one of the highlights of the local cuisine."*

Eduard Frauneder and **Wolfgang Ban** *are the Michelin-starred executive chef–owners of restaurants Edi & the Wolf and Seäsonal Restaurant & Weinbar, cocktail bar the Third Man, and Elderberry Catering in New York City. Eduard began his culinary career at age twelve, working alongside his father in the bakeries and pastry shops he owned in Vienna. Wolfgang was raised in a sleepy market town in the eastern part of Austria, where he developed a taste for fine wines influenced by his grandfather's vineyards and also discovered the art of food. Today, they share a love for Austrian food and wine with New York's dining community.*

"They are traditionally filled with seasonal vegetables and goat cheese, but we chose fresh summer corn and added ricotta to the mix, because the mild ricotta puts the sweet corn more into the spotlight."

🌿

BALLS TO THE WALL (BANGER)

For the Harvey Wallbanger cake

8 tablespoons unsalted butter, softened, plus more for the pan

3 cups unbleached all-purpose flour, plus more for the pan

3 tablespoons cornstarch

4 teaspoons baking powder

1¾ cups granulated sugar

¾ teaspoon fine salt

⅓ cup extra virgin olive oil

1½ teaspoons vanilla bean paste or pure vanilla extract

4 large eggs, at room temperature

¾ cup blood orange juice or regular orange juice

¼ cup Galliano liqueur

¼ cup vodka

2 tablespoons bitter orange marmalade

1 tablespoon grated orange zest

For the "glue"

2 cups sifted confectioners' sugar

⅓ cup bitter orange marmalade

2 tablespoons Galliano liqueur

2 tablespoons vodka

For the frosting

1½ pounds white chocolate, chopped

⅓ cup vegetable oil

Edible silver glitter

Special equipment

Microplane grater

Pastry blender (optional)

Melon baller (optional)

Bamboo skewers or paper lollipop sticks

Styrofoam or florist foam block

In 1978, disco was king, and New York's Studio 54 was where the famous, infamous, illustrious, and ravishing all mingled. Liza, Halston, and Warhol presided over a coke-soaked entourage of models, mavens, and hangers-on under pulsating lights, set to a throbbing disco beat. Everything was larger than life, pumped with sex appeal, bright lights, and more lewd corruption in "the basement" that you could shake a disco ball at.

Most evenings, a large theatrical prop of a crescent moon with a human face would descend over Studio 54's main stage, suspended by invisible wires. From the same wires, a cutout of a gigantic spoon heaped with a suspicious white substance would be hoisted up to the moon's nose, as it were. The man in the moon was really, really, *really* ready to party. The glamour and insanity of disco, Studio 54, and "the Moon and the Spoon" could very well be the twentieth century's highest high.

DISCO CAKE BALLS
RHONDA KAVE

Prepare the cake: Preheat the oven to 350°F. Butter and flour a 9 by 13-inch baking pan. Whisk together the flour, cornstarch, and baking powder. In a large mixing bowl with a hand mixer or in the bowl of a stand mixer, beat together the sugar, 8 tablespoons butter, and salt until fluffy. Beat in the olive oil and vanilla, then add the eggs, one at a time, beating until each is incorporated before adding the next.

In a glass measuring cup, stir together the orange juice, Galliano, vodka, 2 tablespoons marmalade, and orange zest (use a Microplane for maximum flavor punch!). Add ⅓ of the dry ingredient mixture to the butter mixture, mixing until it disappears. Scrape the mixing bowl and add ½ of the liquid, continuing to alternate dry ingredients and liquid, finishing with dry ingredients. Beat until the batter is smooth. Transfer the batter to the prepared pan, smoothing out the top.

Bake the cake for 30 to 35 minutes. Test with a toothpick inserted into the center; it will come out clean when the cake is done. Test about 10 minutes before time to avoid overbaking. Remove the cake from the oven and let it cool in the pan on a wire rack.

When cool, remove the cake from the pan (don't worry about being careful—you're gonna chop it up anyway!) and cut off any crunchy bits from the edges and corners. Now comes the fun part! Crumble the cake into a large bowl with your hands or use a pastry blender or food processor to chop it into bits (the food processor is the easiest and quickest method).

Prepare the glue: This glue will hold the cake balls together. Line a baking sheet with wax paper. Blend the confectioners' sugar, ⅓ cup marmalade, Galliano, and vodka. Using a spoon or your own clean hands, combine into the cake crumbs. To make the balls, scoop out the mixture with a spoon or melon baller and roll with slightly moistened hands to form into firm walnut- to golf ball–size balls. Place them on the baking sheet and freeze for 15 minutes.

Prepare the frosting: When the balls are ready for dipping, combine the white chocolate and vegetable oil in a glass bowl and melt in the microwave on 50% power in 30-second intervals until just melted (do not allow to burn), stirring until all lumps are dissolved. Pour the edible silver glitter into a shallow saucer, where it will be ready to bedazzle your balls!

Finish the cake balls: Before you begin, set your Styrofoam block on the counter and line another baking sheet with wax paper. Put a skewer into a cake ball so you can coat it completely in the chocolate—ideally you want to be able to submerge the cake ball; otherwise, roll it around in the chocolate until completely covered. Allow any excess to drip off, then poke the skewer into the foam block so the pop can set up slightly (about 30 seconds). Quickly roll the still-tacky cake ball in the dish of glitter until completely coated. DISCO MAGIC!!!

Allow the finished cake ball to set up a bit, then gently push it off the skewer onto the prepared sheet pan—you can also leave these on the skewers or substitute lollipop sticks. If you are going to make them into cake pops, before inserting the sticks in the balls, dip the tip in chocolate first to help the ball adhere to the stick. Repeat the process until you have coated all the cake balls. By now the finished dazzlers are set up fully and you're ready to PARTY! 🪡

> *In regard to her twinkling spherical confection, Rhonda says, "Back in the day everybody made Harvey Wallbanger cake with boxed cake mix and other tragic ingredients! Thankfully, the folks in the King Arthur Flour test kitchen came up with this scratch version that I used as a jumping-off point for these crazy, glittery, dazzlingly disco (cake) balls."*

Entrepreneur and chocolatier **Rhonda Kave** *owns and operates Roni-Sue's Chocolates in the historic Essex Street Market in New York. Rhonda has been making chocolates for over twenty-five years, drawing inspiration from her discoveries made by exploring both exotic and local markets in search of special ingredients for her unique handmade treats.*

HAPPIEST MEAL

What did busy parents do before the McDonald's Happy Meal? The multi-course meal was designed to incite the desires of children, but it also served to appease the young-at-heart adult palate. Kemp Minifie's version is sure to please all parties by reconfiguring the combination of meat, bun, potato, and tomato found in this trusty new paper lunch box. Dessert in this happy meal is a second, third, or fourth slice!

MEATBALL AND POTATO PIZZA
KEMP MINIFIE

Prepare the dough: Stir together the yeast, 1 tablespoon of the flour, and ¼ cup warm water in a large bowl. Let stand until the surface appears creamy, about 5 minutes. (If the mixture doesn't appear creamy, discard and start over with new yeast.) Add 1¼ cups flour, the remaining ½ cup water, the salt, and olive oil and stir until smooth. Stir in enough flour (¼ to ⅓ cup) for the dough to begin to pull away from the side of the bowl. (The dough will be slightly wet.) Knead on a floured surface, lightly reflouring when the dough becomes too sticky, until the dough is smooth, soft, and elastic, about 8 minutes. Form into a ball, put in an oiled large bowl, and turn to coat with the oil. Cover with plastic wrap and let rise at warm room temperature until doubled, about 1¼ hours.

Heat a pizza stone while the dough rises. At least 45 minutes before baking the pizza, put the stone on an oven rack in the lower third of an electric oven or on the floor of a gas oven and preheat the oven to 500°F.

Prepare the potatoes: Peel them and cut into ¾-inch cubes. Toss with the olive oil and salt in a bowl and spread out on a parchment paper–lined rimmed baking sheet. Bake them on the pizza stone, stirring and turning them over once or twice, about 20 minutes. Remove from the oven and set aside.

MAKES 4 TO 6 SERVINGS

For the dough
One ¼-ounce envelope active dry yeast (2¼ teaspoons)

1¾ cups unbleached all-purpose flour, plus more for dusting

¾ cup warm water

1 teaspoon fine salt

½ teaspoon olive oil, plus more for the bowl

For the potatoes
¾ pound Yukon gold potatoes

1 tablespoon olive oil

¼ teaspoon fine salt

For the meatballs
3 tablespoons water

½ cup torn pieces of fresh bread from an Italian loaf

½ pound ground beef chuck

⅓ cup finely grated Pecorino Romano or Parmigiano-Reggiano

1 large egg yolk

2 tablespoons finely chopped onion

1 clove garlic, finely chopped

1 tablespoon finely chopped dill pickle (optional)

½ teaspoon fine salt

¼ teaspoon freshly ground black pepper

For the tomatoes and cheese
1 tablespoon olive oil, plus more for brushing on the pizza

6 ounces cherry tomatoes or grape tomatoes (1 packed cup)

⅛ teaspoon fine salt

4 ounces fresh salted mozzarella, diced (¾ cup)

4 ounces whole-milk mozzarella, diced (¾ cup)

Fresh dill sprigs, for garnish

Special equipment

Pizza stone and pizza peel
 (optional; see Note)
Parchment paper

Prepare the meatballs: While roasting the potatoes, pour the water over the bread in a small bowl and stir to moisten evenly. Let stand 5 minutes, then squeeze the bread gently to remove excess liquid.

Combine the bread with the beef, cheese, egg yolk, onion, garlic, pickle (if using), salt, and pepper and blend with your hands until combined (be careful not to overmix). Form slightly rounded tablespoon measures into balls and arrange on another parchment paper–lined rimmed baking sheet. Bake on the hot pizza stone for 5 minutes. (The meatballs will not be cooked through.) Remove from the oven.

Prepare the tomatoes: Heat a heavy medium skillet (not non-stick) over high heat until hot. Swirl the olive oil in the bottom of the pan. Add the tomatoes and salt and cook, covered, shaking the pan several times, until the tomatoes are browned in spots, blistered, and beginning to wilt. Transfer to a bowl and coarsely crush the tomatoes with a fork, leaving big chunks.

Bake the dough: Do not punch down the dough. Dust the dough with flour, then transfer to a parchment paper–lined pizza peel or large baking sheet. Pat out the dough evenly with your fingers and stretch into a 12- to 13-inch round, reflouring your hands when necessary. Lightly prick the dough all over with a fork, brush lightly with oil, and slide (on parchment) onto the stone. Bake until the top is puffed and pale golden in spots, 5 to 6 minutes.

Assemble the pizza: Remove the pizza crust from the oven (use the peel or a baking sheet to slide under the parchment). (Prick any large bubbles with a fork and flatten.) Scatter the cheeses evenly over the pizza and spoon the tomatoes randomly onto it. Slide (still on parchment) onto the pizza stone again. Bake 5 minutes. Remove the pizza from the oven again and top with the meatballs and potatoes. Slide (on parchment) onto the pizza stone a third time and bake until the edge of the crust is deep gold, the cheese is bubbling and golden in spots, and the meatballs are cooked through, 7 to 10 minutes. Remove the pizza from the oven and sprinkle with dill sprigs. ❧

NOTE: If you don't have a pizza stone or peel, you will need 2 large heavy baking sheets (not rimmed). Preheat the oven to 500°F with 1 heavy baking sheet on a rack in the lowest position of the oven (it will not take nearly as long as heating an oven with a pizza stone in it). Form the pizza into an oval (about 14 by 12 inches) on parchment paper on the other baking sheet and continue with the directions above.

Kemp Minifie *joined Epicurious.com as senior editor after thirty-two years wrapped up in all aspects of food at* Gourmet *magazine as well as two years working on the special editions of* Gourmet *and gourmet.com. A graduate of École de Cuisine La Varenne in Paris, Kemp also trained with Madhur Jaffrey, Giuliano Bugialli, Julie Sahni, Diana Kennedy, and Susana Trilling. Although Kemp has accepted her frugal Yankee heritage, she hasn't let it get in the way of her pure enjoyment of all things Italian: chocolate, mascarpone, eggs, basil, olive oil, and Parmigiano-Reggiano, for starters.*

HOW DO YOU LIKE THEM APPLES?

MAKES ABOUT 24 BEIGNETS

For the beignets

2½ cups water

½ pound unsalted butter, cut into pieces

2 teaspoons granulated sugar

2 teaspoons kosher salt

12 ounces all-purpose flour

7 large eggs

1½ cups diced apples (such as Golden Delicious), cut in ⅛-inch cubes.

For the salted caramel sauce

2 cups granulated sugar

1 cup heavy cream

1 teaspoon kosher salt

To serve

Oil, for deep-frying

Confectioners' sugar

Special equipment

Deep-fry candy thermometer

Squeeze bottle with small hole

Slotted spoon

In May 1980, a catastrophic volcanic eruption at Mount Saint Helens caused widespread damage and destruction. The silver lining of the explosion was the release of an ensuing ash plume containing massive amounts of plant-nutritive minerals. Unbeknownst to farmers and fruit tenders, the microscopic materials released in the clouds that roared from the mountain were quietly fertilizing the many surrounding orchards of Washington and Oregon. By the fall of that year, farmers experienced a bountiful bumper crop of apples whose sales were certainly a boon to the disaster-stricken Pacific Northwest.

APPLE AND SALTED CARAMEL BEIGNETS
ANITA LO

Prepare the beignet batter: Bring the water, butter, 2 teaspoons sugar, and 2 teaspoons salt to a rolling boil over high heat. Make sure the butter is completely melted, then all at once, off the heat, add the flour and stir in immediately. Turn the heat to medium and return the pot to the heat. Stir just until the mixture becomes a ball and pulls away from the edges. It should be well mixed. Place the mixture in the bowl of a stand mixer with a paddle attachment and turn to low speed. Allow to stir 1 to 2 minutes, then add the eggs, one at a time, allowing the mixture to fully incorporate each egg before adding another. When all eggs are mixed in, add the apples and mix.

Prepare the caramel sauce: Place the 2 cups sugar in a pot and dissolve in a very small amount of water. Place on high heat and cook until the sugar starts to brown. Do not stir during this process or the sugar will crystallize. When the sugar is a deep, uniform brown, add the cream and cook about 3 minutes. Add the 1 teaspoon salt, taste, and adjust. Transfer to a squeeze bottle and keep warm.

To serve: Fill a deep, heavy-bottomed pot two-thirds with oil, or fill a deep-fryer. Heat the oil to 375°F. Cover a baking sheet with several layers of paper towels. Working in batches, spoon 5 balls of beignet batter into the oil and fry until golden. Remove with a slotted spoon and drain briefly on the paper towels. Pipe a tablespoon of sauce into each beignet with the squeeze bottle. Dust liberally with confectioners' sugar using a small strainer, and serve with the holes up so the sauce don't ooze out. ✦

Anita Lo *is the great American underdog. A first-generation Chinese American, Anita is easily one of the most talented and sophisticated chefs of her generation. At her intimate downtown darling, Annisa, she offers dishes that, in every course, hover somewhere between delectable and phantasmagorical. In an era of dining when restaurant desserts can be dour denouements to avant-garde, creative collations, Anita defies every cliché, playing the whole menu like a pumped pinch hitter from the national anthem to the bottom of the ninth. Her desserts don't accent the meal—they immortalize it. In the weeks following dinner at Annisa, it's likely that you'll find yourself haunted by a mysterious, primal cuisine that has surreptitiously invaded your subconscious, calling you back like an enchanting siren.*

Anita is the author of Cooking Without Borders, *which is required reading for culinary conjurers everywhere.*

Erik Ramirez
Tom Richter
Ruth Reichl
Rachel Wharton
Robert Krueger
Jeremy Spector
Lucas Lin
Scott Hocker
Kyle MacLachlan
Alan Sytsma

80

ALL IN THE ANGLES

MAKES 4 SERVINGS

For the grapefruit leche de tigre

⅛ cup ruby red grapefruit juice

2 teaspoons yuzu juice

2 teaspoons lime juice

Salt

For the scallops

4 very large (U-10) sea scallops

½ cup grapefruit leche de tigre
  (from above recipe)

Maldon salt

4 large segments ruby red grapefruit,
  each cut into 3 pieces

¼ cup toasted blanched hazelnuts,
  cut in half

2 tablespoons Kendall Farms crème
  fraîche (optional)

28 watercress leaves

Special equipment

1½-inch ring cutter

Artist Patrick Nagel created popular illustrations emphasizing the beauty of the female form in a distinctive style reminiscent of Art Deco for the likes of *Playboy* and the cover of Duran Duran's hit album *Rio*. Influenced by Japanese woodblock prints, he forced perspective from flat two-dimensional images and kept simplifying, working to get more across with fewer elements. Erik Ramirez took the artist's sense of refinement to heart, composing a dish with all the minimalist geometry and sensuous beauty of a Nagel Venus.

SCALLOP TIRADITO WITH GRAPEFRUIT, HAZELNUTS, AND WATERCRESS

ERIK RAMIREZ

Prepare the grapefruit leche de tigre: Combine all the juices and season with salt. Refrigerate until ready to use.

Prepare the scallops: Steam the scallops at 155°F for 10 to 15 minutes. Let cool. Once the scallops have cooled, cut them horizontally into ⅛-inch-thick slices. Then, using a 1½-inch ring cutter, punch out perfect circles. You'll use 1 scallop per person. Cover with plastic wrap and set aside in the refrigerator until ready to use.

To plate a single serving: Spoon 2 tablespoons of the ruby red grapefruit leche de tigre into a cold bowl. Arrange scallop slices in a triangle. Season each scallop with Maldon salt. Garnish scallops with 3 pieces of grapefruit, one-quarter of the hazelnuts, 3 dollops of crème fraîche (optional), and 7 watercress leaves. Serve cold and eat with a spoon.

Erik Ramirez *is chef at Richard Sandoval's Raymi in New York City, offering traditional to modern Peruvian fare with an emphasis on small plates and sharing.*

RECKLESS TO THE RIM

With America leaving the dance floor behind, shifting social mores and public health concerns seemed to have taken all of the fun out of nightlife. Enter the Slippery Nipple, Sex on the Beach, and a spate of new cocktails with improbably horny names, meant to evoke a wild and crazy, carefree lifestyle in sharp contrast to most bar patrons' realities. Hey, if you can't do it, why not drink it? The Beagle's Tom Richter reflects on the cocktail's much-maligned period, turning out a totally awesome version of a drink he once disdained, the Appletini.

"FORBIDDEN FRUIT" COCKTAIL
TOM RICHTER

Shake and strain into a coupe glass, with a cherry garnish that will reveal itself as you get closer to the end of the drink.

Tom Richter *balances theatrical pursuits with a showman's flair for classic cocktails at East Village hot spot the Beagle. When not winning countless awards for his craft and writing the "Fresh Pour" column for* Edible Jersey, *Tom spends his time making a quinine tonic bearing his own name, Tom's Tonic.*

MAKES 1 COCKTAIL

½ ounce orgeat
½ ounce lime juice
1 ounce calvados
1¼ ounces blanc vermouth
Cherry, for garnish

YOU BETTER TREAT HER RIGHT...

MAKES 4 SERVINGS

5 matzos
5 large eggs
Salt
8 tablespoons unsalted butter

By 1983, the seventies were really and truly over. But instead of drying up, the frivolity of the previous decade got inflated. Hair, egos, and shoulder pads puffed up alongside the Dow Jones Industrial Average, which tripled in the years between 1980 and 1990, creating the decade's signature villain, the yuppie. Despite the breakneck speed at which the world was growing, life was also changing for the better. Women made leaps ahead in commerce, media, and society at large. The year 1983 saw Sally Ride as the first American woman in space, and Teri Garr juggled family and career on the big screen in the year's blockbuster *Mr. Mom*. However, the year's most memorable girl power moment was the transformation of Donna Summer. Emerging from her sex-kitten "bad girl" persona of the disco era, Summer delivered the ultimate call for respecting the women of the '80s with her triumphant hit, "She Works Hard for the Money."

MATZO BREI
RUTH REICHL

Crumble the matzos into a large sieve placed over a bowl to catch crumbs. Hold the sieve under cold running water until the matzos are moist and softened but not completely disintegrated, about 15 seconds. Transfer the matzos to the bowl with the crumbs. Add the eggs and salt to taste and mix gently with a fork. Heat the butter in a 10- to 12-inch skillet over moderately high heat until the foam subsides. Add the matzo mixture and cook, stirring constantly, until the eggs are scrambled and the matzo has begun to crisp, about 3 minutes.

Ruth Reichl *is best known for being a food writer, food lover, and all-around national treasure. Beginning her career as a writer in 1972, she juggled the transition to chef and co-owner of the famed California restaurant Swallow. Embracing several high-profile editorships, Reichl occupied the roles of restaurant editor of the* Los Angeles Times, *restaurant critic of the* New York Times, *and eventually,*

editor in chief of Gourmet, *where she served from 1999 until the magazine's final issue in 2009. In her decade at the helm of America's beloved culinary and travel publication, she championed the importance of substance and style equally, as well as the numerous endearing qualities of a Gray's Papaya hot dog. As talented a cook as she is a writer and editor, Ruth prepares this beloved recipe, which she says is "basically Jewish French toast" for her family on Christmas morning.*

WELCOME TO BROOKLYN

When The Cosby Show *debuted on NBC in 1984,* television and America at large had had it with stereotypes—which is why the Huxtables were such a breath of fresh air. From their well-to-do Brooklyn Heights home, a doctor dad and lawyer mom tended to a house full of kids and a happy marriage. During its long run, the program presented the humor and hilarity of family life in universal terms that drew in millions of viewers who related to their domestic hijinks; almost everyone saw a little of themselves in *The Cosby Show.* By the end of the program's run, Brooklyn seemed to be back on the map in a way it hadn't been in decades. A loud sweater, however, is still completely optional.

HILDRED'S EASY BROOKLYN BLACKOUT CAKE
RACHEL WHARTON

Prepare the cake layers: Preheat the oven to 350°F. Butter the 3 cake pans. Cream the 12 tablespoons butter and 1½ cups sugar together (a stand mixer makes short work of this). Add the 6 eggs one at a time, incorporating after each addition. Add the chocolate syrup and beat to mix. Add the flour in stages, stirring to mix well. Divide the batter among the cake pans and bake for 30 minutes. Invert and let the layers cool on a wire rack.

Prepare the pudding: Obviously you should just make Jell-O chocolate pudding, but this is a simple homemade version.

Whisk together the 3 eggs and half-and-half in a bowl. Combine the ½ cup sugar, cornstarch, and salt in a heavy-bottomed saucepan. Add the egg mixture and bring to medium heat, whisking to prevent burning and to break up lumps. Stir in the chocolate, then the 2 tablespoons butter. Chill until it thickens up a bit to the texture of frosting.

MAKES 10 TO 12 SERVINGS

For the cake layers
12 tablespoons unsalted butter, plus more for the pans
1½ cups sugar
6 large eggs
One 24-ounce bottle Hershey's Syrup
1½ cups self-rising flour (or you could use all-purpose flour and add 1¾ teaspoons fine salt and 1¾ teaspoons baking powder)
Crushed chocolate wafer cookies

For the pudding
3 large eggs
2½ cups half-and-half
½ cup sugar
3 tablespoons cornstarch
¼ teaspoon fine salt (or more, depending on your preference and your chocolate)
3 ounces dark chocolate, chopped
2 tablespoons unsalted butter, softened

Special equipment
Three 8-inch round cake pans

Assemble the cake: Sandwich the layers and cover the sides and top generously with pudding. Coat with crushed chocolate wafers for extra Brooklyn blackoutness. You should store it, covered, in the fridge, as in my opinion it is actually best a wee bit chilled, thanks both to the pudding and the crazy sugar richness of the syrup. Chilling makes it even denser. ✲

> *Inspired by the Huxtable family, Rachel created a cake that's "exactly the type of thing Cliff could and would make—and Claire would groan over, since she was always after Cliff to go on a diet." She imagines that her recipe, which comes from her great-grandmother, originally came from a can of chocolate sauce.*

Rachel Wharton *is a freelance writer based in Brooklyn, with a master's degree in food studies from New York University. She's contributed to* New York Daily News *and NY1, edited* The Edible Brooklyn Cookbook, *and produced a weekly podcast on food businesses for Heritage Radio Network since 2010. In 2010, she won a James Beard food journalism award for her stories in* Edible Brooklyn *magazine, and one of her profiles from* Edible Manhattan *was included in* Best Food Writing 2012.

BREAKFAST EPIPHANIES

MAKES 5 COCKTAILS

For "the Jock"

2 ounces white rum
1 ounce simple syrup
1 ounce freshly squeezed lemon juice
½ banana, ripe
1 egg yolk
Dash Angostura bitters

For "the Brain"

2 ounces applejack
1 ounce freshly squeezed lemon juice
¾ ounce simple syrup
1 tablespoon strawberry jelly
Peanuts, for garnish

For "the Criminal"

2 ounces Zubrowka Bison Grass vodka
1 ounce freshly squeezed lemon juice
1 ounce simple syrup
1 egg white
Stick licorice candy, for garnish
Fingerless gloves

For "the Princess"

1 ounce vodka
½ ounce simple syrup
½ ounce freshly squeezed lemon juice
Rosé Champagne

For "the Basket Case"

Pixy Stix
2 ounces unaged corn whiskey
1 ounce freshly squeezed lemon juice
1 ounce simple syrup
Coca-Cola

John Hughes's **The Breakfast Club** *premiered in 1985,* and quickly became a symbol for a generation that identified with the group of five archetypal high schoolers struggling with identity and stereotypes throughout a day of detention. We asked Extra Fancy's Robert Krueger to conjure a versatile breakfast cocktail menu that begins with a single common ingredient and through additive ingredients becomes five unique concoctions to start your day. Must be of legal age—or at least sufficiently angst ridden—to enjoy.

"THE JOCK," "THE BRAIN," "THE CRIMINAL," "THE PRINCESS," AND "THE BASKET CASE" COCKTAILS

ROBERT KRUEGER

Prepare "the Jock": Combine all ingredients in a blender with ice. Blend until smooth. Pour into a hurricane glass. Dash Angostura bitters on top. Flex and enjoy.

Prepare "the Brain": Shake the applejack, lemon juice, syrup, and jelly together and strain over ice in a rocks glass. Serve with a plastic "bendy" straw. Garnish with a small dish of roasted peanuts.

Prepare "the Criminal": Combine all ingredients in a mixing glass and shake until the egg white is emulsified. Add ice cubes and shake until chilled and frothy. Strain into a cocktail glass. Float strips of the licorice candy across the drink to make jailbird stripes. Wear the gloves while drinking.

Prepare "the Princess": Shake the vodka, lemon juice, and simple syrup with ice. Strain into a champagne flute. Top with rosé Champagne. Pairs well with sushi.

"The common ingredient is 'sour' made with fresh lemon and sugar," Robert explains, "as the protagonists are decidedly sour about their situation at the start of the film."

Prepare "the Basket Case": Rim a Collins glass by inverting in a shallow dish of water, then dipping in the powder from the Stix. Shake the whiskey, lemon juice, and simple syrup together. Pour with the ice into the glass—carefully, so as not to melt the powder. Top with Coca-Cola. Mix gently.

Robert Krueger *is a partner and bar director of Extra Fancy in Williamsburg, Brooklyn. Previously, he was the bar manager of the famed Manhattan cocktail bar Employees Only, winner of Tales of the Cocktail's 2011 World's Best Cocktail Bar.*

TOTALLY AMAZIN'

Since 1983, the New York Mets had been padding their dugout with heavy hitters and rising stars like Darryl Strawberry, Dwight Gooden, Sid Fernandez, and Lenny Dykstra and by 1986, NYC's "other" baseball team rolled into their twenty-fifth season in the National League. The boys found themselves in a suspense-riddled contest against superrivals the Boston Red Sox on baseball's ultimate stage: the World Series. After losing three of the first five games, the Mets bounced back from the brink of failure to snag the series in an electrifying final two games. The Mets have not since revisited the glory and fame they achieved in 1986.

STRAWBERRY SHORTSTOP
JEREMY SPECTOR

Prepare the dough: Place the potatoes in a saucepan and cover with cold water. Place the saucepan on medium-high heat and bring the water to a boil. Boil the potatoes until soft, remove from the water, and set aside under a kitchen towel.

Sift the flour, granulated sugar, baking powder, and salt together into the bowl of a stand mixer fitted with a dough hook (or mix by hand). In a heavy-bottomed saucepan, bring the milk, butter, cinnamon, allspice, cloves, and orange zest to a simmer; do not allow to boil over.

Peel the slightly cooled potatoes and push them through a ricer, and add to the dry ingredients. Strain the hot milk into a glass measuring cup to remove the spices. Begin mixing the dry ingredients on low speed, and continue mixing while adding the hot milk in a stream (about 1 minute). Add the eggs and continue mixing until smooth (about 5 minutes).

Place the dough in a large floured bowl, cover with plastic wrap or a kitchen towel, and allow to rest in the refrigerator for at least 1 hour.

MAKES A LOT OF DONUTS

For the donuts
4 medium russet potatoes
7 cups all-purpose flour,
  plus more for rolling
⅔ cup granulated sugar
8 teaspoons baking powder
2 teaspoons kosher salt
1⅓ cups whole milk
10 tablespoons unsalted butter
3 whole cinnamon sticks
6 whole allspice berries
10 whole cloves
2 tablespoons grated orange zest
4 large eggs
1 gallon vegetable oil, for deep-frying

For the glaze
10 fresh strawberries, rinsed and hulled,
  or 10 thawed frozen strawberries
2 tablespoons strawberry jam
2 tablespoons whole milk or light cream
2 to 4 cups sifted confectioners' sugar

Special equipment
Potato ricer
Mini food processor, or food mill
Deep-frying thermometer
3½-inch donut cutter
Wire skimmer
Pastry brush (optional)

Prepare the glaze: Slice the strawberries and puree with the jam in a mini food processor or food mill. Pour into a medium bowl and mix in the milk.

Slowly stir in 2 cups sifted confectioners' sugar. Continue adding the remaining confectioners' sugar as needed to form a smooth yet slightly firm glaze.

Prepare the donuts: In a large enameled cast-iron Dutch oven (or similar heavy-bottomed pot), heat the oil to 360°F. Set a wire cooling rack over a baking sheet or cover a baking sheet with paper towels.

Meanwhile, remove the dough from the refrigerator. Roll half the dough out to ½ inch thick on a floured board or pastry marble. Cut out donuts using a donut punch and gently place 4 at a time in the fryer oil. Allow the donuts to cook for 2 to 2½ minutes, until golden brown. Turn the donuts over and cook another 2 minutes.

Remove the donuts with a skimmer and place on the wire rack or paper towels to drain. Continue with the remaining donuts.

Reserve the remaining dough for a second batch of donuts. The dough will keep for a week in the refrigerator.

When the donuts have cooled to room temperature, wipe the glaze onto them with a pastry brush or dip the donuts into the glaze. Let the glaze set before serving.

Jeremy Spector *was never a big fan of school. So after getting kicked out of college, the Queens native decided to follow his one true love, food, which ironically led him back to the classroom at San Francisco's California Culinary Academy. After working at some culinary legends like Straits, Bix, Vivande, and Le Colonial, as well as Balthazar, Gramercy Tavern, Lupa, Schiller's, and Vinegar Hill House, he cofounded Dogmatic and became one of the opening chef-partners at the popular speakeasy Employees Only. Jeremy is the man behind PGB, a restaurant group that includes the Brindle Room, Wonder City Donuts, and DP Pizza. He is also the inventor of PGB Hot Sauce. You can usually find Jeremy cooking in his East Village restaurant, making pizzas by the beach, or napping in his seat at a baseball game. If he had to pick a hero, he'd pick Sylvester Stallone, but then again, who wouldn't?*

MAKES 80 TO 90 DUMPLINGS

For the dough

7 cups all-purpose flour

3 cups hot water (above 200°F)

For the flavoring liquid

5 tablespoons water

¼ teaspoon fine salt

1 teaspoon baking soda

1 little square fermented tofu
(optional; can be replaced with
2 anchovy fillets)

1 teaspoon sugar

1½ teaspoons chicken bouillon powder

3 tablespoons plus 1 teaspoon Shao
hsing wine or dry sherry

3 tablespoons plus 1 teaspoon soy sauce

5 teaspoons oyster sauce

2 teaspoons freshly ground black pepper

3 scallions, coarsely chopped

2 ounces (3 teaspoons) coarsely
chopped ginger

For the filling

2½ pounds ground beef

3 tablespoons vegetable oil

3 medium onions, diced

Pinch sugar

5 teaspoons satay sauce
(the best satay sauce is called simply
"barbecue sauce" on the label; on the
top of the lid it says Bull Head Brand.
This can be replaced with 5 teaspoons
Worcestershire sauce, if necessary.)

1 teaspoon soy sauce

2 large green bell peppers, seeded
and diced small

IF THE COUNTERFEITS...

In the 1980s, commodification of fine art reached new heights. Van Gogh's *Vase with Fifteen Sunflowers* fetched nearly $40 million at auction, and *Irises* grabbed $54 million later in the year. Behind the scenes, notorious forger John Myatt produced as many as two hundred fakes, making a fortune for himself by impersonating masters like Chagall, Matisse, and Le Corbusier. Authenticity is unmistakable . . . until it is mistaken. When one culture's food migrates across borders to another culture where available ingredients and tastes are different, the cuisine must, by necessity, become an interpretation of the original. Is it the real thing, or is it a fake?

BEEF SATAY DUMPLINGS
LUCAS LIN

Prepare the dough: Place the flour in a large bowl. Very slowly drizzle in the hot water, holding a fork while you drizzle, and quickly and evenly stir in the raw flour. You want to "cook" as much flour as you can before using up all the hot water. This dough is very sticky and hard to handle. While the dough is still hot, mix until it is smooth and the bowl is clean. Rest the dough for at least an hour.

Prepare the flavoring liquid: Put all the ingredients in a blender and blend until smooth.

Prepare the filling: Mix the ground beef into the flavoring liquid, and marinate in the refrigerator overnight.

In the vegetable oil in a wok or large skillet over low heat, sauté the onions with the sugar until lightly browned. Add the satay sauce and soy sauce and stir until fragrant. Add the green peppers and stir-fry less than a minute—you want the peppers to stay rather crunchy.

Let the vegetables cool before combining with the marinated beef. This should be enough filling for 80 to 90 dumplings.

Prepare the dumpling wrappers: On a floured surface, roll the dough ⅛ inch thick and punch out 4-inch disks using an inverted drinking glass or cutter.

Prepare the dumplings: Fill each dumpling wrapper with a tablespoon of filling, fold in half, and pinch to close. Bring the ends of the folded piece around to touch and pinch so they hold together. Steam in batches for 8 to 10 minutes. Serve with your favorite sauces. 🪰

Lucas is delighted to share with us this new filling, and says the preparation is a duty best shared among six to eight real friends, part of the joy of eating dumplings.

Lucas Lin *is an NYU graduate and former journalist who opened Dumpling Man on a whim, only to find the demand for his delicious dumplings was widespread and lasting. At the shop on St. Mark's Place in the East Village, you can watch an assembly line of dumpling artisans prepare your order from start to finish.*

HEART AND SEOUL

The second Olympic Summer Games to be held in Asia (the first was in Tokyo in 1964) saw higher numbers of participating countries than any previous games of the 1980s. Some of the twentieth century's best-known athletes, including Flo-Jo, Greg Louganis, and Jackie Joyner-Kersee, would attend and compete. The Korean peninsula and its people were largely undiscovered to generations of Americans. As a result, the intricate platings and divine, opulent preparations of Korean food seemed extraordinary to the average American. Today, Korean cuisine is still woefully underrepresented outside metropolitan East and West Coast cities. Thankfully, the brilliant and polished Scott Hocker has created a dish to introduce the flavor and excitement of Korean cuisine to American cooks and diners.

COLD KOREAN BUCKWHEAT NOODLES
SCOTT HOCKER

In a large bowl, combine ¼ cup rice vinegar, the *gochujang*, *gochugaru*, sugar, and ¼ teaspoon salt. Mix well. Add the radish and toss well to combine. Bring a large saucepan filled with water to a boil. Season with salt until the water tastes like the ocean. Add the noodles and cook until they are just tender.

Meanwhile, in a medium bowl, combine 4 teaspoons of the toasted sesame oil, the garlic, scallions, and the remaining ½ cup rice vinegar. Stir well.

When the noodles are cooked, drain in a colander, rinse well with cold water, and drain again. Divide the noodles among four large bowls, mounding the noodles in the center of each bowl. Drizzle each pile with 2 teaspoons of the remaining toasted sesame oil. Top each pile with scallion-garlic sauce, radish mixture, cucumber, sesame seeds, and *gim*. Pour 1 cup stock around each pile of noodles. Serve with chopsticks and a large, long spoon.

MAKES 4 SERVINGS

¾ cup rice vinegar

¼ cup *gochujang* (Korean red pepper paste)

3 tablespoons fine *gochugaru* (Korean red pepper powder) or hot paprika

¼ teaspoon sugar

Kosher salt

½ pound daikon or Korean radish, peeled and cut into matchsticks

1 pound dried buckwheat noodles

¼ cup toasted sesame oil

2 cloves garlic, finely chopped

2 scallions, finely chopped

2 English cucumbers, peeled and thinly sliced

4 teaspoons toasted sesame seeds

¼ cup shredded toasted *gim* (nori)

1 quart cold stock: chicken, beef, or vegetable

NOTE: If there isn't a Korean or Asian market where you live, all ingredients in this recipe can be obtained easily through mail order.

Scott Hocker *is the editor in chief at Tasting Table, a national media destination for all things epicurean. Previously, Scott was the senior editor at* San Francisco *magazine. During his tenure there, the magazine won a National Magazine Award for General Excellence. His talent is eclipsed only by his enthusiastic and genuine smile.*

MMMMMM... YES

MAKES 6 TO 8 SERVINGS

5 pounds bone-in beef short ribs,
cut crosswise into 2-inch pieces

All-purpose flour

Kosher salt and freshly ground
black pepper

3 tablespoons vegetable oil

3 medium onions, chopped

3 medium carrots, chopped

2 stalks celery, chopped

1 tablespoon tomato paste

One 750-ml bottle dry red wine
(preferably cabernet sauvignon)

10 sprigs flat-leaf parsley

8 sprigs thyme

4 sprigs oregano

2 sprigs rosemary

2 fresh or dried bay leaves

1 head garlic, halved crosswise

1 quart low-salt beef or chicken stock

Creamy polenta or mashed potatoes,
for serving

To create the enthralling aural experience of her sixth album, *The Sensual World*, Kate Bush drew inspiration from James Joyce's *Ulysses* and William Blake's "Jerusalem." Traces of these romantic source materials melded with Kate's expressive voice to create a timeless document of themes close to the core of the human condition.

We sought a dish prepared with that sensual, ancient blood of the earth—wine. In Washington state, we found an aficionado with an appreciation for the sense of drama exemplified by Kate's beloved record in actor and vintner Kyle MacLachlan.

BRAISED SHORT RIBS
KYLE MacLACHLAN

Dredge the short ribs in flour and season with salt and pepper. Heat the oil in a large Dutch oven over medium-high heat. Working in two batches, brown the short ribs on all sides, about 8 minutes per batch. Transfer the short ribs to a plate. Pour off all but 3 tablespoons drippings from the pot, or add more oil to equal 3 tablespoons.

Add the onions, carrots, and celery to the oil and cook over medium-high heat, stirring often, until the onions are browned, about 5 minutes. Add 3 tablespoons flour and the tomato paste, and cook, stirring constantly, until well combined and deep red, 2 to 3 minutes. Stir in the wine, then add the short ribs with any accumulated juices. Bring to a boil. Lower the heat to medium and simmer until the wine is reduced by half, about 25 minutes. While the wine is reducing, preheat the oven to 350°F.

Add the parsley, thyme, oregano, rosemary, and bay leaves to the ribs, along with the garlic. Stir in the stock. Bring to a boil, cover, and transfer to the oven.

Cook until the short ribs are tender, 2 to 2½ hours. Transfer the short ribs to a platter. Strain the sauce into a large heatproof

glass measuring cup. Spoon the fat from the surface of the sauce and discard; season the sauce to taste with salt and pepper.

Serve in shallow bowls over creamy polenta or mashed potatoes, with sauce spooned over.

> *Kyle's long-held fondness for Kate Bush began when he witnessed the singer's performance of "The Man with the Child in His Eyes" on a 1978 episode of* Saturday Night Live.

> *"I was a second-year college student at the U of Washington at the time. Sitting on top of the piano, gold sparkly body suit, pouty lips, provocative undulations—she definitely made an impression on me! I have all her albums and a personalized photograph she sent to me that was in response to the only fan letter I ever sent."*

> *Kyle challenges any viewer to keep a dry eye when Kate's song "This Woman's Work" starts playing over the scene in the hospital in* She's Having a Baby *starring Elizabeth McGovern and Kevin Bacon.*

Kyle MacLachlan *has realized some of this era's most memorable roles on the big screen in* Dune, Blue Velvet, *and* The Doors, *and on the small screen on* Twin Peaks, Sex and the City, *and* Portlandia. *Off-screen, Kyle is a vintner: he is a partner in Pursued by Bear wine and its manufacture in Washington state's Columbia Valley.*

READ MY LIPS

The forty-first president of the United States, George H. W. Bush, was no stranger to having a one-liner of his hung out to dry. From "read my lips" to "a thousand points of light," some of the president's serious intentions transmitted as pure comedy. Audiences laughed at Mr. Bush's childlike remarks during a news conference when he defiantly proclaimed, "I do not like broccoli and I haven't liked it since I was a little kid and my mother made me eat it and I'm president of the United States and I'm not going to eat any more broccoli." Health advocates, dietitians, and housewives sent their displeasure to the White House alongside packages, if not "truckloads," of broccoli and recipes on how it should be prepared. Conversely, President Bush loved hot sauce almost as much as he hated broccoli. But as any good Texan will tell you, hot sauce is good on everything!

ROASTED BROCCOLI RAREBIT WITH TEXAS TOAST

ALAN SYTSMA

Prepare the broccoli: Preheat oven to 450°F. Cut the broccoli into small florets, removing and discarding the stems. In a bowl, toss the florets with the chili flakes, salt, pepper, and enough olive oil to coat. Spread out on a baking sheet. Roast the florets until they're soft and starting to brown on the edges, about 10 minutes.

Prepare the sauce: While the broccoli is roasting, over low heat, combine the butter, flour, and mustard in a medium pot. Cook for 2 minutes, stirring with a wooden spoon. Slowly whisk in the beer and cook quickly until the sauce thickens slightly (raise the heat to medium if necessary). Remove from the heat and, in batches, whisk in the cheese, making sure the mixture stays combined. Add Worcestershire and salt and cayenne pepper to taste. When the broccoli is finished, fold it into the sauce, then set aside.

MAKES 2 SERVINGS

For the broccoli
1½ pounds broccoli
1 teaspoon chili flakes
Salt and freshly ground black pepper
Olive oil, for roasting

For the sauce
1 tablespoon unsalted butter, softened
4 teaspoons all-purpose flour
1 teaspoon dry mustard
1 cup lager beer (don't get too fancy; mass-market stuff works best)
1½ cups shredded cheddar cheese
1 teaspoon Worcestershire sauce
Salt
Cayenne pepper
1 or 2 handfuls chopped fresh herbs (parsley, tarragon, and chives work well)
Maldon salt (optional)

For the Texas toast
4 tablespoons butter, softened
Two 2-inch-thick slices white bread
1 clove garlic, smashed

Prepare the toast: Heat the broiler to high.

Spread the butter on the bread—get both sides—and toast under the broiler, flipping when each side is golden brown (this will take 1 minute at most—keep an eye on it). As soon as the bread is toasted, remove from the broiler and rub the garlic all over each side of the bread.

To serve: Reheat the sauce over low heat. Place the toast in shallow bowls. Stir the herbs into the sauce and spoon the sauce over the toast. Add a couple of flakes of Maldon if you're feeling fancy. ⚘

"How do you rectify a broccoli hater's misguided point of view?" Alan asks. "Mix the green florets into a cheese-and-beer sauce, then slather it all over extra-thick garlic bread (that just so happens to be named after H.W.'s home state)."

Alan Sytsma *is the senior editor of* Grub Street, New York *magazine's award-winning food and restaurant blog. Previously, he worked as an editor at* Food Network Magazine *and* Gourmet *(RIP). Every once in a while, he shows up as a critic on* Top Chef Masters.

If Alan were the White House chef, he'd serve this dish with a salad and beer.

⚘

Andrew Carmellini

David Duran

Daniel Boulud

Kary Goolsby

Aliya Leekong

Yoshi Nonaka

Jessica Wilson

Shanna Pacifico

Greg Seider

Michael Lomonaco

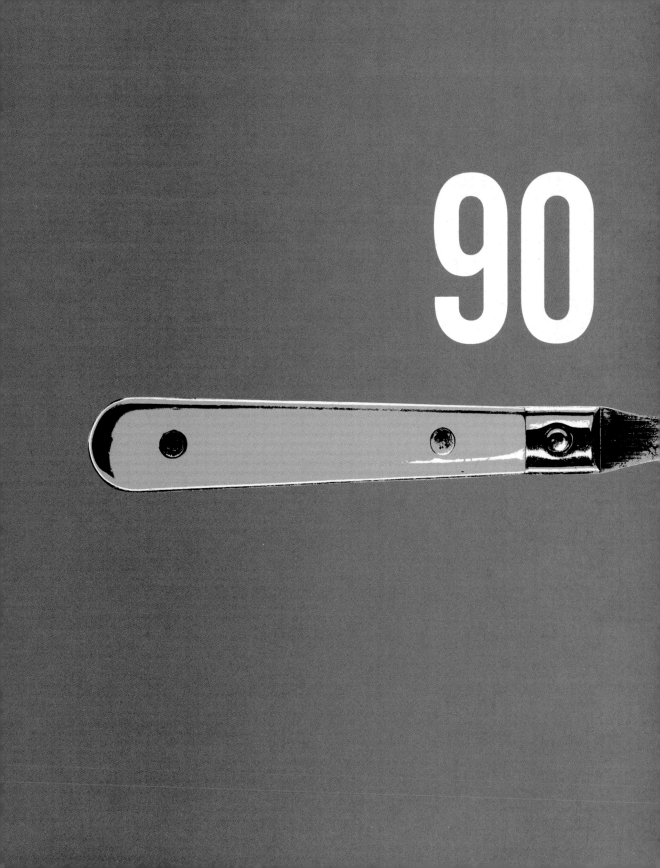

90

MAKES 4 TO 6 SERVINGS

For the tripe

Kosher salt

2½ pounds honeycomb beef (or veal) tripe (2 large or 3 medium pieces)

¼ cup extra virgin olive oil

2 medium onions, sliced thin (about 2 cups)

¼ teaspoon chili flakes

1 tablespoon unsalted butter

1 cup dry white wine

One 28-ounce can peeled tomatoes, chopped, with their juices

3 cups chicken broth

¼ teaspoon coarsely ground black pepper

6 stalks celery, coarsely cut (about 2 cups)

2 medium carrots, sliced (about 1 cup)

For the fried eggs (optional)

2 tablespoons extra virgin olive oil

4 to 6 eggs

Pinch salt

Pinch coarsely ground black pepper

To finish the dish

2 tablespoons sherry vinegar or red wine vinegar

¼ cup grated Parmigiano-Reggiano cheese

2 tablespoons panko bread crumbs

2 tablespoons extra virgin olive oil

THE YEAR PUNK BROKE

By the early '90s, music had finally lost the hair spray, sunglasses, and fingerless gloves. Although Sonic Youth (the influential New York band that *had* been around since the '80s) ironically did not release an album that year, they would be touring with songs from the seminal and touchstone album *Goo*, and filming a concert movie to be released the following year. Now-classic and oft-referenced albums from My Bloody Valentine, the Orb, Slowdive, Nirvana, and Ween would all debut this year, starting a long tradition of deeply eclectic playlists on mixtapes and college radio stations alike. Who better than A.C. to deliver a dish with punk, distortion, and a completely mashed-up, ironic sensibility?

TRIPPA ALLA PARMIGIANA
ANDREW CARMELLINI

Prepare the tripe: Preheat the oven to 375°F.

Bring a large pot of salted water to a boil, place the tripe in the boiling water, and push it under using a spoon or tongs (it will bob up a little bit but should be mostly submerged). Cook the tripe for 15 minutes.

Using tongs, remove the tripe to a bowl and allow it to cool until it can be handled. (To speed things up, put the bowl in the freezer for a few minutes.)

Once the tripe has cooled, pour off any excess water. Cut the tripe pieces roughly into thirds, long 4-inch-wide strips. Cut off any fibrous edges that stick up (they will get tough when cooked). You'll probably end up cutting off about 15 percent of the tripe this way, which is fine. Cut the strips into smaller pieces, about 1 inch wide by 3 to 4 inches long.

Heat the olive oil over medium heat in an ovenproof casserole. Add the onions and slowly cook without allowing them to color until they are soft, about 5 minutes. Add the chili flakes

and butter. Mix well and continue cooking until the butter has melted, about 1 minute.

Add the tripe and stir well to coat every piece in the butter mixture. Turn the heat to high, add the white wine, and cook until the alcohol smell disperses, about 3 minutes. Add the tomatoes, broth, 1½ teaspoons salt, and the pepper.

Cover the casserole and allow the mixture to come up to a simmer. Transfer the casserole to the oven and cook for about 3 hours, stirring occasionally.

Remove the casserole from the oven and place it on the stove. Add the celery and carrots and continue cooking on the stove top, uncovered and at a low simmer, until the liquid has been reduced by half, the vegetables are cooked, and everything has formed a nice sauce (sort of a medium-thick stew), about 1 hour more.

Prepare the fried eggs: When the tripe is nearly done, heat the olive oil in a nonstick pan. Add the eggs, salt, and pepper and fry the eggs to your liking.

To finish the dish: Add the vinegar to the tripe and season with more salt and pepper, if needed. Transfer the tripe to individual serving dishes and sprinkle with the Parmigiano-Reggiano and panko. Drizzle the olive oil over the top.

Serve with a fried egg on top of each dish, if you like.

Born and raised in Seven Hills, Ohio, **Andrew Carmellini** *learned to cook from parents who loved simple, delicious food made well. After graduating from the Culinary Institute of America, he set his sights on Europe and found work in some of its finest restaurants including Valentino Marcattilii's Michelin two-star San Domenico in Emilio-Romagna, Italy.*

Later, during a six-year tenure as chef de cuisine at Café Boulud, Andrew collected two James Beard Awards, a Food & Wine *magazine Best New Chef award, and a three-star review from the* New York Times *in which Frank Bruni described the "first-rate chef's comforting, seductive, and altogether glorious food."*

Andrew has gone on to write the menus at Locanda Verde, the Dutch, the Library, and Lafayette, all to great acclaim. Andrew is the author of two cookbooks with his wife, Gwen Hyman, Urban Italian *and* American Flavor.

HOT MOMMA

Enid Strict may be better known to television audiences as *SNL*'s "the Church Lady." Dana Carvey's sanctimonious character was a hit, hosting notables from Sean Penn to Fred Savage on the sofa of her fictitious *Church Chat* television program. Sporting a powdered wig, cat's-eye glasses, and orthopedic shoes, and looking as though she were clad in iron underpants, Strict proclaimed her devotion to her Lord and savior while swearing against Satan. Carvey's character taught us that all things divine may be complemented by a fiery streak of evil. This breakfast dish is no exception.

HUEVOS DIABLO
DAVID DURAN

Prepare the Coca-Cola carnitas: Steep all the dried chilies in hot water for ½ hour, until softened. Drain the chilies, reserving the soaking water. Working in batches if necessary, in a blender combine the chilies, orange juice, onion, cinnamon, oregano, and bay leaves. Blend until very smoothly pureed, adding soaking water if necessary to keep it moving.

Trim any excess fat and silverskin from the pork. Cut the pork into a few manageable pieces, about 4-inch chunks. Heat the oil in a Dutch oven over medium-high heat until shimmering but not smoking. Add the pork and sear on all sides until browned. Add the chili puree and turn the pork chunks to coat them. Cover the pot, lower the heat, and cook for 1 hour, moving the pork around from time to time so it doesn't stick and burn.

Add the garlic and Coca-Cola and cook uncovered over low heat for about 1 hour more. If the liquid comes close to evaporating too soon, cover the pot. You want the liquid to evaporate out, but nothing should burn.

MAKES 12 TOPPED MUFFINS, 6 SERVINGS

For the Coca-Cola carnitas
3 cascabel chilies
5 guajillo chilies
3 costeño chilies
3 morita chilies
1 cup orange juice (freshly squished)
½ medium sweet onion, diced
½ teaspoon ground cinnamon
½ teaspoon fresh oregano leaves
4 bay leaves
2 pounds pork butt loin
2 tablespoons vegetable oil
¼ cup minced garlic
Two 12-ounce cans Coca-Cola

For the corn muffins
4 tablespoons unsalted butter, softened, plus more for the muffin tin (optional)
9 tablespoons sugar
2 large eggs
½ teaspoon vanilla extract
1½ cups biscuit baking mix (Bisquick)
¼ cup fine yellow cornmeal
⅔ cup whole milk
1 tablespoon finely chopped habanero chilies

For the chipotle "hollandaise" sauce
2 cups heavy cream
One 7-ounce can chipotles in adobo sauce, pureed
6 tablespoons cold water
1 teaspoon kosher salt

For the poached eggs
1 to 2 teaspoons rice vinegar
12 large very fresh eggs

The pork is done when it starts to fall apart when poked with a spoon. Remove the pork with a slotted spoon and shred into smaller chunks. Return the pork to the reduced sauce.

Prepare the corn muffins: Preheat the oven to 375°F. Grease 12 muffin cups or line with paper liners. In a large bowl, cream together the butter and sugar until light and fluffy. Stir in the eggs one at a time, beating well with each addition; then stir in the vanilla.

In a separate bowl, stir together the biscuit baking mix and cornmeal. Blend this mixture into the butter-egg mixture alternately with the milk; stir just until combined. Stir in the habaneros. Spoon the batter into the prepared muffin tin. Bake for 20 to 30 minutes, until golden. Turn out onto a wire rack to cool. Peel off the paper liners, if necessary.

Prepare the chipotle "hollandaise": Heat a saucepan, then pour in the heavy cream. Cook until it is reduced, 5 to 7 minutes. Puree the chipotles and adobo with the water in a blender. Add the chipotle puree to the cream and stir until combined to a nice brownish color and as strong a flavor as you like. Season with the salt. Keep warm.

Prepare the poached eggs: In a shallow pan or wide skillet, bring about 2 inches of water to a bare simmer. Add 1 teaspoon rice vinegar to the water and swirl slightly. Reheat the water to a bare simmer. One at a time, crack the eggs into a very small dish. Gently pour each egg into the pan, using two tablespoons to make sure the egg holds its shape. Let the egg sit for 3 to 4 minutes, until the white has hardened slightly. Lift the egg out with a slotted spoon and place on paper towels to drain.

To serve: Cut off the muffins tops and invert two onto each plate. Top with carnitas, then poached egg, and finally chipotle "hollandaise" sauce. Serve with roasted potatoes. 🌿

David Duran *is the owner of the East Village's El Camion Cantina, where Noah and Paul can be found at least once a week, scarfing down his unpretentious, Mexican-inspired fare. The restaurant is famous for its brunch, when David serves these Huevos Diablo. He likes to say that they're his "best creation in cooking." Once you taste them, you'll likely agree.*

To serve
Roasted potatoes (any roasted potato will work; just add paprika)

Special equipment
Muffin tin

MAKES 12 TO 14 SERVINGS

For the terrine

1 celery root, peeled, cut in six
   4 by ½-inch batons, the rest chopped

6 small carrots, cut in six 4 by ½-inch
   batons, the rest chopped

1 whole beef shank (about 9 pounds),
   trimmed of fat, the bone trimmed short
   enough to fit in a large pot

2 small onions, peeled and each studded
   with 1 whole clove

1 bay leaf

2 sprigs thyme

Kosher salt

10 whole black peppercorns

3 large leeks, trimmed, split lengthwise,
   and rinsed

Two ¼-ounce envelopes unflavored
   gelatin, softened in ½ cup cold water,
   excess water drained when soft

Freshly ground black pepper

Aged Spanish sherry vinegar

6 sprigs tarragon, leaves chopped

For the sauce

1 cup heavy cream

2 tablespoons Dijon mustard

2 tablespoons freshly grated horseradish

2 teaspoons prepared English mustard or
   Colman's dry mustard

1 tablespoon tiny French capers,
   chopped

1 tablespoon chopped cornichons

1 tablespoon chopped fresh chives

1 tablespoon chopped fresh tarragon
   leaves

Special equipment

Large stockpot

1½-quart 12 by 3 by 3-inch terrine mold

BUILD PARIS WHEREVER WE ARE

Daniel Boulud opened Restaurant Daniel on the heels of his James Beard Best Chef, New York City, win in 1992 for his work at Le Cirque. Daniel launched to broad acclaim, garnering *Gourmet*'s Top Table Award, a four-star rating from the *New York Times*, and a Chef of the Year Award for Boulud himself from *Bon Appétit*. On the eve of the restaurant's twentieth anniversary, the chef retrospectively offers one of his signature terrines that appeared on the restaurant's opening menu. The recipe, which originally appeared in his book *Cooking with Daniel Boulud* the same year, has evolved considerably into this version that he makes today. "I love beef, leeks, and mustard and wanted to combine these three ingredients into a recipe inspired by the classic pot-au-feu," Daniel says. "This preparation is essentially a traditional use of leftover meat served cold with a salad. I wanted to create something inspired by that rusticity but with a finesse, so we created a terrine."

BEEF SHANK TERRINE
DANIEL BOULUD

Bring a large pot of salted water to a boil and set a bowl of ice water on the side. Boil the celery root and carrot batons until tender. Chill in the ice water bath and set aside.

Place the shank in a stockpot. Cover with cold water 4 inches above the meat and bring to a boil. Skim the surface and lower the heat to simmer. Add the chopped celery root, chopped carrots, onions, bay leaf, thyme, 6 tablespoons salt, and the peppercorns and gently simmer for 2½ hours or until the beef is tender, skimming as needed. Add the leeks and simmer for another 30 minutes or until the beef is fork-tender. Remove the leeks to a plate and let cool. Remove the beef to a cutting board and let cool. Strain the broth into a large bowl; discard the vegetables, herbs, and spices; and return the broth to the stockpot. Over high heat, reduce to 1 quart liquid. Add the softened gelatin to

the reduced broth while stirring, strain again, and set aside to cool. Adjust the broth seasoning with salt, ground pepper, and sherry vinegar.

Shred the beef into small pieces with your fingers into a large bowl, discarding any fat and nerves. Add enough broth to keep it moist and mix the chopped tarragon leaves with the beef. Season to taste with salt, pepper, and sherry vinegar (remember that once chilled the seasoning will be muted, so be liberal).

Separately coat the leeks, carrot batons, and celery root batons with the broth and season with salt, pepper, and vinegar.

Layer the shredded meat, leeks, and carrot and celery batons in the terrine in an artful pattern. Pour the reduced broth with gelatin into the mold, up to the level of the beef. Press lightly to compact the terrine, cover with plastic wrap, and refrigerate until set (4 hours minimum).

To unmold the terrine, warm its bottom and sides in a bath of hot water for 30 seconds. Then slip the blade of a knife between the terrine and the sides of the mold to separate the terrine from the sides. Place a platter on top of the terrine and, holding it firmly, flip the platter and terrine over. Tap the bottom until the terrine comes loose. Cut ¾-inch slices with an electric knife or a very sharp slicing knife.

For the sauce: Mix together all the ingredients except the chives and tarragon leaves in a small bowl.

Presentation: Place the sauce in a small serving bowl in the middle of a 10-inch round dish. Place terrine slices around the dish and sprinkle with chives and tarragon.

Daniel Boulud *is a chef without equal and a restaurateur known the world over. "Back then, I was part of a new generation of French chefs in New York, looking to impose their style on the dining scene, and I wanted Restaurant Daniel to be one of the best French restaurants in New York of its time," Boulud explains. "Twenty years later, I feel that Daniel is a part of that landmark in New York and American dining."*

HAPPY TOGETHER

Although England and France had been famed "frenemies" for centuries, 1994 saw the historic opening of the "chunnel," an undersea high-speed railway tunnel joining the two nations, allowing the English to easily spend a three-day weekend in Paris, and the French to take a day's shopping trip at Harrods. The chunnel brought both cultures closer together, and around the world, other strange bedfellows cozied up like never before. Tonya Harding and Nancy Kerrigan put on their brightest smiles to compete on the same Olympic figure skating team in Lilleham-mer, ambiguous canine/feline duo Ren and Stimpy won over America's hearts and televisions, and entertainment super couple Lisa Marie Presley and Michael Jackson wed just twelve days after Ms. Presley finalized her divorce from her previous husband. The year 1994 truly was, in all senses, the year of the super couple.

MAKES 4 SERVINGS

1 pound dried linguine
3 tablespoons canola oil
4 shallots, minced
24 littleneck clams, rinsed and cleaned
2 cups white wine
12 ounces fish stock
Freshly ground black pepper
Pinch chili flakes
¼ cup grated Parmesan cheese
4 tablespoons unsalted butter
6 cloves garlic, minced
2 tablespoons bread crumbs
3 tablespoons extra virgin olive oil
1 bunch parsley, chopped

LINGUINE WITH CLAMS
KARY GOOLSBY

Cook the linguine according to package instructions, but slightly undercook, 2 minutes less than directed. Drain and reserve.

In a large sauté pan or pot, heat the canola oil. Add the shallots and cook until translucent. Add the clams, wine, and stock. Cover and steam until the clams open.

Remove the clams. Add the cooked pasta to the sauce and finish cooking the pasta. Season with pepper and chili flakes and place in serving bowls. Sprinkle with Parmesan and place the cooked clams on the half shell on top. Melt the butter with the garlic, bread crumbs, and olive oil and pour the mix over the clams and pasta. Sprinkle with chopped parsley and serve.

Born and raised in Oklahoma, **Kary Goolsby** *relocated to New York to attend the Institute of Culinary Education in 2001. Goolsby is the chef at Upstate, a craft beer and oyster joint owned by Shane*

and Jennifer Covey (the name is a nod to Shane's north-of-the-city upbringing). Fortunately, Upstate is also home to Goolsby's knock-'em-dead linguine with clams, a perfect pairing. To overlook this divine, pure, and pleasing dish would be a mistake, and to prepare a version other than Kary's would be a crime.

MEAT, YOUR MAKER

MAKES 6 BURGERS

For the mint-chili pickled cucumbers

¾ cup rice vinegar

¾ teaspoon kosher salt

1¼ teaspoons sugar

2 Thai chilies, halved

1 shallot, thinly sliced

2 cloves garlic, thinly sliced

2 mini seedless cucumbers, thinly sliced

Handful mint, roughly torn

For the burgers

2 tablespoons unsalted butter

1 tablespoon vegetable oil,
   plus extra for sautéing

1 large yellow onion, thinly sliced

Salt

1½ cups thinly sliced, stemmed shiitake
   mushrooms

2 cups vegetable stock

2 bay leaves

2 or 3 sprigs thyme
   (I like to tie the thyme with a bit of
   kitchen twine, so I can easily toss it
   at the end)

½ teaspoon ground coriander

¼ teaspoon ground cumin

Generous pinch chili flakes
   (I used Aleppo pepper but any will do)

Tiny pinch ground cinnamon

⅓ cup *lentilles du Puy*
   (French green lentils, but brown
   ones work, too)

⅔ cup bulgur wheat

Freshly ground black pepper

2 tablespoons pine nuts, toasted

¼ cup bread crumbs

1 egg, beaten

Extra virgin olive oil

Toasted burger buns, for serving

In the 1990s, Americans—long identified as lovers of and torch-bearers for thick steaks, juicy hamburgers, and racks of ribs—were suddenly seeking meatless alternatives. Tempeh, tofu, and seitan all had renaissances in the '90s, finding themselves not only in the era's superstar, the "veggie burger," but also in desserts, entrées, and lunches. The downside of this newfound quest for health and happiness led to a real dead end for flavor. Bland, depressing versions of favorites like hot dogs and popcorn shrimp masqueraded as the real thing. If anyone can wave a flavorful magic wand over these sad dishes and transform them into something serendipitous, *and* meatless, it's undoubtedly the wise and spicy chef Aliya Leekong.

"MUJADDARA" BURGER WITH SHIITAKE MUSHROOMS, MINT-CHILI PICKLED CUCUMBERS, AND SMOKY YOGURT

ALIYA LEEKONG

Prepare the pickled cucumbers: In a bowl, whisk together the vinegar, salt, and sugar until dissolved. Add the remaining ingredients and toss to coat. I like to put the cucumbers in a wider, shallow container to increase the surface area as they are pickling. Let sit at least an hour before serving, but they can also be refrigerated and will keep for a few days.

Prepare the burgers: Heat a medium skillet over medium heat. Add butter and oil, and when the foam subsides, add the sliced onion and a few pinches of salt to draw out the moisture. Reduce the heat to low and cook for 20 to 25 minutes, until the onion slices deeply caramelize and brown. They should go even darker

For the smoky yogurt

½ cup plain yogurt

2 teaspoons pimentón de la Vera
  (Spanish paprika)

Salt

"Mujaddara is a
Middle Eastern dish
that traditionally pairs
lentils with rice and
caramelized onions,"
Aliya explains. "Certain
versions, like this one,
exchange the rice
for bulgur wheat, which
adds a sweet nuttiness
and beautiful texture
to the dish."

than traditional caramelized onions, just before they start to turn bitter. Remove with a slotted spoon and set aside.

Increase the heat to high and when the oil is hot, add the mushrooms and let sit for 2 to 3 minutes. You want them to develop a nice brown. Stir and sauté for another minute or two and season generously. Remove with a slotted spoon and transfer to a food processor with the onion. Pulse until finely chopped and set aside.

While the onion and shiitake slices are cooking, bring the vegetable stock to a boil with the bay leaves, thyme, coriander, cumin, chili flakes, and cinnamon. Add the lentils; reduce the heat to a simmer; and simmer, covered, for 15 to 20 minutes, until the lentils are almost tender but have a slight bite. Add the bulgur, season generously with salt and freshly ground pepper, and stir to combine thoroughly. Cover and simmer for another 15 minutes. Turn off the heat and let sit for another 10 minutes for the bulgur to finish cooking and turn fluffy and tender.

Remove the bay leaves and thyme. Add the chopped onion and mushrooms to the lentils and bulgur along with the pine nuts. Refrigerate until chilled, 2 to 3 hours or more.

Add the bread crumbs and egg, mixing thoroughly, and adjust seasoning if necessary. Form the mixture into 6 patties. In a medium sauté pan over medium heat, heat enough olive oil to coat the bottom of the pan. Cook the patties 2 to 3 minutes per side.

Prepare the smoky yogurt: Mix together the yogurt and pimentón. Season to taste.

Serve the burgers on toasted buns, topped with a few pickled cucumbers and the smoky yogurt.

> *This burger is not to be overlooked. The ease of preparation and the combination of flavors create an experience more than a meal.*

Aliya Leekong *is the culinary creative director at New York City's Junoon. Her exotic, intense, and revelatory dishes are inspired by Indian, East African, and Pakistani dishes as well as her multicultural upbringing.*

KNOW YOUR CHICKEN

Japanese imports Yuka Honda and Miho Hatori released their second album, as Cibo Matto *Viva! La Woman*, in 1996. The female duo, sometimes joined by musical pals like Sean Lennon, rapped and rhapsodized about all things culinary on memorable songs "Beef Jerky," "Le Pain Perdu," and "White Pepper Ice Cream." Credited as a signature moment for third-wave feminism and female empowerment, the album has also become a cult classic for the food obsessed. Despite its ambiguous lyrics, their signature tune "Know Your Chicken" became the theme song for the new generation of fry hounds.

YFC
YOSHI FRIED CHICKEN
YOSHI NONAKA

Puree the soy sauce, ginger, and garlic in a blender to make a marinade.

Cover the chicken in the marinade and let it marinate for 3 to 24 hours in either a large plastic container or a plastic freezer bag, in the refrigerator.

Drain the chicken and roll it in the cornstarch to get a nice coating on it.

Heat the oil in a Dutch oven to 350°F.

Drop in the chicken a few pieces at a time so they don't stick together, and cook for 6 minutes or until golden. Remove with a wire skimmer and drain briefly on paper towels. Serve hot with lemon wedges.

Yoshi Nonaka is a cook at New York's Hearth restaurant, where he has mastered the family meal with this signature dish. To those unfamiliar with the restaurant business, it's customary for employees to have a meal together before the shift begins. Family meal can be anything

MAKES 6 SERVINGS

1 cup soy sauce
1½ tablespoons grated fresh ginger
1 clove garlic, minced
1 pound boneless, skinless chicken thighs, cut in half
2 cups cornstarch
2 quarts vegetable oil, for frying
1 lemon, cut into wedges, for serving

Special equipment
Dutch oven
Deep-fry thermometer
Wire skimmer

Intensely flavored and salty, the chicken pairs well with a light red or a good cold lager.

from last night's special to a trough of buttered noodles. No matter what your role is at a restaurant, you can step up to offer a hand in creating family meal, and a good one is something worth repeating. At Hearth, Yoshi's fried chicken was cause for celebration. His simple, delicate recipe is worth knowing and perfect for getting your family together.

THE FASHIONABLE LOAF

Designer Bill Blass enjoyed one of the longest and most influential fashion careers of the twentieth century, and his legacy continues to inspire. The year 1997 found Blass readying for retirement, commemorating his $700-million-a-year business with a special edition Barbie doll adorned in his signature stylings. Despite his accomplishments, Blass famously remarked, "I will never be remembered for my clothes. I think my claim to immortality will be my meat loaf." For all of his taste-making strides, Blass was most proud of his homespun, comforting recipes served to small groups of friends at his home for now-legendary dinner parties.

Every designer is reduced to his signature look, and even the most multifaceted chef is invariably held up to a signature dish. We asked Jessica Wilson to harness Blass's self-deprecating, defiant sense of humor and give us a meat loaf worthy of an epitaph. She went one further, and made a twist on one of her signature dishes beloved in the borough of Brooklyn and beyond.

FIG-STUFFED PORK LOAF OVER MUSTARD GREENS WITH SHALLOT-BACON VINAIGRETTE

JESSICA WILSON

Preheat the oven to 350°F.

On medium-low heat in a touch of oil, sweat the garlic and fennel until soft (no color); then let cool completely.

Chop the fennel fronds and parsley together one time across in each direction, and set aside.

In a large bowl, combine the cooled garlic and fennel, ¼ cup bread crumbs, eggs, 1 cup of the oil, ¼ cup of the maple syrup, ¼ cup mustard, the chili powder (optional), nutmeg, and lemon zest and

MAKES 6 TO 8 SERVINGS

1¼ cups olive oil or oil of your choice (blend, vegetable, sunflower), plus a few extra touches

1 clove garlic, minced

1 small bulb fennel, chopped (1 cup, reserve 1 packed cup fronds)

1 small bunch flat-leaf parsley, washed, dried, and picked (1 packed cup)

¼ cup rustic bread crumbs

2 eggs

¾ cup natural maple syrup

¼ cup plus 1 teaspoon whole-grain mustard

1 teaspoon chili powder or chili flakes (optional)

1 teaspoon freshly grated nutmeg

Grated zest and juice of 1 lemon

1½ pounds ground pork

1 tablespoon salt (kosher or coarse sea salt)

Freshly ground black pepper

1½ cups Olde English malt liquor

3 or 4 whole slices bacon, plus 1 cup chopped

1 cup halved fresh figs (dried can be used as well)

4 sprigs thyme

2 small shallots, sliced in thin rings

¼ cup water

½ cup vinegar (red wine, sherry, or champagne)

Cracked black pepper

Tender mustard greens, heavy stems removed, for serving

Fresh herbs (your choice), for serving

Special equipment
Instant-read thermometer

juice. Add the ground pork, salt, pepper (a few turns of the pepper mill), and the malt liquor, and incorporate well.

In a loaf pan lined with aluminum foil or lightly oiled parchment paper, place half of the seasoned pork and spread ½ teaspoon mustard on top. Make a single layer of bacon strips from one end of the loaf to the other, then place the figs flesh side up on top of the bacon. Cover with the remaining pork mixture, and spread the top with the remaining mustard and the thyme sprigs. Wrap with foil, place on a baking sheet, and bake for 25 minutes. Remove the foil and bake for 10 minutes more, or until the internal temperature reaches 160°F and the top is nicely browned. Remove from the oven, unmold, and let stand for 5 to 10 minutes before slicing.

Prepare the vinaigrette: In a small skillet on low heat, render the chopped bacon until the fat has leached out and the bacon is lightly browned. Transfer the bacon to a bowl and add the shallots, water, vinegar, the remaining ¼ cup oil, the remaining ½ cup maple syrup, and 2 teaspoons cracked black pepper, or to your liking (which is a lot for me), and whisk well. Before serving, simmer the vinaigrette in a small saucepan for 4 minutes, stirring.

To plate: Place a few pieces of mustard greens in the center of the plate. Top with a healthy slice of pork loaf. Top with warm bacon vinaigrette and garnish with some freshly picked herbs. ⚘

Jessica Wilson *helms the kitchen at aptly named neighborhood favorite Dear Bushwick. She grew up on her family's farm in Vermont with a sensual, hands-on approach to sustenance that lends her a natural advantage with today's field-to-table appetites. Her pork chop brings all the borough to the yard that Dear Bushwick has out back, but shaking off all expectations with true Blass flair, Jessica here sought to re-form a classic with her own signature imprint. The yield is every bit as memorable.*

THE FACTS OF LIFE

MAKES 12 OYSTERS, 2 SERVINGS

2 cups green Chartreuse
1 cup water
¼ cup freshly squeezed lime juice
2 tablespoons minced cilantro
¼ cup finely diced green apple
12 oysters, shucked, liquor reserved

In 1998, America was still feeling like the golden girl she was in her 1960s. The sexual revolution was once again alive and well and in its "tenth act" or so. Many were still finding sexual taboos to break, mores to burn, and faces to redden. In this case, the blushing faces belonged not to the parents of wild, horny teenagers but to the adult children of senior citizens. On television, in print, and at the dinner table, the sex lives of America's seniors were suddenly no longer off-limits, thanks to the little blue pill named Viagra, which proved to be a game changer in liberating baby boomers' minds, bodies, and g-spots. If you're going to spend a night with Eros, you might as well start off with something to whet the appetite, no matter what your age.

"SPANISH FLY" GRANITA
SHANNA PACIFICO

Mix the Chartreuse, water, lime juice, cilantro, apple, and oyster liquor in a shallow pan and put into the freezer. Using a fork, scrape the mixture occasionally while freezing, until all the liquid is frozen and has small ice crystals, resembling a sno-cone.

Put a small teaspoon of granita on each oyster and serve quickly.

Shanna Pacifico *was raised in a Brazilian American household and her palate is influenced by her cultural roots. After studying at New York's French Culinary Institute, she began her culinary career as a line cook at Peter Hoffman's SoHo restaurant Savoy, where she was imbued with a passion for local and sustainable ingredients.*

Following stints as a cook at Geoffrey Zakarian's Town and restaurants in Spain and Portugal, she reunited with Peter to open the East Village restaurant Back Forty as chef de cuisine. During her tenure, the restaurant received acclaim for its butchering program and full-flavored American regional food. Following the success of Back Forty, in 2011 Shanna moved to Prince Street to become chef at Back Forty West in the former Savoy space, which received a two-star re-view from the New York Times.

CAN'T BREAK THROUGH

In 1999, big blondes Britney Spears, Christina Aguilera, and Jessica Simpson all made their debut recordings, ushering in a new generation of pop stars. But the hot young things made way for seasoned brunette Cher, whose song "Believe" took the number one spot.

"LIFE AFTER LOVE" COCKTAIL
GREG SEIDER

Shake the calvados, agave, and lemon juice in a cocktail shaker with ice. Strain into a champagne flute. Top with Champagne or sparkling wine. Float Amaro Averna on top. Garnish with a lemon twist.

*When Cher's song was playing out of every car and bodega window in New York City, **Greg Seider** was mixing cocktails to the tune of her Autotuned voice. His vision of a mostly bubbly blond concoction capped by a dark and heady float is a fitting metaphor for women in pop music at the end of the century. With accolades and cocktail programs reaching beyond the city, Greg keeps up the innovation at Summit Bar and Prima, both in the East Village, and elsewhere.*

MAKES 1 COCKTAIL

1 ounce calvados
¾ ounce agave mix (equal parts water and agave syrup)
Juice of ½ lemon
Champagne or sparkling wine
Amaro Averna
Lemon twist

1999

TURN OF THE CENTURY

MAKES 4 SERVINGS

For the venison

½ cup brown sugar

2 tablespoons ancho chili powder

2 tablespoons coriander seeds

2 tablespoons cumin seeds

2 tablespoons cardamom seeds, toasted and ground

2 teaspoons celery salt

2 teaspoons dried rosemary

2 teaspoons dried thyme

2 teaspoons granulated garlic

1 teaspoon chili flakes

1 teaspoon freshly grated nutmeg

1 teaspoon whole cloves

1 whole 8-bone Cervena venison rack, cut into 8 chops

½ pound smoked bacon, rind off, in 1 piece

3 to 5 cloves garlic

3 to 5 sprigs thyme, plus more for garnish

½ cup fresh blackberries, or thawed frozen, if that's all that's available

For the chanterelles

2 tablespoons extra virgin olive oil

½ pound chanterelle mushrooms, cleaned, stems lightly peeled (fresh preferred, but rehydrated dry may be substituted)

1 small shallot, finely minced

¼ cup flat-leaf parsley leaves

Freshly grated nutmeg

Salt and freshly ground black pepper

1 tablespoon unsalted butter

By the end of 1999, cell phones were sparse, e-mail was just coming out of its "novelty" phase, and the ladies of *Sex and the City* were here to stay. Crime in New York had fallen dramatically through the 1990s, and by the turn of the century, you'd barely have recognized the place if you'd lived there in the previous decade. Prosperity was on the rise, and the world was looking forward to the new millennium with a little bit of technological anxiety and a whole lot of optimism.

SPICE-ROASTED VENISON CHOPS, CHANTERELLES, AND BLACKBERRIES WITH KALE AND ALMONDS

MICHAEL LOMONACO

 Prepare the venison: Combine the sugar and all the dry spices in a bowl.

Put the venison into a dish, press the spice mixture into the flesh, cover, and reserve.

Prepare the chanterelles: Heat the olive oil in a sauté pan over medium heat for 30 seconds, then add the mushrooms and cook for 3 minutes. Add the shallot and cook 1 minute more before adding the parsley and several grating of nutmeg. Season with salt and pepper, add the butter, and remove from the heat. Reserve warm.

Prepare the red wine and blackberry reduction: Put the grape-seed oil and onion into a saucepan over low heat and cook until lightly caramelized, about 15 minutes. Add the carrot, cinnamon, cloves, chilies, and blackberries and cook until the carrot has softened, about 12 minutes. Add the venison stock and cook until reduced

For the red wine and blackberry reduction

2 tablespoons grape-seed oil

1 Vidalia or other sweet onion, chopped

1 small carrot, chopped

2 cinnamon sticks

2 or 3 cloves

2 or 3 hot fresh chilies

½ cup blackberries

2 cups venison stock

One 750-ml bottle California
    cabernet sauvignon

Fine sea salt and freshly ground
    black pepper

For the kale and honey almonds

½ cup diced bacon

2 pounds kale or other bitter greens,
    washed well in several changes of
    cold water and chopped or shredded
    by hand into small pieces

3 tablespoons unsalted butter

1 cup blanched whole almonds

½ cup water

½ cup honey

by half. Add the wine and cook until reduced by three-quarters. Strain. Season with salt and black pepper. Reserve warm.

Prepare the kale and honey almonds: Put the ½ cup diced bacon in a sauté pan and cook over low-medium heat until the fat has rendered and the bacon is crispy, 6 to 8 minutes. Drain the bacon on a paper towel–lined plate and set aside.

Put the greens in a pot, cover with cold water, and cook until tender, 10 minutes or so. Drain the greens and set aside.

In a wide, heavy-bottomed sauté pan, melt the butter. Add the almonds and sauté until they start to brown, 3 minutes. Pour in the water, then the honey. Stir and cook until the water has evaporated and the honey has caramelized and coated the almonds, approximately 5 minutes. Before the almonds become too dry, add the cooked greens and bacon and cook together, tossing and stirring, to evenly distribute the almonds and bacon.

Cook the venison and assemble the dish: Cut the ½ pound bacon into ½-inch-thick lardons. Heat a skillet and cook the bacon over medium heat until thoroughly cooked and crisp at the edges. Wipe the spices from the venison and pat dry. Heat a heavy skillet, add 1 or 2 tablespoons bacon drippings, add the garlic cloves and thyme sprigs, and sear the venison chops on both sides. Add the bacon lardons to the pan and continue cooking the chops, 5 to 6 minutes in total. When the chops are seared and cooked (rare or medium-rare preferred), assemble the plate with the kale and honey almonds, 2 chops, and some bacon lardons, along with chanterelles to the side. Drizzle some red wine and blackberry reduction around the plate and sprinkle some of the seared garlic cloves and thyme over the venison. Finish with some whole fresh blackberries. 🍃

Michael's venison dish appeared as the entrée on the New Year's Eve menu at Wild Blue, on the 107th floor of the majestic World Trade Center, December 31, 1999. That evening's weather was a mild 39°F, with a visibility of approximately nine miles. Diners were likely to have enjoyed an incredible meal with a spectacular view of the city, welcoming the new millennium.

Michael Lomonaco *is the chef-owner of the highly successful Porterhouse New York at the Time Warner Center. His fans have followed the veteran chef from "21" to Windows on the World, Wild Blue, Noche, Guastavino's, and beyond. Michael was the host of* Epicurious *and* Michael's Place *on the Travel Channel and Food Network, and has published two cookbooks,* The "21" Cookbook *and* Nightly Specials.

Michael is deeply dedicated to community support and charitable causes, and cofounded the Windows of Hope Family Relief Fund in the wake of September 11, 2001. In addition, he participates in fund-raising and events that benefit worthy causes including City Harvest, Autism Speaks, and Share Our Strength.

INDEX

❧

ABOUT THE AUTHORS

NOAH FECKS and PAUL WAGTOUICZ are New York City–based photographers who share a desire to re-create, cook, and capture some of the best recipes of the twentieth century that they either missed the first time around or that they want to experience anew. In 2011 they created the blog *The Way We Ate*, a retrospective look at every recipe ever printed in *Gourmet*, which fed off the burgeoning interest in retro food to become an international phenomenon. As freelance food and dining photographers, Noah and Paul enjoy careers photographing some of the most famous faces and decadent dishes worldwide. Noah earned his BFA from the Parsons School of Design and teaches in the photography department at Parsons, and Paul is also a live performance photographer and a graduate of Sarah Lawrence College. Their blog is www.thewayweate.net.

Early Civilizations in the Americas
Almanac

Early Civilizations in the Americas
Almanac

Volume 2

Sonia Benson

Deborah J. Baker, Project Editor

U·X·L

An imprint of Thomson Gale, a part of The Thomson Corporation

Detroit • New York • San Francisco • San Diego • New Haven, Conn. • Waterville, Maine • London • Munich

THOMSON

GALE

Early Civilizations in the Americas: Almanac

Sonia Benson

Project Editor
Deborah J. Baker

Editorial
Michael D. Lesniak, Sarah Hermsen,
Mary Bonk, Allison McNeill,
Ralph Zerbonia

Rights Acquisitions and Management
Shalice Shah-Caldwell, William Sampson

Imaging and Multimedia
Kelly A. Quin, Lezlie Light, Dan Newell

Product Design
Jennifer Wahi, Pamela Galbreath

Composition and Electronic Prepress
Evi Seoud

Manufacturing
Rita Wimberley

LIBRARY OF CONGRESS CATALOGING-IN-PUBLICATION DATA

Benson, Sonia.

Early civilizations in the Americas. Almanac / Sonia G. Benson ; Deborah J. Baker, project editor.

p. cm. – (Early civilizations in the Americas reference library)

Includes bibliographical references and indexes.

ISBN 0-7876-9252-2 (set : hardcover : alk. paper) – ISBN 0-7876-7679-9 (v. 1) – ISBN—0-7876-7681-0 (v. 2) –
ISBN 0-7876-9395-2 (e-book)

1. Indians–Antiquities–Juvenile literature. 2. America–Antiquities–Juvenile—literature. I. Baker, Deborah J. II.
Title. III. Series.

E77.4.B46 2005

980'.012–dc22   2004020163

Contents

Reader's Guide

Many American history books begin with the year 1492 and the discovery of the Caribbean Islands by Spanish explorer Christopher Columbus (1451–1506). For the great civilizations of Mesoamerica and South America, though, 1492 proved to be the beginning of the end of their civilization. The products of thousands of years of history—the great cities, the architecture, markets, governments, economic systems, legal systems, schools, books, holy shrines—even the daily prayers of the people—were about to be willfully eliminated by the conquering European nations. The rupture would prove so deep that many aspects of pre-Hispanic American culture and tradition were forever deleted from the human memory. Fortunately, some of the important history of the early civilizations has survived and more is being recovered every day.

The three-volume Early Civilizations in the Americas Reference Library provides a comprehensive overview of the history of the regions of the American continents in which two of the world's first civilizations developed: Mesoamerica (the name for the lands in which ancient civilizations arose in Central America and Mexico) and the Andes Mountains region of South America (in present-day Peru and parts of Bolivia, northern Argentina, and Ecuador). In both regions, the history of civilization goes back thousands of years. Recent studies show that the first cities in the Americas may have arisen as early as 2600 B.C.E. in the river valleys of present-day Peru. The earliest evidence of civilization in Mesoamerica dates back to about 2000 B.C.E.

When the Spanish conquistadores (conquerors) arrived in Mesoamerica and the Andes in 1521 and 1531, respectively, they found many native societies, but they were most amazed by two great empires–the Aztecs and the Incas. In the early sixteenth century the Aztecs and the Incas had spectacular cities that could rival those of Europe in size, art and architecture, organization, and engineering. These capital cities ruled over vast empires—the Aztecs with a population of more than 15 million and the Incas with a population of about 12 million—with remarkable efficiency.

The Spaniards at that time could not have understood how many civilizations had preceded those of the Aztecs and the Incas, each one bringing its own advances to the empires they witnessed. In the Andes, many of the key ingredients of civilization were in place by 2600 B.C.E. in early urban centers. From that time forward, the Andean culture was adopted, developed, and slowly transformed by the societies of the Chavín, the Moche, the Nazca, the Wari, the Tiwanaku, and the Chimú, among many others, before the Incas rose to power. Mesoamerican civilization apparently had its roots in the early societies of the Olmecs and Zapotecs, whose ancestors were living in present-day central Mexico by 2000 B.C.E. The Mayas skillfully adopted the calendars, glyph-writing, art and architecture, astronomy, and many other aspects of these earlier civilizations, adding greatly to the mix. The people of the great city of Teotihuacán and later the Toltecs created vast empires that unified the Mesoamerican culture. Later the Aztecs created a government that encompassed all of these early civilizations.

Early Civilizations of the Americas: Almanac presents the story of this development—the dates, locations, sites, history, arts and sciences, religions, economies, governments, and eventual declines of the great ancient American civilizations. Volume 1 features an overview of ancient civilization in general and a brief summary of modern theories about the earliest immigrants and early life in the Americas. The remainder of the volume focuses on the rise of the Andean civilization from the early urban centers to the Inca empire. Volume 2 focuses on the rise of the Mesoamerican civilizations from the Olmecs through the Aztecs.

A note about the use of the word "civilization" in these volumes. The word "civilization" is used here to convey the type of organization and the size of a society, and certainly not to make a quality judgment about whether the society was sophisticated or refined. Besides the civilizations that arose in Mesoamerica and the Andean region, there were thousands of indigenous (native) societies throughout the two American continents with varying levels of the kind of organization experts call "civilization." The civilizations featured in Early Civilizations in the Americas Reference Library are the New World civilizations that developed around the same time and with some patterns similar to the first civilizations of the Old World: Mesopotamia, Egypt, the Indus Valley, and China. Their history has been little known until the last century; indeed, only recent studies have included the Americas in the list of the world's first civilizations.

Features

Early Civilizations in the Americas: Almanac contains numerous sidebar boxes that highlight people and events of special interest, and each chapter offers a list of additional sources that students can consult for more information. The material is illustrated by 192 black-and-white photographs and illustrations. Each volume begins with a timeline of important events in the history of the early American civilizations, a "Words to Know" section that introduces students to difficult or unfamiliar terms, and a "Research and Activity Ideas" section. The volumes conclude with a general bibliography and a subject index so students can easily find the people, places, and events discussed throughout *Early Civilizations in the Americas: Almanac.*

Early Civilizations in the Americas Reference Library

The two-volume *Early Civilizations in the Americas: Almanac* is one of two components of the three-volume U•X•L

Early Civilizations in the Americas Reference Library. The other title in the set is:

- ***Early Civilizations in the Americas: Biographies and Primary Sources*** (one volume) presents a collection of biographies and primary sources—both text and photographs of artifacts—that provide detailed and focused views of the people of the early American civilizations, the artifacts they left behind, and the sources upon which the history of the early American civilizations are based. The volume is divided into three chapters: the Incas, the Mayas and their Ancestors, and the Aztec Empire. Each chapter is arranged loosely by topic and chronology. The biographies include Inca emperor Pachacutec, Maya king Pacal, and Aztec emperor Montezuma II. The primary sources feature artifacts such as the Inca *quipu*, or knotted counting cords, the Maya sacred calendar, and the Aztec Sun Stone. Also included are excerpts from the memoirs and histories compiled by indigenous writers and Spanish missionaries and conquerors in the decades following the conquest.

- A cumulative index of both titles in the U•X•L Early Civilizations in the Americas Reference Library is also available.

Comments and Suggestions

We welcome your comments on *Early Civilizations in the Americas: Almanac* as well as suggestions for other topics to consider. Please write to: Editor, *Early Civilizations in the Americas: Almanac*, U•X•L, 27500 Drake Road, Farmington Hills, Michigan, 48331-3535; call toll-free: 800-877-4253; fax to 248-699-8097; or send e-mail via http://www.gale.com.

Timeline of Events

40,000–15,000 B.C.E. The earliest people to settle in the Americas begin their migrations to the North and South American continents.

c. 15,000–12,000 B.C.E. People leave behind traces of their life at a camp now called Meadowcroft Rockshelter in present-day Pennsylvania.

c. 11,000 B.C.E. People regularly camp at a tiny settlement now called Monte Verde in south-central Chile.

c. 9000 B.C.E. A group of hunter-gatherers called the Clovis culture becomes widespread throughout the present-day United States and Mexico.

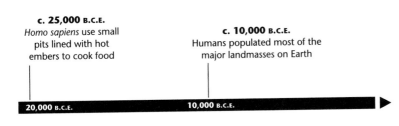

c. 25,000 B.C.E.
Homo sapiens use small pits lined with hot embers to cook food

c. 10,000 B.C.E.
Humans populated most of the major landmasses on Earth

20,000 B.C.E.   10,000 B.C.E.

c. **7000** B.C.E. Worldwide climate change alters the environments of the Americas.

c. **7000–3000** B.C.E. Formerly nomadic people in the Andes Mountain region of South America begin to settle into rough homes, gradually forming tiny villages.

c. **6000–4000** B.C.E. People begin to farm and raise animals in the Andean region.

c. **5000** B.C.E. Simple farming begins in Mesoamerica.

c. **3000** B.C.E. The Andean people in a number of different areas begin building very large ceremonial complexes (large, urban centers where people come to practice their religion) and make advances in art, religion, politics, and trade.

c. **2600** B.C.E. The city of Caral arises in the Supe Valley of Peru. It has thousands of permanent residents, complex architecture, and trade, and small urban centers surround it. Caral may have been the first city of the Americas.

c. **2500–1600** B.C.E. Mesoamericans in some regions form tiny villages.

c. **2500** B.C.E. An engraving of an Andean god known as the Staff God is carved on a bowl made from a gourd in Peru. It is the oldest known religious artifact in the Andean region.

c. **2200** B.C.E. Pottery appears in Mesoamerica.

c. **1800** B.C.E. Andean societies begin to organize themselves by the river valleys in which they live.

c. **1600** B.C.E.–**150** C.E. Large permanent settlements begin to form in Mesoamerica; in the Oaxaca (pronounced wah-HAH-kah) Valley and the Valley of Mexico.

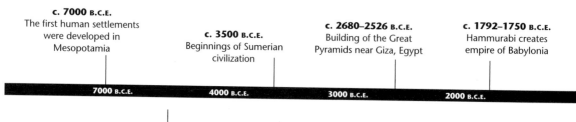

c. 7000 B.C.E.
The first human settlements were developed in Mesopotamia

c. 3500 B.C.E.
Beginnings of Sumerian civilization

c. 2680–2526 B.C.E.
Building of the Great Pyramids near Giza, Egypt

c. 1792–1750 B.C.E.
Hammurabi creates empire of Babylonia

7000 B.C.E.   4000 B.C.E.   3000 B.C.E.   2000 B.C.E.

c. 1500–1200 B.C.E. The earliest distinct Olmec culture emerges in San Lorenzo, along the Gulf of Mexico, south of Veracruz.

c. 800 B.C.E. The Chavín people in the northern highlands of Peru begin to build their ceremonial center, Chavín de Huántar (pronounced cha-VEEN deh WAHN-tar). Their religion and culture spreads through a vast area, unifying many communities of the Andes.

650 B.C.E. The first known example of writing from the Americas is carved by an Olmec artist onto a ceramic stamp bearing what appears to be a royal seal.

600 B.C.E. Another early example of Mesoamerican writing— a glyph, or a figure representing a calendar date was found at a Zapotec site—dates back to this time.

500 B.C.E. Building begins on the Zapotec city of Monte Albán in the Oaxaca Valley.

c. 400 B.C.E. The Olmec city La Venta experiences upheaval and never recovers. The ancient civilization begins a rapid decline.

c. 200 B.C.E. The Chavín culture in the Andean region collapses.

c. 200 B.C.E.–200 C.E. The Zapotec city of Monte Albán rules over the Oaxaca Valley.

c. 150 B.C.E. The Maya cities of Cival and El Mirador arise in the present-day Guatemalan state of Petén.

c. 100 B.C.E.–700 C.E. The Nazca people make large-scale drawings in the desert sands of present-day Peru.

c. 1 C.E. The communities of the Andes mountain valleys create armies for defense; military actions become widespread in some parts of the region.

1000 B.C.E.
The kite is invented in China

776 B.C.E.
Greece's first recorded Olympic games are held at Olympia

c. 528 B.C.E.
Buddhism has its beginnings in India

350 B.C.E.
Greek philosopher Aristotle founds biology, the study of living things

1000 B.C.E.   800 B.C.E.   600 B.C.E.   400 B.C.E.

c. 1 C.E. The Moche people begin to build their state, ruling from Cerro Grande in the southern Andean region and from various northern cities.

c. 200 City of Tiwanaku arises on Lake Titicaca in present-day Bolivia with a population of about 50,000 and advanced arts and religion.

c. 250 The classic Maya era begins, in which the cities of Tikal, Palenque, and Copán flourish in the southern highlands of the Maya world.

400–700 The city of Teotihuacán in the Valley of Mexico rules over a vast economic empire that includes much of the southern two-thirds of Mexico, most of Guatemala and Belize, and some parts of Honduras and El Salvador. The city reaches its height around 500 C.E. with a population between 100,000 and 200,000 people. It is the sixth largest city in the world at this time.

c. 500–600 The city of Wari arises in the south-central area of present-day Peru and begins to spread its rule and influence to surrounding regions.

615 Maya king Pacal begins his rule of Palenque; the city builds its greatest architecture during his long reign.

695 18 Rabbit begins his rule of Copán, bringing about a new age of art and writing in the city.

c. 700–900 The cities of Tiwanaku and Wari both hold influence over large, but separate, areas of the Central Andes in what may have been the first empire-building era in the Americas.

c. 750 The powerful city of Teotihuacán in the Valley of Mexico is destroyed and abandoned.

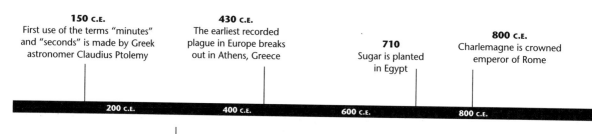

150 C.E.
First use of the terms "minutes" and "seconds" is made by Greek astronomer Claudius Ptolemy

430 C.E.
The earliest recorded plague in Europe breaks out in Athens, Greece

710
Sugar is planted in Egypt

800 C.E.
Charlemagne is crowned emperor of Rome

200 C.E.   400 C.E.   600 C.E.   800 C.E.

850   The Chimú begin to build their capital city of Chan Chan in northern coastal Peru. It will thrive for more than six centuries, with a peak population of 50,000 to 70,000 people.

c. 900   The classic Maya era ends when the dominant cities of the southern highlands, including Tikal, Palenque, and Copán, are abandoned. The Mayas scatter, but Maya cities in the present-day Mexican state of Yucatán, particularly Chichén Itzá (pronounced chee-CHEN eet-SAH) become powerful in the Maya world.

c. 968   Toltec ruler Topiltzin-Quetzalcoatl (pronounced toe-PEEL-tzin kates-ahl-koh-AH-tul) establishes the Toltec capital at Tula in the Valley of Mexico.

1000   A profound Toltec influence takes over Chichén Itzá.

1064   After upheaval in the Toltec capital of Tula, most Toltecs abandon the city.

c. 1100   The Tiwanaku and the Wari abandon their cities.

1150   The Chimú begin to expand their empire. By the fifteenth century, it is the largest pre-Inca empire of the Andean region.

c. 1200   Mayas in the present-day Mexican state of Yucatán shift their capital to the city of Mayapán. Chichén Itzá begins to decline.

1200   The Incas rise to prominence in Cuzco, in the highlands of southeast Peru.

1325   The Aztecs establish their city of Tenochtitlán (pronounced tay-notch-teet-LAHN) on an island in Lake Texcoco in the Valley of Mexico.

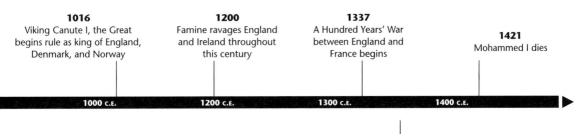

1016
Viking Canute I, the Great begins rule as king of England, Denmark, and Norway

1200
Famine ravages England and Ireland throughout this century

1337
A Hundred Years' War between England and France begins

1421
Mohammed I dies

1000 C.E.   1200 C.E.   1300 C.E.   1400 C.E.

c. 1350 The Incas begin a series of military campaigns, rapidly conquering the communities around them.

1376 The Aztecs select Acamapichtli (pronounced ah-cahm-ah-PEECH-tlee) as their first *huey tlatoani* (ruler).

1428 The Aztecs are the most powerful group in Mesoamerica. They form the Triple Alliance with Texcoco and Tlacopan and rapidly build a vast empire of an estimated 15 million people.

1433 King Nezahualcoyotl (pronounced neza-hwahl-coy-OH-tul) takes the throne in Texcoco in the Valley of Mexico, beginning an era of artistic, educational, and cultural development in that city.

1438 Inca Pachacutec successfully fights the invading Chanca army at Cuzco and becomes the supreme Inca leader, or Sapa Inca, starting the one hundred-year Inca empire.

1440 Montezuma I becomes the ruler of the Aztecs; the empire expands and Tenochtitlán grows more prosperous.

1470 The Incas take control of the Chimú.

1471–1493 Pachacutec's son Tupac Inca Yupanqui rules an ever-expanding Inca empire.

1493–1525 Huayna Capac (pronounced WHY-nah CAH-pahk) rules the Inca empire, but takes up residence in Quito (Ecuador), dividing the Incas.

1502 Montezuma II takes the throne of the Aztec empire.

1517 Mayas successfully fight off the forces of Spanish explorer Francisco Fernández de Córdoba. Soon epidemics of small pox and the measles break out among the Mayas, eventually killing as many as 90 percent of the people.

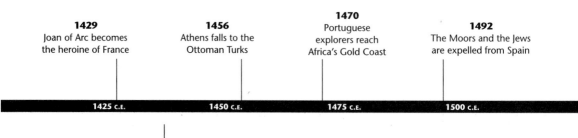

1429 Joan of Arc becomes the heroine of France	**1456** Athens falls to the Ottoman Turks	**1470** Portuguese explorers reach Africa's Gold Coast	**1492** The Moors and the Jews are expelled from Spain
1425 C.E.	1450 C.E.	1475 C.E.	1500 C.E.

March 1519 Spanish conquistador Hernán Cortés receives a "gift" from the Mayas of a young woman called Malinche. She becomes his interpreter and mistress during the Spanish conquest of Tenochtitlán.

September 1519 Cortés enlists the help of the Tlaxcala, who will be his allies against the Aztecs.

November 1519 Cortés' expedition arrives at Tenochtitlán. Within a few weeks the Spanish imprison the Aztec ruler, Montezuma II.

June 1520 Montezuma II is killed during an uprising against the Spaniards. The Spaniards flee from Tenochtitlán.

July 1520 Epidemics of smallpox and measles strike the Aztecs at Tenochtitlán and elsewhere. In the twenty years that follow, the Aztec population will be reduced to one-half its former size.

May 1521 The Cortés forces attack Tenochtitlán.

August 1521 The Aztecs surrender to the Spanish. Spanish conquistadores finish destroying the city of Tenochtitlán and begin building their own capital city, Mexico City, on top of the ruins.

1522 Spanish missionaries begin their efforts to convert the native people of Mesoamerica to Christianity. They destroy thousands of Aztec codices, or painted books, and prohibit all religious practice, hoping to break the people's connections to their religion. Hundreds of thousands of Mesoamericans convert to Catholicism.

1525 Huáscar becomes the Sapa Inca, but his brother Atahuallpa continues to rule the armies in Quito.

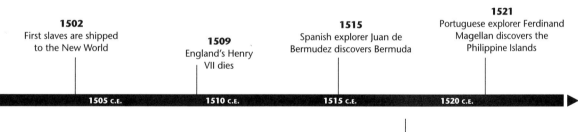

1502
First slaves are shipped to the New World

1509
England's Henry VII dies

1515
Spanish explorer Juan de Bermudez discovers Bermuda

1521
Portuguese explorer Ferdinand Magellan discovers the Philippine Islands

1505 C.E.   1510 C.E.   1515 C.E.   1520 C.E.

1525 A deadly smallpox epidemic strikes the Inca empire. It will eventually kill an estimated 75 percent of the population of the Inca empire.

1526 Another Spanish attack on the Mayas is repelled; once again, the Spanish flee.

1529 Civil war breaks out among the Incas, with the forces of Huáscar fighting the forces of Atahuallpa.

1531 Spanish forces take over the Maya city of Chichén Itzá, but the Mayas rise against them and force them to flee.

1532 Atahuallpa captures Huáscar and becomes the Sapa Inca.

1532 Spanish conquistador Francisco Pizarro and his expedition arrive at Atahuallpa's camp at Cajamarca. The next day they slaughter about six thousand unarmed Incas and capture Atahuallpa.

1532 Spanish priests establish missions in the Maya world and begin strenuous efforts to convert the Maya to Christianity.

1533 Spaniards kill Sapa Inca Atahuallpa and take over the rule of Cuzco and the Inca empire.

1536–1572 The Incas operate a rebel capital in Vilcabamba, a region northwest of Cuzco.

1542 The Spanish set up a capital at Mérida in the present-day Mexican state of Yucatán. Over the next five years they take control of much of the Maya world.

1562 Spanish missionary Diego de Landa begins a book-burning campaign, destroying thousands of Maya codices in his efforts to eliminate the Maya religion. Only three known Maya codices survive.

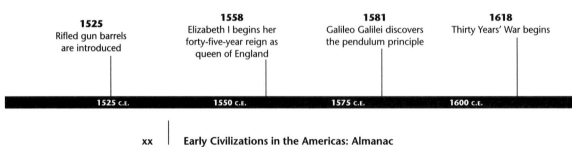

1525
Rifled gun barrels are introduced

1558
Elizabeth I begins her forty-five-year reign as queen of England

1581
Galileo Galilei discovers the pendulum principle

1618
Thirty Years' War begins

1525 C.E.   1550 C.E.   1575 C.E.   1600 C.E.

Words to Know

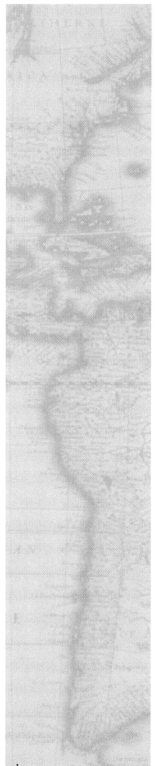

A

aboriginal: Native to the land; having existed in a region from the earliest times.

aclla: A young woman chosen by the Incas to live in isolation from daily Inca life while learning how to weave and how to make *chicha* and foods for festivals; some *acllas* were eventually married to nobles, and others became religious workers.

acllahuaci: A house where young women chosen by the Incas were isolated from daily Inca life; these women were trained in the arts of weaving fine cloth and making *chicha* and foods for festivals, and some went on to become religious workers.

administration: The management and work (rather than the policy making or public relations) of running a public, religious, or business operation.

administrative center: The place in a region or state in which the day-to-day operations of business, government, and religion are carried out.

administrator: A person who manages or supervises the day-to-day operations of business, government, and religious organizations.

adobe: Sun-dried earthen brick used for building.

agriculture: The science, art, and business of cultivating the soil, producing useful crops, and raising livestock; farming.

alliances: Connections between states or other political units based on mutual interests, intermarriage of families, or other relations.

alpaca: A member of the camelid family; a domesticated mammal related to the llama that originated in Peru and is probably descended from the guanaco. The Andeans used the long silky wool of the alpaca in their textiles.

altiplano: A high plateau; also referred to as a puna. In the central Andes Mountains of South America, where early Andean civilizations arose, the altiplano is about 12,000 to 16,500 feet (3,658 to 5,029 meters) high.

Amerindian: An indigenous, or native, person from North or South America.

anthropology: The study of human beings in terms of their social structures, culture, populations, origins, race, and physical characteristics.

aqueducts: Human-made channels that deliver water from a remote source, usually relying on the pull of gravity to transport the water.

archaeological excavation: The scientific process of digging up and examining artifacts, remains, and monuments of past human life by experts in the field.

archaeology: The scientific study of digging up and examining artifacts, remains, and monuments of past human life.

architecture: The art or practice of designing and constructing buildings or other large structures.

Arctic: The areas centered on the North Pole consisting of the Arctic Ocean and the lands in and around it.

artifact: Any item made or used by humans, such as a tool or weapon, that may be found by archaeologists or others who seek clues to the past.

astronomer: A person who studies the planets, sun, moon, and stars and all other celestial bodies.

astronomical observatory: A place designed to help people observe the stars and planets and all celestial phenomena.

astronomy: The science that deals with the study of the planets, sun, moon, and stars and all other celestial bodies.

atlantes: Large stone statues of warriors, often used as columns to support the roofs of Toltec buildings.

atlatls: Spearthrowers.

authoritarian government: Strict rule by the elite; in this type of government, leaders are not constitutionally responsible to the people, and the people have little or no power.

ayllu: A group of extended families who live in the same area, share their land and work, and arrange for marriages and religious rituals as a group; the basic social unit of the Andean peoples.

B

bajo: The Spanish word for "under," referring to lowlands or swampy depressions in the earth's surface. In a rain forest, *bajos* are generally wetlands from July to November and dry the rest of the year.

baptism: A Christian ritual celebrating an individual joining a church, in which sprinkling holy water or dunking signifies his or her spiritual cleansing and rebirth.

barbarian: A word used to describe people from another land; it often has a negative meaning, however, suggesting the people described are inferior to others.

basalt: A fine-grained, dark gray rock used for building.

bas-relief: A carved, three-dimensional picture, usually in stone, wood, or plaster, in which the image is raised above the background.

bioglyph: A symbolic animal or plant figure etched into the earth.

burial offerings: Gifts to the gods that are placed with the body of a deceased person.

C

cacao beans: Beans that grow on an evergreen tree from which cocoa, chocolate, and cocoa butter are made.

callanca: An Inca word meaning "great hall"; a place where people gathered for ceremonies and other events.

calpulli: (The word means "big house"; the plural form is *calpultin.*) Social units consisting of groups of families who were either related in some way or had lived among each other over the generations. *Calpultin* formed the basic social unit for farmers, craftspeople, and merchants. The precise way they worked is not known.

camelid: A family of mammals that, in the Americas, includes the llama, the alpaca, the vicuña, and the guanaco.

cenote: Underground reservoirs or rivers that become accessible from above ground when cave ceilings collapse or erode.

ceque: A Quechua word meaning "border"; *ceques* were imaginary lines that divided Cuzco into sections, creating distinct districts that determined a person's social, economic, and religious duties.

ceremonial centers: Citylike centers usually run by priests and rulers, in which people from surrounding areas gather to practice the ceremonies of their religion, often at large temples and plazas built specifically for this purpose.

chacmool: A stone statue of a man in a reclining position, leaning to one side with his head up in a slightly awkward position; the statue's stomach area forms a kind of platform on which the Toltecs placed a bowl or plate for offerings to the gods—sometimes incense or small animals, but often human hearts.

chasqui: A messenger who was trained to memorize and relay messages. *Chasqui* posts stood about a mile apart along the road system of the Inca empire. When a message was given to a *chasqui,* he would run to the next post and convey the message to the *chasqui* there, who would then run to the next post, and so on.

chicha: A kind of beer that Andean peoples made from maize or other grains.

chiefdom: A social unit larger and more structured than a tribe but smaller and less structured than a state, which is mainly governed by one powerful ruler. Though there are not distinct classes in a chiefdom, people are ranked by how closely they are related to the chief; the closer one is to the chief, the more prestige, wealth, and power one is likely to have.

chinampa: A floating garden in a farming system in which large reed rafts floating on a lake or marshes are covered in mud and used for planting crops.

chronicler: A person who writes down a record of historical events, arranged in order of occurrence.

city-state: An independent self-governing community consisting of a single city and the surrounding area.

codex: (plural: codices) A handmade book written on a long strip of bark paper and folded into accordion-like pages.

colca: Storehouse for food and goods.

colony: A group of people living as a community in a land away from their home that is ruled by their distant home government.

conquistador: (plural: conquistadores) The Spanish word for "conqueror"; in English, the word usually refers to the leaders of the Spanish conquests of Mesoamerica and Peru in the sixteenth century.

controversial: Tending to evoke opposing views; not accepted by everyone.

coya: The Sapa Inca's sister/wife, also known as his principal wife, and queen of the Inca empire.

creole: A person of European descent who is born in the Americas; in this book, a Spaniard who is born in Mexico.

cult: A group that follows a living religious leader (or leaders) who promote new doctrines and practices.

cultural group: A group of people who share customs, history, beliefs, and other traits, such as a racial, ethnic, religious, or social group.

culture: The arts, language, beliefs, customs, institutions and other products of human work and thought shared by a group of people at a particular time.

curaca: A local leader of a region conquered by the Incas; after the conquest, *curacas* were trained to serve their regions as representatives of the Inca government.

D

decipher: To figure out the meaning of something in code or in an ancient language.

deify: Place in a godlike position; treat as a god.

deity: A god or goddess, or a supreme being.

drought: A long period of little or no rainfall.

E

egalitarian: A society or government in which everyone has an equal say in political, social, and economic decisions and no individual or group is considered the leader.

El Niño: An occasional phenomenon in which the waters of the Pacific Ocean along the coast of Ecuador and Peru warm up, usually around late December, sometimes bringing about drastic weather changes like flooding or drought.

elite: A group of people within a society who are in a socially superior position and have more power and privileges than others.

empire: A vast, complex political unit extending across political boundaries and dominated by one central power, which generally takes control of the economy, government, and culture in communities throughout its territory.

encomienda: A grant to Spanish conquistadores giving them privilege to collect tribute from Amerindians in a particular region. The *encomendero* (grant holder) had the responsibility to train Amerindians in Christianity and Spanish, and to protect them from invasion. Most *encomenderos,* however, treated the Amerindians under their grants like slaves, forcing them into inhuman labor conditions often resulting in the collapse or death of the workers.

epidemic: A sudden spreading of a contagious disease among a population, a community, or a region.

evolution: A process of gradual change, from a simple or earlier state to a more complex or more developed state.

excavation: The process of carefully digging out or uncovering artifacts or human remains left behind by past human societies so that they can be viewed and studied.

export: To send or transport goods produced or grown in one's home region to another region in order to trade or sell them there.

F

feline: A member of the cat family; or resembling a member of the cat family.

fertility: The capacity of land to produce crops or, among people, the capacity to reproduce or bear children.

frieze: A band of decoration running around the top part of a wall, often a temple wall.

G

geoglyph: A symbolic figure or character etched into the earth.

glyph: A figure (often carved into stone or wood) used as a symbol to represent words, ideas, or sounds.

government: A political organization, usually consisting of a body of people who exercise authority over a political unit as a whole and carry out many of its social functions, such as law enforcement, collection of taxes, and public affairs.

guanaco: A member of the camelid family; a South American mammal with a soft, thick, fawn-colored coat, related to and resembling the llama.

H

hallucinogenic drug: A mind- and sense-altering drug that may create visions of things not physically present.

heartland: The central region of a cultural group where their traditional values and customs are practiced.

hierarchy: The ranking of a group of people according to their social, economic, or political position.

highlands: A region at high elevation.

huaca: A sacred place, usually used for a temple, pyramid, or shrine.

human sacrifice: Killing a person as an offering to the gods.

I

iconography: A method of relaying meaning through pictures and symbols.

idol: A likeness or image of an object of worship.

import: To bring goods from another region into one's home region, where they can be acquired by trade or purchase.

Inca: The word Inca originally meant "ruler" and referred to the king or leader. It is also used to mean the original group of Inca family clans that arose to prominence in the city of Cuzco. As the empire arose, the supreme ruler was called the "Sapa Inca" and members of the noble class were called "Incas."

indigenous: Native to an area.

L

legend: A legend is a story handed down from earlier times, often believed to be historically true.

llama: A member of the camelid family; a South American mammal that originated in Peru and probably descended from the guanaco. Llamas were used for their soft, fleecy wool, for their meat, and for carrying loads.

logogram: A glyph expressing a whole word or concept.

logosyllabic: A mixed system of writing in which some symbols represent whole words or ideas, while other symbols represent the syllables or units of sound which make up words.

lowlands: An area of land that is low in relation to the surrounding country.

M

mammoth: An extinct massive elephant-like mammal with thick, long hair and long curved tusks.

mass human sacrifices: Large-scale killing of people—or many people being killed at one time—as offerings to the gods.

mercenary soldiers: Warriors who fight wars for another state or nation's army for pay.

Mesoamerica: A term used for the area in the northern part of Central America, including Guatemala, Honduras, El Salvador, and Belize, and the southern and central parts of present-day Mexico, where many ancient civilizations arose.

mestizo: A person having mixed ancestry, specifically European and Amerindian.

missionary: A person, usually working for a religious organization, who tries to convert people, usually in a foreign land, to his or her religion.

mit'a: A tax imposed on the common people by the Inca government; the tax was a labor requirement rather than a monetary sum—the head of every household was obliged to work on public projects (building monuments, repairing roads or bridges, transporting goods) for a set period each year.

mitima: An Inca resettlement policy that required potential rebels in newly conquered regions to leave their villages and settle in distant regions where the majority of people were loyal to the Inca empire; this policy helped the Incas prevent many uprisings.

monogamy: Marriage to one partner only.

monumental architecture: Buildings, usually very large, such as pyramids or temple mounds, that are used for religious or political ceremonies.

mummification: Preservation of a body through a complex procedure that involves taking out the organs, filling the body cavity with preservative substances, and then drying out the body to prevent decay; mummification can also occur naturally when environmental conditions, such as extreme cold or dryness preserve the body.

mummy: A body that has been preserved, either by human technique or unusual environmental conditions, such as extreme cold or dryness.

myth: A traditional, often imaginary story dealing with ancestors, heroes, or supernatural beings, and usually making an attempt to explain a belief, practice, or natural phenomenon.

N

Nahuatl: The language spoken by the Aztecs and many other groups in the Valley of Mexico.

New World: The Western Hemisphere, including North and South America.

nomadic: Roaming from place to place without a fixed home.

O

observatory: A building created for the purpose of observing the stars and planets.

obsidian: Dark, solid glass formed by volcanoes used to make blades, knives, and other tools.

offerings: Gifts for the gods.

oral tradition: History and legend passed from generation to generation through spoken accounts.

outpost: A remote settlement or headquarters through which a central government manages outlying areas.

P

Paleoamerican: A member of a theoretical first population group in the Americas; scholars use this term to make a distinction between this group and the Paleo-Indians, a later group, who are generally considered to be the ancestors of modern Amerindians.

Paleo-Indian: A member of the group of people who migrated to the United States from Asia during the last part of the Great Ice Age, which ended about ten thousand years ago; Paleo-Indians are thought to be the ancestors of modern Amerindians.

pampa: The partly grassy, partly arid plains in the Andean region.

pantheon: All of the gods that a particular group of people worship.

Patagonia: A vast barren flat-land spreading through Argentina and into Chile between the Andes Mountains and the Atlantic Ocean.

Peninsulares: People living in Mexico who were born in Spain.

pilgrim: A person who travels to a holy place to show reverence.

pilgrimage: A journey to a holy place to show faith and reverence.

plateau: A large, elevated level area of land.

polygamy: Marriage in which spouses can have more than one partner; in Inca society, some men had multiple wives, but women could not take multiple husbands.

pre-Columbian American: A person living in the Americas before the arrival of Spanish explorer Christopher Columbus in 1492.

prehistory: The period of time in any given region, beginning with the appearance of the first human beings there and ending with the occurrence of the first written records. All human history that occurred before there was writing to record it is considered prehistoric.

primogeniture: A system in which the oldest son inherits his father's position or possessions.

Q

Quechua: The Inca language, still spoken by Andean people today.

quetzal: A Central American bird with bright green feathers.

quinoa: A high-protein grain grown in the Andes.

quipu: Also *khipu.* A set of multicolored cotton cords knotted at intervals, used for counting and record keeping.

R

radiocarbon dating: A method of testing organic (once living) material to see how old it is. Radiocarbon dating measures the amount of carbon 14 found in a sample. All plant and animal matter has a set amount of carbon 14. When an organism dies, the carbon 14 begins to decay at a specific rate. After measuring the extent of the decay, scientists can apply a series of mathematical formulas to determine the date of the organism's death—and consequently the age of the organic matter that remains.

rain forest: Dense, tropical woodlands that receive a great quantity of rain throughout the year.

religious rites: Established ceremonial practices.

remains: Ancient ruins or fossils, or human corpses or bones.

ritual: A formal act performed the same way each time, usually used as a means of religious worship by a particular group.

S

sacrifice: To make an offering to the gods, through personal possessions like cloth or jewels, or by killing an animal or human as the ultimate gift.

sacrifice rituals: Ceremonies during which something precious is offered to the gods; in early civilizations, sacrifice rituals often involved killing an animal or sometimes even a human being—the life that was taken was offered as a gift to the gods.

Sapa Inca: Supreme ruler of the Incas.

sarcophagus: A stone box used for burial, containing the coffin and body of the deceased, or sometimes only the body.

scribe: Someone hired to write down the language, to copy a manuscript, or record a spoken passage.

script: Writing.

sedentary: Settled; living in one place.

shaman: A religious leader or priest who communicates with the spirit world to influence events on earth.

smallpox: A severe contagious viral disease spread by particles emitted from the mouth when an infected person speaks, coughs, or sneezes.

stela: (plural: stelea) A stone pillar carved with images or writing, often used to provide historical details or for religious or political purposes.

stonemasonry: The work of a skilled builder who expertly lays cut or otherwise fitted units of stone in construction.

subordinate: Subject to someone of greater power; lower in rank.

succession: The system of passing power within the ruling class, usually upon the death of the current ruler.

surplus: The excess above what is needed; the amount remaining after all members of a group have received their share.

syllabograms: Symbols that represent the sounds of a language (usually a combination of a vowel sound and consonants).

T

terrace: One of a series of large horizontal ridges, like stairs, made on a mountain or hillside to create a level space for farming.

theorize: Create an explanation based on scientific evidence or historical analysis that has not yet been proven.

tlatoani: A Nahuatl word meaning "speaker" or "spokesperson" used by the Aztecs to refer to their rulers, or "they who speak for others." The Aztec emperor was often called *huey tlatoani,* or "great speaker."

trance: An altered mental state.

transformation: Changing into something else.

tribute: A payment to a nation or its ruler, usually made by people from a conquered territory as a sign that they surrender to the imposed rule; payment could be made in goods or labor or both.

trophy head: The head of an enemy, carried as a token of victory in combat.

U

urbanization: The process of becoming a city.

ushnu: A large platform in a central part of a city plaza, where the king or noblemen stood to address the public or view public festivities.

V

Valley of Mexico: A huge, oval basin at about 7,500 feet (2,286 meters) above sea level in north central Mexico, covering an area of about 3,000 square miles (7,770 square kilometers) and consisting of some of the most fertile land of Mexico.

vicuña: A South American mammal related to the llama and having a fine silky fleece, often used by the Andeans for making textiles. The early Andeans hunted vicuña for skins and meat.

vigesimal: Based on the number twenty (as a numeric system).

Villac Umu: Inca term for chief priest.

W

welfare state: A state or government that assumes responsibility for the welfare of its citizens.

Y

yanacona: A commoner who was selected and trained in childhood to serve the Inca nobility, priests, or the empire in general; the position was a form of slavery.

Yucatán: A peninsula separating the Caribbean Sea from the Gulf of Mexico, which includes the nation of Belize, the Petén territory of northern Guatemala, and the southeastern Mexican states of Campeche, Quintana Roo, and Yucatán. Yucatán is also the name of a state of Mexico, in the northern portion of the Yucatán peninsula.

Z

ziggurat: A platform or terrace with a tall temple tower or pyramid atop it in ancient Mesopotamia.

Research and Activity Ideas

The following ideas and projects are intended to offer suggestions for complementing your classroom work on understanding various aspects of the early civilizations in the Americas:

Plan a tour of historic Inca sites: Imagine that you are a travel agent and you are preparing a tour for a family that wishes to see the famous historic sites of the ancient Inca civilization in the Andes Mountain region of South America. What Inca cities should they travel to and why? Find a copy of a map of the area of the Inca civilization and plan their tour for them. Make a numbered list of at least six scenic stops they will want to make, marking the map with the corresponding number. Write down the highlights of what they will see there and why it is of interest. When you have completed the Inca tour guidebook and map, you may plan tours for people wishing to see the ancient Maya sites and the ancient Aztec sites as well. Find a map of the Mesoamerican region and start the plans.

Memoirs of a Maya teenager from 750 C.E.: You are a Maya teenager who lives in the year 750. Write an autobiography: what is your name? What city do you live in? Describe the details of everyday existence. What kinds of clothes do you wear and what other adornments do you use to make you look more attractive? Describe the food you eat, the house you live in, and other interesting facts about things like your religion and school. Please feel free to use your imagination to fill in the facts, but base your report on information you find in this book, other books about the Mayas you find at the library, and web sites about the life of the Maya people.

Discussion panel topic—Cities: Some archaeologists believe there were real cities in the Andes Mountains as far back as 2500 B.C.E. Form a group and try, as a group, to come up with a list of factors that make a city. Why is New York or Chicago a city, for example? Then discuss the evidence archaeologists have found in the Andes that might demonstrate that there were cities in the Americas so long ago. In what ways were the ancient cities like modern cities today? In what ways were they different? Can you imagine what life was like in Caral or in Chavín de Huantár?

Research topic—Pyramids: Write a report on the pyramids of the Americas. Research for your report can begin with this reference set, but it should include a trip to the library to find books on the ancient civilizations of the Americas and pyramids in general. You may also use the Internet for your research. What were the biggest pyramids of the Americas? How large were they? When were they built? How do they compare in size and in the time they were built with the pyramids of ancient Egypt? Who built them and how did the builders accomplish their work?

Travel diary of an Aztec merchant: The year is 1460 and you are a trader who has traveled into the Aztec city of Tenochtitlán for the first time to sell your produce. In an essay, describe how you would get into the city and what you would see when you got there.

Maya glyph poster: Make a Maya glyph poster. First you will need to look at some examples. There are some excellent web sites and books at your library that demonstrate Maya glyphs and their use. If possible, check out one of the following:

- "How to Write Your Name in Mayan Glyphs" at http://www. halfmoon.org/names.html

- Ancient Scripts.com http://www.ancientscripts.com/ maya.html

- *Reading the Maya Glyphs,* by Michael D. Coe and Mark Van Stone. London and New York: Thames and Hudson, 2001.

Or find any other resource with pictures of Maya glyphs and explanations of their meanings. Find a glyph or a glyph phrase (your name or the date, for example) that appeals to you and make a poster using the Maya glyph design. Using colored pencils or crayons, draw the glyph and then color it in. Feel free to add your own style to the design. Be sure to label the poster, showing the glyph's meaning.

Early Civilizations of America Food Festival: Plan an Early Civilizations of America Food Festival. Set up booths for Maya, Aztec, and Inca foods. Make a batch of one kind of food and serve it in small portions so everyone can taste it. Read about the foods you are serving: be prepared to tell visitors to your booth all about the way the foods were prepared and eaten by the Mayas, Incas, or Aztecs. You may make any variety of dishes using corn, tortillas, beans, avocados, chili peppers, squash, pumpkin seeds, or chocolate. Here are some suggestions:

Maya booth:

- Popcorn

- Hot chocolate: Recipe

    2 ounces unsweetened bakers' chocolate, chopped into small pieces

    6 cinnamon sticks, broken into several pieces

    4 cups water

    3 tablespoons honey

Heat one cup of water in a saucepan until hot but not boiling and add the chopped chocolate. Stir until the chocolate melts. Add honey. With a wire whisk, beat the hot chocolate while gradually adding 3 cups of hot water from the tap.

When it's good and foamy, pour small portions into cups with cinnamon sticks in each one and serve.

Inca booth:

- Baked sweet potatoes or baked potatoes, cut into large bite-sized pieces with butter, salt, and pepper served on the side

- Quinoa: Recipe

    You will need to purchase a box of quinoa (pronounced KEEN-wah), a grain available in the rice section of most grocery stores. For plain quinoa, simply follow the instructions on the back of the package. For variety, try toasting the quinoa before cooking it. Place 1 teaspoon of vegetable or corn oil on a nonstick frying pan and place over medium heat, stirring constantly until the quinoa is golden brown. Then cook according to package instructions. Try adding canned or frozen corn to the quinoa in the last few minutes of cooking for a real Inca dish.

Aztec booth:

- Corn tortillas (store bought; and cut into pieces) or tortilla chips to serve with refried beans and chilies

- Refried Beans: Recipe

    Open two 15-ounce cans of pinto beans. Heat one tablespoon of vegetable oil in a heavy frying pan over medium heat. When it is hot, put several large spoonfuls of beans into the pan, sprinkle lightly with salt and pepper, and then mash them with a fork until they are hot and mashed. Then place them in a covered bowl and do another batch until the beans are used. Serve on tortilla pieces or tortilla chips with diced chilies, if desired.

- Canned chilies, diced into small pieces, served on the side.

Stage a play—The Historic Meeting of 1519: With a team of eight to ten people, write a short play about the first meeting between Aztec emperor Montezuma II and Spanish conqueror Hernán Cortés in Tenochtitlán in 1519. First do your research: make sure you know who was there and where the meeting took place. Find out whatever you can about how people were dressed and how they spoke with one another. Write the words that you imagine they spoke. Assign roles for each member of the group and then enact the scene for your class.

Debate—The acts of the conquerors: After the Spanish conquerors had defeated the Inca and Aztec empires and the Maya societies, they destroyed many important aspects of the native cultures, including the people's books, arts, and religious buildings and shrines, as they attempted to convert the people to Christianity and to educate them in European customs. Were the intentions of the Spanish honorable, and can their actions be justified? Stage a debate over these questions. Split the class in half; one half debates that the Spanish were not justified and the other half argues that they were (regardless of personal beliefs on these issues). Consider how much damage the Spanish did and what possible causes they might have had for their actions.

Early Civilizations in the Americas
Almanac

Early Mesoamerican Peoples

15

Mesoamericans are people who lived in the civilizations that arose in roughly a 400,000-square-mile (1.04 million-square-kilometer) area in the northern part of Central America (the part of North America that extends from Mexico in the north down to the South American continent at Colombia in the south). Mesoamerican civilizations spanned an area that included the present-day countries of Mexico (mainly in its southern and central parts), Guatemala, Honduras, El Salvador, and Belize. Some experts believe at one time or another in prehistory (the period of time in human history that occurred before there was writing to record it), some thirty civilizations rose and fell in Mesoamerica. Each one had its own distinct culture, but all shared in many Mesoamerican traditions.

Geography

Mesoamerica is bordered by the Atlantic Ocean on the east and the Pacific Ocean on the west. Its climate and geography are very diverse. The weather is warm and dry on

Words to Know

Archaeological excavations: The scientific process of digging up and examining artifacts, remains, and monuments of past human life by experts in this field.

Artifact: Any item made or used by humans, such as a tool or weapon, that may be found by archaeologists or others who seek clues to the past.

Burial offerings: Gifts to the gods that were placed with the body of a deceased person.

Ceremonial centers: Citylike centers usually run by priests and rulers, in which people from surrounding areas gathered to practice the ceremonies of their religion, often at large temples and plazas built specifically for this purpose.

Elite: A group of people within a society who are in a socially superior position and have more power and privileges than others.

Glyph: A figure (often carved into stone or wood) used as a symbol to represent words, ideas, or sounds.

Hybrid: The offspring that results from breeding plants or animals of different varieties, breeds, or species.

Mammoth: An extinct massive elephant-like mammal with thick, long hair and long curved tusks.

Nomadic: Roaming from place to place without a fixed home.

Obsidian: Dark, solid glass formed by volcanoes used to make blades, knives, and other tools.

Plateau: A large, elevated, level area of land.

Prehistory: The period of time in any given region, beginning with the appearance of the first human beings there and ending with the occurrence of the first written records. All human history that occurred before the existence of written records is considered prehistoric.

Religious rites: Established ceremonial practices.

Rock shelter: A shelter formed by overhanging rocks.

the plains along the majority of both coasts. On a large part of the eastern coast, however, heavy rainfall creates dense tropical jungles. Two large mountain ranges run down the length of the area—the eastern and western Sierra Madre mountains. Between the two mountain ranges lie three plateaus (large, elevated, level areas of land) with fertile valleys running in between.

In one of these plateaus is the Valley of Mexico, the site of modern Mexico City and a major center of Mesoamer-

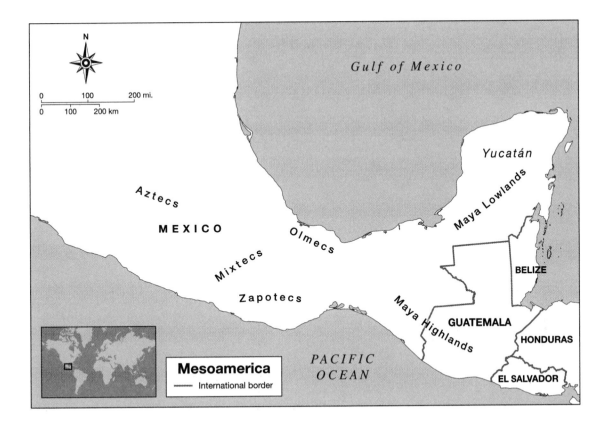

Map showing sites of ancient civilizations in Mexico and parts of Central America (Mesoamerica). *Map by XNR Productions. The Gale Group.*

ican civilizations in former times. In the Valley of Mexico, at an altitude of nearly 7,500 feet (2,286 meters), the climate is generally pleasant and dry except for a few rainy months in the summer. At the time of the Spanish conquest of Mexico in the early 1500s, it is estimated that about 40 percent of the Mesoamerican population lived in the Valley of Mexico.

The first Mesoamericans

At the time the first immigrants arrived in Mesoamerica (the dates of the first migrations are still unknown and open to debate; see Chapter 2 for more information), the climate was very different than today, with heavy rainfall in the Valley of Mexico that created broad, deep lakes and green forests. Ice age mammals such as the wooly mammoth (a now-extinct elephant-like mammal with thick, long hair and long curved tusks) and the horse (which would later become extinct; horses would only reappear in the Americas when the Spanish brought them) roamed the valleys and plateaus of Mesoamerica in large numbers for thousands of years.

The earliest peoples were hunters of big game, who also gathered plants and hunted rodents, snails, and mussels. Most early Mesoamericans lived in small, nomadic (roaming from place to place without a fixed home) family groups. They set up camps and moved from season to season, unable to find enough food in one place to remain for more than a few months. They usually set up portable, temporary shelters or lived in caves and rock shelters (shelters formed by overhanging rocks). Their belongings consisted of things they could carry as they searched for food.

Desert culture

About 7000 B.C.E. the climate changed worldwide. Lands in Mesoamerica that had once been green and lush became dry and desertlike. Many lakes dried up or became smaller and more shallow. Around this time the large mammals disappeared. Mesoamericans were forced to seek new ways of obtaining food and soon took up what is now called the desert culture. Desert culture required new techniques and tools for hunting small animals like rabbits.

People spread out, still in very small groups or bands so each could exploit large amounts of land for enough food to sustain themselves. In the desert culture, plants became a much more central part of the diet; foraging (searching for food) took up more of the Mesoamerican people's time. Emphasis was placed on preparing and preserving foods, particularly grinding seeds and nuts into flour. The bands relocated by the seasons in search of food, carrying with them their few possessions, including baskets and grinding stones.

As time went on, people in the different regions adapted to their environments, each area producing different diets and lifestyles. With a heavier focus on plant foods, many groups learned to plant the vegetables most important to them. By about 5000 B.C.E. Mesoamericans had begun to grow simple crops of avocado, chili peppers, squash, and a grain called amaranth. They began to trade these for plants grown in other regions. Soon they were planting hybrids (the offspring that results from breeding plants or animals of different varieties, breeds, or species) and creating a full set of crops adapted to the weather and soil conditions of each region.

In Mesoamerica, unlike the Andes, few animals were raised for food. Dogs and turkeys were about the only meat regularly eaten. Meat was much less necessary in Mesoamerica by about 4000 B.C.E. because people had cultivated maize, a type of corn, and bean crops. These crops provided most of the nutrients (the elements in food that promote the body's growth and health) the early settlers needed. During the first era of farming, most Mesoamericans remained partially nomadic, leaving their crops for long periods of hunting and only returning in the spring and summer months.

Settling into villages

Although many Mesoamericans had mastered the basics of farming in their region by about 4000 B.C.E. and spent more and more of their time producing and finding plant foods, it was thousands of years before they settled into village life. This significantly separates them from other early civilizations, which went more directly from developing farming techniques to settling into villages.

No one knows why the move to village life was delayed in Mesoamerica. One reason may have been that life was good for the Mesoamericans and they had no real desire to change. From about 5000 B.C.E. to about 2500 B.C.E. most Mesoamericans were growing primary crops—maize, beans, and squash— which they preserved and stored in pits. By about 2500 B.C.E. Mesoamericans spent smaller periods of the year at their hunting camps, and by the end of the era tiny hamlets with about five or ten houses dotted some of the regions.

Pottery

The first practice of firing clay to make pottery in the Americas probably occurred along the northern Caribbean shores of present-day Colombia in about 3100 B.C.E. Pottery's first known appearance in Mesoamerica was around 2200 B.C.E., and its use had become widespread by about 1600 B.C.E. Pottery provided waterproof vessels for food storage; it also aided in cooking and other food preparation, carrying water, and serving.

A display of lifelike figures and objects shows early Mesoamericans cultivating maize in the Valley of Mexico in 3400 B.C.E. © Gianni Dagli Orti/Corbis.

Pottery was easy to make from materials available everywhere. Ceramics arts were also an early and very important form of cultural expression. Pottery was not particularly useful in a nomadic life because it was too heavy to be carried from place to place. Thus the change from nomadic to more settled life went hand in hand with the adoption of pottery in the various regions of Mesoamerica. By 1600 B.C.E. many of the Mesoamericans had settled into village life, but others scattered throughout this vast region had very different lifestyles. The move toward village life did not occur all at once, and many Mesoamericans remained nomadic (roaming from place to place without a fixed home) for centuries.

The pre-Olmec years

Archaeological excavations (the scientific process of digging up and examining artifacts, remains, and monuments of past human life by experts in the field) in

Mesoamerican valleys turned up villages of ever-increasing size that thrived between 1600 B.C.E. and 150 C.E., years when the Olmec (pronounced OLE-meck), the Zapotec, and the city of Teotihuacán (pronounced TAY-uh-tee-wah-KAHN)— were in their infancy. In the Oaxaca (pronounced wah-HAH-kah) Valley of present-day Mexico, archaeologists (scientists who dig up and examine artifacts [any item made or used by humans, such as a tool or weapon, that may be found by archaeologists or others who seek clues to the past], remains, and monuments of past human life) uncovered seventeen permanent settlements from this period.

Most of the settlements were small, but one had a population of about five hundred people in the years between 1300 and 1200 B.C.E. People in the village were farmers living in 20-foot (6.09-meter) rectangular homes. They stored their food in pits and raised dogs and turkeys for meat. Some people in the town clearly had more goods and power than others, which can be deduced from differences in the quality of the food they ate, the homes they lived in, the tools and ornaments they used, and the objects they were buried with. Since some had more than others, scholars believe a class system of some sort existed.

Along with settled life, new cultural traditions developed. In the Valley of Mexico, a town called Tlatilco (pronounced tlah-TEEL-coe) dates back to about 1300 B.C.E. Archaeologists dug up 340 burial sites at Tlatilco. The sites were full of burial offerings (gifts to the gods placed with the body of a deceased person), including artistic objects such as masks and hundreds of small ceramic figurines, mainly in the shape of females. The figurines had unusually elaborate features and hairstyles and were vividly painted in reds, whites, and blacks. The practice of creating elaborate objects and placing them in the grave of the deceased to accompany him or her to the afterlife is evidence of a belief in life after death and of the rise of formal religion as well as an advance in the arts.

By about 1200 B.C.E. the villages in the Valley of Mexico and elsewhere in Mesoamerica were gradually becoming chiefdoms. In these, there was one strong ruler, the chief, who often served as priest or religious leader as well. The chief controlled the food, government, and religion of his people. People most closely related to the ruler had higher

Timeline of Early Mesoamerica

2000 to 1200 B.C.E.: Early pre-Classic era (also called the Pre-Olmec Era). The use of pottery emerges, corresponding to the rise of village life. In San Lorenzo (in the present-day Mexican state of Veracruz), the early Olmec civilization arises with the first real social classes of Mesoamerica. Early Olmec influence spreads to the Pacific Coast of Mexico. The village of San José Mogote dominates the Oaxaca Valley.

1200 to 400 B.C.E.: Middle pre-Classic era (also called the Olmec Era). La Venta, an Olmec civilization, arises in the present-day Mexican state of Tabasco; La Venta's influence spreads throughout Mesoamerica. Monte Albán is created as a capital in Oaxaca Valley. The first lowland Maya (pronounced MY-uh) villages

emerge. The first known Zapotec writings at San José Mogote date back to this era.

400 B.C.E. to 250 C.E.: Late pre-Classic era (also known as Epi-Olmec Era). The two-calendar system featuring the Calendar Round and Long Count calendars and several forms of writing spread throughout Mesoamerica. Construction of the Pyramid of the Sun begins at Teotihuacán. In the Maya lowlands, many pyramids are being built.

250 to 600 C.E.: Early Classic era. City of Teotihuacán is dominant, but Monte Albán shares in influence and trade. The Maya gain influence throughout the large area including present-day Guatemala, Honduras, and eastern Mexico, building new cities of Copán, Tikal, and Kaminaljuyú (pronounced kah-mee-

rank than others, so a few people within these villages were wealthier and more powerful than the ordinary citizens— though rigid social classes had not yet developed.

Burial rituals had become widespread, and the wealthy received more and more elaborate grave offerings as the years passed. Trading, too, gained importance as the Valley of Mexico's villages built a strong trade network, especially in obsidian (dark, solid glass formed by volcanoes used to make blades, knives, and other tools), as well as plants, ceramics, and salt.

As religion spread from village to village throughout Mesoamerica, ceremonial centers arose in strategic locations where they could be reached by several villages. These were places to which people from surrounding areas traveled to

nahl-hoo-YOO) . The period ends with the fall of Teotihuacán. The Monte Albán population scatters.

600 to 900 c.e.: Late Classic era. Southern lowlands Maya civilization flourishes. The great Maya emperor Pacal reigns at Palenque. The period ends with the collapse of the Classic Maya in the southern lowlands. Maya civilization continues in the north in the Yucatán area. Chichén Itzá (pronounced chee-CHEN eet-SAH) is among the important northern Maya sites.

900 to 1200: Early post-Classic era. The Toltecs (pronounced TOHL-tecks) build their capital city of Tula in Mexico and the Toltec states dominate the area. Toltec influences dominate the Maya city of Chichén Itzá in 990. The Toltec

capital of Tula is overthrown at the end of this period.

1200 to 1521: Late post-Classic era. The Maya build a new capital at Mayapán. The Aztecs (Mexicas) create the city of Tenochtitlán (pronounced tay-notch-teet-LAHN) and, under the Triple Alliance with the cities of Texcoco and Tlacopan, build their vast empire.

1521: Spanish Conquest begins. The Spanish destroy the Aztec city of Tenochtitlán in a bloody battle. They go on to destroy the independent governments of fiercely resisting Maya groups in the decades to follow. They also destroy artwork and writings of Mesoamerican peoples, trying to erase the cultural traditions to promote Christianity and European traditions.

perform the rites of their religion under the supervision of the region's great and powerful priests. The centers featured large monuments, public buildings, and large plazas. By about 150 C.E. these religious centers had become widespread throughout Mesoamerica, and they represented some of the area's first cities. The first known Mesoamerican civilization—the Olmecs—arose at the beginning of this period, around 1200 B.C.E.

Connected but distinct

Trade, shared religion, and military conquest ensured that the different cultures of Mesoamerica were in constant contact with each other, so it not surprising they shared

Painting of the Valley of Mexico, with its diverse terrain, in prehistory. *The Art Archive/Museo Ciudad Mexico/Dagli Orti (A).*

many cultural traits. From the time of the Olmecs, Zapotecs, and Teotihuacáns, many of the distinct characteristics of each of the developing civilizations were common to most Mesoamerican civilizations. For example, most cultures had writing and numerical systems, used two calendars, played a ball game in which losers were sacrificed as an offering to the gods, had knowledge of astronomy, built pyramids, ate similar foods, established political structures and sacrificial rites, and worshipped many of the same gods. These ancient Mesoamerican civilizations, however, all notably lacked metal tools, wheels, and beasts of burden, such as horses or oxen, to help do work.

Despite these very important shared traits, the cultures themselves were very distinct, as shall be seen in the Mesoamerican chapters ahead. Looking at the artwork of the various Mesoamerican cultures, differences in style and in the way the people looked and dressed will be quickly recognizable. Differences in what was important to them as a society and how they viewed the universe and the spiritual world were sometimes pronounced, and sometimes subtle, but important.

Prehistory with written documents?

Prehistory is defined as the period of time in which there was no writing to record a given society's history. Though ancient Mesoamerica has traditionally been treated as prehistory, the dawn of the historic period of Mesoamerica was actually in about 600 B.C.E. when the earliest known Mesoamerican artifact with writing was found. The writing was in the form of glyphs (drawn or carved figures used as symbols to represent words, ideas, or sounds), found at an ancient Olmec site. One of the artifact's two glyphs represents the word "king," while the other represents "3 Ajaw," the name of a day on the Mesoamerican calendar. Since people were often named after the day they were born, 3 Ajaw is probably the name of the king.

Glyphs found at Zapotec sites a few centuries later represent dates using the Long Count (a method that started at a "0" year of 3114 B.C.E.; see Chapters 17 and 22 for more information), which historians are able translate into dates on the modern calendar. For the first time, archeologists found artifacts inscribed (written) with dates by their creators. Aside from names and dates, Mesoamerican writing recorded events such as battles or the succession of kings to the throne, and listed Mesoamerican royalty over the generations, with names and important dates.

Although many Mesoamerican societies had glyphs for names, place names, dates, and various other items, only the Mayas developed their writing to cover all of their spoken language. It has taken experts many years to decode the Maya glyphs, but they are now able to read most of the text on the many stelae (plural of stela), or stone pillar monuments, detailing kings and their accomplishments. Histories, using Maya documents, can now be written about the various royal families and the wars and religious practices of Maya cities.

While Maya cities and city-states (self-governing communities consisting of a single city and the surrounding area) developed independently and were never united, this was not the case with the societies of the Valley of Mexico, where the largest cities and empires arose. (An empire is a vast, complex political unit extending across political boundaries and dominated by one central power, which generally takes control of the economy, government, and culture in communities throughout its territory.) By about 500 C.E. the great city of Teotihuacán was at its peak with a population between one hundred thousand and two hundred thousand people, making it the sixth largest city in the world at the time. Through extensive trade and religion, Teotihuacán unified the many peoples of the valley. Teotihuacán became the holiest of places and was still revered as a sacred place long after its inhabitants had disappeared. The Toltecs (pronounced TOHL-tecks) arrived in the valley by the tenth century and forged another loose empire, gaining the distinction of becoming the "chosen" rulers of the Valley of Mexico.

When a rough group of nomadic northerners known as the Aztecs (Mexicas) arrived in the Valley of Mexico in the twelfth century, they learned the traditions of these former civilizations and built upon them. As they became powerful, the Aztecs adopted the widespread belief that the gods had created the present world at Teotihuacán. They also claimed that their leaders were the descendants of the Toltecs and destined to rule the valley and beyond. From their magnificent city of Tenochtitlán, the Aztecs went on to establish a vast empire of about fifteen million people.

While reading about the Mesoamerican civilizations, it is important to remember that not just one group was responsible for the amazing leaps toward civilization occurring in Mesoamerica before the Spanish conquest. These groups were interconnected from the earliest times and continually built upon one another's traditions and innovations. As experts learn more about these ancient societies—particularly by studying artifacts and glyphs—they will be able to trace their connections even further. What these Mesoamerican civilizations might have been had they not been so thoroughly disrupted by the Spanish conquistadores (conquerors) and missionaries remains a mystery. It is, nevertheless, worth thinking about.

For More Information

Books

Adams, Richard E.W. *Ancient Civilizations of the New World.* Boulder, CO: Westview Press, 1997.

Coe, Michael D. *Mexico: From the Olmecs to the Aztecs,* 4th ed. London and New York: Thames and Hudson, 1994.

Katz, Friedrich. *The Ancient American Civilizations.* London: Phoenix Press, 2000.

Morris, Craig, and Adriana Von Hagen. *The Cities of the Ancient Andes.* London and New York: Thames and Hudson, 1998.

Morris, Craig, and Adriana Von Hagen. *The Inka Empire and Its Andean Origins.* New York: Abbeville Press, 1993.

Schobinger, Juan. *The First Americans.* Grand Rapids, MI: William B. Eerdmans Publishing Company, 1994.

Web Sites

Callahan, Kevin L. *Ancient Mesoamerican Civilizations.* http://www.angel fire.com/ca/humanorigins/index.html (accessed on October 18, 2004).

Mesoweb. http://www.mesoweb.com/ (accessed on October 18, 2004).

Olmec Culture

16

In the early 1900s the Olmecs (pronounced OLE-mecks) were a little known cultural group (a group of people who share customs, history, beliefs, and other traits) of ancient Mesoamerica. Scholars had named the group based on the artistic style of a few of their artifacts (things created or used by humans in past times), but no one knew when they had lived. In fact, most people assumed the Olmecs had lived after the ancient Maya (pronounced MY-uh); some believed they were simply a separate grouping of Maya people. Ignorance about the Olmecs was based in part on the geography of their heartland (the central region of a cultural group, where their traditional values and customs are practiced). The hot and swampy jungles in which the Olmecs had lived were so inaccessible that few had ventured there to seek answers about ancient societies. The jungle forests had long ago engulfed the abandoned cities of the Olmecs, hiding them from sight. Over the centuries the heat and moisture combined forces to decay thousands of artifacts and remains of the once-flourishing society.

It was not until the late 1930s that archaeologist Matthew Stirling (1896–1975), long intrigued by the few known Olmec artifacts, began excavating (digging to uncover artifacts and remains) at a site now known as La Venta in Mexico. Under a deep blanket of jungle vegetation he found an astonishing ancient city. Stirling uncovered artifacts proving that the Olmec were a distinct people with a sophisticated society and advanced arts.

The biggest surprise was that the Olmecs had flourished well before the rise of the Mayas. For scholars, the early existence of the Olmecs was hard to believe because there were no other known complex societies in Mesoamerica before the Maya—it seemed as if suddenly and out of nowhere a highly developed society had simply appeared.

In the 1940s, as they excavated La Venta, Stirling and his wife heard a rumor about a huge eye peering up from beneath a trail in the area of San Lorenzo, south of La Venta. Intrigued, they began an excavation there, turning up the second of the seventeen known Olmec colossal heads. Found at several sites, these mammoth sculptures carved from basalt (a fine-grained, dark gray rock used for building) date between 1200 and 900 B.C.E.

The heads weigh up to 30 tons (27.2 metric tons) and measure from about 5 to 11 feet (1.5 to 3.4 meters) in height. All of the heads, which are presumed to be portraits of Olmec priest/rulers, wear tight-fitting helmets. They have distinctive broad-faced, large-lipped features that have caused some people to theorize (create an unproved explanation based on scientific evidence or historical analysis) that the Olmecs had an African or Asian heritage. The colossal heads have become hallmarks (distinguishing characteristics) of the Olmec culture.

For years ancient historians debated amongst themselves about Stirling's discoveries, but by the 1950s most accepted the Olmec culture as the "mother culture of Mesoamerican civilization," meaning that the most important aspects of all later Mesoamerican civilizations originated with the Olmecs. Controversies about the Olmecs continued, and by the 1990s, most historians were persuaded that the Olmecs had *not* been the mother culture of the Mesoamericans. They argued that the different hallmarks of civilization (such as writing, calendars, a ruling elite, organized religion,

Words to Know

Artifact: Any item made or used by humans, such as a tool or weapon, that may be found by archaeologists or others who seek clues to the past.

Basalt: A fine-grained, dark gray rock used for building.

Ceremonial centers: Citylike centers usually run by priests and rulers, in which people from surrounding areas gathered to practice the ceremonies of their religion, often at large temples and plazas built specifically for this purpose.

Cultural group: A group of people who share customs, history, beliefs, and other traits, such as a racial, ethnic, religious, or social group.

Elite: A group of people within a society who are in a socially superior position and have more power and privileges than others.

Excavate: To dig carefully in the earth to uncover artifacts and remains of life from the past.

Glyph: A figure (often carved into stone or wood) used as a symbol to represent words, ideas, or sounds.

Hallucinogenic drug: A mind- and sense-altering drug that may create visions of things not physically present.

Heartland: The central region of a cultural group, where their traditional values and customs are practiced.

Offerings: Gifts for the gods.

Pilgrimage: A journey to a holy place to show faith and reverence.

Ritual: A formal act performed the same way each time, usually used as a means of religious worship by a particular group.

Script: Writing.

Stela: A stone pillar carved with images or writing, often used to provide historical details or for religious or political purposes.

Theorize: Create an explanation based on scientific evidence or historical analysis that has not yet been proven.

and many others) had arisen at different times and in a variety of independent Mesoamerican cultures, of which the Olmecs were just one.

Discoveries in the early 2000s, though, have persuaded a few experts that the Olmecs were probably the originators of some of the most important aspects of Mesoamerican civilization. Olmec artifacts provide the first evidence of many of the Mesoamerican religious themes and political structures central to later civilizations. The Olmecs seem to have been the first Mesoamericans to build ceremonial centers (citylike centers usually run by priests and rulers, in which people from surrounding areas gathered to practice the ceremonies of their religion, often at large temples and plazas built specifically for this purpose). From very recent evidence, it seems possible that Mesoamerican ball games, calendars, math, and even written script had their origins in Olmec times. The jungles of Mesoamerica, however, hold many untapped secrets about the ancient past. Future histories of Mesoamerica will undoubtedly present vital new evidence and theories about the origin of its civilization.

Dates of predominance

c. 1200–400 B.C.E.

Name variations and pronunciation

Pronounced OLE-meck. The name means "rubber people" in Nahuatl (pronounced NAH-wah-tul), the language of the later Aztec (Mexica; pronounced may-SHEE-kah) civilization. The name, given to the Olmecs long after the demise of their culture, refers to their production of rubber by tapping rubber trees. The Olmec people called themselves Xi (pronounced shee). The term Olmec usually refers to people who lived in large settlements in the Olmec tropical heartland, but it is also used in reference to the art style practiced in various other highland regions strongly influenced by the Olmecs.

Location

The Olmec heartland was located in swampy jungle river basins in the tropical coastal plains of the modern-day Mexican states of Veracruz and Tabasco. The three major Olmec centers were San Lorenzo, located on Río Chiquito in southern Veracruz; La Venta, located on an island in the Tonala River in western Tabasco; and Tres Zapotes (pronounced TRACE sah-POE-tays) at the western foot of the Tuxtla Mountains in Veracruz.

Artifacts resembling Olmec ceramics and sculptures have been found in many other regions of Mexico, particularly in the modern-day Mexican states of Oaxaca (pronounced

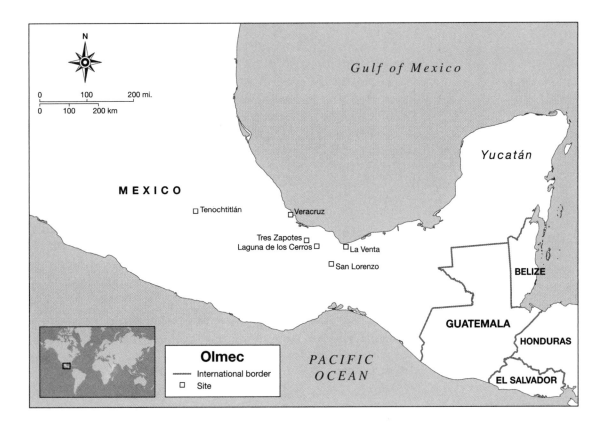

Map showing sites of the ancient Olmec civilization in Mesoamerica. *Map by XNR Productions. The Gale Group.*

wah-HAH-kah), Morelos, Guerrero, and the Federal District, signifying that the Olmecs traded with, or had a high degree of influence over, the people in these highland regions.

Important sites

San Lorenzo

San Lorenzo is the commonly used collective name of three related sites: San Lorenzo Tenochtitlán, Potrero Nuevo, and Loma del Zapote. These sites are located in hot, swampy lowlands in the Coatzacoalcos River basin along the Gulf of Mexico, just south of Veracruz. People had lived in villages around the area of San Lorenzo from about 1750 B.C.E., but by sometime between 1500 and 1200 B.C.E. a distinctive Olmec culture had emerged there.

The site lies upon a plateau (large, elevated, level area of land) that rises about 150 feet (45.7 meters) above the surrounding lowlands. When archaeologist Michael D. Coe (1929–) first surveyed the site in the 1960s, he found to his surprise that a large ridge had been built by human labor on top of a natural plateau. By some estimates, the Olmec laborers who built the artificial ridge had carried more than 1.35 million cubic feet of soil in baskets to the plateau.

San Lorenzo was the oldest of the three primary Olmec sites. Based on the artifacts and remains found, archaeologists (scientists who dig up and examine artifacts, remains, and monuments of past human life) believe San Lorenzo was built to be a center for worship and government. Among the buildings at the site are many ceremonial mounds, large earthen platforms that probably had houses or other buildings upon them. San Lorenzo also had elaborate residences for the elite—the rich and powerful ruling families—as well as a separate area for the houses of common working people.

At its height, San Lorenzo is estimated to have had a population of no more than one thousand people. The number of farmers who lived and worked in the surrounding area, however, is estimated between ten thousand and twenty thousand. The site was clearly once the scene of massive public works projects requiring the work of many laborers. Thousands of hours of work went into building the artificial ridge the village was built upon, as well as the network of stone paved roads, the large basalt drainage systems (rocky channels that carried away wastewater or sewage), and at least twenty human-made water-storage ponds in the city. Because the arts found in the city were so advanced, it is likely that an artisan class was supported in San Lorenzo.

Archaeologists unearthed eight of the seventeen known Olmec colossal basalt heads at San Lorenzo. The colossal heads were carved using stone tools—there were no metal tools as yet in Mesoamerica. The rock had been brought in from the Tuxtla Mountains 60 miles (96.5 kilometers) away. Early Americans did not yet use the wheel or beasts of burden, such as horses or oxen, to help do work; it is believed Olmec workers used log rollers to transport the stone through the jungles with great effort, then floated it down the rivers on rafts to the great cities.

Archaeologists are still making discoveries about the Olmec. El Manatí, a site about 10 miles (16.1 kilometers)

Tres Zapotes

Tres Zapotes, located about 100 miles (160.9 kilometers) northwest of La Venta, flourished around the same time as San Lorenzo and La Venta, but it continued to be occupied well after the fall of La Venta. The site consists of about fifty earthen mounds. Two colossal heads were discovered near Tres Zapotes, including the largest, the Cobata head, which measures more than 11 feet (3.3 meters) tall and about 10 feet (3.04 meters) wide.

Perhaps the most important discovery at Tres Zapotes was Stela C, a carved stone monument from the later days of the Olmecs. Stela C is one of the oldest dated written "documents" of the Americas, dating back to 32 B.C.E. Stela C, along with a few other Olmec artifacts, provides evidence that the Olmecs may have been the creators of Mesoamerican systems of writing as well as the possible originators of a calendar and dating system called the Long Count, which

Olmec jade figurines found in La Venta. *The Art Archive/National Anthropological Museum Mexico/Dagli Orti.*

was used by the Mesoamerican civilizations that followed. Archaeological work around Tres Zapotes is ongoing; several sites have been discovered in the area but have not yet been excavated.

Outlying sites

Archaeologists have found pockets of Olmec or Olmec-influenced artifacts in a wide range of areas, from the modern-day Mexican states of Oaxaca, Morelos, Guerrero, and the Federal District and extending out to places in Guatemala and Honduras. There is plenty of evidence, ranging from weapons to artwork depicting war, that the Olmecs were a warlike society, and it is possible they invaded and ruled over other peoples. Many historians believe, however, that the Olmecs' unquestionable influence over regions near and far was due to three other factors: extensive trade; the efforts of the Olmecs to spread their religious beliefs; and the desire of less-advanced people to acquire or adopt Olmec advances in arts, commerce, and the sciences.

One of the outlying Olmec sites is Teopantecuanitlán (Place of the Temple of the Jaguar Gods), which lies in the hills of Guerrero state at the juncture of the Amacuzac and Balsas Rivers. There, archaeologists have found a sunken courtyard guarded by jaguar heads carved in travertine (a marble-like stone like limestone), as well as early Olmec pottery and figurines. Excavation on this site has revealed that the city's construction began as early as 1400 B.C.E. These early dates have caused some archaeologists to theorize that the Olmecs originated in Teopantecuanitlán and then migrated to their later home in the Olmec heartland.

Another important outlying area with heavy Olmec influence is Chalcatzingo, in the highlands in the eastern part of the modern-day Mexican state of Morales. The ancient city was situated on a stunning cleft (divided in two at the top) volcanic mountain. In the ancient Mesoamerican religions, the cleft mountain was considered the birth place of humans; the great rock cliffs of Chalcatzingo were held sacred. In fact, the name "Chalcatzingo" means "place most revered" in the Nahuatl language.

Chalcatzingo had been occupied by several different groups since about 3000 B.C.E. The Olmec are believed to have had a strong presence there between 700 and 500 B.C.E. Carved into the rock cliffs are spectacular Olmec-style bas-relief (artwork in which part of the design is raised) carvings, providing a wealth of religious imagery that can still be seen today.

It is believed Olmec traders from La Venta used Chalcatzingo as an important outpost and trade center. The city had a great supply of white clay used by the Olmecs in their ceramics. It was also about halfway between the Olmec heartland and mountain sources of obsidian (dark, solid glass formed by lava from volcanoes used to make blades, knives, and other tools) and jade the Olmecs used for their artwork.

History

Because there are no written records from Olmec times to be deciphered and so many artifacts were lost before archaeologists could analyze them, little is known of Olmec history. The earliest Olmec society arose in San Lorenzo in 1700 B.C.E. Most of the common people around the site were maize farmers, but a very profitable trade network was established in San Lorenzo as well. From about 1500 B.C.E. onward, the population grew and so did imports (goods from another region brought into one's home region) of basalt, greenstone, and obsidian from far off places.

As trade grew, it is likely a few family groups profited more than others. These people grabbed the best land for themselves and began to exercise more and more power over others. These few powerful families in San Lorenzo may have formed the first aristocracy (rule by a small, privileged group of people) in Mesoamerica. The amount of strenuous labor it took to build the artificial ridge of San Lorenzo is proof that many laborers were under the control of a governing few.

By about 1250 B.C.E. distinctive Olmec art appeared. Pottery and ceramic figures made from white clay, colossal stone heads and thrones, and many other uniquely Olmec artifacts date back to 1250 B.C.E., and had not appeared before this time. Within a century, San Lorenzo's long-distance trading was flourishing, and the center reigned over a wide area for centuries. Just prior to this era, in about 1200 B.C.E., something mysterious occurred in San Lorenzo. The great monuments and statues that had been built in the city were purposely smashed up and then buried under the city's artificial ridge. Some scholars believe that there was a violent revolution at this time in which rebels destroyed the Olmec monuments. Others think the deliberate destruction of these highly prized monuments may have been done as a part of an important religious ritual (a formal act performed the same way each time, usually used as a means of religious worship by a particular group). Despite this willful destruction of its treasures, San Lorenzo continued to thrive for centuries.

Olmec power passed from San Lorenzo to La Venta around 900 B.C.E. Around this time, huge temples and plazas for religious worship were built in La Venta. The rulers and priests there performed public ceremonies, drawing great crowds to the city. La Venta became a much grander city than San Lorenzo, extending its power farther into outlying areas. It was undoubtedly a sacred place to many, and it is known for the many buried offerings found there. Then, in about 400 B.C.E., La Venta experienced extreme upheaval. Many of its monuments were destroyed or deliberately disfigured. Unlike the upheaval in San Lorenzo of 1200 B.C.E., La Venta never recovered.

The destruction of both San Lorenzo and La Venta greatly weakened the Olmec society. At the site of Tres Zapotes in southern Veracruz, the Olmecs probably carried on in a much less powerful state amid newly emerging civilizations for several more centuries. Experts do not know what finally happened to the Olmecs.

Economy

The three Olmec heartland centers, San Lorenzo, La Venta, and Tres Zapotes, were located in regions with different natural resources and shared these for the mutual benefit of all. San Lorenzo was a farmer's dream. In the lower areas along the river there were flood plains (level land beside a river that sometimes floods) with extremely fertile soil. In the higher areas, with an abundance of rain, the Olmec farmers could produce two maize crops per year on a single piece of land.

With easy access to the rivers, the San Lorenzo Olmecs became able traders. La Venta had access to the resources of the sea (fish, shells, sea animals, and seaweed). La Venta Olmecs probably produced salt, cacao (the dried seeds of an evergreen tree used to make cocoa and chocolate), and rubber. Historians believe the Olmecs were the first to tap rubber trees to make rubber objects. They also extracted basalt from the Tuxtla Mountains near another Olmec center, Laguna de los Cerros. The Olmecs transported the basalt in huge blocks weighing up to 20 tons (18.1 metric tons) to the various ceremonial centers, perhaps by hauling them on log rollers to large wooden rafts and then floating them along the rivers.

The trade of basalt, rubber, shells, and other substances as well as manufactured wares such as the Olmec's fine pottery provided an abundance of goods. Trade extended beyond their own centers. The Olmecs carried on extensive long-distance trade with peoples all over Mesoamerica, including the cities of Monte Albán and Teotihuacán (pro-

The Olmecs transported huge blocks of basalt from outlying areas to create large structures such as this tomb, found at La Venta.
© *Danny Lehman/Corbis.*

nounced TAY-uh-tee-wah-KAHN), developing alliances and trade relations near and far.

Farmers in Olmec times grew maize, yams, squash, beans, grains, gourds, and avocados, although maize was the principal crop. The Olmecs tamed their tropical coastal environment by using slash-and-burn techniques, a way of clearing the land for cultivation by cutting down all the trees and vegetation and then burning them. This added nutrients from the burned vegetation to the soil and prepared it for new crops.

They also used river levees (embankments or walls built along rivers to prevent or control flooding) like those used in ancient times on the Nile River in Egypt to periodically flood their fields. About 7,000 square miles (18,130 square kilometers) of heartland is estimated to have supported about fifty people per square mile. In addition to their crops, the Olmecs ate deer, wild pigs, and fish from nearby lakes and ponds.

Government: A ruling elite

Some scholars of ancient history theorize that it was the successful farming of the Olmecs that led to a government run by a ruling elite. In earlier times, small groups of several families had owned and farmed the lands communally—sharing the work and benefits, with everyone more or less equal in the process. Michael D. Coe and Richard Diehl believe as a few families gained control of the best farmlands, they became wealthy and were then able to rule over others. From this class of families that had gained control through owning the best lands, a group of rulers and priests emerged. In fact, in Olmec society, rulers and priests were often one and the same; there was little difference between religious and civic rule in the Olmec society. As the power became concentrated, the Olmec society fell under the rule of shaman-kings, or priest-kings, who were also probably members of the powerful extended ruling families that owned the best lands and most of the wealth of the area. These shaman-kings were believed to have divine powers. The complex religious system the Olmecs developed in their early years served to justify the absolute rule of these shaman-kings over their people by representing their authority as something ordained by the gods.

The great cities of the Olmecs housed the elite but not the workers. They served as ceremonial centers with religious temples and palaces and had separate areas for trade. The common people lived separately from the ceremonial centers in surrounding areas and made their living as farmers. They provided labor for the ceremonial centers as well as food and goods to the ruling elite. The farmers gathered periodically in the ceremonial centers for religious or governmental celebrations. The farmers belonged to the lower classes in the newly forming class structure. There was a tremendous gap between their condition and that of the upper classes that is apparent in the difference between the lavish burials of the Olmec elite and humble burials of the farmers.

Religion

The Olmec religion associated nature with the supernatural world. Springs, mountaintops, and caves were considered portals (doors) to the supernatural world. Olmec cities were often constructed near natural features, and buildings were sometimes erected to look like a nearby mountain or volcano.

As in many ancient cultures, Olmec shamans, or priests, were believed to have the power to intervene in the supernatural world for the benefit of their people. The Olmecs viewed their shamans with deep respect and willingly honored their great power. Olmec shamans were said to enter trances (states of altered consciousness) by using hallucinogenic drugs (mind- and sense-altering substances that may create visions of things not physically present) and through bloodletting, a process of piercing their skin, often the tongue, ears, or genitals, and losing much blood in the ritual.

While in such a trance, shamans were said to transform themselves into their *naguals,* or animal spirit companions. In this state the shaman might be able to enter the supernatural world through one of its portals. The Olmecs believed that once the shaman had entered the spirit world he could manipulate the forces controlling rain and the growth of crops in order to sustain his people. Some archaeological evidence indicates infants, as symbols of the renewal of life, may have been sacrificed to the gods who were believed to control rain.

The most important symbol in the Olmec belief system, and to subsequent cultures throughout Mesoamerica for centuries to come, was the jaguar. The jaguar was considered the most powerful earthly predator. It navigated well on earth, in the air, and in water—the three vital divisions of the Olmec world. According to the Olmec religion, in early times, a human woman and a jaguar bred, creating a *were-jaguar,* or a creature both human and jaguar, who was the ancestor of all Olmecs. The jaguar was the most common *nagual* to the shamans. Mesoamerican art and architecture features many depictions of shamans in various states of transformation into the *were-jaguar.*

Carving of an Olmec shaman, or priest, making an offering to the gods.
© *Gianni Dagli Orti/Corbis.*

From artwork, archaeologists and historians have been able to piece together some of the framework of the Olmec religion—enough to know that it was highly complex. According to Brian Fagan, in his book *Kingdoms of Gold, Kingdoms of Jade* (1991): "The Olmec took a set of centuries-old tribal beliefs about the spirit world and transformed them into a complex array of beliefs about prestige, success, and control of society that were entirely in tune with American Indian thinking about the nature of the universe. And they, and their successors, ruled with these new beliefs for over 2,500 years."

The Mesoamerican ball game

The Americas can lay claim to one of the world's oldest team sports—the Mesoamerican ball game, called *tlachtli* by the Aztec, *pok-a-tok* by the Mayas, and *ulama* by some other Mexican groups. The game, believed to have originated around 1500 B.C.E., was certainly sport, but it was also an important religious ritual. No one knows whether the Olmecs actually invented the game or if they adopted it from another society, but they were responsible for spreading it to other Mesoamerican cultures. About six hundred ball courts have been found in Mesoamerica, and there are probably many more hidden in the abandoned cities of the jungles.

The ball games were played on large courts with hundreds of spectators watching. The ball courts were often about 120 by 30 feet (36.6 by 9.14 meters) and shaped like the letter I—some courts were even much larger than today's football fields. A big, heavy, solid rubber ball was used, weighing about 6 to 10 pounds (2.72 to 4.54 kilograms). If thrown with force, the ball could seriously injure or even kill a player. Each team tried to score points by getting the ball through stone hoops on the side walls or by causing the other team to drop the ball.

In most versions of the game, only hips, knees, and elbows—no hands or feet—could be used to propel the ball. Players were dressed in uniforms and helmets. At the end of the game, the captain of the defeated team was decapitated (his head was cut off) as a human sacrifice to the gods. The honor to the winning captain was tremendous and evidently made it worth the risk of playing.

The spectators usually made bets on which team would win; sometimes the stakes were very high—people offered themselves or their relatives as slaves if they lost. In some Mesoamerican cultures, the spectators were obligated to give all their clothing and jewelry to the winning team. Thus, when the crowd saw that a team was making the final winning play, they jumped from their seats and ran away so they wouldn't have to give up their belongings.

The Mesoamerican ball game dramatized the religious principles of the Olmecs and the later civilizations who practiced it. The game was seen as a battle between good and evil—the forces of life and death were being played out on the ball court. The human sacrifice at the game's end was viewed as a way to fertilize the earth or to feed the sun with the victim's blood. Sacrifice of all kinds was crucial in the Mesoamerican religion to ensure that the gods were happy and would not destroy life on Earth or cause crop failures, earthquakes, or volcanoes.

Archaeologists have found what may have been Olmec ball courts in the ruins of San Lorenzo and La Venta. Many detailed scenes depicting the game appear in Olmec art, and rubber balls were found in El Manatí. These are the earliest known artifacts of the game.

Arts

The major source of knowledge about the hundreds of years of Olmec civilization is through its surviving artwork. The first discovery of Olmec art was a colossal head, found in the area of Tres Zapotes in 1862. As of 2004 seventeen colossal heads have been located in several sites. These, like much Olmec art, were designed to glorify the Olmec rulers. For the Olmecs, art was meant to give power to the shaman or ruler. The massive "altars" made of enormous carved basalt blocks weighing up to 44 tons (40 metric tons), for instance, are believed to have served as thrones for the Olmec kings.

At the bottom and front of each of these altars was a carved niche. A small human figure sits in the niche, holding either a *were-jaguar* on his lap or a cord in his hand, or both. The niche, according to experts, represents a cave, or the entrance to the supernatural world and the ruler's ties to the gods. The process of entering into the other world—the world of the supernatural—is central to most Olmec art.

Though they were masters at stone carving, the Olmec were also highly skilled potters and stone cutters. Much of their pottery depicts *nagual* transformations—the jaguar in particular, but also the harpy (part bird, part woman), shark, and caiman (a kind of crocodile found in Central and South America). Among Olmec artifacts, archaeologists have found many life-sized ceramic human infants made from white clay. They are realistic portraits and beautifully crafted, but experts are not certain of their significance. They may have celebrated birth but, on the other hand, they may have been portraits of the children about to be sacrificed.

The Olmecs carved some of the hardest stones—jade, serpentine, and jadeite—into figurines, masks, and celts (ground stone axe heads). Because the Olmecs lacked metal tools, the task of carving would have been extremely time

consuming. Jade was especially treasured. One greenstone figurine found in Veracruz is exemplary. The figure is a young man sitting cross-legged with a baby *were-jaguar* lying in his lap. Carved on the young man's shoulders and knees are outlines of the heads of other gods.

A massive Olmec altar depicts a human sitting in a niche. © *Charles & Josette Lenars/Corbis.*

Language and writing

Almost everything about the language and writing of the Olmecs is controversial. There are many speculations about the language spoken among the people, but most scholars believe the Olmecs spoke an ancient form of the Mixe-Zoquean language, which is still spoken in some parts of Mexico today.

Most historians at the turn of the twenty-first century believed that writing in Mesoamerica may have started among the Zapotecs around 400–300 B.C.E. But some scholars think the earliest writing may have originated among the

Olmecs. The evidence of Olmec script (writing) lies mainly in four artifacts: Stela C, dated by its creator at 32 B.C.E. found at Tres Zapotes; La Mojarra stela, dated May 21, 143, and July 13, 156, C.E. found near San Lorenzo, which may be the longest continuous written text passage of Mesoamerica; the Tuxtla statuette, dated 162 C.E., bearing a series of bar-and-dot numbers; and the most recent find, a cylinder (a solid figure bounded by a curved surface and two parallel circles of equal size on the ends) with carved glyphs (figures used as a symbol to represent words, ideas, or sounds) dating back to 650 B.C.E.

The Olmecs dated these "documents" using a system called the Long Count, which was used by many of the civilizations of lowland Mesoamerica. Long Count was made up of a two-calendar system counting back to a starting date of August 13, 3114 B.C.E. No one knows why this date was chosen. The numerals used to express the Long Count on the monuments found in the Olmec heartland were expressed in the bar and dot system, in which a bar had a value of five and a dot had a value of one. Two bars and a dot, for example, would have had a value of eleven.

Experts in Mesoamerican writing had worked with the abundant Maya script for many years before efforts began to interpret Olmec writing. Several small Olmec artifacts had characters that appeared to be writing of some kind, but there was never enough to try to decode them. Then, in 1986, a 4-ton (3.6-metric ton), 8-foot-wide (2.4 meters) by 5-foot-tall (1.5 meters) basalt stela was found at La Mojarra, near San Lorenzo. (A stela is a stone pillar carved with images or writing, used for religious or political purposes.) One side of the monument, called La Mojarra stela, featured an elaborate carving of an Olmec ruler, and next to him were 21 columns of glyphs. Dates from this text were presented in the bar and dot/Long Count system already known to scholars. They were May 21, 143, and July 13, 156 C.E.

In the 1990s linguist Terrence Kaufman (1937–) and anthropologist John Justeson began the task of trying to decipher the text on the monument. Using a mixture of four languages spoken in Veracruz, Tabasco, Oaxaca, and Chiapas, they began to put together patterns and gradually discerned words and grammar. They found additional glyphs on the Tuxtla statuette, a 6-inch (15.2-centimeter) jade-like figurine of a man with a duck mask on his face.

The Tuxtla statuette contained a series of bar and dot numerals as well as some glyphs. Justeson and Kaufman found identical syllables and words on La Mojarra stela and the Tuxtla statuette. Then they discovered that the back of La Mojarra contained hundreds more glyphs. After years of work Kaufman and Justeson were able to create a translation of La Mojarra: The text describes the deeds and accomplishments of a warrior-king named Harvest Mountain Lord.

Though the La Mojarra stela, Stela C, and the Tuxtla statuette are all considered to be examples of Olmec writing, the experts have labeled the writing on them as Epi-Olmec script. This is due to their Long Count dates, from 32 B.C.E. to 162 C.E., which all fall well after the decline of the Olmecs from power. The Olmecs still existed at the time but their society had fallen into a greatly weakened state. The Epi-Olmec glyphs show some notable similarities to Maya glyphs, so many questions remained as to which script came first.

This cylinder with glyph carvings, found near La Venta, Mexico, is considered by many experts to be evidence of the first Mesoamerican writing. *Photograph by Richard Brunck. Courtesy of Dr. Mary Pohl, FSU.*

Some believe the answer to the origins of Mesoamerican writing may have been found in 2002, when a group of archaeologists working near La Venta found a cylinder with raised carvings containing what appear to be glyphs. The cylinder is believed to have been a royal seal probably used to apply the symbols from its carvings to cloth or ceramics. The artifact was scientifically dated to 650 B.C.E. One of the carvings on the cylinder is of a bird with two symbols shown streaming from its beak. This kind of speech scroll, coming out of the mouth of a human or animal and representing the idea of speech or sound, was used widely in Mesoamerican writing and is not much different than dialogue balloons used in contemporary society's comic books and cartoons.

Many believe this is a sign the symbols in the speech scroll are words. Comparing the two symbols within the speech scroll to other Mesoamerican writing, the archeologists found a

strong resemblance to Maya glyphs and translated the symbols on the cylinder as "King 3 Ajaw," which is either the name of a king or a reference to a particular day in the sacred calendar of the Olmec. Because this artifact dates back to pre-Maya times, some believe it is proof the Olmec were the originators of glyph writing in Mesoamerica. The finding remains controversial.

A drawing of what the Olmec glyphs would look like rolled out, with the "speech" coming out of the beak of a bird. *Drawing by Ayax Moreno. Courtesy of Dr. Mary Pohl, FSU.*

Science

Though there are fewer artifacts to confirm the extent of Olmec knowledge in the sciences than found from other groups, the Olmecs were clearly party to, if not the originators of, the amazing advances in mathematics, astronomy, and time measurement shared by most ancient Mesoamerican societies. The Olmecs, as seen in the dating of their monuments, had a written numerical system in which a bar expressed the number five and a dot expressed the number one. They also used zero, which is considered a very advanced mathematical concept. The bar and dot system of numerals was widespread in later Mesoamerican cultures.

The Olmecs observed and recorded the orbits of the planets. They were able to predict eclipses with accuracy. (An eclipse is a partial or total blocking of light from one celestial body as it passes behind or through the shadow of another.) Like later Mesoamericans, they used a combined two-calendar system, with a 260-day sacred calendar and a 365-day solar calendar. Both the calendars and the numerical systems of the Olmecs were based on the number twenty. It is possible the Olmecs were the originators of the time-measuring system used as the basis of all calendars throughout Mesoamerica for centuries, but only a great deal of further investigation will confirm or negate this possibility.

The Olmecs' remarkable advances in arts and sciences, the likes of which no known culture before them had come close to achieving, continue to intrigue archaeologists. Fagan observed:

> *A vast chasm [gap] separates the thousands of farming villages scattered through Central America in 2000 B.C. and the sophisticated*

civilizations that arose with dramatic suddenness only 1,500 years later. It is this chasm that fascinates archaeologists as they search for the origins of the Maya and other Mesoamerican civilizations. Was there one ancestral culture that gave rise to later states of even greater complexity, or did these civilizations emerge from many cultural roots? One candidate may be the mysterious Olmec people....

For More Information

Books

Coe, Michael D. *Mexico: From the Olmecs to the Aztecs,* 4th ed. London and New York: Thames and Hudson, 1994.

Fagan, Brian M. *Kingdoms of Gold, Kingdoms of Jade: The Americas before Columbus.* London and New York: Thames and Hudson, 1991.

Sabloff, Jeremy A. *The Cities of Ancient Mexico: Reconstructing a Lost World,* revised edition. London and New York: Thames and Hudson, 1997.

Web Sites

"The Olmec." *Mesoweb: An Exploration of Mesoamerican Cultures.* http://www.mesoweb.com/olmec/ (accessed on October 5, 2004).

Wright, Micah Ian. "Hey Kids! Giant Olmec Heads!" http://www.micah wright.com/olmec/colossal.html (accessed on October 8, 2004).

Zapotecs and Monte Albán

17

The Zapotecs have lived in the Oaxaca (pronounced wah-HAH-kah) Valley of Mexico since at least 500 B.C.E. and are still there today. Most ancient Zapotec history revolves around the capital city, Monte Albán, which many experts consider the first Mesoamerican city. The Zapotecs, like the Olmecs (pronounced OLE-mecks), are regarded by some current scholars as the possible originators of several key features of the great Mesoamerican civilizations that followed. They were one of the earliest societies to produce a written version of their spoken language and they used the vigesimal, or base-twenty, numerical system (as opposed to the decimal, base-ten system used in contemporary society). They also used bar-and-dot numbers and the two-calendar system of tracking time (see the box on pages 306–307). These were all widespread characteristics of Mesoamerian cultures. (Culture is the arts, language, beliefs, customs, institutions, and other products of human work and thought shared by a group of people at a particular time.)

In seeking the origins of Mesoamerican cultural traits, it is important to remember that the Mesoamerican

Words to Know

Ceremonial centers: Citylike centers usually run by priests and rulers, in which people from surrounding areas gathered to practice the ceremonies of their religion, often at large temples and plazas built specifically for this purpose.

Chiefdom: A social unit larger and more structured than a tribe but smaller and less structured than a state, which is mainly governed by one powerful ruler. Though there are not distinct classes in a chiefdom, people are ranked by how closely they are related to the chief; the closer one is to the chief, the more prestige, wealth, and power one is likely to have.

City-state: An independent self-governing community consisting of a single city and the surrounding area.

Elite: A group of people within a society who are in a socially superior position and have more power and privileges than others.

Glyph: A figure (often carved into stone or wood) used as a symbol to represent words, ideas, or sounds.

Human sacrifice: Killing a person as an offering to the gods.

Observatory: A building created for the purpose of observing the stars and planets.

Pantheon: All of the gods that a particular group of people worship.

Propagandists: People who spread information and ideas designed to further their own cause.

Ritual: A formal act performed the same way each time, usually used as a means of religious worship by a particular group.

Tribute: A payment to a nation or its ruler, usually made by people from a conquered territory as a sign that they surrender to the imposed rule; payment could be made in goods or labor or both.

Vigesimal: Based on the number twenty (as a numeric system).

cultures were strongly connected with each other from ancient times forward. The earliest Zapotecs were heavily influenced by the Olmecs, and later enjoyed strong relations with the great city of Teotihuacán (pronounced TAY-uh-tee-wah-KAHN) in the Valley of Mexico. They also had regular contact with the Mayas (pronounced MY-uhs) at Tikal.

The days when the Zapotecs were the predominant force in the Oaxaca Valley ended with the decline of the city of Monte Albán in about 750 C.E. This chapter is about Zapotec culture during the twelve hundred years it ruled over the valley from its capital city.

Dates of predominance

500 B.C.E.–700 C.E.

Name variations and pronunciation

Twenty-first century Zapotec people usually call themselves *Be'ena'a,* or "The People." In pre-Hispanic times, some of the elite (those who had more power and prestige than others) Zapotecs believed their gods and ancestors lived among the clouds and that, upon death, they themselves would ascend to the clouds. Because of this belief, the Zapotec in some areas were called *Be'ena'a Za'a,* or "Cloud People."

In the sixteenth century, when the Spanish tried to record information about the Mesoamerican peoples they had conquered, they interviewed the Aztec (Mexica; pronounced may-SHEE-kah) people, who called the Zapotec the *Tzapotecatl,* the Nahuatl (pronounced NAH-wah-tul) language word for "Be'ena' Za'a." The Spanish misunderstood the word as *Zapoteca,* and from that time the name Zapotec has been used.

Location

Monte Albán (meaning "White Hill" in Spanish) was the Zapotec capital for many years. It is located in the central Oaxaca Valley in the state of Oaxaca in southern Mexico. The area around the Oaxaca Valley is a rugged section of the Sierra Madre del Sur mountains with some of its highest peaks and several volcanoes.

The Y-shaped valley is set on a wide and fertile plateau beneath these peaks and ridges at an altitude of about 1,300 feet (396 meters) above sea level. The three arms of the valley are formed by smaller valleys: the Etla Valley to the north, the Tlacolula Valley to the east, and the Zimatlán-Ocotlán Valley to the south. The site is 6.2 miles (10 kilometers) west of present-day Oaxaca City.

History

In 1500 B.C.E. the Oaxaca Valley was dotted with small, permanent villages, most of which were made up of

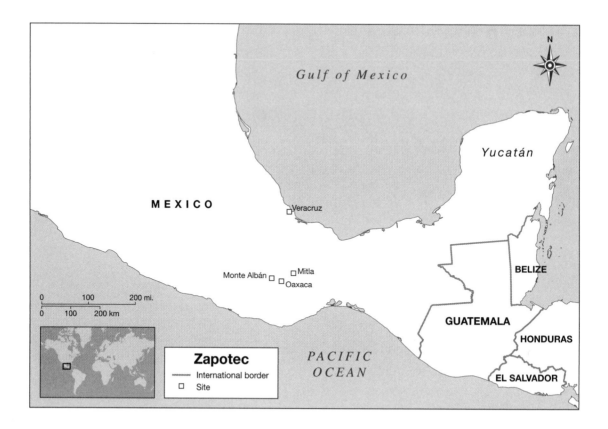

Gulf of Mexico

Yucatán

MEXICO

□ Veracruz

Monte Albán □ □ Mitla
□ Oaxaca

BELIZE

GUATEMALA

HONDURAS

PACIFIC
OCEAN

EL SALVADOR

0   100   200 mi.
0   100   200 km

Zapotec
International border
□   Site

N

**Map showing the sites of
the ancient Zapotec
civilization in Mesoamerica.**
*Map by XNR Productions. The
Gale Group.*

less than a dozen households. People in the valley grew maize (corn) and beans, hunted rabbit and deer, and collected wild plants. The villages gradually became chiefdoms, in which there was one strong ruler. The people most closely related to the ruler had higher rank than others, but there were not distinct social classes. The chiefdoms scattered throughout the Oaxaca Valley had direct connections with chiefdoms all over Mesoamerica. Trade and intermarriage among chiefs' families reinforced these connections. Early Mesoamerican societies were diverse, with distinct languages and customs. Connections among them, however, made it easy to share advances in science and religious systems, as well as art and architecture.

By 1300 B.C.E. one village, San José Mogote, located in the northern arm of the Oaxaca Valley, had grown larger than the others with a population of over six hundred people. San José Mogote was ruled by a few powerful people who had taken over the best farmland and were able to obtain tribute (payment to the ruler in goods or labor) from others. The village quickly became a regional center, in which public buildings were erected and sophisticated art and monuments were created. The center had a strong Olmec influence, especially in its form of government and artistic styles.

San José Mogote attracted people from all over the valley and became a busy center for trade and crafts. Other smaller towns developed in the surrounding Oaxaca Valley, though San José Mogote was the largest. Scholars are uncertain when the Zapotecs arrived in the valley or if they had been there all along, but most believe they were a significant presence in the Oaxaca Valley by about 900 B.C.E. San José Mogote is considered the forerunner of the great Zapotec city of Monte Albán, and many of its artifacts are the first indication of the distinctive Zapotec culture. The most famous of the Zapotec artifacts found at San José Mogote was a stone slab with a carving of a dead body, a victim of human sacrifice (someone killed as an offering to the gods). The carving, which dates back to 600 B.C.E., contains the first known example of Zapotec writing with glyphs (figures, often carved into stone or wood, used as symbols to represent words, ideas, or sounds) writing (see the section on Language and writing in this chapter).

Monte Albán

Around 500 B.C.E., at a point where the three arms of the Y-shaped Oaxaca Valley meet, construction began on the mountaintop city of Monte Albán. By this time, most experts believe the Zapotec culture was dominant in the Oaxaca Valley, though the valley's communities probably had independent governments. Apparently the rulers of the different cities and towns all over the valley agreed to this neutral mountaintop space for a capital city of the region. Why these valley rulers decided to build a city so far above the farmlands and water sources is unknown. Some speculate the city was planned for defense against invaders. Others say its majestic mountaintop setting, close to the divine world of the clouds, was in keeping with the Mesoamerican spirit of creating awe by displaying the power and splendor of the valley's rulers. Whatever the purpose, by about 200 B.C.E. the Zapotecs had completed the massive job of flattening the mountaintop on which the city was to be situated. They

Ruins of the ancient Zapotec civilization of Monte Albán in the Oaxaca Valley, Mexico. © *Paul Thompson; Ecoscen/Corbis.*

eventually built artificial ridges that spanned across to three mountaintops as the city spread out.

Monte Albán was planned from the start as a ceremonial center (a citylike center usually run by priests and rulers, in which people from surrounding areas gathered to practice the ceremonies of their religion, often at large temples and plazas built specifically for this purpose). In fact, the Zapotec name for Monte Albán was *Dani Biaa,* which means "sacred mountain." On the leveled mountaintop, laborers erected great pyramids, temples, and plazas. Two miles (3.2 kilometers) of walls were built around the city center, apparently to separate the sacred or elite (ruler-priests) from the rest of the population. The population in 200 B.C.E. had reached an estimated 10,000 to 15,000 people. The hillsides were terraced (huge steps were cut into them), and many of the common people of Monte Albán lived on the hillside terraces, outside the city walls. At its peak, Monte Albán had a population of about 35,000 people.

Perched over magnificent views, a Great Plaza measuring about 1,300 feet (396 meters) long and 650 feet (198 meters) wide expanded across the city center. The sacred and governmental buildings were built low to the ground and set off by sunken courts and stairways, revealing the great sophistication of the city's architects. To the left of the Great Plaza was the ball court, shaped like an I, in which the Mesoamerican ball game was played. Unlike other Mesoamerican courts, the Monte Albán ball court had no stone rings on its side walls; the Zapotecs evidently played a different kind of ball game at the time, as they still do in the twenty-first century (see Chapter 16 for more information).

Also facing the plaza is the Palace of the Danzantes, a large temple built between 500 and 200 B.C.E. In it are stone slabs with carvings of naked men in odd, contorted (twisted or bent) positions. Each slab has a name glyph at the head level of the portrait. At one time archaeologists (scientists who dig up and examine artifacts, remains, and monuments of past human life) believed the slabs depicted dancers: hence the name *danzantes* (dancers). Now most experts agree the carvings represent the dead bodies of captives the Zapotecs had captured in combat and then sacrificed as an offering to the gods. The *danzante* stones are monuments to Monte Albán's military strength and conquests. They are one of the oldest sets of stone carvings found in Oaxaca.

At the southern end of the plaza is Building J, a mound shaped like an arrow pointing to the southwest. It is believed to have been an observatory (a building created for the purpose of observing the stars and planets). On its outer walls, Building J bears about forty carved stone slabs depicting more bodies of sacrifice victims. Glyphs next to the carvings apparently tell the facts of the conquest: the

The Temple of the Danzantes with its stone slab carvings. © *Charles & Josette Lenars/Corbis.*

The First Mesoamerican Calendar Systems

Based on the evidence available, it appears the earliest writing in Mesoamerica stemmed from attempts to put a date and name on carvings of defeated enemies or victorious battles. No one knows for certain where the first calendar systems arose in Mesoamerica, but two very likely places are the Olmec heartland (the central region of a cultural group, where their traditional values and customs are practiced) and Monte Albán.

Every Mesoamerican society from the Olmecs forward used a calendar system that combined two calendars: the sacred 260-day calendar and the practical 365-day solar calendar. The 260-day calendar was composed of 20 consecutive day-names combined with the numerals 1 to 13. For example, a given day such as 3 Jaguar was formed of two parts: the numeral 3 with the day-name Jaguar. With the 20 day-names and 13 numerals there was a possibility of 260 combinations before the calendar would have to repeat a combination.

The Mesoamericans used this calendar, usually administered by their shamans (priests) to attempt to control, or simply to try to understand, their fate. They used the calendars for planning certain events or for foretelling the destiny of someone born on a particular date. Many groups, including the Zapotecs, named their children after the day-name of their birth—a child born on 6 Monkey, for example, would bear that name.

date, place, and battle. No one is certain of Building J's true function.

Government and economy

The establishment of the capital city of Monte Albán suggests the chiefdoms of the Oaxaca Valley had created a union or alliance. Some historians believe the leaders wanted a neutral capital from which the administration of the whole valley could be carried out. The capital soon became a growing city-state (an independent political unit consisting of a single city and the surrounding area), with increasing populations in its farming areas.

The rulers at Monte Albán managed the farming operations of the valley, keeping their own power by distributing resources to those who competed for their favor and keeping the best farmlands for themselves. The Zapotec rulers de-

The written form of a day-name consisted of a glyph and a bar and dot numeral. In the bar and dot system, a bar represents the number 5 and a dot represents the number 1. Thus one bar with three dots would signify the number 8. The system was vigesimal, meaning base-twenty. (The numeral system used in the twenty-first century is decimal, or base-ten.) Historians believe the Zapotecs first used the 260-day calendar, but later adopted a combined system using both the sacred and the 365-day year.

The 365-day calendar years (often called "vague years") used by the ancient Mesoamericans consisted of eighteen 20-day months with a final 5-day period filling out the end of the year. The calendar was based on the seasons and was useful for farming. When both calendars were used in combination, a new system called the Mesoamerican Calendar Round, emerged. Using both calendars, there were 18,980 possible combinations of dates, making up a unit of 52 solar years.

Mesoamericans viewed time as cyclical. Rather than going forward, they felt they were moving in a large circle that would return to its own beginning. They greatly feared the end of each 52-year unit, believing if the gods were unhappy with humans at that time, they might destroy the world.

manded that the common people pay them tribute, and some farmers were expected to farm the leaders' lands rather than pay them in goods. The Zapotec leaders at Monte Albán also commanded the huge force of laborers it took to build the great city and maintain its irrigation and drainage systems, probably using the tribute system to obtain the labor.

By 200 B.C.E. Monte Albán had developed into a true aristocratic government in which a few rich and powerful families living in its central area governed tens of thousands of commoners. The gap between the upper class and the peasants was great and particularly obvious in the lavish burials of the rulers—buried with precious jewels, metals, arts, and other extravagant belongings—in contrast to the modest burials of peasants.

Among the Zapotec, as with most ancient American cultures, there was little difference between religion, government, and economy—all three were directed by a powerful

Observatory at Monte Albán. © *Danny Lehman/Corbis.*

group of elite ruler-priests. Because people believed their ruler-priests were partly divine and could communicate with the gods, they were happy to accept the leadership; if not, they were probably too afraid to do anything about it.

The ruler-priests at Monte Albán were master propagandists (people who spread information and ideas designed to further their own cause) who took every opportunity to glorify themselves in the public eye. Just as the city itself was built high upon a mountaintop to inspire awe and associate it with the supernatural (divine or spiritual) world of the clouds, so the ruler-priests took care that every piece of art and architecture and every ceremony increased their glory and prestige, and linked them with the gods.

Between 200 B.C.E. and 200 C.E. Monte Albán was at its peak and as powerful as Teotihuacán, the enormous new city growing in the Valley of Mexico. Relations were good and trade between two cities was active. It is believed the Zapotecs occasionally went to war on a small scale, probably for the purpose of capturing prisoners to be sacrificed to the gods. They did not expand into other valleys, but maintained their own power in Oaxaca at a time when Teotihuacán and the early Maya cities were emerging nearby.

Religion

The common people among the Zapotecs believed they had been born from nature itself, directly from rocks, trees, and jaguars. The elite among the Zapotecs believed they had descended from gods who reigned in the world beyond the clouds. They believed their ancestors were in the cloud world and that they, too, would ascend to the clouds upon death.

The sharing of cultures among Mesoamericans meant that more and more gods were introduced to each religion from those of their neighbors. The Zapotec religion had at least fifteen gods in its pantheon (all of the gods that a particular group of people worship) and for each one there were specific rituals (formal acts performed the same way each time). Most of the gods were associated either with farming or fertility. Xipe Totec, "the Flayed One," was the god of sacrifice. The rain god Cocijo was apparently the primary god in the pantheon.

Like all Mesoamerican religions, the Zapotec religion separated the spirit of living things from nonliving things. Anything that lived, breathed, or moved had a life spirit and was treated with reverence. This included many things, such as light, animals, humans, and calendars. The Zapotec practiced ancestor worship and were particularly concerned with the ancestors of their rulers. They believed the dead ancestors of their ruler-priests had the supernatural ability to change the circumstances—particularly with respect to the weather and other natural phenomena—for the entire society. Therefore, the elite were buried in extravagant ceremonies with many jewels, precious gems, and artwork.

With so many gods and complicated calendars requiring sets of rituals for each calendar day, the Zapotec became increasingly dependent on their ruler-priests to oversee

The stone carvings from the Temple of the Danzantes were long believed to depict dancers, although some experts now think they may represent victims of human sacrifice. © *Kevin Schafer/Corbis.*

the extensive ceremonies designed to keep the gods happy. Sometimes this included human sacrifice, often the leaders of enemy cities around them.

Arts

Starting with the gruesome slabs lining the Temple of Danzantes, the stone carvings of the early Zapotecs at Monte Albán that adorned walls, stairs, and doors were primarily used to record the great feats and military victories of Zapotec rulers. Along with scenes of sacrifice victims and their decapitated heads, there are many depictions of the actual rulers, dressed in extravagant finery. Glyphs on these stone carvings describe the leaders' achievements, especially in combat. Throughout the history of Monte Albán, this form of commemoration (making a memorial so someone will always be remembered) used either writing or pictures to represent ideas, was stressed in the art and monuments of the city.

The Zapotecs used their arts to commemorate the living and also to accompany the dead to the afterlife. More than 150 elaborate tombs were found within the ruins of Monte Albán. The elite were buried in chambers adorned with painted murals and stone carvings as well as pottery. Archaeologists have found incredible riches in the Zapotec tombs, including jewelry and figurines made of gold, copper, jade, rock crystal, obsidian (dark, solid glass formed by lava from volcanoes used to make blades, knives, and other tools), and turquoise mosaic. Among the burial goods, as elsewhere in Zapotec society, are glyphs to record the name of the ruler being buried and other facts he would have wished to take with him into the afterlife.

Language and writing

Zapotec is a family of languages within a larger framework called the Otomanguean stock. In present-day Oaxaca more than four hundred thousand people speak some form of the Zapotec language. The language is tonal, meaning that the same word in a different tone will have a different meaning.

In most Zapotec writing, glyphs represented full words, but most experts believe some of the Zapotec glyphs represented sounds, such as syllables or letters. The glyphs were probably read in columns from left to right. From artifacts found in Zapotec ruins, archaeologists have identified more than one hundred glyphs, but still do not know what most of them mean. Those known are mainly day-names from the 260-day calendar. They are easily spotted because they always occur with a bar-and-dot number. Since the Zapotecs often named their children by day-names, most of those found on stone carvings are assumed to represent the name of the person depicted. Most are read in the following manner: 5 Flower; 6 Deer; 1 Monkey.

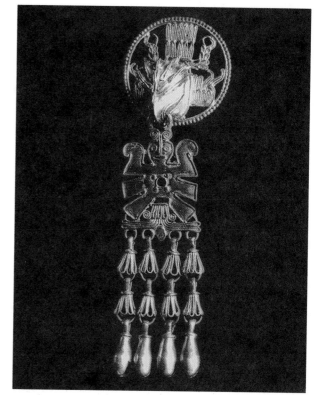

Gold pendant from Monte Albán. *The Library of Congress.*

Archaeologists found an artifact in San José Mogote that many believe is the earliest example of writing in the Americas, dating back to 600 B.C.E. On a stone slab, on the floor of a corridor between two public buildings, is a carving of a dead man with his eyes closed and his mouth open. The man is clearly a victim of human sacrifice, as there is blood flowing out of his chest, indicating his heart had been torn out. At his feet there is a glyph. The glyph is a day-name from the sacred 260-day calendar (see the box on pages 306–307).

The name on the glyph is 1 Earthquake (or, according to some, 1 Motion). The Zapotecs named their children for the day of the year they were born, so the day-name is probably the victim's name, and it is likely he was a chief from a town that the Zapotecs had defeated in a raid or combat. The Zapotecs set the carved slab on the floor to be walked upon by everyone who passed, showing their complete victory over this enemy and glorifying themselves as conquerors.

Scholars believe Zapotec writing originated in this attempt to record and boast about their victories in battle.

Joyce Marcus, one of the primary scholars of Zapotec writing, notes in *Natural History* that over the years the uses of writing in Monte Albán changed. The early glyphs, such as those on the danzante stones, show defeated and often dead captives, listing their names or the places the Zapotecs conquered. Building J, built sometime between 200 B.C.E. and 100 C.E. also had "conquest slabs" depicting conquered enemy leaders. The glyphs on the mysterious Building J include both calendar dates and other glyphs. Later, sometime between 100 and 300 C.E., the Zapotecs built a pyramid with eight stone carvings. While six of these are "conquest slabs," the other two depict what may be a diplomatic meeting between the leaders of Monte Albán and Teotihuacán. The last type of glyph writings of Monte Albán before its decline were records of the genealogy (family history) of the Zapotec rulers.

Sciences

The Calendar Round system of tracking time with a combination of two calendars (see the box on pages 306–307) is one of the most noted Zapotec contributions to the Mesoamerican culture. Zapotec artifacts have provided archaeologists with many more samples of their numerical and calendar systems than were available for the Olmec. The Zapotecs clearly used the Calendar Round before the Maya adopted it. Unlike the Olmecs and the Mayas, the Zapotecs did not use the Long Count system of tracking time, a method that started at a "0" year of 3114 B.C.E. (see Chapter 22 for more information).

Some buildings at Monte Albán are thought by scholars to be observatories. They were built in such a way that the sun would strike them at a certain place on a certain day. With these observatories, the Zapotecs could predict solar and lunar eclipses (a solar eclipse is the concealing of the moon by the sun; a lunar eclipse is the concealing of the sun by the moon) and other phenomena in outer space.

Decline

Around 750 C.E. the rulers of Monte Albán lost power for reasons that remain unknown. At about the same time, the grand city of Teotihuacán collapsed (see Chapter 18). Most of the people of Monte Albán left the city and began living in the surrounding areas of the Oaxaca Valley. About 5,000 people remained in the old city, but it eventually fell into ruin. The Mixtec, another group of people in the Oaxaca Valley, later used the abandoned city as a sacred place in which to bury their own dead. The Zapotecs left their capital city for good, but they did not disappear. Several studies estimate the number of Zapotecs at the time of the Spanish conquest was between 350,000 and 500,000 people.

For More Information

Books

Coe, Michael D. *Mexico: From the Olmecs to the Aztecs,* 4th ed. London and New York: Thames and Hudson, 1994.

Fagan, Brian M. *Kingdoms of Gold, Kingdoms of Jade.* London and New York: Thames and Hudson, 1991.

Sabloff, Jeremy A. *The Cities of Ancient Mexico: Reconstructing a Lost World,* revised ed. London and New York: Thames and Hudson, 1997.

Web Site

Marcus, Joyce. "First Dates: The Maya Calendar and Writing System Were Not the Only Ones in Mesoamerica—or Even the Earliest." *Natural History,* April 1991. Available at http://muweb.millersville.edu/~columbus/data/ant/MARCUS01.ANT (accessed October 6, 2004).

Teotihuacán

18

According to some Aztec (Mexica; pronounced may-SHEE-kah) legends, the city of Teotihuacán (pronounced TAY-uh-tee-wah-KAHN) was built by giants. Who else could have achieved the immense size and scale of building that occurred there more than two thousand years ago? The founders of Teotihuacán remain unknown in the twenty-first century, and observers still look upon the ruins with the same awe and amazement as the Aztecs. At its height in 500 C.E. Teotihuacán's population was somewhere between one hundred thousand and two hundred thousand people, making it the sixth largest city in the world at the time.

Within Teotihuacán's 8 square miles (20.7 square kilometers) were thousands of public buildings and residences, including six hundred pyramids. Among the pyramids was the enormous Pyramid of the Sun, the majestic Pyramid of the Moon, more than one hundred temples and shrines, and thousands of other ceremonial structures. There were also several huge marketplaces and more than two thousand apartment compounds and palaces.

Words to Know

Artifact: Any item made or used by humans, such as a tool or weapon, that may be found by archaeologists or others who seek clues to the past.

Astronomy: The science that deals with the study of the planets, sun, moon, and stars and all other celestial bodies.

Ceremonial centers: Citylike centers usually run by priests and rulers, in which people from surrounding areas gathered to practice the ceremonies of their religion, often at large temples and plazas built specifically for this purpose.

Colony: A group of people living as a community in a land away from their home that is ruled by their distant home government.

Elite: A group of people within a society who are in a socially superior position and have more power and privileges than others.

Empire: A vast, complex political unit extending across political boundaries and dominated by one central power, which generally takes control of the economy, government, and culture in communities throughout its territory.

Excavate: To dig carefully in the earth to uncover artifacts and remains of life from the past.

Fertility: The capacity of land to produce crops or, among people, the capacity to reproduce or bear children.

Glyph: A figure (often carved into stone or wood) used as a symbol to represent words, ideas, or sounds.

Obsidian: Dark, solid glass formed by volcanoes used to make blades, knives, and other tools.

Tribute: A payment to a nation or its ruler, usually made by people from a conquered territory as a sign that they surrender to the imposed rule; payment could be made in goods or labor or both.

Most of the early cities in the Americas were ceremonial centers (citylike centers in which people from surrounding areas gathered to practice the ceremonies of their religion, often at large temples and plazas built specifically for this purpose) to which people traveled for special events. While only the ruler-priests and their staffs actually lived within the ceremonial centers, Teotihuacán was a busy metropolis (city) with all classes of people living and working within its borders. The city was carefully planned and highly organized by its rulers. It served as the center of religion and government for a growing empire that included the entire Valley of Mexico and places beyond. Considered the holiest of places in the world by most Mesoamericans, Teotihuacán had a profound influence over the cultures around it and those that came later.

Although the city of Teotihuacán was vast and its ruins are massive, no significant written artifacts (items made or used by humans that may be found by archaeologists or others who seek clues to the past) have been found there. Some information came from the Aztecs, who reported what they knew about Teotihuacán to missionaries working for the Spanish king in the sixteenth century; many of the names of places in the city are taken from these reports. But even the Aztecs did not have firsthand information since the city had been abandoned centuries before their arrival in the Valley of Mexico. For the Aztecs, the ruins were a sacred part of human history; they believed Teotihuacán was where the gods had created human beings, but they knew little about the actual events that took place in the huge metropolis.

Dates of predominance

150 B.C.E.–750 C.E.

Name variations and pronunciation

Scholars do not know what the people of Teotihuacán called themselves. The name "Teotihuacán" (also Teotihuacan), was the name the Aztecs gave the city. It means either "place of the gods" or "where the men became gods." The name generally refers to the city but it is also used to refer to the civilization ruled by Teotihuacán, primarily within the Valley of Mexico but in some places extending beyond.

Location

Teotihuacán is located in the far northeast section of the Valley of Mexico about 25 miles (40.2 kilometers) northeast of present-day Mexico City. The Valley of Mexico is an oval-shaped basin set between two coastal mountain ranges on a 3,000-square-mile (7,770-square-kilometer) plateau at an altitude of about 7,200 feet (2,195 meters). Inside the Valley

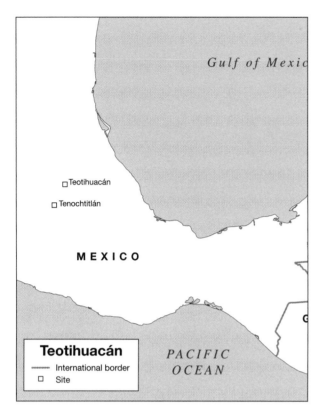

of Mexico there are several large lakes, the largest of which is Lake Texcoco.

Teotihuacán is situated in the Teotihuacán Valley, which is within the larger Valley of Mexico. The Teotihuacán Valley is about 190 square miles (492 square kilometers); about half of this land is good for farming and watered by natural springs.

The site

Besides its enormous size and thousands of buildings, Teotihuacán was unique among ancient Mesoamerican cities in the extremely precise and skillful city planning that went into its layout. The city center was laid out in a gridlike system (a network of evenly spaced horizontal and vertical lines making up a kind of checkerboard) sometime around the first century C.E. The city's layout shows an advanced knowledge of engineering and

Map showing ancient Teotihuacán in Mesoamerica. Teotihuacán influence was also strong in nearby Tenochtitlán, the capital of the Aztec empire. *Map by XNR Productions. The Gale Group.*

may even indicate a detailed knowledge of astronomy (the science that deals with the study of the planets, sun, moon, and stars and all other celestial bodies), according to a few scholars who think the buildings were lined up with the stars and planets above.

Much of Teotihuacán's construction took place between 200 and 300 C.E. The main road running through the city is called the Avenue of the Dead (so named by the Aztecs) and runs north to south for about 3 miles (4.8 kilometers). The Pyramid of the Moon (built around 250 C.E.) is at the northern end of the street, and the Pyramid of the Sun (built around 200 C.E.) is about a half mile to the south.

The four-level Pyramid of the Sun towered over the city. It was more than 200 feet (61 meters) tall and 700 feet (213 meters) wide and is thought to be the ancient world's third largest pyramid. The Pyramids of the Sun and of the Moon were both designed to imitate the look of the moun-

tains surrounding the city. Although they are gray in color today, during the Teotihuacán heyday (its most prosperous and powerful years), they were painted a bright red.

A little farther south on the Avenue of the Dead is the Ciudadela (or Citadel), a sunken plaza measuring about 1,300 feet (396 meters) long, which some believe may once have been the site of the ruler's palace. There are about six hundred small pyramids around the Ciudadela. One of these ceremonial pyramids, found in the city center, is the Temple of Quetzalcoatl (pronounced kates-ahl-koh-AH-tul), the third-largest pyramid in the city, which was built around 200 C.E. This building has six huge steps and is adorned with stone carvings of the Aztec god Quetzalcoatl, the feathered serpent god who plays a vital role in almost every Mesoamerican religion from the time of Teotihuacán forward.

The Temple of Quetzalcoatl is considered by some to be one of the most beautiful pieces of architecture from the

Sculptures of the god Quetzalcoatl adorn this temple in his honor.
© *Charles & Josette Lenars/Corbis.*

Mesoamerican era. In all, there were an estimated five thousand ceremonial buildings in the city. Teotihuacán was also considered a sacred burial ground; many tombs have been found and many more are thought to be still hidden within its ruins.

Teotihuacán was undoubtedly a great religious center, but it was also a place of business with a wide variety of products being made and traded. There were several huge, bustling marketplaces, to which goods and food were brought from places near and far. The common people of the city purchased their food at these marketplaces. There were many kinds of workers besides farmers living in the city; they labored in nearby obsidian (dark, solid glass formed by volcanoes used for chipping stone and making blades, knives, and other tools) mines, made crafts or other manufactured goods, or worked on the huge building projects within the city. Artisans were also plentiful in the city; archaeologists have uncovered about five hundred small workshops.

By about 300 C.E. most of the city's residents lived in apartment compounds—large square buildings comprised of sleeping rooms with kitchens. The rooms were connected by alleyways and outdoor patios. The apartment buildings were set around courtyards and surrounded by high walls. Some had common altars (places where people worshipped and made offerings to the gods), suggesting that extended family groupings (such as grandpar-

Interior courtyard of a Teotihuacán palace.
© *Gianni Dagli Orti/Corbis.*

ents, uncles and aunts, and cousins) existed within these large compounds.

About two thousand apartment compounds have been found in the city to date. Within the compounds, archaeologists have found colorful wall murals. It is believed the residential compounds were arranged in neighborhoods, and that some neighborhoods were reserved for certain groups of immigrants from other lands. For example, a Zapotec and a lowland Maya (pronounced MY-uh) neighborhood could have existed within the city.

The wealthy and powerful lords of Teotihuacán lived in elegant palaces. These large compounds had many rooms and were built, like most of the city's buildings (except for its pyramids), all in one story. They usually had many small courtyards in the front, arranged around a central courtyard. The palaces, like the apartment compounds, were decorated with colorful murals.

History

In 1000 B.C.E. the growing populations of the villages and towns in the Valley of Mexico were engaging in profitable trading with the Olmecs (pronounced OLE-mecks) in San Lorenzo (and later La Venta) and with the Zapotecs in the Valley of Oaxaca (pronounced wah-HAH-kah). They were particularly successful trading the abundant obsidian. As this trade continued, two villages in the valley grew to be small cities. Cuicuilco (pronounced kwee-KWEEL-coe), in the southwest part of the valley (now part of Mexico City) grew the fastest, with a population of about ten thousand by 300 B.C.E.

Teotihuacán was smaller by comparison but grew at a healthy pace. Sometime around 100 B.C.E. Cuicuilco was badly damaged by the eruption of a nearby volcano. At that time, Teotihuacán began to grow at an extremely rapid rate. Though the city of Cuicuilco reestablished itself, it never prospered again, and Teotihuacán, for reasons largely unknown, took its place as the leading city in the valley. By about 1 C.E. a large part of the Valley of Mexico's population had moved to Teotihuacán and its leaders began rebuilding their city, basically starting from scratch with all-new city

plans. The reason for this is not known. They may have re-built in an attempt to accommodate the expanding population, but that end could have been achieved by building outward from the existing structures. It is more likely that the rulers of Teotihuacán had a new vision of the way the city should be set out. The new city was built quickly and immediately prospered.

Why Teotihuacán was so successful is a matter of much interest to scholars. There are several possible reasons. It was close to the best obsidian sources, which provided valued goods to trade and created a strong demand for workers. Its lower parts were situated on good farmlands, which yielded enough crops to feed its population. It was also situated on a well-established trade route, making it a place Mesoamerican traders from far and wide would stop to do business. Teotihuacán was also a prominent holy place, and many believe it was the city's religious significance that drew people from all over the valley.

The Pyramid of the Sun in Teotihuacán with its many steps. © *Richard A. Cooke/Corbis.*

Teotihuacán and the Aztec Legend of the Fifth Sun

In the Aztec religion, it was believed that the world had been created and destroyed four times before the creation of the current world. There are several different accounts of the first four worlds and the people who lived in them. According to one account, the first world was destroyed by jaguars, the second by great winds, the third by fire and volcano, and the fourth by flooding. Each time the world was destroyed, the sun was destroyed with it, and a new sun was needed to create a new world.

In the days after the destruction of the fourth world, the gods met at Teotihuacán to make their plans for a fifth world. There, they chose two gods—one rich and the other poor and sickly—to sacrifice themselves so the world would be renewed. The two chosen gods fasted and prayed for four days, and then all the gods gathered around a great fire. The rich god threw many of his most precious belongings into the fire as sacrifices. The poor god, having no riches to burn, humbly offered weeds drenched in his own blood. When it came time for the gods to sacrifice themselves, the rich god looked into the fire with the intention of

In 1971 people working in the Pyramid of the Sun discovered the monument had been constructed over a natural, four-chambered cave. Inside the cave they found offerings for the gods dating back to before 150 C.E. In Mesoamerican religions, caves are considered very holy and thought of as portals (doors) between the spirit world of the gods and the human world. Some scholars think the ancient Mesoamericans may have believed this particular cave was the place where the first humans emerged into the world.

It is likely the Teotihuacán area was considered sacred throughout Mesoamerica, and its status as a holy site drew thousands of visitors who wished to participate in sacred ceremonies—long before the city, with its pyramids and monuments, was built. The Teotihuacán leaders may have been responsible for spreading the belief that their city was the place of the world's creation. It would have justified their power and the amazing amount of labor they gathered for the city's construction.

Teotihuacán soon became a major force in long-distance trade, and its influence began to spread to other

throwing himself in, but he could not bring himself to do it. The poor god, when it was his time, jumped straight into the sacrificial fire. Not wanting to be outdone, the rich god finally jumped into the fire as well.

The rest of the gods waited after the two sacrifices, but nothing happened. At last, all the gods, one by one, threw themselves into the fire. After their sacrifices, the renewal began. Out of the sacrificial fire, the poor, sickly god arose in great splendor as the new sun, bringing light and life to the world. Sometime later, the rich god rose as the pale moon. The age of the Fifth Sun had begun, brought about at the holy city of Teotihuacán by the sacrifice of the gods.

According to Aztec beliefs, human society was then born in the city. The lords of Teotihuacán, who were wise and understood the ways of the gods, assumed the roles of leaders and priests and the city prospered. Upon the deaths of the lords, the Pyramid of the Sun and the Pyramid of the Moon were built—some said by giants—to serve as their temples.

quarters of Mesoamerica. By the fourth century the rulers of Teotihuacán had begun to look elsewhere for resources, tribute (payment, in goods or labor, to the rulers or conquerors of the state), and markets for their goods. The city's military began to play a stronger role and scenes of war became a common theme of Teotihuacán art.

The leaders of the city had developed a vast economic empire by about 400 C.E., which included much of the southern two-thirds of Mexico, Guatemala, and Belize, as well as some parts of Honduras and El Salvador. Some of the new territories may have been conquered by the Teotihuacán military and then occupied. Scholars believe the manner in which new territories were ruled differed from place to place. Certainly some of Teotihuacán's conquests were gained by military force. Other new regions were probably brought into the empire in a more friendly way, through intermarriage or agreements among the leaders.

In some places, Teotihuacán leaders set up "colonies" (people living in a territory controlled by a central distant power) of their own people in conquered areas. The colonists oversaw things such as mining resources and tribute payments. Many historians believe the Teotihuacán empire was mainly an economic endeavor; the territories under Teotihuacán control may have paid tribute and become trading allies with the large city but they probably continued to rule themselves. In any case, the influence of Teotihuacán deeply impacted the Mesoamerican civilizations.

Government

To build such a sophisticated and massive city, and to ensure that its huge population received the food and goods it needed, the lords of Teotihuacán must have exerted an extraordinary amount of direction and social control. Most historians believe they ruled with iron fists, demanding hard labor as well as complete loyalty and obedience from their people. But it is also clear that the lords ruled with foresight, planning, and a high degree of organization, because the huge city could not have functioned well without this level of management.

Although little is known about the actual rulers and priests of Teotihuacán, it is clear they had a great deal of control over most aspects of the lives of their people. Scholars are not certain whether the rulers were priests, warriors, or both. Twenty-first century information is limited for two reasons in particular: First, there are no writings among Teotihuacán artifacts; second, the Teotihuacáns did not carve memorials or monuments to their leaders like the Zapotecs.

Teotihuacán rulers, however, were mentioned in a few Maya texts. Some members of the Teotihuacán nobility must have traveled on occasion to Maya cities, since intermarriages between noble families of the two cultures had occurred. One Maya text refers to a Teotihuacán emperor named Spear-thrower Owl, who ruled the empire for sixty years.

Economy

Teotihuacán was the center of an amazing amount of trade, producing a wide variety of goods. It is estimated full-time artisans, or craftspeople, working in the city numbered in the tens of thousands, and there were even more who engaged in trading and related businesses. Obsidian production was the city's biggest industry, requiring numerous laborers for mining. There were also artisans who made obsidian blades and fine knives as well as ornaments. Other crafts included ceramics, sculptures, murals, and carvings.

The city was an international hub with excellent routes to other markets. Within the city, the center of activity was the marketplace with thousands of stalls and numerous items being sold by people from all over Mesoamerica. Food, bird feathers, beads, pottery, jewelry, cloth, and much more were sold daily. The marketplace was a great gathering place, where people from many backgrounds shared ideas and culture.

Although many people worked in production or trade, the majority of the valley's inhabitants were farmers who grew the food that fed the hundreds of thousands of people in Teotihuacán. Farms that surrounded the city grew maize (corn), a grain called amaranth, beans, and cactus, among other crops. Maize was revered as the most central food of the Teotihuacán's diet; almost all of the gods of the Teotihuacán religion had some connection to the healthy growth of maize crops.

Religion

Teotihuacán priests were in charge of the huge religious ceremonies their city was built to accommodate. The priests were known to be very scholarly. They are thought to be the group responsible for the skillful observation of the stars and planets and the keeping of calendars for the city and its colonies.

Most of the gods revered by the Teotihuacáns are also found in other Mesoamerican religions. The goddess leading the Teotihuacán pantheon was the Spider Woman, who appeared in many of the painted murals lining the walls of the city. She is thought to be the goddess of the underworld and had influence over darkness, water, war, caves, and possibly creation.

Spider Woman had a spiderlike appearance, with a yellow-colored body and a rectangular nosepiece with three fangs that covered her mouth. Her headdress featured a jaguar image, and her shield was decorated with spider webs.

Mural depicting the rain god, Tlaloc. © *Gianni Dagli Orti/Corbis.*

In many of the murals, there were spiders crawling all over the Spider Woman. Though a goddess of Mesoamerica, Spider Woman can also be found in North America. The Navajo and Pueblo call her Spider Grandmother.

The feathered serpent god of the Teotihuacáns was revered by most Mesoamerican societies under many names and guises. Like the Olmecs, the Teotihuacán artists focused heavily on the jaguar in their religious themes. They combined images of the jaguar, which probably invoked the concepts of the earth and fertility, with images of serpents and birds. Different combinations of these religious images foreshadowed (gave an indication in advance) the Aztec and Toltec (pronounced TOHL-teck) gods Quetzalcoatl, the feathered serpent, and Tlaloc (pronounced TLAH-lock), the rain god. The sun god and the moon goddess are other important gods within the large Teotihuacán pantheon. Unfortunately, without written documents from the city, the names the Teotihuacáns used for their gods have been lost.

Most of what is known about the religion of the Teotihuacáns comes from the religious scenes in their art. An exception is human sacrifice, which was definitely practiced in Teotihuacán, but does not have a significant place in the city's artwork. The remains of sacrificed people have been found in the city's temples.

Arts and sciences

The Teotihuacáns were highly skilled and renowned for their arts. Their artistic style was sophisticated and orderly. It was highly influential and has been found throughout Mesoamerica.

Painted murals lined the interior walls of many of the public and residential buildings of Teotihuacán. Until the last few centuries of the city's existence, most of the murals depicted religious subjects and included pictures of the various gods—Spider Woman, the feathered serpent god, and the rain god—or symbols from the Teotihuacán religion, such as jaguars, butterflies, or birds. Some of the murals depicted scenes of trade with foreign people who had different physical traits and dress than the Teotihuacáns.

Unlike the Zapotecs and the Olmecs, whose artwork was meant to aggrandize (give more power or influence to) their rulers, the Teotihuacán artists did not bother to create likenesses of the city's rulers or warriors in their artwork until the latter part of the city's existence. Sometime around 500 C.E., a shift in artistic style took place in Teotihuacán as the military became a stronger force and conquests of new terri-

Mosaics made from precious stones embellish the face of this Teotihuacán mask. © *Christel Gerstenberg/Corbis.*

tory took center stage. The late Teotihuacán art begins to focus on war and elite warriors and priests.

The Teotihuacán artists produced excellent ceramics, specializing in vessels decorated by cutting away areas and then painting them with religious pictures or symbols. Maize and water, the building blocks of life in Teotihuacán, are frequently depicted in religious scenes on ceramic bowls and vases. Ceramic figurines of humans and animals and ceramic incense burners (objects for burning wood and other substances that produce a pleasant odor) were also very popular and used as trade items.

Stone sculpture was another specialty of some Teotihuacán artists who excelled in making masks of jade or other precious stones. Using shells and obsidian for eyes, these masks had an eerie but often very beautiful look of realistic human expression. Teotihuacán artists specialized in chipping obsidian to produce knives and blades as well as figurines. There were hundreds of obsidian chipping shops in the city and their products were a Teotihuacán mainstay in trade.

In building design, the Teotihuacáns were brilliant engineers, but also expressive architects. Even the walls of buildings were works of art. The predominant architectural style was called *talud-tablero,* in which rectangular framed panels with carved designs were placed over sloping walls. The walls of the city, including the enormous pyramids, were painted in bright shades of red and even the streets were whitewashed or polished so everything looked bright and clean.

Although not enough Teotihuacán artifacts with writing have been found to allow experts to decode them, most historians believe Teotihuacán had some basic form of writing using glyphs—figures (often carved into stone or wood) used as a symbol to represent words, ideas, or sounds. Like most Mesoamericans, they used the 260-day sacred calendar to track time. The 260-day calendar was composed of 20 consecutive day-names combined with the numerals 1 to 13. For example, a given day such as 3 Jaguar was formed of two parts: the numeral 3 with the day-name Jaguar. With the 20 day-names and 13 numerals there was a possibility of 260 combinations before the calendar would have to repeat a combination.

For numerals the Teotihuacáns used the bar-and-dot system, in which a bar represented the number 5 and a dot represented the number 1. Thus one bar with three dots would signify the number 8. Evidence further indicates the Teotihuacáns, particularly their scholarly priests, were highly skilled in astronomy.

Decline

From its peak as the largest and most influential city of Mesoamerica in the fifth and sixth centuries, Teotihuacán quickly fell in the seventh century—some say around 650 C.E. Around this time, a fire swept the city. The fire may have been accidental, due to an invasion by enemies, or a strike against the ruling powers from within. The economy may have declined because of bad weather or competition, and perhaps the city's people lost faith in their leaders.

After the initial fire, the people of Teotihuacán began to abandon the city in large numbers. From about 750 C.E. the people who remained participated in ceremonial burnings of the city's temples and monuments. No one tried to restore the destroyed buildings. Before long, the once-great city lay in ruins.

For More Information

Books

Adams, Richard E.W. *Ancient Civilizations of the New World.* Boulder, CO: Westview Press, 1997.

Coe, Michael D. *Mexico: From the Olmecs to the Aztecs,* 4th ed. London and New York, Thames and Hudson, 1994.

Fagan, Brian M. *Kingdoms of Gold, Kingdoms of Jade.* London and New York: Thames and Hudson, 1991.

Sabloff, Jeremy A. *The Cities of Ancient Mexico: Reconstructing a Lost World,* revised ed. London and New York: Thames and Hudson, 1997.

Web Site

Schuster, Angela M.H. "New Tomb at Teotihuacán." *Archaeology, Online Features.* http://www.archaeology.org/online/features/mexico/ (accessed on October 7, 2004).

Mystery of the Maya

19

When the Spanish conquistadores (Spanish word for "conquerors") arrived in the Americas at the beginning of the sixteenth century, they found a people known as the Maya (pronounced MY-uh) living on the Yucatán peninsula (a large area separating the Caribbean Sea from the Gulf of Mexico, which includes the nation of Belize, the Petén territory of northern Guatemala, and the southeastern Mexican states of Campeche, Quintana Roo, and Yucatán). These lands had been the home of Maya people for thousands of years.

At the time of the Spanish conquest there were hundreds of Maya villages and towns, but the magnificent cities of earlier days—Tikal in northern Guatemala, Copán in northern Honduras, and Palenque, in Chiapas, Mexico, as well as Chichén Itzá (pronounced chee-CHEN eet-SAH) and Mayapán in the Mexican state of Yucatán—had long been abandoned. The once-great Maya civilization had fallen centuries before.

In the years after the conquest of Mesoamerica, the ruins of the ancient Maya were largely forgotten. Some were known to a few experts. Early Spanish conquerors and missionaries reported on the spectacular ruins of some ancient Maya cities, but their reports were largely ignored. Maya descendents living near old ruins certainly knew of their existence, but rarely shared this information. The tropical forests engulfed most of the ruins, and the great Maya civilization seemed to disappear.

Rediscovering ancient Maya cities

In 1839 John Lloyd Stephens (1805–1852), a U.S. travel writer and lawyer with a fascination for ancient sites, arranged a trip to Central America with his friend and partner, English architect and artist Frederick Catherwood (1799–1854). The two men had heard rumors of mysterious ancient temples hidden deep within the rain forests (dense, tropical woodlands that receive a great quantity of rain throughout the year) and were determined to find them.

Landing at Belize, Stephens and Catherwood made their way to Guatemala and then traveled by mule across difficult mountain passages to reach the rain forests of northern

and have more power and privileges than others.

Glyph: A figure (often carved into stone or wood) used as a symbol to represent words, ideas, or sounds.

Highlands: A region at high elevation.

Lowlands: An area of land that is low in relation to the surrounding country.

Malaria: A infectious disease transmitted by mosquitoes, causing chills and fever.

Prehistory: The period of time in any given region, beginning with the appearance of the first human beings there and ending with the occurrence of the first written records. All human history that oc-curred before the existence of written records is considered prehistoric.

Rain forest: Dense, tropical woodlands that receive a great quantity of rain throughout the year.

Stela: A stone pillar carved with images or writing, often used to provide historical details or for religious or political purposes.

Yucatán: A peninsula separating the Caribbean Sea from the Gulf of Mexico, which includes the nation of Belize, the Petén territory of northern Guatemala, and the southeastern Mexican states of Campeche, Quintana Roo, and Yucatán. Yucatán is also the name of a state of Mexico, in the northern portion of the Yucatán peninsula.

Honduras. It was an exhausting trip, traveling through the overgrown, steamy, mosquito-infested tropical jungles. Finally, they reached a small and very humble Amerindian (an indigenous, or native, person from North or South America) village called Copán.

The people of the village told them about a nearby site where there were many piles of stones. Stephens and Catherwood asked some locals to take them there. When they came upon the massive ruins of the ancient Maya city of Copán, with its intricately carved pyramids, sophisticated architecture, and monuments adorned with what appeared to be some kind of picture writing, they were amazed.

Stephens wrote, as quoted in *Early Archaeology in the Maya Lowlands:*

> *The City was desolate. No remnant of this race [the ancient people of Copán] hangs around the ruins, with the traditions handed down from father to son and from generation to genera-*

Maya ruins at Copán, Honduras. © *Tonay Arruza/Corbis.*

tion. It lay before us like a shattered bark [ship] in the midst of the ocean, her masts gone, her name effaced [erased], her crew perished, and none to tell whence she came ... the place where we were sitting, was it a citadel [fortress] from which an unknown people had sounded the trumpet of war? Or a temple for the worship of the God of peace? Or did the inhabitants worship idols made with their own hands and offer sacrifices to the stone before them? All was mystery, dark impenetrable mystery, and every circumstance increased it.

The two men spent many days among the great stone monuments of the ancient city of Copán—Stephens writing his observations and Catherwood drawing exact copies of the architecture and stone carvings. The jungle made these tasks almost impossible. The mosquitoes devoured them and the heavy vegetation blocked their light and access to monuments. Nonetheless, utterly fascinated with the ancient city, the two men kept at their work.

After their stay at Copán, Catherwood and Stephens searched for other ruins and encountered the ancient city of

Palenque in Chiapas, Mexico. Again, their keen enthusiasm was dampened by the extremely harsh conditions—sweltering heat and humidity, torrential rains, snakes, scorpions—awaiting them each day. They left Palenque for Uxmal (pronounced oosh-MAHL), an ancient site in the Mexican state of Yucatán. There, Catherwood collapsed from malaria (an infectious disease transmitted by mosquitoes, causing chills and fever) and the two had to return to the United States.

Back in New York Stephens wrote and Catherwood illustrated a book chronicling their amazing finds. The two-volume *Incidents of Travel in Central America, Chiapas, and Yucatán* appeared in 1841, taking the world by storm. Most scholars and the public were surprised there had been such a highly sophisticated civilization in Central America. Most historians at the time believed civilization was an Old World (Eastern Hemisphere) invention. They viewed the native peoples of Central America with a good deal of prejudice and had trouble believing that Maya ancestors had been re-

Palenque, nestled amidst the harsh tropical jungles of Chiapas, Mexico. *The Library of Congress.*

sponsible for great advances similar to those of ancient Egypt and Greece.

Stephens and Catherwood returned a year later to the Maya world, this time observing ruins at Uxmal, Tulúm, and about forty other sites in the Yucatán. In 1843 they published another very popular two-volume book set about their expedition. It would be their last trip to the ancient Maya sites, but their discoveries had a profound impact on the field of archaeology (the scientific study of digging up and examining artifacts, remains, and monuments of past human life) as a whole. These two amateur archaeologists had introduced the public to the forgotten world of the Maya.

After Catherwood and Stephens paved the way, many explorers traveled to Central America to observe and write about the Maya ruins. Fifty years later, from 1891 to 1895, the first real archaeological excavation (digging up and examining artifacts, remains, and monuments of past human life by experts in the field) of a Maya site took place at Copán. Decades later, from 1926 to 1937, a groundbreaking excavation of the Uaxactún (pronounced wah-shahk-TOON) ruins in the southern lowland (area of land that is low in relation to the surrounding country) region of Guatemala provided information on when and where the cities of the Maya civilization flourished. Universities around the world began to study the Maya and experts began to uncover this magnificent, sophisticated, and long-lasting civilization.

Who were the Maya?

The Maya have lived continuously in the vast Maya regions of Mesoamerica from about 3000 B.C.E. or earlier, right up until today. The Maya had many cultures (arts, language, beliefs, customs, institutions and other products of human work and thought shared by a group of people at a particular time) and never joined together in a unified state. The common people were, for the most part, farmers living in rural areas. During the long history of Maya civilization, a series of powerful and highly sophisticated independent city-states (independent self-governing communities consisting of a single city and the surrounding area) and small cities rose and fell.

Experts believe about four thousand years ago there was a single Mayan language, which they call Proto-Mayan. The

Proto-Mayan-speaking people separated into groups with distinct cultures and, over the years, at least thirty-one distinct Mayan languages developed. These languages were related to each other, but the groups of people who spoke them were always politically independent of each other and sometimes even at war with one another.

Mayan languages were so different from each other that someone from one Maya group could not understand the language of a person from another group. Some of these Maya groups and languages were: Yucatec, Itzá, Lacandón, Mopan, Chorti, Chontal, Chol, Cholti, Tzotzil (pronounced so-TSEEL), Tzeltal (pronounced sel-TALL), Coxoh, Tojolabal, Chuj, Jacaltec, Kanhobal, Mocho, Tuzantec, Mam, Aguacateca, Huaxtec, Ixil, Quiche, Tzutuhil, Cakchiquel, Uspantec, Achi, Pocomam, Pocomchi, and Kekchi. All of these groups, though distinct, shared religion, arts, and traditions and had similar forms of government.

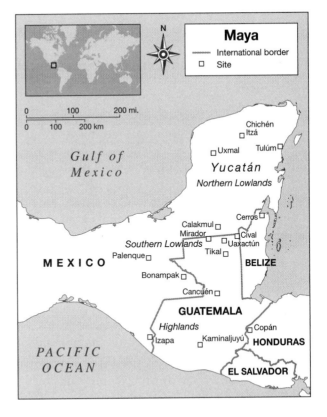

Map showing the major sites of Maya civilization in Mesoamerica. *Map by XNR Productions. The Gale Group.*

Name variations and pronunciation

The word "Maya" (pronounced MY-uh) is used as both noun and adjective. It is appropriate to speak, for example, of the Mayas or of a Maya monument. The word "Mayan" refers to the language.

Dates of predominance and location

El Mundo Maya (Spanish for "the Maya world"), was a vast area of about 200,000 square miles (518,000 square kilometers) located mainly on the Yucatán peninsula, a peninsula (a large body of land extending out into the water) that separates the Caribbean Sea from the Gulf of Mexico. On the

A Note about Rain Forests

Most of the Maya civilization arose in rain forest areas. A rain forest is a dense, tropical woodland area that receives a great quantity of rain throughout each year. It is made up of trees with large, broad leaves that form a tent over the entire forest. Under this tent covering, rain forests maintain an even climate—the hot and very humid climate of the tropics—becoming natural greenhouses. Many different kinds of plants can be grown, and all kinds of exotic animals can thrive. The soil, however, is usually poor so only plants with highly developed root structures will survive. It is extremely difficult to clear rain forest land for farming.

The hardships encountered by Stephens and Catherwood in their trips to the Maya world were only small examples of how difficult it is for humans to exist in the environment where the Maya built their world. Throughout history, few civilizations were built in the jungle, but almost all of the Maya's large, urban centers were located in the tropical rain forests.

According to Richard Hooker, as quoted from his Web site *Civilizations in America,* the tropical rain forests were a very significant factor in the shape of Maya civilization:

> *While plant and animal growth seems almost out of control and the rains never stop, tropical rain forest makes extremely poor agricultural land. As a consequence, a greater amount of area is required to support each person—this encourages population dispersal [spreading out] rather than the concentration [gathering together] necessary to do things like build cities and temples and such.*
>
> *It has been estimated that there were never more than 30 people* per *square mile during the Classic period. So the Maya accomplishment is truly awe-inspiring! With a difficult life, with heat and humidity that would melt the hardiest North American, and with a very sparse population, the Mayas built incredibly sophisticated urban centers.*

The Mayas, like other Mesoamericans, built tall pyramids and other massive structures without the benefit of the wheel or beasts of burden (animals to help with work). In rain forest terrain, though, the wheel would have been quite useless.

peninsula are the southeastern Mexican states of Campeche, Quintana Roo, and Yucatán; the nation of Belize; and the northern Guatemalan state of El Petén. The Maya world extends beyond the peninsula into the western portions of Honduras and El Salvador and into the Mexican states of Chiapas and Tabasco as well.

Modern historians divide the history of Maya societies prior to the invasion of the Spanish in the 1500s into three eras. During each of these eras, the predominant or most important centers of Maya civilization changed regions, as follows:

- Pre-Classic era: c. 2000 B.C.E. to 250 C.E.—predominant centers were in the southern region, often called the southern highlands (region at high elevation), an area consisting of the highlands in Guatemala extending to the Pacific Coast, the western part of the Mexican state of Chiapas, and the eastern part of El Salvador.

- Classic era: c. 250 to 900 C.E.—major urban centers were in the southern lowlands, particularly in the area surrounding the Guatemalan state of Petén.

- Post-Classic era: 900 to 1521 C.E.—major urban centers were in the northern lowlands of the present-day Mexican state of Yucatán.

The dense rainforest region of Mexico's Yucatán.
Photograph by Kelly A. Quin.
Copyright © Kelly A. Quin.

Not prehistory, but ...

Of all the fascinating artifacts (items made by humans, such as tools or weapons) left behind by the ancient Maya civilization, perhaps none have held so much interest as the glyphs (figures used as symbols to represent words, ideas, or sounds) found carved into stone monuments and artwork or written in ink in books (see Chapter 22 for more information). The Mayas had a highly sophisticated system of writing and were avid recorders of their own history. Even their calendar system was extremely accurate. So why, with such an advanced system of writing in place, is Maya history so frequently studied as prehistory? (Prehistory is the period of time in any given region, beginning with the appearance of the first human beings there and ending with the occurrence of the first written records. All human history that occurred before the existence of written records is considered

A trademark of the Maya civilization is its glyphs, often carved into stone monuments. © Kevin Schafer/Corbis.

prehistoric.) To answer this question, it is necessary to consider some of the effects of the Spanish conquest.

The Bishop Landa

In 1546, after a bitter fight, the Spanish occupied most of the Yucatán. Their treatment of the Mayas was often cruel; some were enslaved or forced into hard labor. The Spanish wanted the land, the gold and precious gems, and to use the Amerindians as slaves. They also wanted to convert the Mayas to Christianity. Many Spanish of the day believed the best way to convert non-Christians to Christianity was to erase their culture and traditions—by brutal force, if necessary.

In 1549 a missionary (someone who works to spread religious beliefs) named Diego de Landa (1524–1579) arrived in the Yucatán, taking up residence in a monastery in the new Spanish capital, Mérida. Like other missionaries, Landa believed it was necessary to wipe out the Maya heritage and culture in order to convert the Mayas to Christian beliefs. He was ruthless in his pursuit of this goal, beginning with the destruction of hundreds of sacred Maya shrines.

After Landa became the head of the monastery in 1562, he learned some Mayas in a village called Mani were still practicing their traditional religion. Landa had the people of the village put in a prison where they were tortured, and some mutilated, to get them to confess their "sins." Many died on this terrible day.

As Landa knew, Maya writing was not limited to stone monuments. The Mayas also had beautiful handwritten books called codices (plural of the word "codex"), many of which had been passed down over the generations. The paper for these codices was made from the inner bark of fig trees and then treated with a lime coating. A Maya scribe wrote columns of glyphs on a long strip of this paper with a brush dipped in ink. When the book was done, the paper was folded like an accordion to form pages. Scholars believe these codices contained vast amounts of Maya learning and culture, including history, sciences, literature, and religion.

After Landa had persecuted the people of Mani for practicing their religion, he rounded up all the Maya codices that could be found and threw them into a huge bonfire. In this raid and later ones, it is believed Landa destroyed several thousand Maya books. His own description of this act (as quoted by Brian M. Fagan in *Kingdoms of Gold, Kingdoms of Jade,* 1991) has become known as an example of the worst kind of intolerance and zealotry (fanaticism, or an excess of eagerness in the pursuit of a goal): "We found a great number of books in these characters [Maya glyphs] and, as they contained nothing in which there was not to be seen superstition and lies of the devil, we burned them all, which they [the Mayas] regretted to an amazing degree and caused them affliction."

Only three (or possibly four) Maya codices survived Landa's religious purge. If more of the codices had survived, the books probably would have revealed many details of the Maya civilization. Oddly, Landa's writings, long overlooked, have become one of the sources to which scholars now turn for clues about Maya writing. Landa thought he would be

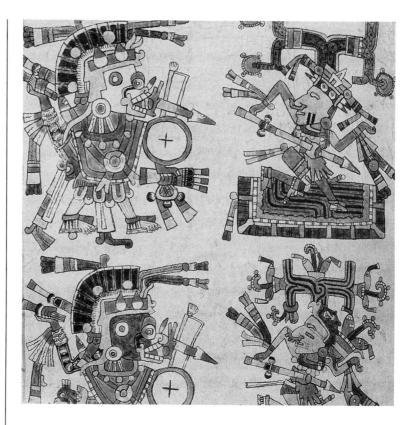

more effective in his efforts to destroy the Maya culture if he knew more about his target. He began studying the Yucatec language as soon as he arrived in the Yucatán and learned to speak it fluently.

Landa interviewed the locals about their ways of life, their language, and their system of writing. He even attempted to create an alphabet to write down the Mayan language by asking Maya scribes to write symbols to correspond to each of the sounds of the Spanish alphabet. His book about the Maya, *Relación de las Cosas de Yucatán* (1566; roughly translated as "History of Yucatán Things") is full of accounts of the culture as described by people who lived it before the Spanish conquest.

Landa's book also provided some of the greatest clues for deciphering the few Maya glyphs available to historians. Ironically, the man who was most responsible for destroying Maya literature was also partially responsible for its eventual translation by scholars and historians.

The glyphs today

The relentless efforts to convert the Mayas and force them to accept European ways, the destruction of the Maya codices and the looting of their shrines prevented the Maya's written history from enduring after the conquest. Since the days of Stephens and Catherwood's expedition, archaeologists have found about eight hundred different glyphs on stelae (plural of stela; stone pillars carved with images or writing, often used to provide historical details or for religious or political purposes) and other carvings. These remained largely undeciphered (no one was able to read them) for many years. Then, in the 1980s, experts began to crack the Maya code, finally reading a number of the glyphs and opening the door to Maya recorded history.

By the end of the 1990s scientists were able to translate much of the Maya writing that still exists today. The insight gained by reading these documents, many of which present histories of Maya rulers and their deeds, has caused scientists once again to change some of their views about the Mayas. It is important to remember, though, that only the elite (a group of people within a society who are in a socially superior position and have more power and privileges than others) Mayas could write. Most scholars believe the kings frequently required their scribes to write history in a way that justified their power and glorified their deeds. Both archaeological excavations and deciphering Maya codes have continued into the twenty-first century, and will slowly solve some of the many mysteries Stephens and Catherwood uncovered more than 150 years ago.

For More Information

Books

Fagan, Brian M. *Kingdoms of Gold, Kingdoms of Jade: The Americas before Columbus.* London and New York: Thames and Hudson, 1991.

Galvin, Irene Flum. *The Ancient Maya.* New York: Benchmark Books, 1997.

Henderson, John S. *The World of the Ancient Maya,* 2nd ed. Ithaca and London: Cornell University Press, 1997.

Meyer, Carolyn. *The Mystery of the Ancient Maya,* revised ed. New York: Margaret K. McElderry Books, 1995.

Web Sites

"Early Archaeology in the Maya Lowlands." *University of California.* http://id-archserve.ucsb.edu/Anth3/Courseware/History/Maya.html (accessed on October 18, 2004).

Hooker, Richard. "Civilizations in America: The Mayas." *World Civilizations, Washington State University.* http://www.wsu.edu/~dee/CIVAMRCA/MAYAS.HTM (accessed on October 18, 2004).

The Rise and Fall of Maya Cities

20

The Mayas (pronounced MY-uhs) were never a single group of people. The amazing fifteen-hundred-year civilization consisted of multiple groups who shared religion, arts, writing, scientific advances, and many other cultural traits, but who never lived under one unified government. Rather, the Maya civilization consisted of the rise and fall of a series of independent city-states (independent self-governing communities consisting of a single city and the surrounding area) and smaller cities, each with its own line of rulers. There were many Maya histories rather than just one.

The huge 200,000-square-mile (518,000-square-kilometer) region that makes up the Maya world has remained their home for thousands of years, but throughout history different regions flourished at different times. Large cities like Tikal in the Petén area of Guatemala or Chichén Itzá (pronounced chee-CHEN eet-SAH) in the present-day Mexican state of Yucatán were extremely influential for hundreds of years and then were abandoned.

When the cities of the Petén area were abandoned at the end of the Classic era around 900, a portion of the Maya popula-

Words to Know

Bajo: The Spanish word for "under," referring to lowlands or swampy depressions in the earth's surface. In a rain forest, *bajos* are generally wetlands from July to November and dry the rest of the year.

Cenote: Underground reservoirs or rivers that become accessible from above ground when cave ceilings collapse or erode.

Ceremonial centers: Citylike centers usually run by priests and rulers, in which people from surrounding areas gathered to practice the ceremonies of their religion, often at large temples and plazas built specifically for this purpose.

Chiefdom: A social unit larger and more structured than a tribe but smaller and less structured than a state, which is mainly governed by one powerful ruler. Though there are not distinct classes in a chiefdom, people are ranked by how closely they are related to the chief; the closer one is to the chief, the more prestige, wealth, and power one is likely to have.

City-state: An independent self-governing community consisting of a single city and the surrounding area.

Conquistador: The Spanish word for "conqueror"; in English, the word usually refers to the leaders of the Spanish conquests of Mesoamerica and Peru in the sixteenth century.

Equinox: The two times each year—March 21 and September 23—when the sun crosses the equator and day and night are of equal length.

Glyph: A figure (often carved into stone or wood) used as a symbol to represent words, ideas, or sounds.

Observatory: A building created for the purpose of observing the stars and planets.

Rain forest: Dense, tropical woodlands that receive a great quantity of rain throughout the year.

Ritual: A formal act performed the same way each time, usually used as a means of religious worship by a particular group.

Solstice: The two times each year—June 21 and December 21—when the sun is farthest from the equator and days and nights are most unequal in length.

Stela: A stone pillar carved with images or writing, often used to provide historical details or for religious or political purposes.

tion moved to the northern Yucatán. The great Maya cities, however, were principally ceremonial centers, places designed for people to gather to practice their religion, often at large temples and plazas built for this purpose. The rulers, priests, and their staffs lived within the city, but the common people did not. Frequently, farming communities that supported large cities remained in place even after the city was abandoned.

Pre-Classic era: c. 2000 B.C.E. to 250 C.E.

The earliest evidence of Maya civilization is found around 2000 B.C.E., generally in the southern region, which is often called the southern highlands (a region at high elevation). This area consists of the highlands in Guatemala extending to the Pacific Coast, the western part of the Mexican state of Chiapas, and the eastern part of El Salvador. Because of its altitude, this region is significantly cooler than the other two Maya regions. The highlands feature many large lakes and have ample wildlife and natural resources.

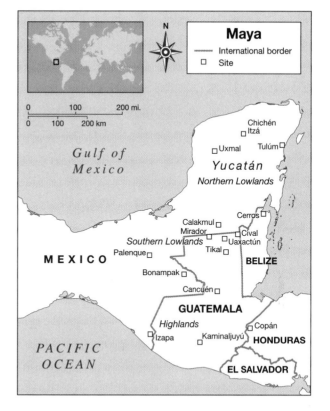

The highlands area was strongly influenced by the Olmec (pronounced OLE-meck). Toward the end of the pre-Classic era, major cities began to develop in the southern lowlands (an area of land that is low in relation to the surrounding country) particularly in the area surrounding the Guatemalan department (state) of Petén. These included Cival and El Mirador (pronounced MEER-a-door) in Guatemala as well as Cerros in Belize and Kaminaljuyú (pronounced kah-mee-nahl-hoo-YOO) in highland Guatemala.

Map showing the major sites of Maya civilization in Mesoamerica. *Map by XNR Productions. The Gale Group.*

Cival

Excavations beginning in 2001 at Cival, a site in the Guatemalan state of Petén, have revised views about the chronology of the rise of Maya civilizations. Historians had long believed that the pre-classic Mayas—those living before 250 C.E.—were simple folk living in farming villages, without the sophistication of the Olmecs, Zapotecs, and Teotihuacáns (pronounced TAY-uh-tee-wah-KAHNS) who were building cities in other Mesoamerican areas.

Historians previously thought it was only in the Classic era (250–900 C.E.), with the rise of cities like Tikal and Palenque, that the Mayas rose to the height of their great civilization. Reports from Cival and El Mirador, as well as other towns and cities in Petén have shown this to be an error.

Cival thrived as a ceremonial center and city in the years 150 B.C.E. (or possibly well before that) to about 100 C.E. Recent excavations show the urban center was fairly large—extending about a half mile—and the city probably had a population of about ten thousand. Cival had many of the features of later classic Maya civilization: it was ruled by a line of kings and had highly refined arts, organized religion, and complex monumental architecture that included five pyramids (one nearly 100 feet or 30.5 meters tall), a central plaza, and other buildings and palaces.

Cival's ruling class was also advanced in astronomy (study of the planets, sun, moon, and stars and all other celestial bodies). According to archaeologist Francisco Estrada-Belli, who has directed the excavations at Cival, the city's buildings were carefully positioned to face the sunrise around the time of the equinoxes (the two times each year—March 21 and September 23—when the sun crosses the equator and day and night are of equal length) and the solstices (the two times each year—June 21 and December 21—when the sun is farthest from the equator and days and nights are most unequal in length). Estrada-Belli believed the buildings were used to measure time; the Maya were masters with calendars and measuring time and seasons. These discoveries at Cival prove the most fundamental advances of the Maya civilization preceded the Classic era by several hundred years.

During his excavation at Cival, Estrada-Belli made several fascinating discoveries. Under some stairs inside a pyramid the archaeologist found a huge, 15- by 9-foot (4.6- by 2.8-meter) stucco (plaster or cement) mask carved into the shape of the Maya sun god. The face on the mask had one eye visible, and was surrounded by images of cornhusks, connecting it to maize (corn), which was central to the Maya life. The mask had snake's fangs and a square mouth.

Excavators later found a nearly identical mask on the other side of the stairs; some believe there were probably four masks at one time. The masks were probably placed on opposite sides of the stairs leading into a room where rituals were performed. The masks date back to 150 B.C.E. A stela, or stone pillar carved with images or writing, was found at the center of the pyramid and dated back to 300 B.C.E. On the stela was a carving believed to be the earliest known Maya portrait of a king.

In a recess within one of the pyramid's walls the archaeological team found five jars that seemed to have been smashed deliberately at the time they were placed there. Under one of them there were 120 round and polished pieces of jade, a precious green stone, and five jade axes. These objects date back to 500 B.C.E. and are believed to be artifacts of a ceremony performed as a new king began his reign.

If indeed a royal dynasty had been established as early as 500 B.C.E., it signifies that Maya civilization has been around much longer than has ever been thought. Much more excavation at Cival and in many towns surrounding it will be necessary to find answers to the questions this discovery has raised.

A defensive wall surrounds the city of Cival, indicating that at some point in its history it came under attack from outside. Cival was abandoned about 100 C.E.

El Mirador

The city of El Mirador, deep in the rain forests (dense, tropical woodlands that receive a great quantity of rain throughout the year) in the northern part of Guatemala's Petén area, was the largest of the pre-Classic Maya cities. At its peak, from about 150 B.C.E. to 150 C.E., El Mirador may have had a population of one hundred thousand people. El Mirador covered a 6-square-mile (15.5-square-kilometer) area and is believed to have had the most buildings of any pre-Classic Maya city—about 250 known and probably about one thousand more that have yet to be mapped by archaeologists.

The Mayas of El Mirador built two of the largest pyramids in the Americas. La Danta Pyramid in El Mirador is 230 feet tall (70.1 meters) and El Tigre Pyramid is more than 180 feet (54.9 meters) tall. The latter is set within a notably massive, 57,000-square-foot (5,301 square-meter) complex (about the size of three football fields). Archaeologists have also

San Bartolo

In 2001 archaeologist William Saturno wandered into a tunnel at a small site of ruins called San Bartolo in a very remote and inaccessible part of the Petén region of Guatemala. Trying to escape the oppressive heat of the jungle, he followed the cool tunnel. It brought him to a small room built under an 80-foot (24.4-meter) pyramid. There, by the light of his flashlight, Saturno discovered an ancient but very beautiful Maya mural in excellent condition.

The mural dated back to 100 C.E., making it the earliest Maya wall mural ever found. Excavations have continued at San Bartolo, but so far only a 6-foot (1.8-meter) portion of the mural has been revealed. Archaeologists believe the painting wraps around the entire room. The discovery has been hailed as one of the most important Maya artifacts and many are anxious to see the rest of the mural.

The San Bartolo mural depicts a scene from a Maya creation myth known to scholars only from the artifacts of much later times. A report from Harvard University's Peabody Museum of Archaeology and Ethnology describes the exposed scene as follows:

The principal standing figure is the bejeweled Maize God whose distinctive head shape replicates [copies], albeit stylistically, the foliation [leaves] of the corn plant. Arms outstretched, his hands seem to hold an object still hidden by the fill of the tunnel. The Maize God has turned his head and looks over his shoulder at the woman kneeling behind him, who in turn has her arms upraised. Another female figure with flowing black hair "floats" above her. In front of the Maize God is a somewhat obscure [vague or indistinct] figure of a kneeling man, painted black, and other figures seem to be arranged in a procession-like line at left.

Until the San Bartolo mural was found, there were no artistic depictions of Maya mythology or history, nor any storytelling art dating back to this early time. Scholars were surprised to find such sophisticated art from the pre-Classic era. Archaeologist David Freidel, as quoted in *National Geographic News*, calls the painting a "masterpiece," with "fine-line exquisite details all perfectly rendered." The view of experts about the pre-Classic Maya has been greatly revised by this discovery, which proves that the culture was already highly advanced in these early years.

found some of the earliest known examples of Maya writing in the city.

Experts believe that in its earliest phases El Mirador was ruled as a chiefdom (a social unit larger and more structured than a tribe but smaller and less structured than a state, which is mainly governed by one powerful ruler) and was already well populated by about 400 B.C.E. It was a busy trading center with frequent contact with the highlands, especially in obsidian (a dark, solid glass used for making fine blades and knives). By 150 B.C.E. El Mirador had apparently become a regional center from which a series of very powerful kings oversaw the rule of the city and of the towns and villages surrounding it.

Archaeologists have located more than two dozen towns or settlements near El Mirador that may have been controlled or influenced by its kings, with more settlements in the area yet to be identified. An extensive *sacbe,* or roadway system, connected El Mirador to neighboring towns and centers. For reasons unknown, El Mirador was abandoned sometime before 100 C.E.

Classic era: c. 250 to 900 C.E.

In the southern lowlands, particularly in the area surrounding the Guatemalan department of Petén, the Maya reached the peak of their civilization in the Classic era. This central region also included most of Belize, parts of eastern Honduras, most of the Mexican states of Chiapas and Tabasco, and the extreme southern part of the Yucatán peninsula.

Tropical rain forests spread across the Petén area; the climate is hot and humid and several major rivers flow through the southern lowlands. The region is extremely fertile, with a variety of plants and animals in its forests. Maya cities that flourished during the Classic era include Tikal, Palenque, Copán, Uaxactún (pronounced wah-shahk-TOON), Quiriguá, and Calakmul.

At the height of the late Classic era (600 to 900 C.E.) the total Maya population reached about twenty million. Between 900 and 1000 the populations living in the Classic era cities abandoned them and, in the post-Classic era, many Maya people moved northward up the Yucatán peninsula.

Tikal

There is evidence of human presence at Tikal, a settlement about 60 miles (96.5 kilometers) in northern present-day Guatemala in Petén, as early as 800 B.C.E. During the pre-

Classic years when El Mirador and Cival were at their peak, Tikal was advancing from its origins as a cluster of farming communities. The settlement was built on a series of ridges in the rain forest overlooking the swampy Bajo de Santa Fe. *Bajo,* the Spanish word for "under" refers to lowlands, or swampy depressions in the earth's surface.

In a rain forest, *bajos* are generally wet from July to November each year and dry the rest of the time. Scientists believe the *bajos* around Tikal and other Maya cities of this region were once wet year-round, making them very useful for farming and obtaining other resources.

By the Classic era, Tikal had become the dominant urban center of the region and the largest Maya city ever to be built. At its peak from about 500 to 899 C.E. Tikal probably had a population of about 60,000 or more within the city. The common people, mainly farmers, lived in rural areas surrounding the city; archaeological excavations have estimated at least about 30,000 people lived around the city during peak times. The population of Tikal and its immediate surroundings was probably between 90,000 and 100,000 people, though some believe it was much higher. From its origins as a farming village to its abandonment in about 899 Tikal endured as a community for an unusually long time—at least fifteen hundred years. Tikal covered about 25 square miles (64.8 square kilometers), with its city center taking up about 6 square miles (15.5 square kilometers). Building, of course, took place over hundreds of years.

A complex called the "Lost World" (named after Sir Arthur Conan Doyle's [1859–1930] 1912 novel about a remote jungle where dinosaurs still roamed), though recently discovered, is the most ancient complex in the city. The Lost World is made up of about forty buildings, including the 100-foot-tall (30.5-meter-tall) Great Pyramid, which was built as long ago as 500 B.C.E. The Great Pyramid has stairways on all four sides with large masks mounted over them. One set of buildings in the Lost World is called the Complex for Astronomical Commemoration. This very early construction was built in connection with the movements of the stars. This structure, like the observatory at Cival, was probably created to calculate the equinox and solstice; such astrological observation served as the basis for the incredibly sophisticated Maya calendar system.

At the very center of the city is the Great Plaza, a huge plaster floor first built in about 100 B.C.E. There are several other large plazas, including the East Plaza and the Plaza of the Seven Temples. All of the plazas feature ball courts for playing the Maya version of the Mesoamerican ball game, which was called *pok-a-tok*. Played by teams on a large court, the purpose of the ball game was to bounce a solid rubber ball through a stone ring without using hands or feet. Maya people took the game very seriously, often betting with high stakes—in many cities, the losers of the game were beheaded as sacrifices to the gods.

The Great Plaza was surrounded by the Central Acropolis, the North Acropolis ("acropolis" is a Greek word that means fortress on a hill or high rock), and hundreds of temples and palaces. One building in the city's center is believed to have served as a jail, with wooden bars across its windows. Archaeologists are currently aware of about three thousand buildings in the center of Tikal.

The Great Plaza and view of the North Acropolis and Temple at the ruins of Tikal.
© ML Sinibaldi/Corbis.

It was not until the last few hundred years of Tikal's
history that the enormous temples and pyramids were erected. The tallest of the buildings in the city were the six terraced pyramids with temples built upon their tops. These
were built in the last centuries of the city's existence, between 696 and 766 C.E. The largest of these pyramids, called
simply Pyramid IV, was 230 feet (70.1 meters) high. Built in
720, it was the largest building in the pre-Spanish Americas.

In its earliest years, Tikal began burying its dead at
the North Acropolis, which became a sacred site. As the years
went on, the North Acropolis became the burial site for all
the city's rulers, and their burials became more and more
elaborate, with pyramids or temples built over their tombs.
Temples were constructed on top of existing buildings in a
process that changed the city's skyline over and over. The
pyramids, of course, were only erected for the rulers and
other members of the elite (people within a society who are
in a socially superior position and have more power and priv-

ileges than others). The people who lived in and around the city generally buried their dead under their houses, often placing everyday objects with them to help in their afterlife. Ceramics found with the dead at Tikal are noted for their craftsmanship and beauty.

The stelae. In the city's main core about two hundred carved stone shaft monuments, known as stelae (plural of stela), have been found. Many were once painted red. A large group of the stelae at Tikal were dedicated to specific rulers of the city. These portraits, showing their subjects in elaborate dress, were carved on one side of the stelae.

The sides and the back of the stelae were often carved with columns of glyphs (figures representing words, ideas, or sounds) presenting the history and genealogy (family descent) of the ruler. Scholars believe the Maya of Tikal had been using carved glyphs to write since about 200 B.C.E., but the earliest dated stela to be found in the city so far is Stela 29, dated by its creator at 292 C.E.

The glyphs on the stelae found at Tikal have been interpreted, for the most part, in recent years. They present the history of at least thirty lords of the city. The founder of Tikal, according to the text on some stelae, was Yax Eb' Xook, or Yax Ch'aktel Xok (First Step Shark) who ruled during the first century C.E. His tomb, Burial 125 in Tikal, has been found in the North Acropolis. Rulers of Tikal were defined by a "successor glyph," which counted the number of successions there had been since the first king, Yax Eb' Xook, founded the royal dynasty.

In its early years, Tikal was just one of many Maya cities in the central Maya lowlands, but by about 500 C.E. it dominated the entire region. The stelae tell of major wars, as well as alliances Tikal formed with other cities.

Decline. During the height of the Classic era, Tikal and the city of Calakmul were frequently at war as the two major powers of the lowland Maya. At the end of the ninth century, however, many of the great Maya cities of the central lowlands were deserted by their inhabitants. In Tikal the abandonment was slow and may have been the result of drought (long period with little or no rainfall), climate changes, or the depletion of soil. It is also likely that many of the trade networks that had supported the city moved to the coasts. In truth, no one knows what caused the collapse of the city.

Tikal holds a profound place in the hearts of the Maya people. The word "Tikal" means "place of voices" in Mayan; the name was probably given well after the city's abandonment by the locals who were haunted by the ancient ruins.

By the twenty-first century the rain forests had grown over most of the ancient buildings. From a distance, only the extremely tall pyramids of Tikal are visible; the thick forest canopy hides the rest. The ancient site, though, has captured the imaginations of many over the years. Visiting Tikal in the deep jungle invokes an eerie sensation of the colorful, bustling world that once thrived in its now silent ruins. The site has become a popular tourist spot, and filmmaker George Lucas (1944–) used Tikal's magical presence as background scenery in his 1977 science fiction classic *Star Wars*.

Palenque

Palenque lies upon a ridge in the foothills in Chiapas, Mexico, overlooking the swampy floodplains (plains bordering a river and subject to flooding) of the Usumacinta River and the tropical plains extending to the Mexican Gulf Coast. Palenque was a medium-sized city, much smaller than Tikal. It is thought to be the most beautiful of Maya ceremonial centers, with some of the finest architecture, sculpture, and bas-relief carvings (three-dimensional pictures, usually in stone, wood, or plaster, in which the image is raised above the background).

Although Palenque's history goes back to about 100 B.C.E., it did not become a major population center until about 600 C.E. For the next two hundred years the city flourished under very strong leadership, becoming a dominant force in the Maya world.

Probably the best-known Maya king, Pacal (the name means "shield"), began his rule in Palenque in 615 C.E. Normally, Maya kingship was passed from father to son. In Pacal's case, it was his mother who had ruled the city before him and passed the rule to her son. Pacal justified his unconventional succession to the kingship by claiming his mother was a goddess in human form. As the son of a goddess, he

had an absolute claim to be king. During his long rule, which lasted until his death in 695 C.E., Pacal was responsible for the construction of much of Palenque's grandest architecture—his effort, no doubt, to inspire the people in his city with awe and reverence for his power.

Pacal put great care into the building in which he was to be buried. The Temple of Inscriptions, as it came to be called, was a temple set atop a tall step pyramid. Although Pacal built the pyramid and prepared it for his burial, it was his son, Chan Bahlum, who finished construction of the temple at the top of the pyramid. Within two chambers in the temple, archaeologists found three panels carved with columns of glyphs providing a detailed history of the ruling family of Palenque and the Maya people in general.

The Temple of Inscriptions' panels have the second longest series of Maya carvings known to exist (the longest inscription is found on the Hieroglyphic Staircase at Copán).

Temple of Inscriptions in Palenque—burial site of the Maya king, Pacal.
© *MacDuff Everton/Corbis.*

Ruins of Pacal's palace stand in the background in Palenque. © ML Sinibaldi/Corbis.

A stairway leading from the temple was found in the 1950s and descends into the pyramid and down to Pacal's tomb. In the tomb is Pacal's huge carved sarcophagus (a stone box used for burial, containing the coffin and body of the deceased, or sometimes only the body).

The massive lid of the sarcophagus is carved with a portrait of the king entering the afterlife and glyphs identifying it as Pacal's tomb. The remains of Pacal's body were still inside; he was wearing an exquisite mosaic jade face mask and an entire suit made of jade pieces held together by gold wires. Surrounding him was a collection of jade burial offerings. In addition, the tomb held the remains of several young people who were probably sacrificed to accompany him to the afterlife. Pacal's tomb represents the most elaborate Maya burial discovered.

Besides building his future place of burial, Pacal also began the construction of a set of connected buildings and courtyards on top of a mound called the Palace. Pacal's sons and successors, Chan Bahlum and Kan Xul, continued construction on this complex over the next generations. The Palace may have provided residences for the lords or priests of the city, but most experts believe it housed governmental and religious offices.

The Palace has many rooms, all adorned with fine stone or stucco carvings depicting Maya gods, the rulers of the city, and a variety of ceremonies. The Palace stands out from the rest of the city because of its 4-story square tower. Other notable buildings in Palenque's city center are the Temple of the Cross, the Temple of the Sun, and the Temple of the Foliated Cross. All three are set on top of step pyramids and are adorned with stone carvings, many depicting the succession ceremonies of Pacal's two sons, as each one took the throne.

Like other cities at the end of the Classic era, building stopped in Palenque around 800 C.E. The city itself was abandoned sometime later. The farmers surrounding the city continued to live there for a couple of centuries, but then they, too, abandoned the area. No one knows the reasons for these abandonments. Palenque has undergone intensive excavation, but in the twenty-first century only about thirty-five of its buildings have been examined. An estimated five hundred more buildings lie under the rain forest's thick canopy.

Copán

The ruins of Copán (place of the clouds) are located in a fertile valley on Río Copán, in northwestern Honduras near the Guatemala border. The city, which had been populated since about 2000 B.C.E., was situated on an ancient trade route from the Pacific Coast to the Montagua River. Copán did not become a prominent center of art and ceremony until about 465 C.E. Like Palenque, Copán only had few centuries of peak existence before it was abandoned around 800 C.E.

During these peak years, however, the city made remarkable contributions in the arts, astronomy, and architecture. People often call Copán the "Athens of the Maya world," comparing it to the ancient city in Greece where art and astronomy flourished. Copán was the first city John Lloyd

Stephens (1805–1852) and Frederick Catherwood (1799–1854) encountered in the Maya world, and they believed it was the most important of all Maya cities. (See Chapter 19 for more information on Stephens and Catherwood.)

Copán was never a big city like Tikal. At its height it is believed to have supported between ten and twenty thousand residents. Its buildings are not as extravagant as those in Tikal or Palenque, though Copán artists were masters of intricate stone carvings and glyph texts. Their art, which is found throughout the city, tells a very detailed history of the kings, wars, and other events.

Stelae rise up along the walkways of Copán's Great Plaza. Some stelae are as high as 14 feet (4.2 meters) tall. Most were created as portraits of rulers. Accompanying the carved pictures were glyphs telling the names, dates, and historic details of the rulers portrayed in each stelae.

Copán had come under the rule of a royal family in 426 C.E. Its first king was named Mah K'ina K'uk' Mo' (Great Sun Lord Quetzal Macaw). In 628 C.E. Copán was ruled by Smoke Imix (Smoke Jaguar), a strong ruler who built the city's economy through trade. Many of the stelae found in the Great Plaza refer to Copán's famous thirteenth king, 18 Rabbit, who ruled from 695–738 C.E.

During 18 Rabbit's long rule, the city became one of the Maya's most sophisticated, especially in terms of its glyphic writing, intricate carving and sculpture, and discoveries in astronomy. Although the specific details are not known, 18 Rabbit was captured by the neighboring Maya city of Quiriguá, perhaps during an armed conflict. Though Quiriguá was a smaller and weaker city than Copán, the great king 18 Rabbit was beheaded as a sacrifice to the gods according to Quiriguá writings.

In 749 C.E. the magnificent Hieroglyphic Stairway was built in Copán. It had been started by 18 Rabbit, but was finished by a king named Smoke Shell after 18 Rabbit's death. The Hieroglyphic Stairway has been called one of the greatest ancient achievements in the world. Its sixty-three steps contain more than one thousand individual Maya glyphs, making it the longest inscription of the Maya civilization. The glyphs describe the royal successions and the deeds of

Copán's Altar Q, with its detailed carvings. © *Gianni Dagli Orti/Corbis.*

the city's rulers, particularly in battle. Unfortunately, many of the glyph blocks have fallen from the stairway, and it may take experts a long time to determine their order.

The "golden age" of Copán under its succession of kings was beautifully depicted on a large block of carved stone called Altar Q, an artifact that captivated Stephens and Catherwood in 1839. Carvings of four men appear on each of the four sides of the block. These sixteen figures represent the kings who ruled Copán from 426 to about 820 C.E., seated in the order of their reigns. The kings appear to be sitting on their name glyphs. On one side of Altar Q, Copán's founder, Mah K'ina K'uk' Mo', is seen passing the scepter of kingship to Copán's last king, Yax Pasah.

Set between the founder and Yax Pasah is a glyph representing a Maya date of 6 Kaban 10 Mol, or July 2, 763 C.E., which commemorates Yax Pasah's inauguration as king. By showing the founder of the dynasty handing him his power,

Altar Q proves the absolute right of Yax Pasah to rule. Yax Pasah was the last king to rule Copán. No writings explained what happened to the king, or to the city, which had been abandoned by about 820 C.E.

Post-Classic era: c. 900 to 1521 C.E.

The northern lowlands were particularly prominent in Maya history during the post-Classic era. The region consists mainly of the present-day Mexican state of Yucatán. This part of Mexico is flat, dry, and rocky, with few rivers or lakes. Parts of the region are covered with large rain forests. Maya cities that flourished during the post-Classic era were Uxmal (pronounced oosh-MAHL) and Chichén Itzá.

In the early thirteenth century, Uxmal and Chichén Itzá were abandoned and Mayapán became the Maya's capital of the northern lowlands. By this time the northern lowlands were caught up in heavy warfare. Mayapán collapsed in the 1400s and no great cities replaced it before the arrival of the Spanish in the early 1500s.

Chichén Itzá

Chichén Itzá was a city on the northern Yucatán peninsula, far north of Tikal, Palenque, and Copán. Scholars believe a group of Mayas called the Itzá arrived in the Yucatán in about the eighth century C.E. They discovered three cenotes (underground reservoirs or rivers that become accessible from above ground when cave ceilings collapse or erode) at Chichén Itzá and settled there. In this land where there were no above ground rivers, cenotes were important water sources to Mayas and they were also considered sacred places. From Chichén Itzá the Itzá Maya ruled much of the Yucatán peninsula. The name of the city means "mouth of the well of Itzá."

While Copán, Tikal, and Palenque in the central region to the south flourished during the last two centuries of the Classic era (around 600–800 C.E.), so, too, did Chichén Itzá. The northern city was a center of arts and astronomy, but it also became a very influential religious center. Its buildings—the Red House, the House of the Deer, the Nun-

Ruins of the Temple of the Warriors, at the ancient Maya city of Chichén Itzá.
Photograph by Kelly A. Quin.
Copyright © Kelly A. Quin.

nery and Annex, the Church, the Akab Dzib, the Temple of the Three Lintels, and the House of Phalli—all supported its function as a ceremonial center.

When the cities of the central region began to lose their populations at the end of the Classic era, the people of Chichén Itzá took notice. Maya scholars Linda Schele and David Freidel stated in Martin Gray's *Sacred Sites* Web site:

> In the wake of this upheaval, the Maya of the northern lowlands tried a different style of government. They centered their world around a single capital at Chichén Itzá. Not quite ruler of an empire, Chichén Itzá became, for a time, first among the many allied cities of the north and the pivot [central point] of the lowland Maya world.

Historians report a great change in the culture (arts, language, beliefs, customs, institutions, and other products of human work and thought) of Chichén Itzá around 1000 C.E. At that time the Toltecs, who were rising in power in present-day Mexico, began to have a significant influence on the city and

its surrounding areas. Most experts believe the Toltec influence was due to strong trade and diplomatic connections between the Toltec city of Tula and the Maya city of Chichén Itzá.

During this era magnificent new buildings and plazas were erected in the city, all showing a new look, including Kukulcán's Pyramid; the Temple of the Warriors; the Great Ball Court (the largest known in the Maya world) as well as eight smaller courts; the Group of the Thousand Columns; and the Observatory (Caracol; a place used for observing the stars). The best known among these is Kukulcán's Pyramid, a 75-foot (22.9-meter) tall pyramid. The pyramid was built to observe the movements of the stars. The buildings were situated so that during the spring and autumn equinoxes, the sun would cast its shadow down the main stairway, appearing like a snake making its way down the pyramid's steps.

The Toltec religion spread to the city as well, influencing Maya art and religious practices. Some believe the

Kukulcán's Pyramid in Chichén Itzá was built to observe the movements of the stars. *Photograph by Andrea Henderson. Reproduced by permission.*

scale of human sacrifice rose significantly under Toltec influence, although the Mayas had long been accustomed to the practice. The cenote at Chichén Itzá became one of the central places for sacrifice. People threw their most valuable possessions into the cenote, usually in the hopes of convincing the gods to bring rain to their land.

Human sacrifice at the cenote was probably less common, but a regular practice nonetheless. The bones of children, young men and women, and the elderly have been found in the depths under the opening. The Great Ball Court of Chichén Itzá was also the site of many sacrifices, since the losers of the ball game were usually sacrificed.

There is evidence that violence erupted in Chichén Itzá in the early 1200s. Some of the great buildings and markets were burned. Many scholars believe there was a rebellion among the city's people against its rulers. Around this time the new Maya capital of Mayapán, about 70 miles (112.6 kilometers) west of Chichén Itzá, was formed by an alliance (the joining of two or more people or groups for the benefit of all) of Maya lords in the Yucatán.

Mayapán, a walled city of about twelve thousand, was the capital city of the northern lowlands for the next two hundred years, though it was never as grand in the arts and architecture as prior Maya cities had been. People of Chichén Itzá and the neighboring Uxmal gradually abandoned their cities, either moving near Mayapán or to more rural areas. In Chichén Itzá, the only part of the city that remained active was the Sacred Cenote, to which the Maya made frequent pilgrimages (journeys to a holy place to show faith and reverence).

The conquest

When the Spanish arrived in the Maya world in the early sixteenth century, the Maya were in a weakened state. Their large cities had been abandoned and they had divided into small groups who sometimes fought amongst themselves. Despite these skirmishes, the Maya still put up fierce resistance when Spanish explorer Francisco Fernández de Córdoba (c. 1475–1525) arrived in the Yucatán in 1517. De Córdoba wanted to replace slaves who had died during his travels in Cuba; the Maya resisted and defeated de Córdoba, killing him in battle and forcing his troops to flee.

The Maya victory against the gun-bearing Europeans, however, could not save them from the spread of the terrible diseases these men brought—including smallpox, measles, and influenza. (Smallpox is a severe contagious viral disease spread by particles emitted from the mouth when an infected person speaks, coughs, or sneezes.) The native Mesoamericans had no immunity or resistance to diseases common in Europe. By some estimates, within the next hundred years about 90 percent of the Mesoamerican population had died of disease or were killed in battle.

The Spanish had come to the Americas seeking gold, though the Maya did not have it in vast quantities. For a while, the Spanish troops in Mesoamerica were busy in their efforts to subdue the Toltecs and Aztecs and did not bother with the Maya. Then, in 1526, Spanish conquistador (conqueror) Francisco de Montejo (c. 1479–1548) petitioned for the right to conquer the Yucatán region.

When Montejo arrived, a few Maya chiefs were friendly but most Mayas fled. The Spanish gave chase and the Maya attacked them. Spanish troops killed more than twelve hundred Maya, but the Mayas still did not give up. Though Montejo's expedition was forced to leave the Yucatán, his son renewed the attempt in 1531, taking the city of Chichén Itzá. Once again the Mayas rebelled and the Spanish were forced to flee.

The younger Montejo returned with a larger force in 1542 and set up the Spanish capital city of Mérida. The Maya continued to revolt, but during the next five years the northern Yucatán fell under the control of the Spanish. Mayas in the Petén region, however, resisted the Spanish until 1697, maintaining their own government, culture, and religion. Few expected the Maya could so successfully fight off armed European invaders; only by fierce determination could they have prevailed for so long.

For More Information

Books

Henderson, John S. *The World of the Ancient Maya,* 2nd ed. Ithaca and London: Cornell University Press, 1997.

Meyer, Carolyn. *The Mystery of the Ancient Maya,* revised ed. New York: Margaret K. McElderry Books, 1995.

Montgomery, John. *Tikal: An Illustrated History.* New York: Hippocrene Books, 2001.

Web Sites

"The Early Maya Murals at San Bartolo, Guatemala." *Peabody Museum of Archaeology and Ethnology.* http://www.peabody.harvard.edu/SanBartolo.htm (accessed on October 16, 2004).

Gray, Martin. "Places of Peace and Power." *Sacred Sites.com.* http://www.sacredsites.com/americas/mexico/chichen_itza.html (accessed on October 16, 2004).

Lovgren, Stefan. "Masks, Other Finds Suggest Early Maya Flourished." *National Geographic News,* May 5, 2004. Available at http://news.nationalgeographic.com/news/2004/05/0504_040505_mayamasks.html (accessed on October 16, 2004).

Parsell, D.L. "Oldest Intact Maya Mural Found in Guatemala." *National Geographic News,* March 22, 2002. Available at http://news.nationalgeographic.com/news/2002/03/0312_0314_mayamurals.html (accessed on October 16, 2004).

Maya Religion and Government

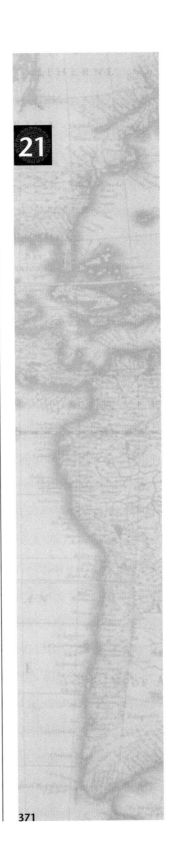

21

Like many pre-Hispanic cultures, the Mayas (pronounced MY-uhs) did not distinguish between religion and government. While they considered the gods to be the rulers of their everyday life, they depended on their mortal rulers to ensure that the gods did not destroy the earth or extinguish the life-providing sun. The Maya religion required a highly complicated worship, including bloodletting and sacrifice rituals often fulfilled by the kings and queens. These efforts were believed to "feed" the gods. The rulers were also believed to have the power to pass in and out of the spirit world, where they could communicate with the gods and ask them to bring prosperity to their people. The Maya kings actively promoted themselves as the descendants of the gods in order to maintain and increase their power over the people. These efforts at persuasion resulted in many of the characteristic aspects of Maya culture, from the towering pyramids to the sophisticated methods of writing developed to record the kings' names and important dates as well as to prove their royal descent stemming from the gods.

Words to Know

Administrator: A person who manages or supervises the day-to-day operations of business, government, and religious organizations.

Charisma: Natural charm and an attractive personality able to persuade, inspire, and win the devotion of people.

City-state: An independent self-governing community consisting of a single city and the surrounding area.

Elite: A group of people within a society who are in a socially superior position and have more power and privileges than others.

Glyph: A figure (often carved into stone or wood) used as a symbol to represent words, ideas, or sounds.

Hallucinogenic drug: A mind- and sense-altering drug that may create visions of things not physically present.

Pantheon: All of the gods that a particular group of people worship.

Primogeniture: A system in which the oldest son inherits his father's position or possessions.

Ritual: A formal act performed the same way each time, usually used as a means of religious worship by a particular group.

Sacrifice: To make an offering to the gods, through personal possessions like cloth or jewels, or by killing an animal or human as the ultimate gift.

Shaman: A religious leader or priest who communicates with the spirit world to influence events on earth.

Stela: A stone pillar carved with images or writing, often used to provide historical details or for religious or political purposes.

Trance: An altered mental state.

Transformation: Changing into something else.

Religion

Government, arts, sciences, and every aspect of daily life in the ancient Maya civilization were determined by the all-encompassing Maya religion. The Maya believed everything in the world had a sacred spirit nature—mountains, rocks, plants, insects, trees, animals, and people. The stars were thought to be manifestations (living symbols or images) of the gods, weather was controlled by gods, and even the maize (corn) that sustained Maya life was represented by a god. The four directions—east, west, north, and south—had gods associated with them; there were gods who reigned over fishing, hunting, weaving, and other daily activities, including gods who represented the days of the month. According to some accounts, there were at least 166 Maya gods.

Most of the deities of the Maya are difficult to identify individually, especially because the names and faces of certain gods varied from city to city. In addition, most of the gods had more than one face or identity. A few of the best-known gods of the Maya pantheon (all of their gods together) are as follows:

- **Hunab Ku:** (pronounced WAHN-ab kwa) According to some, the supreme god and possibly the creator of the human race. Some scholars believe Hunab Ku was created by the Mayas after the Spanish conquest (the Spanish conquered most of the Maya lands in 1542) and the introduction of Christianity. Others think he might be Itzamná, or possibly his father.

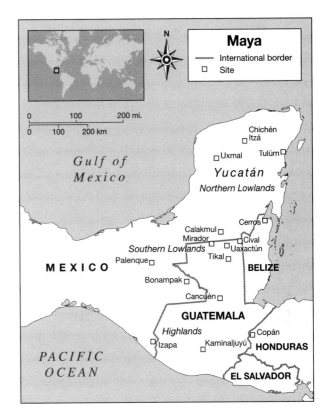

- **Itzamná:** (pronounced eets-ahm-NAH) The supreme god of the Maya, creator of human life, lord of day and night, and the ruler of all gods. Itzamná invented writing and was responsible for Maya science and learning. He was usually associated with the Maya elite (people in a socially superior position who have more power and privileges than others). He was portrayed in two ways: as an old, toothless man with hollow cheeks, and as a reptile. Itzamná was probably the god who came to be known in the post-Classic era as Kukulcán (pronounced koo-kool-CAHN) by the Toltecs (pronounced TOHL-tecks), and as Quetzalcoatl (pronounced kates-ahl-koh-AH-tul) by the Aztecs, or Mexica (pronounced may-SHEE-kah).

- **Ix Chel:** (pronounced eesh SHELL) The wife of Itzamná sometimes depicted as a moon goddess, sometimes as the rainbow goddess. Ix Chel was associated with medicine, childbirth, weaving, and telling the future. She had a mean side, sometimes associated with destruction, and was depicted as an old woman with a serpent in her hand.

Map showing the major sites of Maya civilization in Mesoamerica. *Map by XNR Productions. The Gale Group.*

Large sculpture of the head of the god Itzamná, depicted as an old man.
© Charles & Josette Lenars/Corbis.

- **Kinich Ahaw:** (pronounced KEE-neesh AH-haw) The sun god; often identified as the father of Itzamná. He was frequently depicted as a firebird (a bright red bird with black wings and tail). The Maya believed the sun underwent a heroic transformation (changing into something else) on a daily basis. Every evening when it set in the west, the sun was thought to pass into the underworld (Xibalbá, pronounced shee-bahl-BAH) where it then transformed into a jaguar that navigated the evils of the night. At dawn, the sun was resurrected from the underworld (reborn) as it rose in the east.

- **Chac:** (pronounced chahck) The rain god and the god of the farmers, associated with creation and life. Chac was often depicted with a reptile face and fangs, carrying a lightning axe.

- **Yum Kaax:** (pronounced yoom kAHSH) The god of maize and patron of farmers. Yum Kaax was usually depicted as a young man with an ear of corn growing out of his head.

All the Maya gods had their own individual traits but they were also interconnected, coming from a powerful spiritual force. The gods could be kind to human beings, but they could also be vicious or destructive. The Maya believed the only way to save themselves and their world was to soothe the gods by performing specific rituals (formal acts performed the same way each time, usually used as a means of religious worship) at specific times. The most essential part of Maya life was to make the gods happy. A very complicated system of ceremonial rituals was created for this purpose.

Although the Maya gods were very powerful, they needed people as much as people needed them, and the system between gods and humans was one of mutual generosity. When the gods were happy, they brought rain and sun for crops, allowed human beings to give birth to healthy children, and limited earthquakes, volcanic eruptions, and disease. The gods desired two things only humans could give them—reverence and blood. The Maya showed their reverence individually through prayers and burning incense (substance, such as wood, that emits a pleasant odor when burned) on a daily basis. They also held large festivals to honor the gods, feeding them the blood they craved (see the box on pages 376–377).

The Maya universe

Maya artists represented the universe in three levels: Xibalbá, the underworld; the earth; and the heavens. They usually depicted the earth sitting atop either a turtle or a crocodile in water. The earth was a large, flat square; each

The Epic Tale of the Hero Twins

The myth of the two ball-playing young men known as the Hero Twins was a major cornerstone of the Maya belief system. The Hero Twins appear frequently in Maya art, and the Maya ball game was considered a reenactment of their deeds. The most complete tales of their adventures are taken from the *Popol Vuh* (Book of Counsel), a book presenting the traditional mythology (traditional, often imaginary stories dealing with ancestors, heroes, or supernatural beings, usually making an attempt to explain a belief, practice, or natural phenomenon) of the Mayas.

The *Popol Vuh* was probably written in glyphs (figures used as symbols to represent words, ideas, or sounds) in the Quiche Mayan language (one of the Mayan language groups) long before Europeans arrived in the Americas. Sometime after the Spanish conquest in 1542, someone copied the original book, still in the Quiche Mayan language, but written in the Latin alphabet. The manuscript was discovered many years later in a university library in Guatemala.

The tale of the Hero Twins actually begins with their father, Hun Hunapu (pronounced wan wan-a-PWA) who was also a twin. He and his twin brother were playing the Maya ball game one day and disturbed the Lords of Death by making too much noise. The lords called them down to Xibalbá and challenged them to a ball game. When the twins lost, the lords cut off their heads.

Hun Hunapu's head was placed in a tree, where the daughter of one of the Xibalbá lords found it. When she stretched out her hand to it, the head spit into her hand. This made her become pregnant with the Hero Twins. Escaping from the Lords of Death, she went to live with Hun Hunapu's mother until the twins—Hunahpu and Xbalanque (pronouced shpah-LAHN-kay)—were born.

When the twins became young men, they found the ball gear of their fa-

corner had a specific color. There was also a specific god, called Bacad, who ruled each corner of the planet.

According to the Maya, the heavens were comprised of thirteen layers, while Xibalbá, the dark, watery world below, was comprised of nine layers. At the center of all things was the World Tree. Its roots reached deep into the underworld, its trunk rose up to the earth, and its branches soared into the heavens. The tree demonstrated the Maya belief that the three levels of the universe were interconnected and humans could communicate with the spirit world on

ther and uncle and decided to play. Like their elders before them, they disturbed the Lords of Death with their noise. The lords challenged the twins to come to Xibalbá for a ball game. In Xibalbá the lords put the twins through many tests and ordeals, and in some of them the twins died, but they were able to quickly come back to life. Through their quick-thinking, trickery, and courage, the twins outsmarted the Lords of Death several times. In the end they allowed themselves to lose the game, knowing it was their fate to be sacrificed (offered to the gods).

When the lords challenged them to jump over a fire, the twins jumped right into it and burned to death. The lords, delighted to have finally won a victory, took no chances. They ground the twins' bones into powder and threw the bone dust into a river. At the bottom of the river the bones knit together and transformed back into the living twins. Over and over, the Hero Twins used their magic and wits, al-lowing themselves to be sacrificed in a variety of ways and then coming back to life.

The Lords of Death became so intrigued with the twins' power to defeat death that they asked the twins to show them how it was done. After watching the twins die and come back to life so many times, the lords wanted to try it themselves. The Hero Twins seized the opportunity—they killed the Lords of Death as they had requested, but refused to bring them back to life.

Having defeated death, the twins brought their father and uncle back to life. The Hero Twins then ascended into the sky from the underworld, becoming the sun and the moon, making the maize grow, and bringing balance to the world. Their story brought the message that there is always hope—one may defeat death in the afterlife. Their adventures mirrored the journey of the sun, which disappeared, or died, every night in the underworld and was resurrected each morning to bring light and life to the Maya people.

any of the three levels. This belief was also represented by the worship of caves as sacred portals (doors or gates) leading from the earth to the spirit world.

The Maya religion focused heavily on measuring time. Using earlier Mesoamerican calendars as a base, the early Mayas developed an incredibly accurate three-calendar system. The system combined a 260-day sacred calendar; a solar calendar made of eighteen months of twenty days each, plus five extra days; and a 52-year solar cycle (see Chapter 22 for more information on the calendar system). The primary purpose of these calendars was to determine the proper times to perform rituals and ceremonies to keep the gods happy.

According to the Maya religion, the world had been created and destroyed several times before the present age. Time was viewed very differently than today—instead of running straight forward into the future, it ran in long cycles that would eventually return to their starting points. The ends of these cycles were greatly feared as a time when the gods might destroy the world.

Passing through portals

The complexity of the Maya religion, with its numerous gods and hundreds of rituals, demanded that a group of privileged people spend most of their time learning about the Maya universe and creating ways to communicate with the gods. The people who did this were priests or shamans (religious leaders who communicate with the spirit world to influence events on earth). Most scholars believe these early shamans created the remarkable Maya calendar, numeral, and writing systems. They were also responsible for curing illnesses and healing injuries, listening to confessions, and teaching new shamans. Their most important function, however, was to communicate with the gods—and for this they found several ways to travel through portals and into the spirit world.

The Maya believed every person had an animal companion spirit, a soul identical to his or her own within the body of an animal. The two souls would share the same fate—if the person was killed, the animal would die, and the reverse was true as well. By entering into a trance (an altered mental state), a skilled shaman could transform into his or her animal spirit—good shamans probably had several animal companion spirits—in order to enter the supernatural world.

Sometimes shamans achieved transformations through the use of hallucinogenic drugs (mind- and sense-altering drugs that may create visions of things not physically present) or fasting (not eating for a long period of time). Often, though, the transformations were done along with Maya blood ceremonies.

The Maya believed it was the job of human beings to regularly feed the gods with blood. This was done through bloodletting—piercing one's own skin to draw blood—and

through sacrifice, either animal or human. The Mayas believed if the gods were properly nourished, the world would be in harmony. This demanded pain and sacrifice on the part of humans.

Nobles and shamans performed bloodletting during ceremonies. Males frequently pierced the skin of their genitals, tongues, or ears to draw blood. They used the spines of stingrays (sea creatures with sharp, barbed tails) or knives made of obsidian (dark, solid glass created by volcanoes and often used to make sharp instruments). The blood dripped onto strips of paper, which were then burned. The smoke from the bloody paper was believed to bring the blood directly to the gods, along with the Maya people's prayers.

One famous mural depicts the wife of a king pulling a thorny rope through a hole she has pierced in her tongue. The blood flows out of her mouth and onto paper strips in a basket. Bloodletting rituals such as that were sometimes performed in public ceremonies, in which the viewers could watch as the loss of blood induced a trance in the person spilling his or her blood. While in the trance, the bloodletter was believed to be transporting him or herself into the spirit world to communicate with the gods.

Sacrifice to the gods often consisted of offerings, usually of animals, but of human sacrifice, too. The victims of sacrifice were usually prisoners of war. During Classic times (from about 250 to 900 C.E.), wars were waged simply for the purpose of obtaining captives for sacrifice (the Maya tended not to sacrifice people from their own city). The Maya also sacrificed criminals and children, usually orphans, whom they brought from cities nearby.

There were many methods of sacrifice. None were humane (gentle or caring) and some involved unthinkable kinds of torture. The most common sacrifice method was to paint the victim blue and place him or her on a stone altar, with four people stationed to hold down the arms and legs. With a sharp knife a priest then cut open the chest and reached between the ribs to pull out the victim's beating heart and offer it to the gods. The heart was smeared on carved figurines made in the image of the gods and then the corpse was thrown down the temple stairs.

The practice of human sacrifice was important to Maya beliefs. Despite its horror, sacrifice must have seemed necessary to people who felt it was the only way to influence the powerful forces around them. In the Maya set of beliefs, death was required to sustain life.

The institution of *ahaw* kingship

Sometime in the pre-Classic era, the institution of kingship arose. Prior to about 300 B.C.E. experts believe most

Maya people lived in small, egalitarian societies (everyone had an equal say in decisions affecting the community), with perhaps an elder or the head of a large family providing guidance. Toward the end of this period, the Maya were exposed to people from the grand cities of Teotihuacán (pronounced TAY-uh-tee-wah-KAHN) in the Valley of Mexico and Monte Albán in the Oaxaca (pronounced wah-HAH-kah) Valley. These cities were wealthy and advanced, thriving under the direction of very powerful ruler-priests and select noblemen who claimed to have the power to control the forces of good and evil, could monitor time through their elaborate calendar systems, and could record history as they wished.

Near the end of the pre-Classic era, after 300 B.C.E., the focus of art began to change in some Maya communities, particularly those in the southern lowlands (a region that included the area surrounding the Guatemalan department [state] of Petén, most of Belize, parts of eastern Honduras, most of the Mexican states of Chiapas and Tabasco, and the extreme southern part of the Yucatán peninsula).

While art had previously depicted the gods and religious symbols, it began to focus on specific kings, called *ahaws* (pronounced AH-haw, also spelled "ahau") and their royal family lines.

In particular, portrait stelae (stone pillars carved with images or writing, often used to provide historical details or for religious or political purposes) began to appear in many cities. These featured a carved portrait of the king in elaborate dress on one side, with glyphs representing his name, the important dates of his reign, and other details on the other side. The art signaled a new cult or extreme devotion to the *ahaws;* this intense loyalty formerly reserved for religious figures was instead channeled to one powerful man who the Maya believed descended from the gods and had the power to influence them on behalf of his people.

Soaring city kingdoms

As the power of the kings grew, there was a sudden explosion of building in the Maya cities. The kings were eager to prove their godlike power. The common people were willing to provide the hard labor to fulfill the wishes of the *ahaw,* as this was their chance to please the gods and do sacred work. Most of the big building projects did not have a practical function. Some structures served as ceremonial monuments from which the *ahaw* might appear to his people to perform bloodletting and other rituals. Many were simply to glorify the king with their size and artistry. One grand building would serve as the *ahaw's* burial place.

Many scholars believe the development of the powerful and godlike kingship was a major factor in the spectacular rise of Maya civilization that followed. All across the Maya world monuments rose to the heavens to announce the power of the king who had them built. They inspired awe in his subjects and continue to inspire observers in the twenty-first century. The art, the pyramids, the extravagant royal tombs, the stelae with their glyphs—all were constructed through millions of hours of exhausting human labor for the purpose of demonstrating the *ahaw's* immense power.

The *ahaw* and nobility had a price to pay for all their glory. The *ahaw's* role as ruler was to serve as the living World Tree, connecting the three levels of the universe (the underworld, the earth, and heavens). It was up to the nobility to transform themselves to their spirit form so they could communicate with their ancestors and the gods. On significant occasions, of which there were many, the *ahaw* was expected to pass through the portal between the human and the spirit world in order to ensure the outcome of certain events such as military conquests, the growth of crops, or that the sun would return after a solar eclipse (partial or total blocking of light from the sun when then moon crosses its path).

It was also up to the *ahaw* to feed the gods the blood they required. At public ceremonies, the *ahaw* and often his wife, too, would perform bloodletting rituals. According to Linda Schele and Mary Miller in *The Blood of Kings: Dynasty and Ritual in Maya Art* (1986), "Blood was the mortar of ancient Maya ritual life. Rulers were viewed as descendants of the gods. It was considered their duty to bleed and mutilate themselves on ritual occasions … to cement their divine lineage [family line] and sustain the universe." The *ahaws* not only spilled their own blood, but fasted and prayed to communicate with the gods. If the crops failed or a war was lost, it was considered the fault of the *ahaw*.

By the late Classic period, the *ahaw*s had become extremely skillful in their leadership. They staged spectacular public ceremonies, drawing people from far and wide to witness bloodletting rituals in festivals featuring magic, music, and sacrifice. The lords sacrificed jaguars, dogs, crocodiles, and many other animals, but human sacrifice was the supreme gift to the gods. They dazzled the common people with these huge festivals of splendor and blood that were surely enough to satisfy the gods.

One of the popular festivities the *ahaw*s sponsored was the Maya ball game. The ball game had been part of Mesoamerican life since 3000 B.C.E. Large ball courts shaped like the letter I and measuring about 75-feet (22.9-meters) long and 25-feet (7.6-meters) wide were built for this purpose within the sacred core of every city. Some cities had several courts. The object of the game was to keep a heavy, solid rubber ball in the air without using hands or feet. There were also stone hoops through which to shoot the ball.

The Maya ball game involved hitting a hard rubber ball through this stone ring without using hands or feet. This hoop ring is located in the ball court at Chichén Itzá.
Photograph by Deborah J. Baker. Copyright © Deborah J. Baker.

Perhaps these games were played for pleasure by the nobles of the city. But from the evidence provided in Maya art, the game was regularly used as a ritual that led to human sacrifice. Maya murals depict the game being played between two teams—both teams could be made up of captives taken during warfare, or one team might be made up of captives and the other of the city's noblemen.

The captives forced to play the game were usually nobles, perhaps even the king, of a defeated neighboring city. In the murals, the members of the losing team are forced to become victims of sacrifice, often by decapitation (having their heads cut off). The ball games were seen as reenactments of the tales of the Hero Twins (see the box on pages 376–377) and considered a sacred ritual that celebrated victory over evil and death.

The elite world

The succession of a new king upon the death of the old king was central to the stability of Maya cities. The model for succession in Classic times was primogeniture, a system in which the oldest son inherited his father's position. The success of the Maya *ahaw* system, however, demanded having a ruler who could convince masses of people to do hard labor for the state without being forced into it by the military.

The head of a Maya city needed to have proper lineage as well as charisma—a natural charm and an attractive personality to persuade and inspire people to serve him loyally and without question. Sometimes the more magnetic personalities from the royal families took power. Some royal families created bonds with other cities by arranging marriages among the nobility or royalty, and in some cases, women from the nobility held high offices. In the city of Palenque, for example, two *ahaws* were women.

During the Classic Maya era, the social hierarchy (ranking of people in terms of power, wealth, and prestige) was clear. At the top, there was a king and a small group of nobles. The nobility was a very small group—perhaps 5 percent of the population in the early Classic era. Though the king was generally the supreme ruler over all others, the nobles, too, were considered divine.

Nobles were born into their positions; they ran the governments, ruled cities, led ceremonies, and performed many other jobs. They, too, were responsible for interacting with the spirit world and making sure the gods treated the city and its citizens favorably. In exchange for this, the common people continued to provide unimaginable amounts of labor to build magnificent, massive pyramids, ceremonial buildings, and tombs; to clear jungles for either construction or farming; and to provide food through farming.

From city-state to state

As the city kingdoms became stronger and wealthier during the Classic era, they ruled over larger populations of common people who farmed the lands surrounding the city. Eventually, the larger Maya cities incorporated smaller cities nearby into their rule, becoming city-states.

By the late Classic era, the neighboring cities of Tikal and Calakmul in the Petén region of Guatemala had become regional capitals and ruled over many smaller cities and communities. The Maya lowland civilization had become a patchwork of several very powerful, but independent, city-states that ruled over increasingly extensive areas. The *ahaw* of the large regional centers usually appointed noblemen called *batabs* (meaning axe bearers) to govern outlying cities.

Pyramidal depiction of Maya social organization, with the king and his nobility at the top and the common people at the bottom. *The Art Archive/National Anthropological Museum Mexico/Dagli Orti.*

The end of the Classic era kingdoms

By the end of the Classic era, the numbers of nobility had swelled; they constituted about 25 percent of the population. The nobles served in a wider range of capacities, as regional governors, military commanders, priests, scholars, building project managers, trade regulators, and administrators in the city-state. They lived in luxury and began to build their own stelae, carving their portraits and history into stone, and built monuments and temples for their own burials. Some scholars believe this rise in power led to divisions within the government and weakened the strength of the *ahaws*.

Warfare became widespread as the Classic era drew to a close. For most of their history Maya warriors from one city would attack another only for the purpose of gathering sacrifice victims. But as time went on, the armies of the big city-states became professional and competitive. Though led by nobles, Maya soldiers in the Classic era were enlisted from among the peasants. They were armed with knives, spears, clubs, and shields.

With large trained armies at their disposal, the nobility began to seek conquests. While earlier warfare had resulted in the death of some captured nobles, warfare after about 750 C.E. caused terrible destruction to cities and surrounding areas. Bitter conflicts between cities could last for decades and result in thousands of lost lives and destroyed homes and crops.

By about 900 C.E., the great cities of the Maya southern lowlands had been abandoned. The populations from the cities and some people of the surrounding farmlands moved north to the northern lowlands in the present-day Mexican state of Yucatán. The exact reasons for this desertion are not known and continue to puzzle historians. It is likely overpopulation—too many people for the land and its farms to support—might have been a factor. Inadequate farming might have contributed as well (see Chapter 23 for more information on the Maya economy), since there is evidence severe drought (long period of little or no rainfall) may have destroyed crops. In some cities there is also evidence of violence from either internal rebellion or raids from outside.

Because the *ahaw* and nobility were responsible for making the gods happy, a natural disaster such as a drought or devastated crops would have been considered a failure to perform their duties. This could have caused an uprising among the common people. Starvation could have forced some Maya to leave their cities long before the final years of abandonment. It is likely many factors contributed to the demise of the Classic era's Maya kingdoms.

Post-Classic governments

During the Classic era, while great cities and states like Tikal, Copán, and Calakmul flourished in the southern lowlands of Petén, cities in the northern highlands of the Yucatán were thriving as well. Chichén Itzá (pronounced chee-CHEN eet-SAH), which had been settled in the sixth century, was by far the most powerful of the northern cities around 1000 C.E., but there were other large cities—Uxmal (pronounced oosh-MAHL), Cobá, and Sayil, to name a few.

Influences from other Mesoamerican peoples, particularly the Toltec, prevailed in the northern cities; their art and architecture differed in many ways from cities in the south. Chichén Itzá, with its powerful military, had probably conquered many of the cities in a large area but they joined together without hostility after the conquests. By 1000, there was a strong alliance among Uxmal, Cobá, and Chichén Itzá.

Ruins of Chichén Itzá's Temple of the Warriors. The city, with its powerful military, ruled the northern lowlands during the post-Classic Maya era.
Photograph by Kelly A. Quin. Copyright © Kelly A. Quin.

Chichén Itzá ruled the northern lowlands until about the thirteenth century. Inscriptions on monumental stones at Chichén Itzá relate that the city and its outposts were not ruled by a single *ahaw,* as the southern cities had been. There was apparently a group of five nobles (or possibly more), some or all of whom may have been brothers. These nobles shared the rule of the large kingdom, acting as a supreme council over the strong and expanding military state. Under the council's rule, the cities in the region of the present-day Mexican state Yucatán prospered.

The social hierarchy in the post-Classic era (900 C.E. to 1521 C.E.) was more complex than in the Classic era. There were four basic classes: nobles, priests, common people, and slaves. Nobles were born into their position, and common people were, for the most part, farmers who were required to provide crops and labor to the nobility of the city. Slaves were usually commoners from other cities who had been captured in war. When prisoners were taken during battle, the captives from the nobility were usually sacrificed, while the common soldiers became slaves. Criminals and orphaned children, however, sometimes became slaves as well.

Around 1200 C.E. Chichén Itzá's population began to desert the city for unknown reasons. Many are thought to have moved down to the Petén region of Guatemala—the land of the former Classic civilization. Around this time a smaller city to the west, Mayapán, replaced Chichén Itzá as the capital in the region.

Mayapán was walled, an unusual feature for a Maya city, and an indication warfare was widespread during this era. It had few ceremonial structures, inferior architecture, and was apparently built in a hurry. With rampant warfare, there was little time for feeding the gods, producing great art, writing histories and mythology, and working with the intricate and accurate calendar systems. The hallmarks of the great civilization were rapidly disappearing.

In 1441 C.E. there was a terrible uprising in Mayapán, which destroyed the city. The population of Mayapán scattered; some went to the city of Mani, which became a new capital. Though the Maya survived and went on to new lives, the glory of their civilization was over. About sixteen small city-states remained in the Yucatán area, but they were in constant warfare with each other. When the Spanish arrived only fifty years after the fall of Mayapán, the Maya put up surprising resistance to the invaders, but had been greatly weakened by the recent collapse of their governments.

For More Information

Books

Gallenkamp, Charles. *Maya: The Riddle and Rediscovery of a Lost Civilization,* 3rd ed. New York: Viking, 1985.

Galvin, Irene Flum. *The Ancient Maya.* New York: Benchmark Books, 1997.

Henderson, John S. *The World of the Ancient Maya,* 2nd ed. Ithaca and London: Cornell University Press, 1997.

The Magnificent Maya. Alexandria, VA: Time-Life Books, 1993.

Schele, Linda, and Mary Miller. *The Blood of Kings: Dynasty and Ritual in Maya Art.* New York: W.W. Norton, 1986.

Web Sites

"Early Archaeology in the Maya Lowlands." *University of California.* http://id-archserve.ucsb.edu/Anth3/Courseware/History/Maya.html (accessed on October 18, 2004).

Hooker, Richard. "Civilizations in America: The Mayas." *World Civilizations, Washington State University.* http://www.wsu.edu/~dee/CIVAMRCA/MAYAS.HTM (accessed on October 18, 2004).

Maya Arts and Sciences

22

Maya (pronounced MY-uh) mythology (traditional, often imaginary stories dealing with ancestors, heroes, or supernatural beings, and usually making an attempt to explain a belief, practice, or natural phenomenon) features two brothers, Hun Batz and Hun Chuen, who angered the Hero Twins long ago and were transformed into monkeys. These brothers came to be known as the "monkey scribes," and they were the patrons (supporters) of Maya art and writing—the skills involved in telling the Maya's story. In the ancient Mayan language, there was no distinction between writing and painting; the word *ts' ib* was used for both.

The Maya scribes created writing and artwork on surfaces all over their cities, particularly in the Classic era from 250 to 900 C.E. Some inscribed (carved) the stone pillar monuments—called stelae—in the plazas, door lintels (horizontal structures over doors), stone or stucco buildings and pyramids, thrones, altars, and even jade jewelry; the painter-scribes worked on wall murals and pottery; those who used a pen worked in handmade books known as codices. Glyph-

Words to Know

Astronomer: A person who studies the planets, sun, moon, and stars and all other celestial bodies.

Bas-relief: A carved, three-dimensional picture, usually in stone, wood, or plaster, in which the image is raised above the background.

Codex: A handmade book written on a long strip of bark paper and folded into accordion-like pages.

Decipher: To figure out the meaning of something in code or in an ancient language.

Elite: A group of people within a society who are in a socially superior position and have more power and privileges than others.

Equinox: The two times each year—March 21 and September 23—when the sun crosses the equator and day and night are of equal length.

Glyph: A figure (often carved into stone or wood) used as a symbol to represent words, ideas, or sounds.

Logogram: A glyph expressing a whole word or concept.

Logosyllabic: A mixed system of writing in which some symbols represent whole words or ideas, while other symbols represent the syllables or units of sound that make up words.

Pre-Columbian American: A person living in the Americas before the arrival of Spanish explorer Christopher Columbus in 1492.

Prehistory: The period of time in any given region, beginning with the appearance of the first human beings there and ending with the occurrence of the first written records. All human history that occurred before the existence of written records is considered prehistoric.

Ritual: A formal act performed the same way each time, usually used as a means of religious worship by a particular group.

Sarcophagus: A stone box used for burial, containing the coffin and body of the deceased, or sometimes only the body.

Scribe: Someone hired to write down the language, to copy a manuscript, or record a spoken passage.

Solstice: The two times each year—June 21 and December 21—when the sun is farthest from the equator and days and nights most unequal in length.

Stela: A stone pillar carved with images or writing, often used to provide historical details or for religious or political purposes.

Syllabograms: Symbols that represent the sounds of a language (usually a combination of a vowel sound and consonants).

Vigesimal: Based on the number twenty (as a numeric system).

writing was almost always accompanied by pictures that added to the meaning of the words.

Maya scribes were members of the noble classes and were treated with great respect. According to Michael Coe and Mark Van Stone in their book *Reading the Maya Glyphs* (2001), they did more than create art and writing—Maya scribes probably played a role in society similar to priests, and many may have actually been priests. Priests were responsible for many scholarly activities: observing the stars and planets, creating the calendar systems used by the Mayas for timing religious rituals, seeing into the future, and recording Maya history. All of these functions involved the writing and painting done by scribes.

Scribes and priests formed an elite (people within a society who are in a socially superior position and have more power and privileges than others) and educated group who were gifted thinkers, writers, and artists. The scribes were given a good deal of creative leeway and were encouraged to excel in their fields by the ruling class. In the end, however, the purpose of their work was to glorify the Maya gods and kings.

Map showing the major sites of Maya civilization in Mesoamerica. *Map by XNR Productions. The Gale Group.*

It was in the realm of these elite Maya scribes that the Maya civilization excelled beyond all other pre-Columbian Americans (people living in the Americas before the arrival of Spanish explorer Christopher Columbus in 1492) and many Old World (Eastern Hemisphere) civilizations as well. Though many of the Maya achievements in language, the arts, and science originated in other Mesoamerican societies, no other group put together all the advances so well, or as early, as the Mayas.

Maya glyphs and writing

The Maya glyph system of writing was unique among all the languages of the pre-Columbian Americas in that it could fully reproduce the spoken language. Maya scribes could express abstract thoughts in glyphs without referring to pictures. Their writing reflected the complex grammar of

Deciphering the Work of Scribes

The Maya clearly meant to leave behind full records of their lives, beliefs, customs, and sciences. The scribes had written the story of the Maya everywhere. But between the determination of the Spanish missionaries and conquistadores (conquerors) to eliminate the old, non-Christian traditions and the rapid growth of the jungle forests over abandoned cities, Maya art and writing were lost for centuries. No survivors managed to hang onto the art of reading and writing in the distinctive Maya script.

Attempts to decipher (figure out the meaning of something in code or in an ancient language) Maya glyphs have taken years and are ongoing. British anthropologist J. Eric Thompson (1898–1975) started the process of deciphering Maya writing in the early 1950s when he cataloged all known glyphs into three divisions: main signs, affixes, and portraits. Thompson believed (incorrectly) that all glyphs were logograms. He also believed Maya writing was religious in nature.

Russian linguist Yuri Valentinovich Knorozov (1922–1999), however, argued correctly that many Maya glyphs stood for syllables. Knorozov worked with Spanish bishop Diego de Landa's (1524–1579; see Chapter 19 for more information) "alphabet." Landa had developed this alphabet soon after the Spanish conquest by asking Maya scribes to write down glyphs for the sounds of the Spanish alphabet. With his understanding of Landa's work, Knorozov was able to identify many syllable glyphs. Unfortunately, most scholars ignored him, and Thompson's incorrect views were accepted for many years.

In the late 1950s German-Mexican Heinrich Berlin (d. 1981) added to the un-

the classic Mayan language—an early version of the language used for most reading and writing even after Mayan broke into more than thirty distinct languages.

A glyph is a symbol that stands for either an entire word or for one of the sound units that makes up a word. Glyphs expressing a whole word or concept are called logograms. Scholars point out that if only logograms were used in any writing system, there would need to be thousands of them—too many for the writing system to function properly. Therefore most writing systems included symbols representing the sounds of the language, either by using an alphabet to represent the individual letter sounds, or using symbols to represent the syllable sounds. Glyphs representing syllable sounds are called syllabograms.

derstanding of Maya glyphs with his observation that some glyphs seemed to be place-names referring to specific cities. He called these emblem glyphs.

In the 1960s Russian American archaeologist Tatiana Proskouriakoff (1909–1985) opened the door for decipherment. In a study of glyphs on Stela 14 at the ancient Maya city of Piedras Negras in Guatemala, Proskouriakoff found patterns of dates that never spanned a period of time longer than a human life. Once she correctly guessed that one glyph, which looked like an upside down frog, stood for birth, she was able to identify birth and death glyphs. Using common sense, she went on to identify the name glyphs of rulers, the royal family lineage, details of war and enemy captives, and other historical details written in glyphs on the stela.

In this manner she was able to identify a sequence of glyphs presenting the historical succession of seven rulers spanning two hundred years. Proskouriakoff had provided an essential key to all who followed—that most of the Maya's writing was a recording of their history. From there, many more scholars worked together successfully, cracking the Maya code.

After years of treating the Maya's masterful historians as a prehistoric group (a people whose history occurred before there was writing to record it), archeologists finally had written text to work with. In the last three decades of the twentieth century, most of the Maya glyphs were translated and there are now names and faces for many of the Maya kings and details of the wars, successions, and religious ceremonies which would have been lost forever.

Maya writing was logosyllabic—it used both kinds of glyphs. Many words could be written either way by using a single logogram glyph or by using several syllabogram glyphs to create the sound of the word. For example, if the Maya had a logogram for the word "ladder" it would be a single figure representing the entire word (quite possibly a picture of a ladder). If they wished to write it in syllabograms, there would be a glyph for each of its two syllables, "lad" and "der."

The Canadian Museum of Civilization Corporation's *Maya Civilization* Web site provides another example: the name of the great king of Palenque, Pacal (603–683 C.E.) means "shield." Sometimes to write his name the scribes created a picture of a shield; sometimes they wrote it in syllabograms (pah-ca-la; the final, extra "a" sound at the end of the

| cacao | atole | tamale/bread | honey | turkey tamale |

word is common in Maya writing—the glyph providing the "l" sound is provided by the full syllable "la"), and sometimes it was written as a combination of pictures and sounds.

Archaeologists believe the earliest Maya glyphs date back to about 400 B.C.E. The first known dated Maya monuments were created in the first century C.E. There are about eight hundred known glyphs in the Maya writing system; about five hundred signs were in common use at any given time.

Glyphs are generally square figures with rounded corners. Although some glyphs are made up of only one element or sign, most have several. The largest element is called a main sign, and the smaller ones are called affixes. The main signs are larger and squarer in shape, while the affixes appear to be squashed onto the main sign. Glyphs were usually arranged within a kind of grid (rows and columns in a checkerboard fashion) in double or paired columns running from top to bottom.

On a grid, a reader would start with the glyph in the left upper corner and proceed to the paired glyph to its right. Then the reader would go to the pair of glyphs directly under the first pair, to the pair of glyphs under it, and so on to the bottom. Then the reader would begin at the top again with the pair of glyphs in the third and fourth position of the top row, and go to the pair directly below. As if this were not complicated enough, each individual glyph, with its main element and affix components, had a reading order as well.

The Maya concept of art

Art and writing were considered one and the same in the Maya world. The Maya probably did not think of art in the way most people in the modern world do. For them, art

Carved glyphs adorn this Maya stone slab, or stela.
© *Charles & Josette Lenars/Corbis.*

was not an expression of feelings or a personal statement. Most art fell into one of two categories: historical or religious. Historical art depicted kings taking the throne, the bloodlines of the royal families, particularly the descent of the king from the gods, and battles in war and other triumphant historic events (not the defeats, however). Religious art depicted rituals (formal acts performed the same way each time, usually used as a means of religious worship to make the gods happy), such as human sacrifice, ball games, or bloodletting rituals.

Religious art also depicted the gods and other religious symbols, and gave visual detail to the calendars that dominated Maya life and religion. In the Classic era, art was used to promote the image of the king as a divine or partly divine ruler. In addition, art, like writing, was used to record history. The kings and nobles of the Classic Maya cities in particular tried to make certain that people in future times would know about them.

Stone monuments

The large Maya cities of pre-Classic and Classic times are immediately notable for their huge stone buildings with grand staircases in the front. Most cities had tall pyramids soaring into the skies with brightly painted temples built on top. The pyramids were monuments to the kings who were buried beneath them, often in elaborate tombs with precious jade and stone offerings to the gods.

The plazas, monuments, and buildings in Classic Maya cities were highly decorated, inside and out, with stone carvings of all types, sizes, and shapes. Detailed sculptures of gods, animals, prisoners, and kings stood in the plazas, some made of stone, some made of clay. Bas-reliefs (carved, three-dimensional pictures in which the image is raised above the background) depicting similar subjects lined the walls. Huge carved stone thrones and benches, usually called altars, were another form of monument typically bearing an image of a king or noble conversing in some way with the spirit world.

The age of the stela

One of the main distinguishing characteristics of the Classic Maya era (from about 250 to 900 C.E.) was the stela cult—the widespread creation of carved stone monuments known as stelae. These huge, inscribed slabs or pillars of stone were anywhere from 3 to 35 feet (0.9 to 10.7 meters) tall. Most stelae were carved with the portrait of a ruler or other nobleman dressed in elaborate headdresses and surrounded by symbolic images.

These stelae featured long text passages in glyphs that provided the birth and death dates of the king, as well as relating other information: the history of a significant event involving him and his achievements or some aspect of the city's history. Stelae were a tremendously important form of communication for rulers, who used them to promote and justify their powerful positions within the city-states (independent self-governing communities consisting of a single city and the surrounding area).

All of the great Maya cities had stone stelae commemorating their rulers and historic events, particularly in the late Classic era. The Maya city Copán, in northwestern Honduras near the Guatemala border, is particularly famous for its stelae. The city's Great Plaza is crowded with the elaborately inscribed pillars, most depicting the king known as 18 Rabbit, who ruled from 695–738 C.E. During 18 Rabbit's long rule, the city became one of the Maya's most sophisticated in terms of its glyphic writing and intricate carving and sculpture.

The architecture of Maya cities was adorned with bas-reliefs. *The Library of Congress.*

In 725 C.E., the nearby city of Quiriguá came under the power of Copán. One of its noblemen, Cauac Sky, was appointed by 18 Rabbit to rule the small city. Thirteen years later 18 Rabbit was captured by Quiriguá and beheaded as a sacrifice to the gods. After the death of 18 Rabbit, Quiriguá became a center for beautifully sculptured stelae. One of its stelae, built in 771, is the largest known stela in existence, weighing 65 tons (59 metric tons) and measuring more than 35 feet (10.7 meters) tall.

18 Rabbit was responsible for the construction of the famous Hieroglyphic Staircase in Copán. The giant staircase was comprised of some 1,250 or more blocks inscribed with glyphs. The blocks were arranged on the staircase to commemorate the kings of Copán and their lineage. Unfortunately, the blocks crumbled and fell long before archaeologists found the staircase, and it has been difficult to restore them to their proper order. One of the items the staircase records is the death of 18 Rabbit. A later ruler of Copán,

Smoke Shell (ruled 749–763 C.E.), was responsible for finishing the project. The stairway is believed to be the longest passage of glyph writing in the Western Hemisphere.

The tomb of Pacal, who ruled from 600 to 683 C.E., is in the city of Palenque, located in present-day Chiapas, Mexico. Its intricately carved sarcophagus (a stone box containing the coffin and body of the deceased) lid are an extravagant example of stone images and glyphs commemorating a Maya king. The image carved on the lid is an illustration of Pacal falling into the jaws of the underworld, which is portrayed as a monster. Pacal is shown falling along the World Tree, an important image of the Maya religion.

The World Tree was the center of all things, with roots reaching deep into the underworld, trunk rising up to Earth, and branches soaring into the heavens. The tree demonstrated the Maya belief that all three levels were interconnected and Pacal, as a partly divine king, could travel between Earth and the spirit world. Along with the images on the sarcophagus lid, there were glyphs providing the dates of Pacal's birth and death and his royal family lineage.

Pacal's tomb is located deep beneath the Temple of Inscriptions in Palenque, a temple set atop a tall step pyramid. Within two chambers of the temple, archaeologists found three panels carved with columns of glyphs, which provided a detailed history of Palenque's ruling family and its people. The panels are the second longest inscription (words carved into something) known to exist from the ancient Maya civilization.

Codices

The cities in the southern lowlands that flourished during the Classic era, such as Tikal, Uaxactún, Palenque, and Copán, were abandoned by about 900 C.E. In the post-Classic era (900 to 1521 C.E.), cities in the northern lowlands of Yucatán became the centers of Maya art. Few stelae, however, were found in the northern cities like Chichén Itzá (pronounced chee-CHEN eet-SAH) or Uxmal (pronounced oosh-MAHL); instead artwork and glyphs were found in Maya codices.

The paper for a Maya codex was usually made from the inner bark of fig trees and treated with a lime coating.

Scribes crafted their glyphs and illustrations onto a long strip of this paper with a brush dipped in ink. When the book was done, the paper was folded like an accordion to form pages.

In their attempt to wipe out the Maya religion and its traditions and convert the Mayas to Catholicism, Spanish missionaries—particularly Bishop Diego de Landa—were responsible for burning thousands of Maya codices. Only three or four codices survived, probably because they had been shipped off to Europe before the missionaries got hold of them.

Three of these rare books—the Dresden, Paris, and Madrid codices (all named for the cities in which they are now located)—offer an amazing glimpse into post-Classic Maya life. A fourth codex, called the Grolier, which was found in fragments in Mexico, remains controversial because of its origins. Because the codices were written on paper that could not withstand time and the elements, no other codices have been discovered at Maya excavations. Pictures on ceramics of the Classic era, however, indicate there were codices before 900 C.E., but none have ever been found.

The Maya tradition of commemorating royalty and nobles with art and glyphs disappeared with the Classic era. In the post-Classic cities, priests and scribes used their arts to record the information they needed to conduct Maya rituals in accordance with the Maya calendar. The codices recorded the positions of the sun, moon, and planets and kept track of solar and lunar eclipses (the times when the sun and moon crossed paths and blocked the view of the either the sun or the moon for the people on Earth). These books were called "priest's handbooks" by one scholar. Scholars believe the Maya codices that were destroyed or lost contained vast amounts of learning and culture, including history, sciences, literature, and religion.

Ceramics

Like scribes and stone carvers, Maya potters probably came from the educated elite and were allowed to focus on their arts. They created a great variety of vessels—pots for cooking and storing food; small figurines representing humans, animals, and gods; objects to be placed with a body in

Maya pottery, such as this bowl, was often highly decorated.
© *Bettmann/Corbis.*

its burial; beverage holders, and much more. The process began with finding the right color and consistency of clay, usually located in riverbeds. The clay was mixed with hard elements, such as rocks or sand, to make it stronger. Then it was kneaded by hand until it was ready to be shaped. Some potters would then create long coiled ropes of clay and smooth them together to make the walls of their pottery pieces. After the vessel was formed, it was allowed to dry.

The Maya mixed clays, minerals, and water to create paints for ceramics. Though some Maya artists preferred to paint only in red and black, their paints could be mixed into a variety of colors—orange, red, purple, and yellow. Certain mixtures would turn into the colors of blue and green during the firing process. Many potters carved designs into their creations as well. The decorations of Maya pottery ranged from geometric designs to ritual scenes of sacrifice or bloodletting (see Chapter 21 for more information on bloodletting). Maya glyphs frequently appeared on ceramic pots as well.

Maya scribes and artists wrote on a variety of surfaces and objects. Some of the pottery from the Classic era is covered with long columns of glyphs, presenting some of the most sophisticated writing of the era. One such ceramic vessel, a 10-inch (25.4-centimeter) high rectangular object with sides representing the pages of a book, is called the Wright Codex and dates back to about 600 C.E.

Michael Coe and Mark Van Stone noted in their book *Reading the Maya Glyphs* that the text on classic Maya ceramics had "the subtlety and complexity of what may have once been contained in the now-disappeared Maya books of the Classic period." They also observed that some of this text records the speech of real people, whether a statement by one person or a dialogue between two.

Painted murals

Two sets of Maya painted murals had been found by the early twenty-first century. The famous set of three room-sized murals at Bonampak were found in the 1940s in Chiapas, Mexico. The murals at Bonampak are unique among Maya art in that they depict everyday scenes. These beautifully painted murals date back to about 800 C.E. and have given archaeologists and historians a great deal of information about the details of Maya existence—clothes, music, rituals, courtly life, war, sacrifice, and much more. The three murals, when viewed together, tell a story that moves forward in time (see the box on pages 404–405).

More recently, a far earlier mural was found in the tiny city of San Bartolo in Guatemala dating back to 50 B.C.E. Although the excavation is not yet complete and only portions of the mural have been exposed, the mural appears to be a skillfully painted portrayal of Maya mythology as ex-

The Bonampak Murals

In the eastern part of the Mexican state of Chiapas, a group of Maya people known as the Lacandón have managed to live in relative isolation from the modern world, still practicing many of the ancient Maya traditions (see Chapter 23 for more information on the Lacandón). The Lacandón made pilgrimages (journeys to sacred places) to the ancient ruins known in the twenty-first century as Bonampak, which remained unknown to the rest of the world until the 1940s. There is much controversy about who, among non-natives, actually "discovered" Bonampak.

Among many exciting artifacts of the ancient town's ruins was a small temple with three rooms. Every surface in all three rooms of the temple was painted. Together, the three murals, each encompassing a room, form a narrative or story. The first mural is a scene at the Bonampak court, centering around what appears to be a supreme ruler and his family. There are also elaborately dressed nobles wearing headdresses and dancers putting on costumes, all seeming to prepare for some kind of ceremony.

In a panel below the elite are warriors and servants, as well as musicians playing drums and trumpets and wearing masks to portray gods. The second mural features a furious battle in which an enemy city is being raided. Warriors in full costume are shown as

---

pressed in the *Popol Vuh* (title translated as "Book of Council"), which presents the traditional mythology of the Mayas. The art is far more sophisticated than expected, and archaeologists believe there were many other murals from the pre-Classic era that did not survive the centuries of damp, tropical weather. The mural at San Bartolo also contains sixteen glyphs, some of the earliest ever found.

Maya numbers

The Mayas used the bar and dot system of writing numbers, which had been in use among early Mesoamerican peoples for some time. The Mayas were able to express all numerals through three symbols. A shell represented 0, a dot represented the value of 1, and a bar represented the value of 5. Numbers were usually written from bottom up, unlike modern numbers, which run horizontally. For example, to

they attack. The defeated prisoners of the battle are shown on another wall. They have been stripped of their clothing and sit before their judges, who will determine whether they will be sacrificed or become slaves.

The third mural depicts musicians and people dancing in elaborate costumes. A human sacrifice is taking place; a prisoner, apparently already dead, is being held down while his body is being beaten. Men dressed in long white feathered capes look upon the scene.

The murals were painted around 800 C.E. Like many Maya cities, Bonampak had been warring with its neighbor city, Yaxchilan, for centuries, but peace was established sometime at the end of the eighth century when the king of Bonampak, Chaan Muwan, married a princess from Yaxchilan. The king then commissioned the murals. By the time the murals had been painted, the city of Bonampak, like many other Classic era Maya cities, was being deserted by its people.

The Bonampak murals differ from almost all other Maya art in that they clearly, and in much detail, depict daily life. Most Maya art presents gods, kings, and abstract symbols. In these murals, it is almost as if the painter was recording the reality of life so later generations could see what it was like.

write the number 7 in the Maya system, a bar running horizontally is placed at the bottom; over it are two dots running horizontally. Thirteen would be written with two bars, one on top of the other, on the bottom position, and three dots directly over the bars.

The Maya number system was vigesimal—based on the number 20. Most scholars believe the Mesoamericans chose 20 as their base because people have 20 fingers and toes with which to count. The number system of the modern-day world is decimal-based, or based on 10. In Maya mathematics, numbers larger than 20 were written in powers of 20, just as modern numbers are written in powers of 10.

To illustrate, take the example of the numeral 1,424. In the decimal system, the number at the far right position, 4, is in the ones column (4 x 1 = 4). The number to the left of it, the 2, is in the tens column (2 x 10 = 20). The 4 in the hundreds column means 4 x 100 or 400, and the 1 in the thousands column means 1,000.

In the vigesimal system the columns, which go from bottom to top, present ones, twenties, 400s, 8,000, 160,000, and so on. In the number 1,424, the bottom line or ones column would be represented by four dots (representing, in the decimal system, 4). On top of the ones would be the twenties column. This would be two bars and a dot (representing, in the decimal system, 11 x 20 = 220). On top of the twenties is the 400s column, in which there would be three dots (representing, in the decimal system, 3 x 400 = 1,200). So 1,200 + 220 + 4 = 1,424.

The number 45 would be represented by a bar on the bottom (1 x 5) and two dots (2 x 20) over the bar. It was easy to add numbers written in the Maya bar and dot system. The numbers were set side by side and then combined by columns. Subtraction is a process of eliminating, rather than combining, the dots and bars. The Maya did not use fractions.

In the Maya number system, 80 would be represented by a shell on the bottom row, representing zero ones, and with four dots in the twenties column. The Maya are often credited with being the first people of the world to have created the concept of zero, which is very necessary to complex arithmetic and numeric expression. However, it is possible that the Mayas adopted the concept from the Olmecs (pronounced OLE-mecks) or another earlier Mesoamerican culture. The concept of zero as a placeholder in written numbers did not reach European countries until around 800 C.E. Despite the simplicity of the bar and dot system, the Maya also used glyphs and pictures of gods to express numbers as well. This led to some confusion when scholars deciphered Maya artifacts.

The Maya calendar system

Diego de Landa, the Spanish bishop in Yucatán responsible for the destruction of many Maya cultural objects, was also the author of one of the fullest accounts of Maya culture (for more information on Landa, see Chapter 19: The Mystery of the Maya). In his book about the Maya, *Relación de las Cosas de Yucatán* (written in 1566; title roughly translated as "History of Yucatán Things"), Landa described the

Maya calendar in detail and included drawings of glyphs. Scholars in the twentieth century used Landa's book to help determine how the Maya calendar system worked.

The priests were the primary calendar experts among the Mayas. They used a combination of three basic calendars: the sacred round, the solar calendar, and the Long Count. The system was based on calendars of other early Mesoamerican groups, such as the Olmec, Zapotec, and Teotihuacáns (pronounced TAY-uh-tee-wah-KAHNS). Scholars believe the Maya system dates back to about 100 B.C.E. It was so accurate that many believe Maya dates were actually more exact than those of contemporary calendars.

The sacred round calendar

The sacred round calendar, or *tzolkin,* which was used to plan religious ceremonies, measured a 260-day year. There were 20 day names and 13 day numbers used for this calendar. Every one of the 260 days in the sacred round had a unique day name/day number combination. The day names, and their possible meanings in English, are as follows:

- Imix: water, wine, or waterlily
- Ik': air, wind
- Ak 'bal: night
- K' an: corn
- Chicchan (or Chikchan): serpent, snake
- Cimi (or Kimi): death
- Manik': deer or hand
- Lamat: Venus or rabbit
- Muluc: water or rain
- Oc: dog
- Chuen: frog or monkey
- Eb: skull or broom
- Ben: reed or cornstalk
- Ix: jaguar, magician
- Men: eagle
- Cib (or Kib): owl or shell
- Caban: Earth
- Etz 'nab: flint or knife

- Cauac: storm
- Ahaw (or Ahau): lord

The first day of the sacred calendar year is 1 Imix. Day 2 is combined with the second day name, and so the second day is 2 Ik', the third day is 3 Ak 'bal, and so forth in the order they are presented in the list. After the first twenty days, the sequence begins again as 2 Imix, 3 Ik', 4 Ak 'bal, and so forth throughout the 260 possible combinations. Each one of these day name/day number combinations was associated with a deity. In the sacred round, every day had meanings and associations used to foresee the future when planning for war, marriage, or large ceremonies. People were named by the day name and day number of the particular day they were born.

The solar calendar

The solar calendar, or *haab* (often called the "vague calendar"), measured a 365-day year. There were eighteen 20-day months, each with a month name and a 5-day period at the end to finish out the year, called Uayeb (Wayeb). This last short period was considered a very unlucky time. The month names and their possible meanings in English are listed below:

- Pop: mat
- Uo (or Wo): frog
- Zip: stag
- Zotz: bat
- Tzec: skull
- Xul: termination or dog
- Yaxk 'in: red or new sun
- Mol: gather or water
- Ch 'en: well or black
- Yax: green
- Sac (or Zac): white
- Ceh: forest
- Mac: cover
- K' ank' in: yellow or skeleton
- Muan: falcon or owl
- Pax: drum

- Kayab: turtle
- Cumhu: dark
- Uayeb (Wayeb, the 5-day period to finish the year): ghost

In the solar year, the days were numbered 0 to 19 and combined with the month name. The first day of the year, therefore, was 0 Pop, then 1 Pop, 2 Pop, and so on through 19 Pop, and then the second month began: 0 Uo, 1 Uo, and

Illustration of the *tzolkin*, or the Maya sacred round calendar. *Calendario Maya (www.calendariomaya.com).*

so on. 0 Pop, New Year's Day on this calendar, is thought to have been sometime in the month of July. The solar calendar measured seasons and was used primarily for farming.

The 52-year cycle

The Maya priests combined the sacred round calendar and the solar calendar. Every day had two names—its name on the sacred round and its name on the solar calendar. Both names were usually used on stelae. An event, for example, may have happened on 9 Imix 5 Zotz. Using both names of the two calendar systems, it would be 52 years before 9 Imix 5 Zotz, or any other date using both calendars would recur.

For the Maya, history happened in "bundles" of 52 years, like centuries are to us today. If they had just used these two calendar systems, there would have been no way to place their dates in any larger time frame than the 52-year cycles. During a term of two hundred years, for example, there would be three 9 Imix 5 Zotz days and no way to tell which was which. To resolve this problem, the Maya devised a third calendar, called the Long Count.

The Long Count

With the Long Count, the Maya priests devised a way to count back to the beginning of the world. The Maya believed the world had been created and destroyed several times before the present era. For reasons unknown, they placed the first day of the present era on a date that would be August 13, 3114 B.C.E. (some sources say) on the Gregorian calendar (the calendar used by contemporary society). On Maya calendars the first day of creation, or day zero, was expressed as 4 Ahaw 8 Cumhu.

Long Count dates count back to the zero year in special time periods (like twenty-first century months, years, and centuries). These are modified forms of the vigesimal system, as follows:

- 1 kin = 1 day
- 1 uinal = 20 days
- 1 tun = 360 days (approximately 1 year)
- 1 katun = 7,200 days (approximately 20 years)

- 1 baktun = 144,000 days (approximately 395 years)
- 1 pictun = 2,880,000 days (approximately 7,885 years)

A Long Count date was usually expressed from the largest time period (baktun or katun; pictuns were rarely used) to the smallest (kin) using the bar and dot numeral system. After the Long Count date, Maya scribes wrote the sacred round and solar calendar date as well. In an example from the Canadian Museum of Civilization Corporation's *Maya Civilization* Web site, a typical Maya date would be 9.10.19.5.11, which is the expression in bar and dot format of 10 Chuen 4 Cumhu.

The numbers relate to the time periods as follows: 9 baktuns (1,296,000 days), 10 katuns (72,000 days), 19 tuns (6,840 days), 5 uinals (100 days), 11 kins (11 days). This adds up to 1,374,951 days, or approximately 3,767 solar years since the first day of creation, and falls at the sacred calendar round day named 10 Chuen, and at the solar day named 4 Cumhu. It would be sometime in the modern calendar year around 651 or 652 C.E.

Astronomy

In order to develop such accurate calendars, Maya astronomers (people who study the planets, sun, moon, and stars and other celestial bodies) had to have an amazing grasp of the movement of the heavenly bodies. Most scholars agree Maya priests obtained this knowledge through a careful study of the cosmos, and particularly its cycles, over long periods of time. The Maya priests were probably not aiming for the kind of accuracy as desired in the twenty-first century. Because they believed time was laid out in a set of interconnected cycles, they wanted to learn about the cycles in the heavens that corresponded to the cycles of their calendars. Many of the Maya's measurements of the heavenly cycles are preserved in the Dresden codex.

The Maya charted their observations and, with tables for the various movements of the stars and planets, attempted to understand the universe with mathematical precision. Among the primary observations made by Maya astronomers was the passage of the sun through its zenith (the point di-

An astronomical observatory used by the Mayas for observing movements of the planet Venus. *Photograph by Deborah J. Baker. Copyright © Deborah J. Baker.*

rectly above them in the sky). In Mesoamerica, the sun could be observed directly overhead two days each year. On those days, no shadows were cast at noon.

The Mayas also charted eclipses of the sun and moon. Many Maya buildings were constructed in such a way to cast certain shadows during the solstices (two times each year—June 21 and December 21—when the sun is farthest from the equator and days and nights are at their most unequal in length) and equinoxes (two times each year—March 21 and September 23—when the sun crosses the equator and day and night are of equal length) each year. The Maya were also extremely interested in Venus, and knew its movements and cyclical positions in relation to the sun and Earth. They also observed the positions of the Milky Way.

The Maya used their knowledge of the cosmos to attempt to see into the future and to time their rituals and ceremonies based on the cycles of the heavenly bodies. For example, if the end of a katun, a 20-year calendar period, came at the same time as a particular planetary cycle or position, it might signal to Maya kings that it was time to go to war with a neighboring city. In classic Maya times, the ends of cycles were celebrated with rituals, sometimes involving putting up stelae to commemorate the day and the ruling Maya king.

The discoveries continue ...

From the concept of zero to a writing system that represented a full spoken language to a wide range of advanced artwork to a highly accurate calendar system, the advances of the Mayas in the arts and sciences have never failed to amaze. Scholars have spent lifetimes trying to solve just a few of the mysteries the Mayas left behind. Despite the destruction of the Maya codices and other written and artistic monuments, in recent decades they have made great steps forward in this search to understand the American past. While some Maya experts have made remarkable progress in deciphering the Maya glyphs carved into stelae and painted on ceramics, others have made discoveries like the uncovering of the murals at San Bartolo. Their work will almost certainly continue to shake up the current beliefs about the Maya culture for many years to come.

For More Information

Books

Coe, Michael D., and Mark Van Stone. *Reading the Maya Glyphs.* London and New York: Thames and Hudson, 2001.

Gallenkamp, Charles. *Maya: The Riddle and Rediscovery of a Lost Civilization,* 3rd revised ed. New York: Viking, 1985.

Galvin, Irene Flum. *The Ancient Maya.* New York: Benchmark Books, 1997.

Newsome, Elizabeth A. *Trees of Paradise and Pillars of the World: The Serial Stela Cycle of "18-Rabbit-God K," King of Copán.* Austin, TX: University of Texas Press, 2001.

Web Sites

"Maya Civilization: The Maya Calendar." *Canadian Museum of Civilization.* http://www.civilization.ca/civil/maya/mmc06eng.html (accessed on September 21, 2004).

"Maya Civilization: Writing and Hieroglyphics." *Canadian Museum of Civilization.* http://www.civilization.ca/civil/maya/mmc04eng.html (accessed on September 21, 2004).

Maya Economy and Daily Life

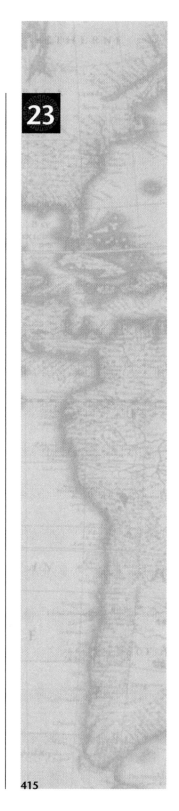

23

From the Classic Maya (pronounced MY-uh) era, beginning about 250 C.E., Maya artists and scribes (people who wrote glyphs—the Maya writing system using figures for words and sounds—on monuments and in books) focused their writing on the lives of the rich and powerful of their time. Almost all of the writing and art left behind portrays the heroic deeds and courtly lives of the nobles of ancient Maya cities.

The upper classes of Maya society represented only a tiny portion of the population. Most people lived in humble farming villages and towns ruled by one of the large Maya cities. The farmers worked hard to feed themselves and to provide the enormous amount of food, goods, and labor necessary to support the cities and their elite or ruling classes.

With the breakthroughs in deciphering (figuring out the meaning of) Maya glyphs, many historians in the last decades of the twentieth century focused on the royal families whose lives were chronicled by Maya historians. There are many unexplored ancient cities and villages, untouched by modern hands, lying beneath the tropical jungles—especially those without huge pyramids or ornate temples to draw at-

Words to Know

Alliances: Connections between states or other political units based on mutual interests, intermarriage of families, or other relations.

Cacao beans: Beans that grow on an evergreen tree from which cocoa, chocolate, and cocoa butter are made.

Cenote: Underground reservoirs or rivers that become accessible from above ground when cave ceilings collapse or erode.

Decipher: To figure out the meaning of something in code or in an ancient language.

Elite: A group of people within a society who are in a socially superior position

and have more power and privileges than others.

Glyph: A figure (often carved into stone or wood) used as a symbol to represent words, ideas, or sounds.

Milpa: Cornfield.

Obsidian: Dark, solid glass formed by volcanoes used to make blades, knives, and other tools.

Scribe: Someone hired to write down the language, to copy a manuscript, or record a spoken passage.

Stela: A stone pillar carved with images or writing, often used to provide historical details or for religious or political purposes.

tention to them. There is little known about the daily lives of ordinary Mayas: were they poor or comfortable in their lives? How strict was the rule of the royal families? What were the roles of women? How did their economies work?

Many fascinating new clues to the daily existence of the Maya are being discovered as excavations continue in the twenty-first century. In the early 2000s new archeological evidence revealed not only a thriving trade network, but a wealthy merchant class during the Classic Maya era—both of which had been previously unknown to scholars.

Cancuen: Place of serpents

In April 2000, U.S. archaeologist Arthur Demarest and a team of Guatemalan scientists were walking through what they assumed was a small set of ruins in a remote area of Guatemala's tropical jungles. After some stelae (upright slabs or pillars of stone carved with pictures and glyphs) found in the Maya cities of Tikal and Dos Pilas in the Petén jungles of Guatemala had referred to a great marketplace known as Cancuen (pronounced CAN-coo-win), Demarest and his team led an expedition deep into the jungle to find the site.

As Demarest ascended a hill, he suddenly fell shoulder-deep into a leafy hole, which he quickly realized was a snake nest. Forced to remain perfectly still to avoid being bitten by the poisonous snakes, he had plenty of time to survey his surroundings. He discovered that the hill he had climbed was not a hill at all, but rather the roof of a huge palace completely covered over by the tropical forests. Demarest had stumbled upon the great city of Cancuen, which meant "the Place of the Serpents" in Mayan.

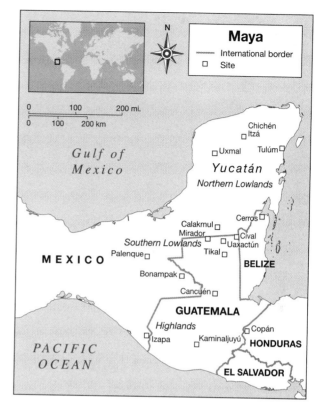

Map showing the major sites of Maya civilization in Mesoamerica. *Map by XNR Productions. The Gale Group.*

Early investigations proved Demarest had indeed discovered a huge, 3-story palace covering nearly 250,000 square feet (23,250 square meters)—about the size of six football fields. Inside there were nearly two hundred rooms, most with 20-foot-high (6.1-meter) ceilings, and at least eleven courtyards. The palace's solid limestone walls had been well-preserved by the tropical forests, holding up far better than the Maya's usual walls made of concrete and mud.

It was immediately clear that the king who had reigned during the design and construction of the palace must have had great power; the palace would have dazzled any visitors who entered the maze-like building. Outside the palace were houses where artisans (craftspeople) and merchants lived. There were also hundreds of workshops, where the artisans carved jade (a green gemstone) ornaments and jewelry, and made knives and tools out of obsidian (a solid, dark glass created by volcanoes). It is believed that Cancuen's

Ruins of the once three-story palace at Cancuen, Guatemala. *AP/Wide World Photos.*

population ranged between about one thousand to three thousand people at its peak.

Cancuen was located at the foot of the highlands, on a small natural harbor at the beginning of the Passion River. Its location at the head of the river allowed the city to control trade between the southern highlands of Central America and the Classic Maya city-states (independent self-governing communities consisting of a single city and the surrounding area) of Tikal, Palenque, and Copán further north. The business of trade had been ongoing in Cancuen since 300 C.E. or earlier, making the city and most of its people, both workers and nobles, very wealthy. The city became extremely powerful because it controlled the area's natural resources, such as jade, which was highly valued by the Mayas. (Jade was considered as valuable as gold was to other civilizations.)

In a Public Broadcasting System interview available on the PBS *Online Newshour* Web site in 2000, Demarest described much evidence of Cancuen's thriving trade, including a 35-pound (16-kilogram) jade boulder used for making plaques and other artifacts, as well as pyrite (fool's gold) and obsidian workshops. According to Demarest, many "of the most precious things in the Maya world were being controlled by [the king of Cancuen]," most of which were then "worked into fine artifacts by his artisans, and then traded down river."

While other Maya cities derived their power from religious activities and warfare, scholars were surprised to find no sign of warfare in Cancuen. Instead, its rulers forged strong trade alliances (connections based on mutual interests, intermarriage of families, or other relations) with other cities throughout the Maya world. Trade, and the wealth it brought, made the city strong until, like other Maya cities in the Classic era, it was abandoned in the ninth century for reasons that remain uncertain.

Trade

In pre-Classic times, before about 300 C.E., scholars believe the Maya probably traded only locally among themselves. By 400, however, the city of Teotihuacán (pronounced TAY-uh-tee-wah-KAHN) in the far northeastern section of the Valley of Mexico (about 25 miles [40.2 kilometers] northeast of present-day Mexico City) had developed a vast economic empire (a vast, complex unit extending across boundaries and dominated by one central power) covering much of the southern two-thirds of Mexico, Guatemala and Belize, as well as some parts of Honduras and El Salvador. The Maya world was strongly influenced by the Teotihuacáns, and the Classic Maya cities were clearly a part of the Teotihuacán trading network for a significant period of time. From then forward, long-distance trade was central to the Maya and remained so until the Spanish conquest in the sixteenth century.

The first known encounter between the Mayas and the Europeans provides a view of the trading activities in the Maya world. When Spanish explorer Christopher Columbus (1451–1506) and his crew were on their fourth voyage to the Americas (still looking for the Indies, or Asia) in 1502, they spotted a large seagoing canoe off the coast of Honduras. The canoe was very wide and cut from a single, giant tree. It was

Cacao beans were highly prized by the Mayas, both as food as well as a type of money. *Birchbank Press Photo Bank. Reproduced by permission.*

loaded with goods including wooden obsidian-edged swords, copper tools, textiles, embroidered and painted clothing, ceramics, and cacao beans (beans that grow on an evergreen tree from which cocoa, chocolate, and cocoa butter are made). The men and women aboard the canoe were clearly transporting goods for trade. They told the Spaniards they had come from *Maia,* and this is how the Spanish came to call them the "Mayas."

In the Classic era, trade was central to the economy of the numerous independent city-states. Every region had its own special products to export (sell to other places). Areas that had control of the resources of the highland areas (like Cancuen), exported jade, obsidian, and quetzal feathers (highly valued green tropical bird feathers). The lowlands exported ceramics, honey, and rubber. Coastal Maya traders exported salt, shells, and dried fish. The exchange of these products usually involved a direct trade of items, such as jade for ceramics. Sometimes, though, Maya merchants paid for goods with cacao beans, which were used as a kind of money.

Cities that did not have direct access to resources like obsidian or jade were still major centers of the large Maya trading network. Tikal, for example, the largest of the Classic era cities, served as a vital trade center where products like salt were brought in from the coast and traded for obsidian brought in from the highlands. Merchants in Tikal purchased raw materials, such as obsidian, and made products to sell, creating a very large and profitable industry in the city. Tikal had about one hundred obsidian workshops, where knives and tools were made, and many other industries as well.

By the post-Classic era after 900 C.E. (when Chichén Itzá [pronounced chee-CHEN eet-SAH], Mayapán, and Uxmal [pronounced oosh-MAHL] in the northern lowlands were

powerful cities), many scholars believe prosperous long-distance trading had prompted a new class to emerge—a large and strong middle class. In the northern lowlands of Yucatán after about 1000 C.E., a few merchant families grew very wealthy through trade. They often established trading alliances with families in other cities.

Commoners, it seems, were able to rise through the social ranks through successful trade. Soon merchants from both the noble and common working classes came into political power. The middle-class ranks swelled even more in the industrial cities, where craftspeople made up a significant portion of the population and assumed higher status and more wealth than the common workers or farmers.

Traders were highly respected by the Maya people. They were not taxed and were often provided food and lodging by locals while traveling. In ancient Maya times, there were no pack animals to help with transporting goods to faraway places, so most traders acquired slaves to carry their goods. Slaves were usually people who had been captured during warfare, or sometimes they were criminals or orphans.

The Maya had an excellent road system for traveling between cities. Traders and merchants, as well as their slaves and other people they employed, traveled to cities both within and outside the Maya world. The traders came back with exciting new ideas and many stories to tell. In their travels, they acquired the foods, tools, jewelry, clothing, and arts of the many lands and peoples of Mesoamerica.

Farming

Trade was important to the economy of the Maya city-states, but the single most important economic activity was farming. The city-states could not have survived without enough crops to sustain their people, such as those involved in trade and crafts, as well as construction of city buildings and monuments. The majority of the ancient Maya population was made up of farmers.

Maize (corn) was the primary crop in the Maya world. Maize was considered a gift of the gods to the people. It was part of most Maya religious ceremonies, appeared in much of their art, and even in their personal adornments. Maya headdresses, for example, were often shaped like ears of corn. In stories about the creation of the Maya people, it was believed the gods created humans from maize. Both nobles and common people ate maize on a daily basis, often three times a day with each meal.

Maya farmers also grew other crops: black and red beans, sweet potatoes, squash, pumpkins, cacao, avocados, tomatoes, chili peppers, guavas, papayas, bananas, melons, and cotton. They grew cacao trees for their favorite drink, called *xocoatl*, or chocolate (see the box on pages 430–431), which was generally only available to the ruling classes.

Most Maya farmers lived outside the cities in small villages ruled by local chieftains (leader or head of a group) who were responsible to the nobility of the city-states. The land surrounding these villages was owned by all the people in common. Local leaders, appointed by the nobility, divided the village land up among families based on need. The farmers received a plot to farm and most had a kitchen garden as well. There was also a communal plot tended to by all of a village's farmers. Village land was not simply to be used for the benefit of the farmers; Maya farmers gave about two-thirds of their crops and much of their labor to the nobility of the nearby city.

Milpa farming

The small plot of land—called a *milpa,* or cornfield—received by each villager was about the right size to provide for their needs. These *milpa* sites were temporary because the Maya use a farming system called "slash and burn" agriculture. Initially, *milpas* were sections of the tropical forest that had not been farmed for many years. Once a family received their *milpa,* they cut down all the jungle growth and the trees, allowing the cuttings to dry out on the land. After burning the cuttings, ashes from the fires provided necessary nutrients to boost the poor soil and farmers could then plant crops on the land.

Maize, or corn, was the primary crop of Maya farmers. *U.S. Agricultural Research Service, USDA.*

Farmers usually planted crops during the rainy season, from May to October. After the *milpas* were farmed for a few years, the soil would lose its nutrients and would be abandoned for a time to "rest." In the Petén area of Guatemala and other parts of the southern lowlands, land was left to rest for about four to seven years; in the northern lowlands of the Yucatán peninsula, where the soil is even thinner, the fields had to be left to rest for about fifteen to twenty years.

When a farmer left a *milpa,* he would clear another section from the forests. Over time, and as the population grew, more and more of the rainforests were cleared for farming to support the needs of the growing Maya world. This rapid clearing may actually have been responsible for climate

A field prepared for planting crops by burning, according to the Maya farming custom. © *Charles & Josette Lenars/Corbis.*

changes in the region, which in turn led to the abandonment of some Classic era cities in the eighth and ninth centuries.

Another challenge faced by Maya farmers was obtaining enough water for their crops. In hilly or mountainous areas of the highlands, the Maya dug terraces (large steps used to create level ground for farming) into the slopes, where water supplies were more plentiful. In some lowland areas where the land was swampy, they developed canal systems in gridlike patterns throughout the farmlands, carrying water, and perhaps even permitting canoe travel, throughout vast areas.

Fields were raised above the canals, receiving a controlled amount of moisture to produce larger crops. In the northern lowlands, villages often formed around cenotes (underground reservoirs or rivers that become accessible from above ground when cave ceilings collapse or erode). The Maya also developed excellent systems for collecting rainwater, building large tanks to hold water through frequently occurring droughts (long periods of little or no rain). Water was collected during the tropical downpours, which sometimes dumped up to 100 inches (254 centimeters) in a few months.

The Maya did not raise many animals for meat. The exceptions were dogs, kept as pets and sometimes eaten, and turkeys. They did hunt for meat, though, using bows and arrows or blowguns (long narrow pipes through which pellets or poison darts can be blown). Meat gathered from hunting included monkey, deer, iguana, and armadillo. Many Maya farmers also kept bees for honey.

Maya scholar Richard E.W. Adams urged people studying the Maya not to romanticize them. Farmers, under the direction of elite groups in the city, were forced to produce more and more food for the growing populations of the cities. Adams believes—and many other scientists agree—that the Mayas eventually destroyed the tropical rainforest environment, causing the food shortages that marked the end of the Classic era. He described his findings in a 1996 *Cosmos Journal* article:

> *Maya cities were sustained by large rural populations. Based on intensive ground surveys (mine and others), there were as many as 450 people per square mile. This astounding density is similar to that found today in crowded rural zones.... One current fallacy [something untrue] is that native American populations lived in harmony with nature with relatively little deleterious [bad] effect. It is simply not true for the Maya or many other Mesoamerican groups, nor probably for the New World as a whole. Thirteen hundred years after their entry into the lowlands around 750 C.E. nearly every square meter of land had been modified. This was done first by slash-and-burn farming and later by intensive agricultural systems such as swamp drainage, hillside terracing, and field rotation systems. The vast tropical forests of recent times are a result of 1100 years of recovery after the catastrophic Maya collapse [in] about 840.*

Daily life

Marriage, family, and child rearing

Marriage and family were very important to the Mayas. Marriages were often arranged by parents, who would consult a matchmaker with knowledge of the Maya calendar cycles and the positions of the stars and planets. Couples were matched by their dates of birth. The day of the wedding was also planned around calendar cycles.

The young couple lived with the female's parents for several years after the marriage so the husband could prove his worth to the wife's parents. If the marriage was not working out, it was permissible for the couple to divorce simply by agreeing to it. Both were then free to marry someone else. Among noblemen, it was acceptable to have as many wives as one could afford. Among the common people, however, monogamy (one spouse) was the rule.

The Mayas loved large families. Maya couples greeted the news of a new baby with joy and celebration. Parents would consult a priest when the baby was born to find out about the alignment of the stars and the calendar cycles involved in the child's birth. Priests gave children their names, though children would also get a nickname from their families, and later, a formal name. Male names always began with the prefix *Ah,* which was changed to *Na* after marriage. Female names began with the prefix *Ix.*

When Maya boys reached the age of five, a white shell was braided into their hair. Girls of the same age received a red shell on a string tied around their waists. These symbols of childhood and purity remained in place until the boy was fourteen and the girl reached twelve. At this time, a puberty ceremony was conducted by a priest, assisted by several respected members of the community. After clearing the room of evil spirits, the priest would ask the child to confess any evil acts he or she may have done, and, if all was in order, performed rituals and prayers upon the child ending with the removal of the child's childhood shell. Gifts were exchanged and the adults would then drink *pulque* (pronounced PUHL-kay), a fermented ceremonial drink made from agave cactus, to toast the child's future.

After the puberty ceremony, Maya boys often left home to live in houses with other young, unmarried men. There they learned crafts, played games, and were trained in warfare. They still went daily into the cornfields to work with their fathers. They painted themselves black to show they were single. Boys generally did not marry until the age of eighteen. Girls remained with their parents after puberty, learning the work they would be expected to perform as wives. They learned to grind maize and cook, spin and weave textiles, sew and embroider, and to do other crafts and household duties. Girls generally were married by the age of fourteen.

When a couple married, they divided the household labor. The man was usually the principal farmer, but the woman worked in the fields too. Men hunted and fished. In the off-seasons, the men were obligated to join huge construction groups who built giant monuments, irrigation canals, roads, and other public works requiring vast amounts of labor.

Women were in charge of home maintenance, cooking, childrearing, and the production of crafts, such as cloth and often pottery. The hardworking Maya women were, for the most part, respected. They were sometimes allowed to own property, and in a few instances, noble Maya women became rulers of the great city-states. Like many societies, however, the Mayas did not treat women as the equals of men. Women were not supposed to look directly at a man, and they were not allowed to eat their meals with men. The women served men their dinners, and ate later.

Houses

When many people think of Maya homes they are likely to think of great palaces or temples. These were the homes of the very small noble class, who lived in the cities. The vast majority of Mayas lived in the outskirts of the cities or in farming villages. Their homes were usually built in complexes, with several homes surrounding a central courtyard. The complex was often made up of the homes of extended family members (the relatives beyond the parents and children, including aunts and uncles, grandparents, and cousins).

The houses of the common people were usually rectangular, with one or two rooms each. They were made from either wood or stone, depending on the materials available. Some houses were made from poles (the trunks of young trees, stripped of their bark) tied together and set on a stone foundation. Most had two doors standing across the house from each other so a breeze could flow through. They did not actually use doors in these doorways, but sometimes hung a blanket across

for privacy. The weather in the tropics was usually warm so there was generally no need to keep out the breezes. Roofs were made of thick palm thatch (plant stocks used for roofing).

There was little furniture in a Maya house. If the house had two rooms, one was used by the whole family for sleeping. Beds were woven straw mats placed on the floor in a low, wooden frame. The other room was used as a kitchen and living room. There were benches and stools along with pottery, baskets, and hanging chili peppers in the room.

Food

In the farming villages and towns throughout the Maya world, women and girls rose very early each day to begin making breakfast, usually with some form of maize. Because maize has tough kernels that are difficult to digest, the Maya women were continually processing it. They soaked the dry kernels in water and lime overnight or longer, then ground the soaked mixture with stone tools, using a *mano* (a long tube-shaped stone) and a *metate* (a smooth stone surface). This created a thick dough called *zacan*. The Mayas found many ways to use *zacan*. They added water to make *atole*, a thin gruel they drank for breakfast. The women would often put a lump of the *zacan* mixed with a little water into a gourd and send it with the men in the family to eat as a meal while working in the fields.

Maize was also cooked in stews or baked inside corn husks with other ingredients, such as beans, chilies, or turkey meat, to make *tamales*. The most common use for the maize in the twenty-first century is to make the ground meal into tortillas, flat corn pancakes. Many people believe the Mayas have been making tortillas for thousands of years, but some scholars believe the Spanish brought the concept of tortillas to the Americas.

The Maya frequently ate beans with their tortillas, or with *zacan* in soups and stews. The Maya cooks often added hot chili peppers to beans to give them flavor. Beans added important protein to the maize-based diet. Since the Mayas did not eat much meat, protein was very important to their health.

Clothing

For Maya men, the standard item of clothing was the *ex*, a loincloth formed from a long strip of cotton wound around the waist several times and then passed between the legs, with flaps hanging both in front and in back. If the weather was cool, they might also wear a *pati*, a cotton square draped over their shoulders like a cape. Maya women usually wore a short skirtlike garment. Sometimes they wore a shawl, but women were not expected to wear clothing on their upper bodies unless it was cool. Maya women also sometimes wore dresses. Their clothing was often dyed in bright colors and patterns.

Children usually did not wear clothes. Maya people went barefoot much of the time, but they also wore sandals, usually made from deer skin and tied with cords. Jewelry was very common, even among the poor farming people. Most Maya children had multiple body piercings for jewelry—the nose, ears, and various other parts of the face; the holes were gradually enlarged to hold ornamental tubes and plugs.

Xocolatl: The Drink of the Gods

Either the Mayas or the Olmecs (pronounced OLE-mecks) were the probable "inventors" of chocolate. The Mayas have been consuming it as a drink since 100 C.E. or before. The early Mesoamericans discovered the cacao tree, *theobroma cacao* (which means "food of the gods" in Greek), in the tropical forests. At first they removed the pods from the wild trees, but soon the Mayas (in the present-day Mexican state of Tabasco) began transplanting cacao trees to their own land to harvest a steady supply of cacao beans.

Cacao trees produce green pods filled with a wet white pulp and cacao beans. The Mayas removed the seeds from the pod and allowed them to ferment (a process of breaking down their elements) until they turned dark brown. Then the seeds were dried, roasted, and ground to form a thick paste. For the drink the Mayas called *xocolatl,* meaning "bitter water" (since they usually did not sweeten their cocoa) they added chili and ground maize.

There was no whipped cream in the Maya world, since there were no cows, but the Mayas liked foam on their chocolate. To achieve this, they placed an empty pot on the ground and, from a standing position, poured the chocolate into the pot below. They repeated this, pouring the

All Mayas, except slaves, wore their hair long. Their hairstyles tended to show off the long foreheads specially shaped with the use of boards in infancy. Women wore ponytails gathered at the top of their head, or sometimes they braided their hair using colorful ornaments. Men often burned an area in the middle of their scalp to make it bald, but they let all the hair around the bare spot grow long. They often created elaborate hairstyles with many ponytails, ties, and bands. Huge headdresses were often worn.

Village administration and military duty

By the Classic Maya era beginning in 250 C.E., most villages and farmland were under the rule of one of the large Maya city-states nearby. The king of the city and his priests and nobles were the supreme rulers of the farmers. The laws, taxes, and decisions about war all came from the city. Commoners did not deal directly with the elite; local leaders were

A cacao tree with beans. © *Robert van der Hilst/Corbis.*

chocolate from pot to pot until there was a good head of foam. They usually drank their chocolate hot.

Chocolate was mainly consumed by the upper class Mayas in the Classic era, but its use probably spread to the common people in later years. Some Maya people drank chocolate with every meal.

Cacao beans were also used as currency, or money, in the Maya world. Bijal P. Trivedi noted a few Maya prices in a *National Geographic* (2002) article stating, "Early explorers to the region found that four [cacao] beans could get you a pumpkin, 10 a rabbit and 100 would buy you a slave."

appointed by the king to make sure taxes were paid, labor duties fulfilled, and the laws of the city-state obeyed.

Another function of the appointed local leaders was to assemble and maintain local armies. The Maya city-states generally kept their store of weapons in the city, but they took their soldiers from local militias made up of the men and boys of farming towns. The men were trained in hand-to-hand combat, using spears and axes with stone or obsidian blades, and throwing weapons, like lances, slings, and even bows and arrows. Soldiers usually wore a kind of armor made of cotton. In battle, most soldiers painted their faces. Officers of the armies were from the city's nobility.

Entertainment

Though they worked hard most of their days, farmers and craftspeople who lived outside large city-states were not isolated from the city and its culture (arts, language, beliefs,

In the Eye of the Beholder

The ancient Maya had a strong sense of personal beauty. Some of their standards of beauty and style might stand out in twenty-first-century fashion, but certainly many examples of contemporary fashion would probably have shocked them, too.

- While a Maya baby was still young, its parents placed its head between two boards and then bound them very tightly together. The babies were left like this for a few days. Baby's heads are very soft and quite easy to reshape. This procedure flattened the forehead and caused the head to slope backward, creating the distinctive head shape seen in Maya art. The Mayas found this very attractive.

- The Mayas thought being cross-eyed was very appealing, so mothers of young children tied a bead to a hair or string hanging between the child's eyes. The eyes, drawn to the bead between them, would cross, and it was every mother's hope her child's eyes would remain crossed.

- Mayas often decorated their teeth. They began by filing the front teeth to a sharp point, then attached small plates of jade or obsidian into holes on the front of the filed teeth.

- Tattoos were also very popular among the Mayas. Both men and women had intricate designs and pictures tattooed all over their faces and bodies. The process was quite painful—after the artist painted the tattoo on the skin with vegetable dyes, he or she would cut into the skin so the tattoo would be permanently absorbed into the skin. This cutting frequently caused infections and illness.

customs, institutions, and other products of human work and thought shared by a group of people at a particular time). Huge festivals were held on a regular basis—generally at the end of every twenty-day month and on other important occasions as well. Thousands of people from miles around would gather in the city's plaza. Religious ceremonies, led by priests in elaborate costumes, usually began the festivities, which often featured ritual bloodlettings or human sacrifice (see Chapter 21 for more information). After the solemn ceremonies, though, there was generally a great deal of music with everyone joining in the dancing and singing. In the plaza, traders would also bring out their goods from far and wide.

Other than festivals, the Maya attended Mesoamerican ball games called *pok-a-tok* in some Mayan languages (see Chapter 21 for more information on the Maya ball game). Maya children played their own versions of the ball game, and played with dolls and board games as well.

The survival of the Maya

Throughout the long history of the Maya, the powerful and wealthy city-states were built through the intense labor of the common workers. The cities thrived, and their people ate the maize and beans the farmers grew. But eventually, one by one, all of the great Maya cities and city-states collapsed and were abandoned. The farmers in many cases were forced to move to another location, mainly to be around a secure water source. In many of the Petén (Guatemala) regions, farming communities were either severely reduced by malnutrition (sickness due to starvation) and disease after the decline of the city-states, or the people simply moved away.

Maya sculpture of the head of a man with tattoos.
© *Gianni Dagli Orti/Corbis.*

In the northern Yucatán lowlands, and in isolated areas throughout the Maya world, the rise and fall of the Maya city-states may not have had the same devastating impact on farmers' lives. Archeologists have found evidence some farming villages continued to exist in Petén long after the Classic era. At the time of the Spanish conquest in the mid-sixteenth century, many Maya villages were still leading the same lives and practicing the same traditions that had been in existence for many centuries.

The Spanish, in their enthusiasm to convert the Maya to Christianity and to incorporate them into the Spanish culture, caused great changes. The new economic and political systems exploited the native people and caused devastation

among the Mayas. When Spanish control ended, the new governments were just as bad or worse. The Maya population and its culture, however, did not disappear. Their culture had been disrupted from outside, but the Maya found ways to live on.

In the early 2000s there were about six million Maya people living in Mexico, Guatemala, and Belize. The largest group, the Yucatecs, number around three hundred thousand and live in the Mexican state of Yucatán. Two other large groups, the Tzotzil (pronounced so-TSEEL) and the Tzeltal (pronounced sel-TALL), numbering around two hundred thousand combined, live in the Mexican state of Chiapas. In Guatemala, Mayas make up about half of the population. About 40 percent of the Guatemalan population speaks an Amerindian language (language of an indigenous, or native, person from North or South America)—mostly the Mayan languages—as their first or primary language. The modern Maya religion, however, has become a mix of Christianity and Maya spirituality and traditions.

The Lacandón Maya

The Mayas strongly resisted the Spanish invasion of their lands in the early 1500s. One group of Mayas escaped the Spanish influence altogether, having fled when they learned the Spaniards had arrived. This group hid out in the Lacandón tropical wilderness of Chiapas and lived their lives hidden from the Europeans.

More than two centuries later, in 1790, the Spanish made a last attempt to defeat the Lacandón Maya in order to convert them to Christianity and assimilate them into New Spain. Even then, the Lacandón Mayas were able to resist the Spanish and were left in peace until the mid-twentieth century. They continued to practice Maya traditions and a distinctive form of their religion.

By the 1940s people were coming into the jungles of Chiapas to tap chicle trees for their rubbery sap, the main ingredient in chewing gum. There were also people seeking to cut down the forests' mahogany trees for their wood. This new invasion of Maya land proved to be a disaster for the Lacandón. The strangers entering their environment exposed the Lacandón to new diseases, causing terrible epidemics that killed many.

For a time in the 1980s, there were only about two hundred surviving Lacandón members, and their forests rapidly disappeared due to growing demands for lumber. Researchers continue to make great efforts to observe the Lacandón Maya in their own environment. Small parcels of forest have been set aside for their use, but rapid deforestation (cutting down the rainforests) threatens the Lacandón Maya and other peoples as well.

For More Information

Books

Gallenkamp, Charles. *Maya: The Riddle and Rediscovery of a Lost Civilization,* 3rd revised edition. New York: Viking, 1985.

Galvin, Irene Flum. *The Ancient Maya.* New York: Benchmark Books, 1997.

The Magnificent Maya. Alexandria, VA: Time-Life Books, 1993.

Web Sites

Adams, Richard E.W. "Romance Versus Reality in the Ancient Maya Civilization." *Cosmos Club Journal.* http://www.cosmos-club.org/journals/ 1996/adams.html (accessed on September 22, 2004).

Ebersole, Rene S. "What Lies Beneath: Discovery of a Maya Palace in Guatemala, and Insights into the Maya Civilization around Cancuen." *Current Science,* November 17, 2000. Available at http://www.findarticles.com/p/articles/mi_m0BFU/is_6_86/ai_67326281 (accessed on September 22, 2004).

Gugliotta, Guy. "In Guatemalan Jungle, A Mayan Wall Street? Enormous Palace Was Major Trading Center." *Washington Post,* September 8, 2000. Available at http://www.hartford-hwp.com/archives/41/204.html (accessed on September 22, 2004).

Saurez, Ray. "Lost and Found: Interview with Arthur Demarest." *PBS Online Newshour,* September 11, 2000. Available at http://www.pbs.org/newshour/bb/latin_america/july-dec00/mayan_9-11.html (accessed on September 22, 2004).

Trivedi, Bijal P. "Ancient Chocolate Found in Maya 'Teapot.'" *National Geographic Today,* July 17, 2002. Available at http://news.nationalgeographic.com/news/2002/07/0717_020717_TVchocolate.html (accessed on September 22, 2004).

Toltec Culture

24

Much of what is known about the Toltecs (pronounced TOHL-tecks) comes from the Aztecs (Mexicas; pronounced may-SHEE-kahs), who later succeeded the Toltecs as the rulers of the Valley of Mexico. The Aztecs revered the Toltecs and, when interviewed by the conquering Spanish in the sixteenth century, told a detailed history of Toltec heroism. The Aztecs frequently portrayed the Toltecs idealistically as the great masters of nearly everything they did: architecture, the arts, religious worship, and warfare. In fact, the Aztec reports often credited all the inventions and triumphs of the Mesoamerican past to the Toltecs. Spanish missionary Fray Bernardino de Sahagún (c. 1500–1590), who interviewed the Aztecs and wrote down their stories in the mid-sixteenth century, recorded the words of one Aztec man who summed up the feelings of awe the Aztecs held toward the Toltecs: "The Tolteca were wise. Their works were all good, all perfect, all marvelous … in truth they invented all the wonderful, precious, and marvelous things which they made" (quoted from Brian M. Fagan's *Kingdoms of Gold, Kingdoms of Jade*). The advances the Aztecs credited to the Toltecs, such as the invention

Words to Know

Artifact: Any item made or used by humans, such as a tool or weapon, that may be found by archaeologists or others who seek clues to the past.

Atlantes: Large stone statues of warriors, often used as columns to support the roofs of Toltec buildings.

Barbarian: A word used to describe people from another land; it often has a negative meaning, however, suggesting the people described are inferior to others.

Bas-relief: A carved, three-dimensional picture, usually in stone, wood, or plaster, in which the image is raised above the background.

Chacmool: A stone statue of a man in a reclining position, leaning to one side with his head up in a slightly awkward position; the statue's stomach area forms a kind of platform on which the Toltecs placed a bowl or plate for offerings to the gods—sometimes incense or small animals, but often human hearts.

Chiefdom: A social unit larger and more structured than a tribe but smaller and less structured than a state, which is mainly governed by one powerful ruler. Though there are not distinct classes in a chiefdom, people are ranked by how closely they are related to the chief; the closer one is to the chief, the more prestige, wealth, and power one is likely to have.

Elite: A group of people within a society who are in a socially superior position and have more power and privileges than others.

Mass human sacrifices: Large-scale killing of people—or many people being killed at one time—as offerings to the gods.

Obsidian: Dark, solid glass formed by volcanoes used to make blades, knives, and other tools.

Pantheon: All of the gods that a particular group of people worship.

Quetzal: A Central American bird with bright green feathers.

Sacrifice: To make an offering to the gods, through personal possessions like cloth or jewels, or by killing an animal or human as the ultimate gift.

Tribute: A payment to a nation or its ruler, usually made by people from a conquered territory as a sign that they surrender to the imposed rule; payment could be made in goods or labor or both.

of the calendar and techniques in architecture and the arts, had actually been the work of earlier groups in Mesoamerica—the Olmecs (pronounced OLE-mecks), Zapotecs, Teotihuacáns (pronounced TAY-uh-tee-wah-KAHNS), Mayas (pronounced MY-uhs), and many other societies preceding the Toltecs.

A lack of artifacts (items made or used by humans, such as tools or weapons) from the Toltec empire has made it extremely difficult for archaeologists to restore the ancient sites or learn details about their history. The artifacts they have found, however, seem to conflict with Aztec accounts. While the Aztecs described the remarkable beauty and wonder of the city of Tula, the ancient capital of the Toltecs, archaeologists found little there to inspire such awe. The actual site of Tula was not recognized as the Toltec capital until the 1940s, largely because the ruins were not magnificent at all. Tula was never as grand or as large as the nearby ancient ruins of Teotihuacán. Besides, its ruins were looted by the Aztecs when they were building their own capital city, Tenochtitlán (pronounced tay-notch-teet-LAHN). If there once was great art there, it has long since disappeared.

Nonetheless, the story of the warrior nobles who brought together a diverse and divided empire by waging war and spreading their religion is of monumental importance in the background of ancient Mexico and its people. It is probably important to remember, however, that the Toltec history told by the Aztecs tells us as much about the Aztecs as it does about the Toltecs.

Dates of predominance
c. 900–1200 C.E.

Name variations and pronunciation
Toltec; sometimes Tolteca. Pronounced TOHL-teck. The original name the Toltecs used for themselves is not known. They received the name *Toltecs* from the Aztecs; it means "the artificers" or "master builders" in Nahuatl (pronounced NAH-wah-tul), the language of both the Toltecs and the Aztecs.

The first Toltecs were called the Toltec-Chichimec. During the days of the great Teotihuacán empire, based in the Valley of Mexico from about 400 to 700 C.E., Mesoamericans called the people who lived to the north of the Valley of Mexico the "Chichimecs" and considered them "barbarians"

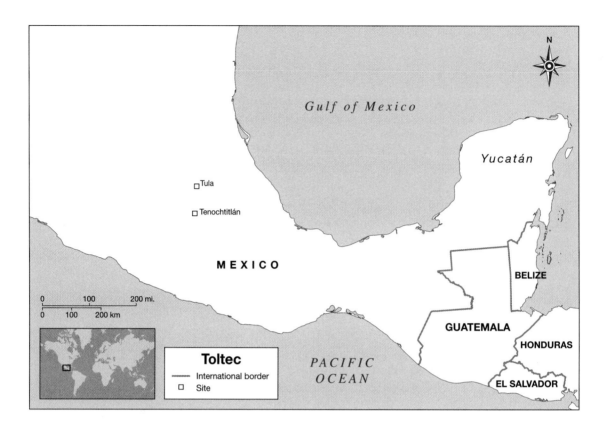

Map showing the sites of the ancient Toltec civilization in Mesoamerica.
Map by XNR Productions. The Gale Group.

(a word used to describe people from another land; it often has a negative meaning, however, suggesting the people described are inferior to others) because they were nomads and had not developed a full farming culture.

After the fall of Teotihuacán around 700 C.E., there were invasions into the valley by groups from the north. The earliest was led by the Toltec-Chichimecs, but other groups joined them as they settled in the Valley of Mexico. These groups gradually united as the Toltecs, though their union was not one of culture but of a shared need for a thriving community and the strength it provided for wars or conquests.

Location

The Toltec base was their capital city of Tula, in the far north of the Valley of Mexico in the present-day Mexican state of Hidalgo, about 50 miles (80 kilometers) north of Mexico City.

There is debate, however, about the extent of the Toltec empire. While some scholars believe the Toltecs ruled only a portion of the Valley of Mexico, others believe the Toltec empire (a vast, complex political unit extending across political boundaries and dominated by one central power) extended from the Chichimec territory to the north down to Monte Albán in the south, with other conquests or areas of influence reaching into the Maya lands at Chichén Itzá (pronounced chee-CHEN eet-SAH) in the present-day Mexican state of Yucatán.

Important Sites

Tula

It is difficult for archaeologists to reconstruct the ruins of the Toltec capital city, Tula. The city was burned and destroyed by the invading Chichimec groups who forced the Toltecs out in the twelfth century. Two centuries later the Aztecs, who were building their capital 50 miles (80 kilometers) away at Tenochtitlán, carried off the artwork and architectural structures of Tula to use in their construction.

Tula was known in the Nahuatl language as Tollan—the Place of Reeds. It was situated on a high rocky promontory (elevated place) protected by steep slopes on three sides. There had been villages located at the site from very early times, and by about 800 C.E. many bands of nomadic peoples had settled in the area. It became a crafts center for making pottery and obsidian (dark, solid glass formed by volcanoes) tools and knives.

The city reached its peak in the tenth century; then, beginning about 950 C.E., the rulers of Tula completely rebuilt the city in a century-long project. By this time Tula's population was somewhere between thirty-five thousand and sixty thousand people, and the city sprawled over about 5.5 miles (8.8 kilometers). During this rebuilding, according to Michael D. Coe in *Mexico: From the Olmecs to the Aztecs* (1994), all the streets were reoriented from true north to 15° east of north. A large plaza and ceremonial center (place peo-

Ruins of the Toltec city of Tula, Mexico. © *Danny Lehman/Corbis.*

ple gather to practice their religion) were added with ornate pyramids, temples, and ball courts.

The largest structure in Tula is known as Pyramid C. It was so badly vandalized (willfully destroyed or disfigured) that there are no sculptures or artwork left to examine for clues about the culture. The smaller Pyramid B, though, shows why the Toltecs were considered master builders. Pyramid B is a stepped pyramid. Extending from the front is a grand and ornate colonnade (hall with evenly spaced columns); inside the colonnade the walls are lined with bas-relief (carved three-dimensional pictures of stone, wood, or plaster, in which the image is raised above the background) carvings of warriors. A stairway leads to a two-room temple on top of the pyramid. At the doorway to the temple there are two stone columns representing the feathered serpent god Quetzalcoatl (pronounced kates-ahl-koh-AH-tul). There are two rooms inside the temple featuring tall pillars in the form of warriors that serve as roof supports. Giant stone fig-

Remains of the "Serpent Wall" in Tula depicting snakes devouring humans. © Paul Almasy/Corbis.

ures of warriors like these are found throughout Tula, and are called *atlantes*. *Atlantes* are just one of the art forms at Tula demonstrating the Toltec emphasis on the warrior cult.

Another common form of sculpture found within Pyramid B's temple are *chacmools*, statues of men reclining or lying down at an angle, with their heads up in a slightly awkward position. The stomach area of these statues forms a kind of platform on which a bowl or plate was placed as offerings to the gods—sometimes incense (a substance, such as wood, that emits a pleasant odor when burned) or small animals, but often human hearts. Pyramid B is flanked with bas-reliefs depicting the symbols of warriors, including eagles eating hearts, jaguars, and coyotes.

There are other pyramids, two ball courts, and many colonnades around the plaza. One 130-foot (39.6-meter) wall, called the "Serpent Wall," gruesomely depicts a serpent eating a human being. A low building at the border of the plaza features a wall called the *tzompantli* (pronounced

Illustration of a Toltec woman. *The Library of Congress.*

tzome-PAHN-tlee), a rack on which hundreds of decapitated human heads were mounted, perhaps in association with the sacrifices (offerings to the gods) of the defeated players in the ball games.

People lived in and around the capital city in complexes, or groups of about five houses built together with walls around the grouping. Each complex had a central courtyard and a place of worship. The houses were usually rectangular with several rooms for a family's use.

Archaeologists found the art at Tula focused mostly on the grim subjects of war and sacrifice. The Aztecs, on the other hand, reported a city of incomparable beauty and majesty. Michael C. Meyer and William L. Sherman, in their book *The Course of Mexican History* (1995), sum up the very different views of the city that emerged from the many Aztec reports: "Palace interiors were decked with the brilliant plumage of exotic birds, while various salons were lined with sheets of gold, jewels, and rare seashells. Residents' ears were soothed by the sweet singing of pet birds."

It is likely that a great deal of Tula's beauty simply did not endure. Many of the adornments that disintegrated over time or were whisked away by looters probably brightened the city and eased the somber tone most people find in its ruins. But Meyer and Williams also caution that the Aztec "version of paradise on earth, in which there was an abundance of all things, was embellished in the retelling over the centuries."

Toltec influence in Chichén Itzá

Archaeologists have reported a striking similarity between the Toltec capital of Tula and the northern lowlands Maya center of Chichén Itzá (pronounced chee-CHEN eet-SAH). The cities have similar layouts and share many characteristic features. These included architectural style, with rounded temples not seen elsewhere, and features like *atlantes, chacmools,* ball courts, and *tzompantlis.*

Though the connection between the post-Classic (900–1521 C.E.) Mayas and the Toltecs is very obvious, the nature of this connection has long been a matter of speculation. To some it seems clear the Toltecs invaded the Maya at Chichén Itzá and ruled the city as a conquest. Others think it is equally likely the Maya traders absorbed some of the Toltec styles during their extensive travels. Some theorize that the Mayas at some point brought the city of Tula under their power.

History

From about 400 to about 700 C.E. the city of Teotihuacán, located in the Valley of Mexico, ruled over a vast economic empire that included much of the southern two-thirds of Mexico, most of Guatemala and Belize, and some parts of Honduras and El Salvador. Teotihuacán was powerful and prosperous and kept the diverse warlike tribes, called the Chichimecs, to the north of the Valley of Mexico from attacking within the empire.

When Teotihuacán fell a turbulent period ensued, lasting from about 700 to 900 C.E. Some have called this period the "dark ages" of Mesoamerica. Most of the cities that had once flourished within the Teotihuacán trade network were reduced to villages, and constant war between small factions made life difficult. There was less expression in the arts and less skill in the crafts. Only a few cities, notably Cholula in the present-day state of Puebla, Xochicalco (pronounced zoe-chee-CAHL-coe) in the state of Morelos, and El Tajín in the northern part of the state of Veracruz, maintained rule over small states.

The ancient Mesoamericans distinguished between the "civilized" area of settled agricultural peoples of the Valley of Mexico and regions to the south and the "barbarians" to the north, where people hunted and gathered and did not live in settled villages or towns. The northerners were called the Chichimecs, a diverse group who, during times of drought (long period of little or no rainfall) or famine in the past, had attempted unsuccessfully to invade the towns and villages around the Teotihuacán empire.

Without the unifying force of Teotihuacán, there was little to prevent the Chichimecs from invading. Sometime in the early 900s, a group of Chichimecs arrived in the Valley of Mexico and one of their first acts was to invade Teotihuacán. They then burned and destroyed the remains of the abandoned city.

According to Aztec history, a leader from the north named Mixcoatl (pronounced meesh-COE-waht-tul; meaning "Cloud Serpent") led the invasion of Teotihuacán. He then established a new city in the Valley of Mexico called Culhuacán (pronounced cool-whah-CAHN) around 930 C.E. The people he initially led were the Toltec-Chichimecs, a specific group of Chichimecs who spoke the Nahuatl language and had lived at the borders of the Teotihuacán empire in western Mexico. Later other groups would join the Toltec-Chichimecs to form the group known as the Toltecs.

There are many conflicting stories about Mixcoatl and his military campaigns through Mesoamerica, his death, and the birth of his son, Topiltzin. Topiltzin (his given name, Ce Acatl, means "1 Reed" in Nahuatl) would become the most famous Toltec leader. As a young man he studied in the city of Xochicalco, where he became a high priest in the cult (a group that follows a living religious leader, or leaders, who promote new principles and practices) of Quetzalcoatl, a god whose name he adopted.

Topiltzin-Quetzalcoatl rose to power as the king of the Toltecs and began his reign by founding the capital city of Tula around 968 C.E. From Tula, Topiltzin-Quetzalcoatl began to establish control over a number of small states of various ethnic origins. According to some historians, he slowly turned his conquests into the Toltec empire. For about two centuries the Toltecs conquered regions throughout Mesoamerica. They either ruled the territories directly or demanded huge tributes (payments to a nation or its ruler made by people from a conquered territory as a sign that they surrender to the imposed rule; payment could be made in goods or labor or both) and took many young men as prisoners of war.

Topiltzin-Quetzalcoatl

Legends about the ruler Top-iltzin-Quetzalcoatl abound. (A legend is a story handed down from earlier times, often believed to be historically true.) Many scholars believe he actual-ly existed (though Mixcoatl's exis-tence is more strongly questioned) and there is evidence he was a very strong and able ruler-priest. Neverthe-less, scholars have found that over the years legends about Topiltzin the ruler can no longer be separated from those of the god whose name he took.

The Quetzalcoatl religious cult is believed to have become popular during the dark ages after the fall of Teotihuacán. When Topiltzin-Quetzal-coatl became king, he became a holy and moralistic religious reformer for the people of Tula. One of his reforms was to put an end to the practice of human sacrifice—claiming the god Quetzalcoatl wanted nothing more

Toltec representation of the god Quetzalcoatl. © *Werner Forman/Corbis.*

than butterflies or snakes. Tula was full of people from differ-ent areas and backgrounds, however, and a large number worshiped the god Tezcatlipoca (pronounced tez-caht-lee-POE-cah; meaning "Smoked Mirror" or "Smoking Mirror"). While Quetzalcoatl stood for human life, rebirth after death, culture, and peaceful existence, Tezcatlipoca represented night, death, sorcery, and war.

According to some Aztec accounts, those who wor-shiped Tezcatlipoca planned an uprising against Topiltzin-Quetzalcoatl. They knew that as a priest, Topiltzin had sworn to remain celibate (refrain from sexual relations) and to re-main pure in his deeds. They tried to trick the virtuous king into committing shameful acts that would discredit him in front of his people. In one tale Topiltzin-Quetzalcoatl is tricked into drinking *pulque* (pronounced PUHL-kay), an al-coholic beverage made from cactus juice, and becomes very drunk. In the morning he wakes up next to his sister, appar-ently having broken his vow of celibacy. Ashamed, he decides he is no longer fit to rule his empire and sails east into exile from his land.

In another tale Topiltzin-Quetzalcoatl kills Tezcatlipoca, but the god of sorcery casts a spell on his own body before he dies, making it impossible for the people of Tula to remove the rotting corpse (dead body) from their city. The body begins to smell very badly, and anyone who goes near it dies, but no amount of effort can move Tezcatlipoca's cursed corpse. Topiltzin-Quetzalcoatl realizes he has to leave the city to save it from the curse and, again, he sails off to the east.

Topiltzin-Quetzalcoatl goes into exile in both tales, sailing off on a raft made of serpents. The exile is said to have taken place, by modern calendars, in the year 987 C.E. The defeated ruler promises to return in the year 1 Reed as a man with fair skin and a beard (most of the natives of the Americas did not have facial hair).

Five centuries later in 1519—the Aztec year 1 Reed—Spanish conqueror Hernán Cortés (1485–1547), a man with fair skin and a beard, arrived in Mexico. Aztec leader Montezuma II (pronounced mohk-the-ZOO-mah; 1466–1520; ruled 1502–1520) welcomed Cortés, believing he was the powerful and revered Quetzalcoatl in his predicted return. The lack of Aztec resistance against the Spanish signaled the end of the Aztec civilization.

Another possible historical connection to Topiltzin-Quetzalcoatl's exile from Tula involves post-Classic (after about 900 C.E.) Maya history. At the end of the tenth century a conqueror called Kukulcán was said to have invaded the Maya world in the northern lowlands of Yucatán. The Maya had been expecting Kukulcán, the serpent god, to return to them. Many historians believe Kukulcán was none other than the exiled Topiltzin-Quetzalcoatl. His arrival may have been the beginning of a Toltec-Maya era at Chichén Itzá.

The warrior empire

According to Aztec legends, Topiltzin-Quetzalcoatl died around the turn of the tenth century. After his death, the fierce warlike factions of Tula took power, setting the tone for the four kings who followed him. The empire continued to expand through conquests, but the people under the Toltec rule were by no means unified. War became standard fare for everyone in Mesoamerica, and it became more vicious and bloody. About a century after Topiltzin-Quetzalcoatl's death, the last Toltec king, Huemac, or "Big Hand," took the throne. By most accounts, the worst violence took place during his reign. Famine gripped the Toltec people and fighting broke out among the different factions of Tula. Toltec warriors forced the impoverished conquered nations to pay them tribute. Prisoners of war proved valuable, as Toltec religious practices demanded more and more human sacrifices. It was during this time that mass human sacrifices (killing many people at once as an offering to the gods) first began to take place in Mesoamerica.

By 1064 evidence shows there was rebellion from within the city and probably some invasions from outsiders as well. Most Toltecs had abandoned their capital city and moved to new areas of Mexico. King Huemac and a group of people remaining loyal to him fled and attempted to establish a new city. Unable to stand the shame of his failed reign, Huemac committed suicide. Some Toltecs remained at Tula for a couple more decades, but the government and its kings were gone.

Government

The lack of Toltec artifacts has led to many scholarly debates about the Toltecs and arguments about the range and nature of their government. Some experts believe the Toltec ruled over a large empire in Mesoamerica, either directly through conquest or through their influence as traders. Others believe the Toltec state consisted of only a small area in the northern part of the Valley of Mexico, that the Toltec led violent raids and exacted tribute, but did not rule other regions.

The Toltec people came from a wide variety of backgrounds and practiced different customs. While the early Toltec rulers seem to have adopted the Teotihuacán culture, a later Toltec nation was notably different from the Teotihuacáns and other early Mesoamericans. The Toltecs placed supreme emphasis on war. While rulers of prior Mesoamerican societies often came from the ranks of the priesthood, the elite of the Toltec were always warriors first. Any male in

Atlantes are just one of the forms of Toltec architecture showing the society's emphasis on warfare. © *Paul Almasy/Corbis.*

their society, no matter what the background, could succeed only if he had proved himself in battle.

Toltec soldiers were divided up into several military orders: the Coyote, the Jaguar, and the Eagle. Territorial conquests and the bringing of prisoners to be sacrificed to the gods were the measure of worthiness and honor, bringing rewards to the soldier. The major function of the government at Tula may have been to bring together the many different peoples in their region to join in their wars, and to reap the benefit of the tributes or territory gained in this manner.

Economy

Farming in the area around Tula required extensive irrigation because there was little rain. The Toltecs built dams to capture water during the rainy seasons and then moved it to their fields through small canals. Toltec warriors also sent conquered peoples to live in well-guarded irrigated lands, where they produced crops for Tula and its warrior elite (people within a society who are in a socially superior position and have more power and privileges than others). Though farming and trade probably produced a good portion of the food and supplies needed by the Toltecs, it is likely they brought in a significant portion by collecting tribute from conquests.

The Aztecs considered the Toltecs master craftspeople. They are said to have been the first metalworkers in Mesoamerica, but none of the metalwork has been found by archaeologists at Tula. The Toltecs controlled some major obsidian mines, and within the city there were hundreds of obsidian workshops in which weapons, knives, and other tools of war were made. Other tools were also made for trade: the Toltecs are believed to have carried on extensive long-distance trade.

Religion

The Toltecs worshiped many gods, but from the later accounts, there were two gods who reigned supreme during the peak years of the empire: Quetzalcoatl and Tezcatlipoca. The rivalry between these two gods parallels the history of what is known about Tula.

Quetzalcoatl versus Tezcatlipoca

Quetzalcoatl was a god in every Mesoamerican pantheon (all of the gods that a particular group of people worship) and is particularly associated with Teotihuacán, the Toltecs, and the Aztecs, as well as the Mayas in Chichén Itzá. His name literally means "quetzal bird-snake." Because the quetzal was considered sacred, the name probably means divine serpent, but he is usually referred to as the "feathered serpent."

To the Toltecs, Quetzalcoatl was the creator god. In one legend, Quetzalcoatl and his friend or twin brother Xoloti, a god with the head of a dog, traveled to the underworld to collect the bones of dead human beings. Quetzalcoatl then dripped his own blood onto the bones, and human beings were restored to life. Quetzalcoatl was also the god of civilization, holiness, and peace. The Teotihuacáns had worshiped

Two Early Societies of the United States

Pre-Columbian societies are groups that existed during the period before Spanish explorer Christopher Columbus arrived in the Americas in 1492. Using strict standards of classifying peoples as civilizations, the pre-Columbian societies in the area of what is now the United States, no matter how complex, do not exactly fit into the category of "civilization" created by experts in ancient history. Two groups, however, that could be and sometimes are considered to be among the early civilizations in the United States are the Mississippians from the moundbuilding tradition in the southeast and the Anasazi from what is the present-day U.S. Southwest. These two groups also happen to have had regular contact with Toltec traders, according to some experts.

The Moundbuilders

In the East of what is now the United States in around 1500 B.C.E. a series of complex societies known as the "moundbuilders" arose. They had advanced farming skills and the ability to store their grains in pottery. The moundbuilders participated in ritualistic (formal acts performed the same way each time) burial practices that involved building large, intricate earthen mounds. Over the centuries they built thousands of these mounds throughout the southeast and Mississippi River Valley.

The first moundbuilding societies arose at Poverty Point, located in present-day northeastern Louisiana. The people who built them were hunter-gatherers, but their capacity for trade spread some of their religious and cultural traditions up the rivers through the Mississippi and Ohio River valleys. Eventually, the hunter-gatherers evolved into moundbuilders and flourished as a series of chiefdoms (social units mainly governed by one powerful ruler; the units that are larger and more structured than tribes but smaller and less structured than states) along the Mississippi River from Illinois and Wisconsin in the north down to Louisiana in the south.

Mississippians built several large cities around the great mounds through the years. Because of some uniquely Toltec features found in the design and imagery of some of the moundbuilders' art and architecture, archaeologist Michael C. Coe stated in *Mexico: From the Olmecs to the Aztecs,* that these sites, with their "huge temple mounds and ceremonial plazas, and their associated pottery and other artifacts, show Toltec influence." Throughout the history

Quetzalcoatl alongside their rain god for bringing farming and especially maize (corn) to the people of Mesoamerica. While the Toltecs seem to have initially accepted the Teotihuacán version of Quetzalcoatl, at some point they transformed him from the god of nature and farming into their god of holiness

of archaeological research into Amerindians, there has been speculation that the Toltecs were closely related to the moundbuilders, either as their descendants or their ancestors. One moundbuilder site in Arkansas was erroneously named the Toltec site, though it was later proved that there was no connection to the Mesoamericans. Many current scholars have concluded that the speculations connecting the Toltecs and the moundbuilders are wrong. Any Toltec influence on the moundbuilders that exists probably stems from trade relations.

The Anasazi

The Anasazi emerged in about 400 C.E. in the Four Corners region of present-day Arizona, New Mexico, Utah, and Colorado. (Meaning "Ancient Ones," the Anasazi are believed to have been the ancestors of today's Pueblo Indians.) They were originally hunter-gatherers with a nomadic way of life. But during the first century C.E. they settled down as farmers, raising crops such as maize, beans, and squash. They also became highly skilled artists, making beautiful baskets and pottery with distinctive black-on-white geometric patterns.

Beginning around 1 C.E. the Anasazi developed a highly complex society, eventually building great architecture. By the 1100s, at the peak of the Toltec empire, the Anasazi lived in large cliff dwellings and huge adobe apartment buildings, some of which had more than twelve hundred rooms. They had built extensive roads in the canyons and the southwestern countryside, connecting urban populations with villages over a wide area. One of the goods they traded was turquoise (a bluish-green gemstone) in exchange for quetzal (a Central American bird with bright green feathers) feathers and obsidian tools. The Anasazi culture disappeared in about the thirteenth century, about the same time as the Toltecs. Some scholars theorize the end of trade with Mexico may have contributed to the Anasazi's collapse.

Some experts believe Toltec traders may have ventured as far as the Southwest of the present-day United States, exchanging obsidian with the Anasazi for turquoise. The Toltec's feathered serpent imagery is still found among some of the New Mexican pueblos. Via another route, the Toltecs may have been trading with the Mississippian moundbuilding tribes of the southeastern United States as well.

and peace. By some accounts the Toltecs associated the god with Venus, the morning star. In one legend, after Quetzalcoatl was driven from Tula, he went into exile on the east coast of Mexico. Promising to return one day, he set himself on fire, and his heart rose as the morning star.

Images of Quetzalcoatl vary, but along with depictions of him as a feathered serpent, Quetzalcoatl was also represented as a human man with a beard. In 1519, by many accounts, Aztec emperor Montezuma II mistook the bearded and fair-skinned Spanish conqueror Hernán Cortés for the god Quetzalcoatl and welcomed him into the center of his city.

Tezcatlipoca was the Toltec god who opposed and rivaled Quetzalcoatl, and he probably shared equally in his power over human beings. The shield he carried was a dark mirror with which he could view or reflect human activities, and he may have functioned as a judge who wielded the arm of justice over people. Tezcatlipoca was also the god of night and sorcery, known for his warlike nature. He was said to have the power to destroy the world, and it was considered very dangerous not to worship him. Many credit the god Tezcatlipoca with the introduction of mass human sacrifices. A great deal of what is written about this god has to do with his sending Quetzalcoatl into exile through his sorcery or trickery.

Many scholars believe the accounts of Tezcatlipoca's banishment of Quetzalcoatl follow the historical facts of the Toltec empire. The original group of northerners who arrived in the Valley of Mexico adopted the peaceful ways of the Teotihuacáns—rulers were priests, as they had been in earlier times, and Quetzalcoatl, the peaceful god, was their representative.

As various ethnic groups from the north came upon the city of Tula, however, a more warlike culture arose. These groups were probably responsible for eliminating the ruler-priests and replacing them with warriors. The new, warlike state was represented by Tezcatlipoca. Accounts of the exile of Quetzalcoatl, god and ruler, relate the beginning of a new, more violent and bloody era in the Valley of Mexico.

Arts and sciences

Despite few artifacts to support their views, most archaeologists agree with the Aztecs about the Toltec mastery of arts and crafts. The arts of the Toltecs seem to reflect a major shift from the predominantly religious focus of art in the earlier ages to a focus on war and death. Many observers have noticed the difference between earlier Mesoamerican architecture, which used sacred imagery and seemed to be reaching up to the gods, and Toltec architecture, which appeared to have been created either to serve its function or to inspire fear in those who beheld it. Such views, however, may be missing the truth—no one knows what may have been taken from Tula by the Aztecs or others many years ago.

Some of the most prominent features of the ruins of Tula are the *atlantes,* colossal stone statues in the form of warriors standing guard over the temple, used to support the temple roof. These warriors also appear in the many bas-reliefs and other sculptures throughout the city. According to Brian Fagen, author os *Kingdoms of Gold, Kingdons of Jade* (1991): "Everywhere, fierce warriors strut, men carrying feather-decorated *atlatls* (spearthrowers) in their right hands, bundles of darts in the other. They wear quilted armor, round shields on their backs, hats topped by quetzal feather plumes."

A Toltec *chacmool* sits in front of the Temple of Quetzalcoatl in Tula. *© Paul Almasy/Corbis.*

Walls and columns throughout Tula are decorated with carved images of skulls and ferocious animals, such as the jaguar. Snakes are depicted eating humans or their hearts. One distinctive form of art found in Tula and Chichén Itzá is the *chacmool,* a large stone carving of a man lying down with his head up and sometimes holding a tray on his stomach. These are found in front of the temples, and are believed to have been used for offerings, particularly of human hearts in sacrifice ceremonies.

Decline

Sometime during in the 1100s, Tula met a violent and destructive end after famine and factional fighting within the empire. Legends report that Toltec king Huemac fled with those loyal to him, while other city residents moved to other parts of Mexico. Most experts believe a group of Chichimecs invaded and thoroughly sacked the city. This region of central Mexico again entered a dark age, in which no single power was able to unify the different cities and peoples. Warfare was widespread and ferocious, as people competed for scarce resources—this would remain the state of Mesoamerica until the rise of the Aztecs in the fourteenth century.

According to the Aztec legends, only a few noble Toltec families were thought to have remained in the Valley of Mexico after the fall of Tula. Since these Toltecs were said to be descended from Quetzalcoatl, most Mesoamerican rulers after the fall, regardless of their actual background, claimed descent from the Toltec kings whose reputation as gods and warriors could only add to their glory. Despite their relatively short period of time as a major Mesoamerican force, the Toltecs had become a huge presence in the hearts and minds of the Mexicans who came after them.

For More Information

Books

Coe, Michael C. *Mexico: From the Olmecs to the Aztecs*, 4th ed. London and New York: Thames and Hudson, 1994.

Fagan, Brian. *Kingdoms of Gold, Kingdoms of Jade*. London and New York: Thames and Hudson, 1991.

Meyer, Michael C., and William L. Sherman. *The Course of Mexican History*, 5th ed. New York and Oxford: Oxford University Press, 1995.

Sabloff, Jeremy A. *The Cities of Ancient Mexico: Reconstructing a Lost World*, revised ed. London and New York: Thames and Hudson, 1997.

Web Sites

Quetzalcoatl. http://www.rjames.com/Toltec/toltecs.asp (accessed on October 16, 2004).

The Toltecs. http://www.elbalero.gob.mx/kids/history/html/conquista/tolte.html (accessed on October 18, 2004).

The Rise of the Aztecs

25

The Aztec empire was at its peak when the Spanish conquistadores (conquerors) arrived in 1519. The first soldiers who arrived with the expedition of Spanish commander Hernán Cortés (1485–1547) were amazed by the civilization they found in the Valley of Mexico. The size, magnificence, beauty, wealth, order, cleanliness, and sophistication of the capital city of Tenochtitlán (pronounced tay-notch-teet-LAHN) rivaled the top European cities of the time, and outdid them in many ways.

At the same time, however, the conquistadors were horrified by the massive human sacrifices (killing many people as an offering to the gods) practiced by the Aztecs, usually in very gruesome ways. Many noted (as most people still do today) the odd combination of sophistication and brutality of the Aztecs. Few of the Spanish conquistadores who described the Aztecs noted that they—who were busily recording information about the civilization they had found—had recently killed thousands of Aztec people themselves and were taking part in the destruction of the most cherished

Barbarian: A word used to describe people from another land; it often has a negative meaning, however, suggesting the people described are inferior to others.

Chinampa: A floating garden in a farming system in which large reed rafts floating on a lake or marshes are covered in mud and used for planting crops.

City-state: An independent self-governing community consisting of a single city and the surrounding area.

Codex: A handmade book written on a long strip of bark paper and folded into accordion-like pages.

Empire: A vast, complex political unit extending across political boundaries and dominated by one central power, which generally takes control of the economy, government, and culture in communities throughout its territory.

Mass human sacrifices: Large-scale killing of people—or many people being killed at one time—as offerings to the gods.

Mercenary soldiers: Warriors who fight wars for another state or nation's army for pay.

Nahuatl: The language spoken by the Aztecs and many other groups in the Valley of Mexico.

Sacrifice: To make an offering to the gods, through personal possessions like cloth or jewels, or by killing an animal or human as the ultimate gift.

Tlatoani: A Nahuatl word meaning "speaker" or "spokesperson" used by the Aztecs to refer to their rulers, or "they who speak for others." The Aztec emperor was often called *huey tlatoani,* or "great speaker."

Tribute: A payment to a nation or its ruler, usually made by people from a conquered territory as a sign that they surrender to the imposed rule; payment could be made in goods or labor or both.

parts of Aztec culture (arts, language, beliefs, customs, institutions, and other products of human work and thought).

The Aztec empire arose very quickly, and its reign over Mexico was short-lived. The Aztecs arrived in the Valley of Mexico from humble, nomadic origins (wanderers with no fixed home) and were scorned as ruffians by most of its societies. Their main claim to fame from the beginning was their expertise as warriors. They established their island city of Tenochtitlán in 1325 and spent much of their first century there serving as warriors for another, larger and more powerful city-state (an independent self-governing community consisting of a single city and the surrounding area).

Soon the Aztecs' own city grew, and they learned the ways of the valley. By their second century at Tenochtitlán, from about 1428 to 1521, the Aztecs were able to take over as the most powerful group in Mesoamerica and prevailed over an empire of an estimated fifteen million people. (An empire is a vast, complex political unit extending across political boundaries and dominated by one central power, which generally takes control of the economy, government, and culture in communities throughout its territory.) The civilization brought together in this two-hundred-year period was a remarkable accomplishment for this unknown group from the north.

Dates of predominance
1325–1521 C.E.

Name variations and pronunciation
The name "Aztec" was bestowed upon the earliest members of the group at the time they arrived to settle in the Valley of Mexico. It meant "people from Aztlán." The people of the valley meant the name "Aztec" as an insult, indicating the Aztecs came from remote, humble origins. By the time the first Spanish writers began to describe the Aztecs in the sixteenth century, the name used for them had long been "Mexica" (pronounced may-SHEE-kah), or more specifically Culua-Mexica, which pointed to an association with the Toltec (pronounced TOHL-teck) rulers.

Sometime in the eighteenth century a writer used the word "Aztec" to describe the rulers of Tenochtitlán and the Aztec empire who called themselves Mexicas. Although it is not considered the correct term, since then "Aztec" has been used in many histories and the popular media. Scholars hope that in the not-too-distant future everyone will easily recognize the group by the more appropriate term, "Mexica." For the sake of recognition and simplicity, this book continues to use the term "Aztec."

The term "Aztec," used properly, refers to the peoples in the entire empire the Aztecs conquered, who were associ-

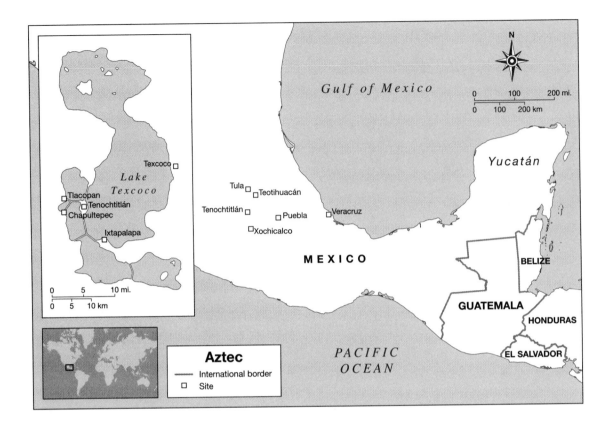

Map showing the sites of the ancient Aztec civilization in Mesoamerica.
Map by XNR Productions. The Gale Group.

ated with the founders of Tenochtitlán by trade, conquest, or traditions. This included not only the Nahuatl-speaking groups of the valley (pronounced NAH-wah-tul), but also the Zapotecs, Otomí, Mixtecs, and many others.

Location

At its peak, the Aztec empire extended from Guatemala in the south up to northern Mexico, spanning across Mexico from the Pacific Coast on the west to the Gulf of Mexico on the east. The empire included about five hundred cities, some very large, though none were nearly as large as Tenochtitlán, the capital of the Aztecs and the base of their rule. Tenochtitlán was located on an island in Lake Texcoco in the Valley of Mexico. Present-day Mexico City now occupies this area, as Mexico City was built on top of Tenochtitlán after the Spanish conquered it.

The Valley of Mexico is a huge, oval basin about 7,500 feet (2,286 meters) above sea level. It is set in the middle of the continent, less than 200 miles (322 kilometers) from the coasts to the east and west. It covers an area of about 3,000 square miles (7,770 square kilometers) and consists of some of the most fertile land in Mexico. At the time of the Aztec empire, lakes covered a large area of the basin's floor. A large portion of the Mesoamerican population in the sixteenth century lived in the valley. It was the most densely populated region of Mexico, consisting of groups with many backgrounds.

Tenochtitlán

Tenochtitlán was a huge and magnificent city of about two hundred thousand people at the time the Spanish conquistadors first arrived in 1519. It was one of the largest cities in the world at its peak, and it was compared by the Spaniards to the Italian city of Venice, which was built on canals like Tenochtitlán. Tenochtitlán was built on two small, swampy islands in the middle of Lake Texcoco.

Over several generations the islands had been built up by land refill. The Aztec workers drove long stakes into the bottom of the lake surrounding the island to create foundations. They filled in around the stakes with large rocks dragged in from the lakeshores and covered the rocks with mud they had painstakingly dredged up from the bottom of the lake. After many generations, the island of Tenochtitlán had expanded enough to merge with the island called Tlatelolco, which had been settled by another sect of Aztecs. Both islands together had expanded to be about 5 square miles (13 square kilometers) in area.

In order to support their population, the early settlers in Tenochtitlán needed more land for farming. They solved this problem by digging canals into the islands' salty marshes, cutting back the plants growing in the wetlands, and then piling these reeds on top of each other to form a large raft floating in the shallow water. They then brought mud from the bottom of the swamps to cover the rafts and planted willows underneath to anchor them. These became garden plots, called *chinampas*. With water always available, *chinampas* could produce crops year round. On these fertile floating

Tenochtitlán, the capital of the Aztec empire, with its canals and causeways.
© *Gianni Dagli Orti/Corbis.*

gardens the Aztecs raised maize (corn), beans, chili, tomatoes, squash, and flowers. When enough roots of the plants became established in the lake bottom, the *chinampas* formed small islands. The Aztecs also built light cane and thatch houses on top of *chinampas*.

Making good use of their watery environment, the Aztecs built canals in the city through which canoes could travel, bringing in food and supplies and carrying out waste. Three great causeways (roads built over the water) connected the island to the shore at various points. Each one was several miles long and around 25 or 30 feet (8 or 9 meters) wide. The causeways were constructed of wood beams fitted together like a jigsaw puzzle, and they could be taken apart in a hurry if an enemy approached. Until the Spanish arrived, no one had ever attacked the city.

The emperor Ahuitzotl (pronounced ah-weet-ZOH-tul; ruled c. 1486–1502) decided to thoroughly renovate the city around 1487. A new city plan was formed. In the massive rebuilding of Tenochtitlán, the Aztecs built the city on a grid (a system of rows and columns creating a checkerboard effect) with perfect, ruler-sharp straight lines in their streets, canals, and buildings. The sacred temple of the city was oriented to the four directions. In the center was Templo Mayor, a great double pyramid, with one tower dedicated to the god of war and sun, Huitzilopochtli (pronounced hweets-ee-loh-PAWCH-tlee), and the other dedicated to the rain god, Tlaloc (pronounced TLAH-lock). The steps of Templo Mayor were stained with the blood of thousands of human sacrifice victims. A *tzompantli,* a rack on which the heads of sacrifice victims were mounted and left to rot, stood near the temple, holding about ten thousand mounted human heads when the Spanish arrived. In the city center there were about eighty structures, including a ball court and temples dedicated to various gods such as Quetzalcoatl (pronounced kates-ahl-koh-AH-tul; the feathered serpent and creator god), Tezcatlipoca (pronounced tez-caht-lee-POE-cah; the god of night, sorcery, and war), and Ehecatl (the god of wind).

There were schools for the priests called *calmecac,* and schools for warriors called *telpochcalli.* There were also residences for the five thousand priests who tended Huitzilopochtli's temple. Near the Templo Mayor were the lavish palaces that housed royalty and the highest nobles of Tenochtitlán, complete with exotic flower gardens, parks, and ponds with swans. The architectural style used in the city was borrowed from earlier civilizations, particularly Teotihuacán (pronounced TAY-uh-tee-wah-KAHN).

Tenochtitlán had a local market in each of its four quarters, plus two other huge markets: one in the city center and one in the northern sector of Tlatelolco. All markets operated five days a week. An amazing assortment of foods, crafts, clothing, jewelry, animals, and even slaves were available in these lively markets, with as many as sixty thousand people busily buying and trading their wares on a given day. A constant flow of canoes laden with trade goods came in and out of the canals to the city. There was also heavy foot traffic on the causeways consisting of slaves and traders carrying their goods back and forth between the city and the lake shores.

The ruins of the ancient city of Tenochtitlán stand amidst the buildings of present-day Mexico City.
© Charles & Josette Lenars/Corbis.

Canals led out of the sacred center and into the city districts in each of the four directions. Perfectly parallel to the canals were streets for people on foot. All around these streets and canals there were lush, fragrant flower gardens. There were even zoos, with all kinds of mammals, snakes, and birds.

The city was divided into five districts, each with its own central plaza. The neighborhoods where most of the city's people lived were organized within these districts. The wealthy people lived around the market areas in houses made of stone or stucco (a plaster used to cover exterior walls). The common people lived farther out, usually in adobe (sun-baked brick) houses. All of the houses were painted white. Though its population was dense and traffic was heavy, Tenochtitlán was extremely clean and orderly.

Since the water in Lake Texcoco was salty, the people living in Tenochtitlán could not drink it. For their drinking water, they built an aqueduct, a pair of pipelines that used gravity to transport water to the island from natural springs near the lake's shores. The Aztecs had also devised an ingenious system of dealing with human waste. Their public latrines (bathrooms) were little huts built on canoes stationed along the canals. The canoes periodically transported the waste to the *chinampas*, where it served as fertilizer.

With its population of about two hundred thousand, Tenochtitlán was far larger than other cities around the Valley of Mexico and Lake Texcoco, but there were many other good-sized cities, and some were highly sophisticated. It is estimated there were about fifty cities in the Valley of Mexico. Just the cities surrounding Lake Texcoco that served as suburbs to Tenochtitlán had a combined population of about one and a half million people. The entire Aztec empire is thought to have had a population of about fifteen million people. Although the rulers at Tenochtitlán did not rule directly over all these cities, they were all related by trade, common religious celebrations, and the payment of tribute (goods or labor paid to a nation or its ruler, usually made by people from a conquered territory as a sign that they surrender to the imposed rule) to the capital.

History

The Valley of Mexico

The Valley of Mexico was called Anáhuac (meaning "near the water") by the people living there. It had been a center of civilization long before the Aztecs arrived around 1325. The great city of Teotihuacán had flourished from about 500 to 700, ruling its huge empire from the valley (see Chapter 18 for more information). The period that followed the fall of Teotihuacán was chaotic, with the valley's many smaller cities and communities at war with each other, competing for resources and territory.

In about 1000 the militaristic (warlike) Toltec empire, with its strong armies and healthy long-distance trade network, brought unity to Anáhuac for two more centuries (see Chapter 24 for more information). When the Toltecs fell, the Valley of

Mexico became a patchwork of independent city-states, most with only a small amount of surrounding territory.

Ancient Mesoamericans distinguished between what they considered the "civilized" peoples who were settled into agricultural life in the Valley of Mexico and certain areas south of it and the "barbarians" (used to describe people from another land; it often has a negative meaning, however, suggesting the people described are inferior to others) of the area north of the Valley of Mexico, where nomadic people hunted and gathered and did not live in settled villages or towns. These northerners were a diverse group called the Chichimecs.

To the people of the Valley of Mexico, the Chichimecs seemed coarse or uncouth. They did not have the architecture, arts, calendars, writing, and education people in the densely populated valley had known for many centuries. Despite their humble Chichimec roots, however, the Toltecs became legendary rulers of the valley. Both during the Toltec reign and after its fall, many other groups migrated to the valley from the north, including a group of about ten thousand Nahuatl-speaking people known as the Aztecs.

At the time the Aztecs arrived, most of the independent city-states in the Valley of Mexico had similar systems of government. Each was ruled by a supreme leader called the *tlatoani* (pronounced tlah-too-AH-nee), which means "speaker" or "spokesperson" in Nahuatl. Since the fall of the Toltecs, the belief throughout the valley was that the people destined to lead the cities should be descendants of the Toltec royal family. Most *tlatoanis* therefore claimed to be of the ancient royal Toltec descent, although in many cases this was questionable.

Every community in the valley, whether a large city or small town, had its own *tlatoani* and its own supreme gods. People, rich or poor, were fiercely loyal to their communities. The city-states used their armies to force smaller surrounding communities to pay tribute. These were often hostile arrangements; to defend themselves against unwanted conquests, smaller communities sometimes allied themselves with larger ones, willingly paying tribute for defense purposes. As new groups of outsiders settled into the valley, the competition for territory and resources increased.

The Aztec background

Much of what follows is taken from the Aztecs' accounts of their own history as they had learned it and passed it along from generation to generation; however, much of this history may have come from the Spanish conquistadores and missionaries of the sixteenth century. There are many conflicts among the different versions of the history, and yet many of the events described have been verified by other historical and archaeological records.

It is impossible to separate what many people consider the distinct fields of mythology and history included in the accounts. (Mythology is the field of scholarship that deals with the study of myths—traditional, often imaginary stories about ancestors, heroes, or supernatural beings that usually make an attempt to explain a belief, practice, or natural phenomenon.) The ancient historians did not distinguish between religion and fact in the way most historians do in the twenty-first century; their idea of what constituted reality was different than that of contemporary society. In addition, Aztec rulers willfully rewrote Aztec history to unify all groups within their empire. It is helpful to remember that history is never purely factual (based strictly on the facts). It is always shaped by the beliefs and views of the people who tell it. Nevertheless, the Aztec myths and descriptions provide a distinctive portrait of their historical and cultural background.

According to the Aztecs, they arrived on Earth through the openings of seven caves. They later settled on an island in the middle of a large lake called Aztlán ("the place of the white herons" or "the place of whiteness"). The exact location of Aztlán has never been determined. The supreme god of the Aztecs was named Huitzilopochtli; the name means "Hummingbird of the South or Left," the god of war and sun. Sometime in the twelfth century, the Aztec people set off from Aztlán in search of a new home. Four priests carried Huitzilopochtli, in hummingbird form, and the god occasionally twittered out directions to them as they traveled. The Aztec people wandered into the Valley of Mexico early in their travels and settled there in various places over the years.

One of the places the Aztecs stayed was Culhuacán (pronounced cool-whah-CAHN), which had been an early home of the Toltecs. After their stay, the Aztecs called them-

Two Spanish Sources: Díaz and Sahagún

As a rule, accounts of the defeated by their conquerors should always be viewed with some suspicion. It usually isn't in the interest of the conquerors to present the defeated in a sympathetic light or to portray them as equal in sophistication to themselves. The following writers, Bernal Díaz (del Castillo; pronounced cah-STEE-yoe; c. 1492–1581), a conquistador, and Bernardino de Sahagún (c. 1499–1590), a Franciscan missionary (a person, usually working for a religious organization, who tries to convert people, usually in a foreign land, to his or her religion), were both Spanish eyewitnesses to the Aztec culture around the time of the Spanish conquest. Their works have the biases (partialities or judgments) of their times and circumstances, but both had good powers of observation. Their works have shaped the current understanding of the Aztecs and their history. Some excellent Aztec sources survived the conquest (see Chapter 27 for more information on Aztec books and oral traditions), but the works of these two Spaniards present several central elements of Aztec history and culture not recorded elsewhere.

Bernal Díaz was a Spanish soldier who joined the expedition of Spanish conquistador Hernán Cortés in 1519 and took part in the conquest of the native peoples of the Americas. He was in Tenochtitlán when it fell to the Spanish, and Díaz remained in Mesoamerica for the rest of his life. Many years after the conquest, he felt compelled to respond to a book about the conquest published by Cortés's secretary, who overstated the heroism of Cortés and had, in fact, never been to the Americas.

In 1552 Díaz began work on his own account, *Historia verdadera de la conquista de Nueva España* (title translates as *The True History of the Conquest of New Spain*). Díaz, however, was not highly educated and his work was considered crude. It was not published during his lifetime. A version of the book was published in Spain in 1632, but only after an editor had considerably altered the text. It was not until 1904 or 1905 that an edition prepared from the original manuscript appeared and somehow survived in Guatemala.

Díaz's history focuses on the events from 1519 to 1521, when the Aztecs were

selves the Culhua-Mexicas to associate themselves with the renowned Toltecs, the chosen rulers of the valley. By this time the Aztecs had aspired to rule the great land they were traversing, even though the other inhabitants of the valley considered them vulgar nomads.

Despite their crude behavior, the Aztecs had gained a reputation as skilled warriors. In several of the places they stayed,

conquered by the Spanish. Though the style is rough and many of Díaz's interpretations seem naïve, the elderly soldier wrote with deep honesty and remarkable memory. In many cases he has provided descriptions of things for which there are no other sources.

In 1529 a young Spanish Catholic missionary, Bernardino de Sahagún, was sent by his church to Mexico, where he taught young native Americans at a missionary school near Tenochtitlán. As he taught his students religion and the arts in Spanish and Latin, Sahagún took pains to learn their language, Nahuatl. He became fascinated by the Aztecs and soon began researching their history and culture.

Sahagún's research began with a series of interviews with the Aztec elders (people who have authority because of their age and experience) in the 1540s. He soon found that the Aztec orators— the people whose job it was to pass on the history of their people from generation to generation—relied on codices (plural of codex), books on birch bark paper filled with pictures and symbols. Most of the codices in existence at the time of the Spanish conquest in 1521 had been destroyed by the conquerors, who believed the books were full of pagan (non-Christian and therefore evil to them) instruction.

A few surviving codices were brought out for Sahagún, and the elders showed him how they were used. Bit by bit, the elders described the history and traditions of the Aztec people and Sahagún, with the help of Nahuatl-speaking assistants, recorded the words of the elders in their own language. By about 1580, Sahagún's great work, the twelve-volume manuscript of the *Florentine Codex* was complete. Its pages presented a column of Nahuatl text on the right and comments in Spanish in a column on the left. In between were illustrations to accompany the text. The *Florentine Codex* was organized by subject matter, with volumes dedicated to such topics as history, the gods, the calendar, Aztec society, and the Aztec perception of the natural world.

they became mercenary soldiers (warriors who fight wars for another state or nation's army for pay) for rulers in the area. Most of the valley's inhabitants found many Aztec practices revolting, particularly their methods of performing human sacrifices and their habit of raiding other communities to take their women. After several run-ins with other communities, the Aztecs had been chased out of most of the settled areas in the valley.

With nowhere else to go, the Aztecs camped out on the marshy shores of Lake Texcoco where no one else considered living. It was there, according to their later accounts, that the Aztecs received a sign foretelling they had found the location of their new home: On a small island on the lake, they saw an eagle perched on a cactus bearing large red fruit; the eagle was eating a snake. The Aztecs settled on the lake island in the year 1325 after wandering for more than two hundred years.

Building a home

As the Aztecs began building their city, sometime around 1345 a conflict erupted, dividing them into two groups. One group settled on the island they called Tenochtitlán, while the other group settled on a nearby island to the north they called Tlatelolco. The two islands eventually merged as the Aztecs built them up with landfill. They quickly outgrew the tiny islands, however, and with amazing resolve and a tremendous amount of labor gathered mud from the bottom of the lake to build up the land area of the islands. They drove long stakes into the lake bottom and filled in the cavities with rocks and mud to make the islands even larger.

As they settled into their new home, the Aztecs began trading with other communities for supplies and protection. Soon young Aztec warriors were hired as mercenary soldiers by the Tepanecs of Azcapotzalco, one of the most powerful communities of the valley. With the help of the fierce Aztec warriors, Azcapotzalco conquered many city-states in the valley and shared their tribute and loot with the Aztecs. The arrangement eventually turned into a partnership between the two groups. The Aztecs learned a great deal about the valley's culture from the Tepanecs; they also learned about building an empire.

By 1375 the Aztecs had built a very large city and had placed their first *huey tlatoani,* or "great speaker," Acamapichtli (pronounced ah-cahm-ah-PEECH-tlee; ruled 1376–1396), on the Aztec throne. Neighboring communities feared and respected them.

From independence to empire

In 1427 Itzcoatl (pronounced eetz-coe-WAH-tul; translates to "Obsidian Snake"; ruled c. 1427–1440), a new Aztec *tlatoani,* took the throne. The Tepanecs had begun to fear the great growth of their partner, the Aztecs. Itzcoatl no longer trusted the Tepanecs and decided to crush them. In 1428 the Aztecs formed the Triple Alliance, joining with the nearby cities of Texcoco, ruled by Nezahualcoyotl (pronounced ne-za-hwahl-COY-oh-tul; 1403–1473), the poet king, and the city of Tlacopan on the western side of the lake. The three cities joined together to thoroughly destroy the city of Azcapotzalco. Thereafter, the Aztecs had the strongest state in Mexico.

The new ruler, Itzcoatl, decided upon a number of reforms for the Aztec people. He began by changing history. Most of the people of the Valley of Mexico had special orators who were trained to tell their stories. They relied mainly on memory, but they also used books with pictures that served to jog their memories as they related their tales. Itz-

The Man behind the Emperors

The Aztec *huey tlatoanis,* like any other rulers or governments, had trusted counselor/assistants to help them organize their empires and make crucial decisions about trade, law, and war. Many historians believe one such adviser to the Aztec *huey tlatoanis,* Tlacaelel ("Manly Heart"), may have been largely responsible for their remarkable rise to power. Tlacaelel was the nephew of Itzcoatl and the brother of Montezuma I, (pronounced mohk-the-ZOO-mah; c. 1390– c. 1464; ruled 1440–1469) and probably could have taken the post of *tlatoani* had he desired. Instead, he led from behind the scenes, but it was reported that Tlacaelel's orders were always followed immediately.

Tlacaelel is credited with formulating the plan by which Itzcoatl was able to recreate the empire's history, imposing a world view in which the Aztecs were the chosen leaders and heirs of the Toltecs. Along with burning the old books for this purpose, Tlacaelel made strong reforms in the workings of the government and transformed the Aztec religion. He is also thought to be responsible for the concept of "flower wars," battles staged by two cities that agreed to fight for the sole purpose of providing each other with captives for sacrifice. Tlacaelel was also the mastermind behind the Triple Alliance with Texcoco and Tlacopan.

coatl had all the books collected and burned, since they did not tell the story as he wished it to be remembered. He provided orators with a new history of the Aztecs, in which the Aztec rulers were the undisputed descendants of the Toltecs and the only true rulers of Mexico. Part of his new vision of the Aztec people was that it was their duty to provide the hearts and blood of their prisoners of war to the gods so the sun would have the fuel it needed to rise and light up the earth every morning.

In 1440 Itzcoatl was succeeded by his nephew Montezuma I, a renowned general in the Aztec army. Under his leadership, the Aztecs conquered many new lands and put together a central state government to administer all holdings. As the city of Tenochtitlán grew in population, it became more and more dependent on the tribute coming in from the cities defeated by Aztec warriors. The Aztec army attacked cities and communities farther away. From each city they demanded tribute in many forms, bringing wealth to

Tenochtitlán. In general, they did not rule the communities they conquered.

An era of mass human sacrifice

In the mid-fifteenth century one catastrophe after another occurred: first, locusts ate crops; then, the lake flooded the fields; and later, frosts killed more crops. Many Aztecs died from hunger and disease while others fled to different regions. During the years of catastrophe, the Aztec priests began to practice human sacrifice on a scale never known before, killing thousands of prisoners of war as offerings to the gods. When the famine ended in 1455, the Aztecs probably reasoned that the sacrifices had worked, and they continued the practice of human sacrifice on a huge and horrific scale from this time forward. From every battle, they captured many soldiers to sacrifice to the gods.

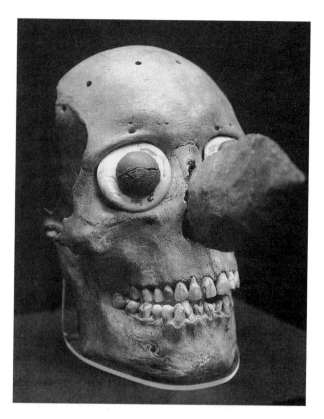

The Aztecs killed thousands of prisoners of war as human sacrifices to the gods. This skull was once an Aztec sacrifice victim. *AP/Wide World Photos.*

During the occasional periods when there were no wars being fought, the Aztecs would arrange to enter into battles, called "flower wars," with a neighboring city, usually Tlaxcala. These were staged battles fought solely for the purpose of taking prisoners to sacrifice. Although the arrangement with Tlaxcala was agreed to by both sides, at some point the Aztecs must have angered their partner in ritual war. When the Spanish attacked the Aztecs, an estimated two hundred thousand Tlaxcala soldiers were fighting alongside the Spanish, providing invaluable help in the conquest.

According to the Aztec religion, the world had been created and destroyed four times before the present world. Each of these worlds had its own sun, which died as the world ended. The Aztecs believed their sun—the fifth sun—would be extinguished and the world would end if they did not supply the gods with enough blood and beating hearts from human sacrifice (see Chapter 27 for more information).

When the emperor Ahuitzotl organized a ceremony to dedicate the building of a pyramid and temple to Huitzilopochtli, the Aztec army, along with its allies from Texcoco and Tlacopan, rode off to start a flower war with the cities of Tlaxcala and Huejotzingo. The war was waged solely for the purpose of bringing sacrifice victims to the dedication ceremony. In 1487 the Aztec army was said to have brought twenty thousand prisoners of war from the battle. The captives were lined up in columns that spanned the long streets of Tenochtitlán as each awaited their turn to be sacrificed on the temple stairs.

The end of the era

Ahuitzotl expanded the empire to its fullest, gaining territory south all the way to Guatemala, and holding most of central Mexico, including large portions of the present-day Mexican states of Oaxaca (pronounced wah-HAH-kah), Morelos, Veracruz, and Puebla. In 1502 Montezuma II (1466–1520; ruled 1502–1520) took the throne. He was known to be a great warrior whose forces were constantly at war, but Montezuma was also a thoughtful and quiet man, with a strong religious sensibility.

According to some, Montezuma II was also quite superstitious. By the time of his reign, there were signs the Aztec people were tiring of constant war and sacrifice. Aztec poetry from the last years of the empire expressed a longing for human kindness and mercy and an end to the blood and violence. On what new paths Montezuma might have led his empire, had it not been invaded by the Spanish, will never be known. The Aztec empire was conquered during Montezuma's reign and he was the last of the great Aztec *huey tlatoanis*.

For More Information

Books

Clendinnen, Inga. *Aztecs: An Interpretation*. Cambridge, UK: Cambridge University Press, 1991.

Coe, Michael D. *Mexico: From the Olmecs to the Aztecs*, 4th ed. London and New York: Thames and Hudson, 1994.

Fagan, Brian M. *Kingdoms of Gold, Kingdoms of Jade: The Americas before Columbus*. London and New York: Thames and Hudson, 1991.

Meyer, Michael C., and William L. Sherman. *The Course of Mexican History,* 5th ed. New York and Oxford: Oxford University Press, 1995.

Thomas, Hugh. *Conquest: Montezuma, Cortés, and the Fall of Old Mexico.* New York: Simon & Schuster, 1993.

Web Sites

The Aztecs. http://www.elbalero.gob.mx/kids/history/html/conquista/aztecas.html (accessed on October 18, 2004).

Hooker, Richard. "Civilizations in America: The Mexica/Aztecs." *World Civilizations, Washington State University* http://www.wsu.edu/~dee/CIVAMRCA/AZTECS.HTM (accessed on October 18, 2004).

Aztec Government and Economy

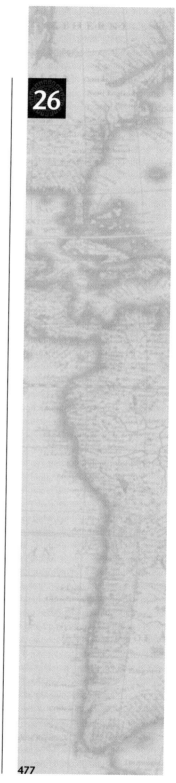

26

From the time the Aztecs settled in Tenochtitlán (pronounced tay-notch-teet-LAHN) in 1325 until the day the Spanish conquered the city in 1521 was a period of just less than two hundred years. There were two distinct eras of government and economy during this time, each about one hundred years long. During the period from 1325 until 1427, the Aztecs were under the domination of the Tepanecs. As subjects of a more powerful people, they gradually built their monarchy and established an economy at least partly based on the spoils they brought in from the battles they fought with the Tepanecs. In the second hundred years, the Aztecs, under the Triple Alliance formed with the nearby cities of Texcoco and Tlacopan, were the unquestioned military power and dominated the Valley of Mexico.

With their highly skilled military forces, they went on to conquer vast territories beyond the valley, forcing the conquered people to pay hefty annual tribute payments in the form of goods sent to the capital city. (A tribute is a payment by one nation to a conquering nation, often occurring on a regular basis like a tax.) War became an economic neces-

Words to Know

Atlatls: Spearthrowers.

Cacao beans: Beans that grow on an evergreen tree from which cocoa, chocolate, and cocoa butter are made.

Calpulli: (The word means "big house"; the plural form is *calpultin*.) Social units consisting of groups of families who were either related in some way or had lived among each other over the generations. *Calpultin* formed the basic social unit for farmers, craftspeople, and merchants. The precise way they worked is not known.

Chinampa: A floating garden in a farming system in which large reed rafts floating on top of a lake or marshes are covered in mud and used for planting crops.

Empire: A vast, complex political unit extending across political boundaries and dominated by one central power, which generally takes control of the economy, government, and culture in communities throughout its territory.

Hierarchy: The ranking of a group of people according to their social, economic, or political position.

Mercenary soldiers: Warriors who fight wars for another state or nation's army for pay.

Nahuatl: The language spoken by the Aztecs and many other groups in the Valley of Mexico.

Nomadic: Roaming from place to place without a fixed home.

Subordinate: Subject to someone of greater power; lower in rank.

Succession: The system of passing power within the ruling class, usually upon the death of the current ruler.

Tlatoani: A Nahuatl word meaning "speaker" or "spokesperson" used by the Aztecs to refer to their rulers, or "they who speak for others." The Aztec emperor was often called *huey tlatoani,* or "great speaker."

Tribute: A payment to a nation or its ruler, usually made by people from a conquered territory as a sign that they surrender to the imposed rule; payment could be made in goods or labor or both.

sity for the empire (a vast, complex political unit extending across political boundaries and dominated by one central power, which generally takes control of the economy, government, and culture in communities throughout its territory). As the population of Tenochtitlán grew, the resources surrounding it were inadequate to support its people, and the Aztecs became increasingly dependent on tribute payments. The Aztecs were highly successful in maintaining a flow of

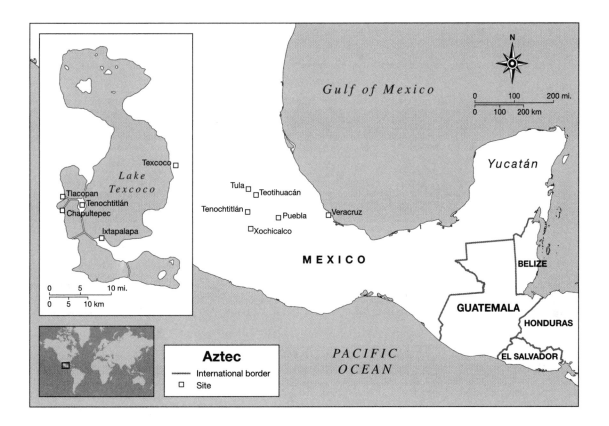

materials into Tenochtitlán from afar, though, and their capital city experienced a high level of prosperity.

Government

The early years

During the centuries before 1325, while the Aztecs wandered Mexico in search of a home, they practiced a form of democracy. The elders (people who have authority because of their age and experience) of their group elected a leader on the basis of his power and skills. Accomplishments on the battlefield were always the primary test of a potential leader's strength. In its nomadic times, the Aztec society had only a few powerful people: the leader, some priests, and some war commanders. The rest of the population was made up of peasant farmers and warriors.

In their first hundred years at Tenochtitlán, the Aztecs were subordinate (subject to someone of greater power) to the

Tepanecs, a very powerful group who lived on the west shore of Lake Texcoco in the cities of Azcapotzalco and Tlacopan. The Tepanecs had hired the Aztec warriors as mercenary soldiers (warriors who fight wars for another state or nation's army for pay). When the Aztecs helped the Tepanecs conquer other territories, they were entitled to share in the tribute paid by the defeated cities. During these years, Tenochtitlán and its government grew in wealth and power.

For their first fifty years at Tenochtitlán, the Aztecs were ruled by a chieftain (the leader of a tribe). In 1376 they formed a monarchy, installing a king named Acamapichtli (pronounced ah-cahm-ah-PEECH-tlee; ruled c. 1376 to 1395), who claimed descent from the Toltecs (pronounced TOHL-tecks), a group who had ruled the Valley of Mexico from around 900 to 1200. Many people in the Valley of Mexico believed the Toltecs had been chosen by the gods to rule over the valley. In fact, almost all Mesoamerican rulers claimed descent from the Toltec kings, regardless of their actual background. From Acamapichtli's reign until the end of the empire, the supreme leader of the Aztecs was always chosen from this founding royal family.

The Aztec empire: 1427 to 1521

At the end of their first hundred years in Tenochtitlán, the Aztec kings were still under the control of the Tepanec emperors of Azcapotzalco. With the help of Aztec warriors the Tepanecs had become the most powerful people of the Valley of Mexico. The arrangement between the Aztecs and Tepanecs had been satisfactory to both for many years, but as Tenochtitlán grew in power, its leaders wanted to rule the valley. The Tepanec leaders, fearing the increasing power of the Aztecs, tried to suppress them, demanding greater amounts of tribute.

The Triple Alliance

The Alcohuans, a Nahuatl-speaking (pronounced NAH-wah-tul; the language spoken by the Aztecs and many other groups in the Valley of Mexico) people who had migrated to the Valley of Mexico about the same time as the Aztecs, lived on the eastern side of Lake Texcoco. During the fourteenth century, their city, Texcoco, had grown and thrived independently of the Tepanecs. Under the new name of Texcocans, they were rapidly gaining a reputation for their cultural refinement. When the Tepanecs conquered Texcoco in 1418, they killed its king. His son and heir, fifteen-year-old Nezahualcoyotl (pronounced ne-za-hwahl-COY-oh-tul, meaning "Hungry Coyote"; 1403–1473) was forced to flee. Years later, Nezahualcoyotl returned to claim his position as king, killing the Tepanec lord who had taken his father's throne.

In 1426 Nezahualcoyotl teamed up with the Aztec emperor Itzcoatl (pronounced eetz-coe-WAH-tul; ruled c. 1427–1440) and together they defeated the Tepanec city of Azcapotzalco, killing most of its population. They then formed the Triple Alliance, bringing the formerly Tepanec-dominated town of Tlacopan into the alliance. These triumphs marked the beginning of the Aztec empire, and Itzcoatl became its first emperor, or *huey tlatoani* (pronounced WHO-ee tlah-too-AH-nee; "great speaker"). From this time until the Spanish conquest—nearly one hundred years—the Aztecs were unquestionably the most powerful people in Mesoamerica.

With the Aztecs always in the lead, the Triple Alliance remained intact for years. Texcoco and Tlacopan followed the bidding of the Aztec emperor in Tenochtitlán in matters of war only; they were independent on other matters. The alliance imposed its rule on cities throughout an ever-expanding area of central Mexico, demanding tribute in the form of certain amounts of goods on certain dates. Under their alliance agreement, Tenochtitlán and Texcoco received two-fifths of the tribute, while Tlacopan received one-fifth. The cities became rich and according to Robert Hull in his book *The Aztecs* (1998): "Each year Tenochtitlán received 7,000 tons of corn, 4,000 tons each of beans, chia seeds, and grain, an unbelievable 2 million cotton cloaks, and a huge quantity of war costumes, shields, and feather headdresses."

Texcoco

Under King Nezahualcoyotl, who ruled from about 1433 to 1470, Texcoco became the second most important city in the Aztec empire. Not long after he recovered the throne of his kingdom, Nezahualcoyotl created a code of laws so well regarded that it became the standard throughout

Illustration of villagers in Texcoco greeting King Nezahualcoyotl. *The Art Archive/National Archives of Mexico/Mireille Vautier.*

the empire. During the ninety-one years in which Nezahualcoyotl and his son, Nezahualpilli (1460–1515) reigned, Texcoco was the legal center for the entire empire. King Nezahualcoyotl was also a great poet, philosopher, biologist, and engineer. With his promotion of culture and education, Texcoco drew great artists—poets, dancers, and musicians—and the top thinkers from all over Mesoamerica, quickly becoming the empire's center of learning.

Texcoco remained a very strong city during the life of Nezahualcoyotl, but gradually during the reign of his son, Nezahualpilli, Texcoco became increasingly dominated by the powerful Tenochtitlán. Texcoco was not alone in becoming subordinate to Tenochtitlán. When Tenochtitlán had first been established, a sect of the Aztecs broke off from the main group and established their own city on a nearby island they called Tlatelolco. The two cities remained separate and were somewhat hostile to one another for years. In 1473 the Aztecs of Tenochtitlán overthrew the Tlatelolco government and incorporated the island into their city. One of their largest markets was on Tlatelolco.

Expanding throughout Mexico

The Aztecs were not content to remain in the Valley of Mexico, and within decades of forming the Triple Alliance their armies had conquered most of central and southern Mexico. The Aztecs never controlled any of the Maya (pronounced MY-uh) lands, nor did they ever conquer the southern part of the Mexican state of Veracruz. Nevertheless, their empire covered a vast area compared to the size of many large European nations.

Unlike the European nations, however, the Triple Alliance did not actually rule most of the peoples it conquered. Instead the empire installed an official tax collector in the conquered city or center and expected prompt payment of tribute on a regular basis. Submitting to the Aztecs largely meant making hefty tribute payments and acknowledging their supreme authority in the area. In times of war, the defeated city might also have to send soldiers to fight for the empire.

In general, though, conquered cities and city-states continued to rule themselves. Although they did have to agree to recognize the Aztec war and sun god Huitzilopochtli as the supreme god, they continued to practice their traditional religions. If, however, a conquered people did not send their tribute payments, they would face an army of Aztec warriors in violent combat, and everyone knew the Aztecs excelled most in military matters.

At its height, the empire was a very loose coalition (a union of different peoples under an agreement) of different peoples with vast populations. The people of the empire, according to Michael D. Coe in *Mexico: From the Olmecs to the Aztecs* (1994) were "held in a mighty system whose main purpose was to provide tribute to the Valley of Mexico." In all there were probably about fifteen million people in this coalition. Many of them spoke Nahuatl and worshiped, for the most part, the same gods as their conquerors.

There were people of many different backgrounds and languages within the empire. For example, in 1379 the Aztec warriors conquered a non-Nahuatl speaking farming

The Aztec Kings and Emperors, 1376 to 1521

- Acamapichtli (pronounced ah-cahm-ah-PEECH-tlee; ruled c. 1376–1395): The founder of the royal Aztec dynasty and the first chieftain of Tenochtitlán. In 1376 the leader of the Tepanecs, Tezozomoc, allowed the Aztec leaders to establish their own monarchy. They elected Acamapichtli as their new leader, whose father was Aztec but whose mother was apparently a direct descendant of the Toltecs. Acamapichtli is said to have taken a wife from each Aztec *calpulli*, or district. With his claim to Toltec blood, his offspring became the new Aztec/Toltec nobility, ready to be rulers of a great empire in Mexico.

- Huitzilihuitl (pronounced wheet-zeel-ee-WHEE-tul; ruled c. 1395–1417): The son of Acamapichtli, Huitzilihuitl married the daughter of the powerful Tepanec king, Tezozomoc.

- Chimalpopoca (pronounced chee-mahl-poe-POE-cah; ruled c. 1417–1427): The grandson of Aztec royal founder Acamapichtli and Tepanec ruler Tezozomoc. Chimalpopoca plotted against the heir to the Tepanec throne, and after Tezozomoc died, the Tepanecs captured and murdered him.

- Itzcoatl (pronounced eetz-coe-WAH-tul; means "obsidian serpent"; c. 1380–1440; ruled c. 1427–1440): An illegitimate son of Acamapichtli (his mother was a slave) and the uncle of Chimalpopoca, Itzcoatl had been prominent in the council and as a warrior for several decades before taking the throne. In his second year as *tlatoani,* the Aztecs overthrew the Tepanecs and formed the Triple Alliance with the cities of Texcoco and Tlacopan. The destruction of Azcapotzalco, one of the most powerful communities of the valley, marked the beginning of the Aztec empire; Itzcoatl was the first of the empire's six emperors, or *huey tlatoanis*. Itzcoatl's adviser Tlacaelel is credited (and blamed) for many significant transformations in Aztec life and culture taking place at this time. Tlacaelel also served under Montezuma I (pronounced mohk-the-ZOO-mah), Axayácatl (pronounced ash-eye-AH-catl), and Tizoc (pronounced TEEZ-ohk).

society in the area that is now the state of Morelos. The Aztecs named the people the *Tlahuica* (meaning in Nahuatl, "people who work the land"). The largest Tlahuica cities were Cuauhnahuac (now Cuernevaca) and Huaxtepec. After the Aztecs defeated them in battle, the Tlahuicans were required to pay an annual tribute. According to careful records left behind by the Aztecs, the Tlahuicans sent eight

- Montezuma I, or Montezuma Ilhuicamina (also spelled Moctezuma; ruled c. 1440–1469): Nephew of Itzcoatl and a leading general of the Aztecs, Montezuma I led his armies to many triumphs in the battlefield, greatly expanding the Aztec empire. In the 1450s the Valley of Mexico suffered from heavy flooding that led to crop failures and famine. Montezuma began making conquests in unaffected areas outside of the Valley of Mexico, including Mixtec regions in the present-day Mexican state of Oaxaca (pronounced wah-HAH-cah), and Huastec and Totonac territory on the Gulf Coast.

- Axayácatl (ruled c. 1469–1481): Grandson of Montezuma I, Axayácatl spent much of his reign battling to reconquer rebelling territories; he also added vast areas to the empire. In the course of combat, he lost a leg.

- Tizoc (ruled c. 1481–1486): Grandson of Montezuma I and brother of Axayácatl, Tizoc was known as a weak ruler. During his reign, however, the empire continued to grow.

- Ahuitzotl (pronounced ah-weet-ZOH-tul; ruled c. 1486–1502): Grandson of Montezuma I and brother of Axayácatl and Tizoc, Ahuitzotl was a fierce and warlike emperor, responsible for adding vast regions to the empire. The new territories under his reign ran from Guatemala up the coast of the Gulf of Mexico, doubling the size of the empire. Ahuitzotl undertook a rebuilding of Tenochtitlán, including the building of the Templo Mayor, a set of twin pyramids dedicated to the war god Huitzilopochtli (pronounced hweets-ee-loh-PAWCH-tlee) and the rain god Tlaloc. The estimated number of human sacrifices in the four-day dedication ceremony for the new temple was twenty thousand.

- Montezuma II (also Moctezuma Xocoyótzin; ruled 1502–1520): Son of Axayácatl, Montezuma II ruled over the empire for seventeen years. He was responsible for several major advances in the social, political, economic, and cultural arenas. He died in 1520 while battling Spanish conquistadores (conquerors).

thousand sets of clothing, sixteen thousand sheets of bark paper, and twenty thousand bushels of maize to Tenochtitlán annually.

Even though the Tlahuicans were forced to pay hefty tributes for more than a century, they grew wealthy and enjoyed a stable government as part of the Aztec empire. They were strong enough to conquer a few cities around them and established a very profitable trade business. The Tlahuicans remained loyal to the Aztecs to the end, coming to their defense against the Spanish in 1520. This was not the case with some of the other peoples of the empire. Aztec warriors were continually fighting rebellions from cities and regions that deeply resented paying tribute.

A couple of groups successfully repelled the attacks of the Aztecs. One was the Tarascans, who had settled in Tzintzuntzan, in the present-day Mexican state of Michoán. The city of Tzintzuntzan had a population of about thirty thousand and was advanced in the arts, particularly weaving. The Tarascans were not Nahuatl speakers. In 1479 an Aztec army of twenty-four thousand soldiers under the command of the emperor Axayácatl attacked the Tarascans in their homeland.

The Aztecs probably anticipated an easy success, but over the years the Tarascans had grown very powerful, though they had avoided contact with others. In the long and bloody battle, the fierce Tarascan army slaughtered thousands of Aztecs. The surviving Aztecs retreated, never again trying to conquer the Tarascans.

The Tlaxcalan people lived much closer to Tenochtitlán in the Valley of Mexico. Their territory was surrounded by the empire, but somehow Tlaxcala avoided coming under the rule of the Aztecs. The Tlaxcalans had been allies of the Aztecs off and on during the fifteenth century. During the great famine in the Valley of Mexico in 1454, both societies were running low on victims for sacrifice. The Tlaxcalans agreed to enter into "flower wars" with the Aztec army—wars waged only for the purpose of taking victims to be sacrificed to the gods. These wars were waged with the mutual consent of both groups, and strict rules were followed.

At some point in their history together, the Tlaxcalans began to view the Aztecs as mortal enemies. Perhaps the Aztecs broke the rules or continued the wars after Tlaxcala withdrew its consent, but this is not known. In 1520 after the Tlaxcala fought and lost a battle with the invading Spanish, a huge force of the Tlaxcalan army joined forces with the Spaniards to help defeat the Aztecs.

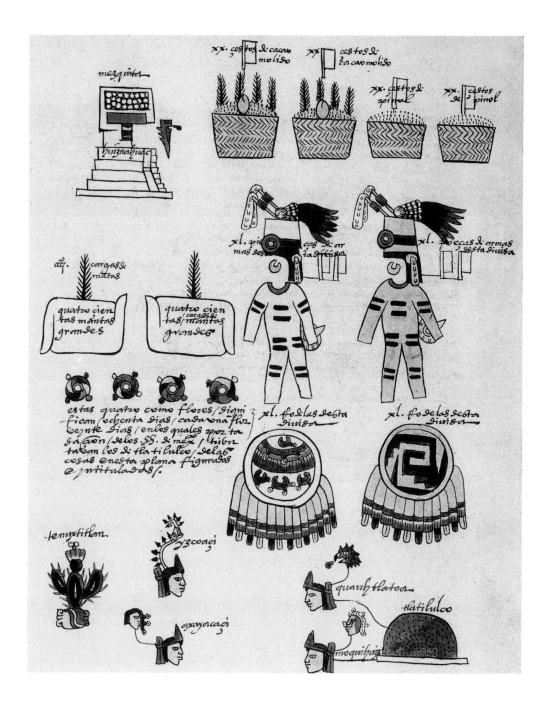

A record of tribute items—in labor and in goods—given to the Aztec empire from one of its conquered cities. Items include: repairs to a temple, 40 baskets of cacao, 40 baskets of maize flour, and 40 costumes and shields. *The Art Archive/Bodleian Library of Oxford/The Bodleian Library.*

The governmental and social hierarchy

The Great Speaker

The succession (the system of passing power within the ruling class, usually upon the death of the current rule) of Aztec emperors was a stable process throughout the years of the empire. The rulers and their top lords and priests all came from the royal family and were usually closely related. The Aztecs did not hand the throne to the oldest son as was done in some European countries at the time. Being born into Aztec royalty did not assure one of special privilege; the royal family was huge. Emperors frequently had hundreds of wives and some were said to have thousands of children. Only the top performers in combat and in managing the affairs of the government were considered for top offices.

A council of about thirty nobles chose the emperor from among four nobles who had held the top positions under the deceased former emperor. At the same time they chose a new emperor, the council selected four other royal leaders who were sons, nephews, or brothers of the newly elected emperor. These four lords would maintain their positions until the emperor died, and at that time one of them would be elected to replace him.

The emperors of the Aztec empire were expected to behave in a very dignified manner and live a virtuous life as an example to their people. They were rarely seen in public. Aztec emperors lived in royal palaces in a walled-off section of the Tenochtitlán temple district. Inside the palace compounds were lavish gardens and beautiful buildings filled with gold, arts, and other treasures of the empire. There were about three thousand servants to tend to the palace and the needs of the royal family.

Whenever the emperor appeared, he was dressed elaborately in a headdress made from the brilliant green feathers of quetzal birds. His robes were made from the finest woven textiles and his sandals were made of gold. He was carried by his servants on a litter (an enclosed platform with a couch or bench carried on long poles), and when he stood, cloaks or mats were laid out in front of him so his feet never touched the ground. People around him were expected to bow three times as he passed and were never to look directly into his face.

The nobility

The Aztec emperor's top lords took responsibility for much of the daily management of running the empire. Among the top advisers to the emperor were four army generals, each one in charge of the armies of the four districts of Tenochtitlán. Just under the emperor was the *cihuacoatl* (meaning "Snake Woman," though the position was filled by men), a very powerful adviser who ruled over the domestic affairs of the empire as a kind of deputy to the emperor. Serving the emperor and his top lords was a council of advisers.

Under the top advisers to the emperor was a larger class of nobles of different ranks. These included priests of many ranks and positions. Every city and city-state within the empire had its own *tlatoani*, or supreme ruler, from the Aztec nobility, who reported to the *cihuacoatl*. All of the provinces (territories located at a distance from the capital city) had their own administrators, or *tecuhtlis*, who ran public works, enforced laws, and punished criminals.

Illustration of Aztec nobles. Nobles had to earn their prestige through military feats or proven leadership.
© *Stapleton Collection/Corbis.*

Though Aztec lords usually came from noble families, being born as the son or daughter of a nobleman was not enough to ensure one's future. The prestige and power of being a noble were given only to those who had proven themselves as leaders, particularly in the military. Nobles, like the emperor, were expected to provide an example for the rest of the population. Good manners, extreme cleanliness, and modesty were standard. The Aztec nobles had changed a great deal since their wandering years, when they were considered ruffians by the other peoples of the Valley of Mexico. In fact, historian Leopold Castedo, as quoted in Michael C. Meyer and William L. Sherman's *The Course of Mexican History* (1995), observed that "the nobles were so extraordinarily refined that when they were forced to come near the Spaniards, they screened their nasal passages with branches of fragrant flowers," because the smell of the unwashed conquistadores offended them so much.

The *pochteca*

The *pochteca,* Aztec long-distance traders and merchants, held a crucial position within the Aztec empire. Carrying goods made by the artisans (craftspeople) of Tenochtitlán and other cities, they traveled as far south as present-day Guatemala into Maya lands and throughout the Mesoamerican regions, selling their wares. From these distant markets they brought back the materials Tenochtitlán craftspeople needed to make their goods. Without the *pochteca,* the economy of Tenochtitlán would not have prospered.

The *pochteca* were an unusually knowledgeable group who learned the languages and customs of the many peoples on their trade routes. They were also a daring and brave group. As they passed through foreign lands gathering the goods that would bring them wealth in a faraway market, they had to avoid being hit by the spears and arrows of hostile and suspicious peoples. The *pochteca* often served as spies, informing the emperor about the activities and military strength of the peoples in the far reaches of the empire. Because their work was so important to the empire, the emperor gave them military escorts to keep them from harm, but they also had to rely on their wits and charm to survive in dangerous and unknown places.

The *pochteca* usually became exceedingly rich from their trade, but even though they performed a service to all, they were not accepted by the people of Tenochtitlán. The *pochteca* lived together in the sidelines of the city. Perhaps due to fear of robbery or to prevent jealousy, they dressed in ragged clothes and brought their caravans (groups of people traveling together and carrying goods) in and out of the city under the cover of darkness. The children of the *pochteca* married only within the group, and the *pochteca* remained a small but very rich and knowledgeable society unto themselves.

Common folk

The common people of the Aztec empire made up the great majority of the Aztec population. They were mainly farmers, artisans, servants, and other laborers. The Aztecs were organized into social units called *calpulli*, meaning "big house." *Calpultin* (plural of *calpulli*) were groups of families who were either related in some way or had simply lived among each other over the generations. The precise way a *calpulli* worked is not known, but each *calpulli* generally held land its members used for farming or other industry. Thus, many *calpultin* were divided by the trades of their members, such as farming or pottery-making. In the cities the *calpultin* formed a kind of neighborhood, with the group living within its own district and taking responsibility for the district's maintenance. The *calpulli* had a leader called the *calpullec;* like the emperor, the *calpullec* worked with a governing council. Each *calpulli* had its own traditions and its people socialized together and usually married within their group. Men in the *calpulli* formed their own military unit, fighting in wars together. The farming *calpultin* gave a proportion of their crops to the emperor as tribute, and the artisan *calpultin* paid a tax on their sales. The *pochteca* formed their own *calpultin*.

Slaves

At the bottom of the social ladder in the Aztec empire were the slaves, who usually worked for nobles in the fields or as servants in their homes. The bonds of slavery were never passed from parents to children, and servitude was often temporary in the Aztec empire. Some of the Aztec slaves were people who had been taken captive in battles, but there were many other ways for people to become slaves.

An Aztec might become a slave, for example, if he or she fell into debt. Punishment for certain crimes was to serve a term as a slave. Sometimes when people gambled, they pledged themselves as slaves if they lost the bet. People who had no food sometimes sold themselves into slavery out of desperation. Slaves could marry people who were not slaves. It was not, however, customary to treat slaves harshly though they were sometimes used for human sacrifice ceremonies.

War and warriors

Every man in the Aztec empire was expected to fight in the wars, from the emperor down to the common people. Constant war was central to the day-to-day operations of the empire; war was, in effect, the empire's purpose. The economy of Tenochtitlán depended upon the constant receipt of tribute from conquered lands. In addition, the religion of the Aztecs required massive human sacrifice to keep the sun rising and to satisfy the gods to prevent the final destruction of the earth.

Prisoners of war brought home by Aztec soldiers were sacrificed on the temple steps, and they were believed to be vital to the very existence of the Aztec civilization. In early times, Aztecs may have waged wars to conquer new territories and exert their role as the rulers of the empire, but in the later years they were often compelled to fight simply to maintain the status quo (keep things as they were) through more and more human sacrifice.

Every Aztec male was trained to be a warrior. Inga Clendinnen, in her book *Aztecs: An Interpretation* (1991), observed how deeply invested the Aztec society was into its warrior cult:

> To be born a male in Tenochtitlán was to be designated a warrior. The attending midwife met the birth of a boy child with war-cries, and lifted the baby, still slippery from the birth fluid, away from his mother's body to dedicate him to the Sun, and to the 'flowery death' of the warrior in battle or on the killing stone [where humans were sacrificed].

The Aztec emperor was the chief military commander and often went out into the battlefields to fight with his

armies. If he was unable to go to war himself, he sent one of his top generals, usually a brother, nephew, or uncle. The emperor had the authority to compel all of the cities under his control to send him all their able-bodied men to serve as warriors. It is believed Aztec emperors in the last century of the empire were able to gather an army of about one hundred thousand men at any given time.

Serving under the emperor or his general were the Aztec knights. The knights were members of very prestigious military orders—the Arrow Knights, the Eagle Knights, and the Jaguar Knights. Knights were chosen from among the best warriors and enjoyed the greatest honors. Other commanding officers were usually picked from among nobles, who had extensive military training.

Nobles sent their sons to the *calmecac,* or religious school. Even though the young nobles were taught by priests, the main focus of the education at the *calmecac* was

An Aztec priest performing a sacrificial offering of a prisoner's heart to the war and sun god, Huitzilopochtli. *The Library of Congress.*

Aztec warriors, such as those depicted in this illustration, were honored and often rewarded with special gifts for their successes in battle. © Archivo Iconografico, S.A./Corbis.

to train them as warriors; by the age of fifteen the boys were in very rigorous military training. After proving their merit in battle, some young nobles would go on to become administrators or government officials. Many, though, would spend most of their lives on the battlefield.

The majority of soldiers were from the common people. They farmed or worked in trades or services until there was a call to war. When the emperor called for soldiers, all males over the age of fifteen marched off with the men of their *calpulli*, and the group would fight together as a unit.

From childhood, Aztec males were taught to dream about the honor they would gain as soldiers in battle. Boys were taught that it was their life's mission to provide captives for sacrifice in order to feed the earth and please the gods. At age ten, boys had their hair cut short except for one long lock. This lock would only be cut when the boy had brought home his first prisoner of war.

For common people, the military was the only way to rise up in Aztec society. If a common soldier did well in battle, he was rewarded with land, slaves, or loot from the defeated. If he managed to capture several enemies to be offered for sacrifice, he had a chance to become a noble or to join the ranks of the knights. If he died in battle, his family received gifts. As a reward, soldiers who died in battle were thought to go to a special part of the heavens reserved only for them.

Starting wars

The Aztec armies did not attack other peoples without warning. If they decided to conquer a city or region, they sent their ambassadors (diplomatic officials who represent a government or a society) out to the leaders to inform them they were to begin paying tribute. They offered the city their military protection and the benefits of trading within the empire in return. In some cases, when the ambassadors made these offers to a region's leaders, the leaders responded by killing the ambassadors and mutilating their bodies to show their scorn of the offer.

If the region in question did not accept the Aztecs' offer after a significant amount of talking and threatening, it was time for war. The emperor called on the cities in his realm to send their soldiers. The war drums resounded around the empire, and soldiers everywhere made their way to the arsenals where weapons were stored. There they received a variety of arms. The most deadly weapon was likely a *macuahuitl*, a three-foot combination sword and club with sharp obsidian (dark, solid glass formed by volcanoes used to make tools and weapons) blades set into its edges. Legend has it that the Aztec soldiers were able to chop off a horse's head with just one blow from this mighty club. There were also *atlatls*, or spear throwers, from which Aztec warriors flung darts and spears at their enemies. Some warriors had bows and arrows.

The Aztec coat of armor was made from tightly fitted quilted cotton that had been stiffened by soaking in salt water. These suits could often stop an arrow or soften the impact of a spear. The army officers had specific ways of dressing, using feathers and certain designs so soldiers would recognize them and follow their lead in battle. Some wore full animal skins complete with the animal's head. The purpose of such costumes was to instill fear in the enemy.

The warriors would arrive in Tenochtitlán in their *calpulli* groupings. There they participated in ceremonies to the gods before embarking on their journey on foot across the land to the enemy region. When they arrived, the knights and other officers ran ahead, leading the attack, followed by massive numbers of soldiers. They usually tried not to kill their opponents in battle. Rather, large groups would try to circle and then surround the enemy to capture and bring them home for sacrifice.

Economy

As it grew, the city of Tenochtitlán, with its population of hundreds of thousands of people, needed more food and goods than could be grown or found in the area. The island was short of land for farming and there were few sources of metal, stone, feathers, or shells—the commodities craftspeople needed—to be found nearby. The city was forced to wage constant wars to bring in goods in the form of tribute. The *pochteca,* with their extensive long-distance trading were also responsible for bringing in resources from remote places. With these goods, Tenochtitlán developed a very large class of urban (city) tradespeople who made products for use in the city or for export out to distant lands.

Chinampas and farming

For many of the years of Tenochtitlán's existence, local farmers were able to provide the city with most of its food. Around the island city there were many swampy areas, which might have seemed useless to most farmers. Aztec farmers, however, developed an ingenious method for farming in these swamps. They began by digging canals to run from the marshy waters near the shores into the island, then cut down the swamp vegetation and dried it out, creating reeds.

The reeds were woven together into large floating mats. Getting mud from the lake bottom, the Aztecs heaped the mats with the fertile soil, creating raised garden beds. Stakes were often driven into the ground to anchor the floating gardens. Willow trees were then planted around the corners of the mats in the lake bottom to provide permanent anchors. The farmers planted crops on these *chinampas* or floating gardens, including maize (corn), squash, beans, grains, chili peppers, avocados, tomatoes, and flowers. Because the climate was usually good and there was an unending supply of water for irrigation, the *chinampas* usually produced crops year-round.

The lake was just one of the Aztec farming environments. The Aztecs cut terraces (steps to make level fields for farming) into the hillsides to keep the soil from eroding during heavy rains and were able to farm the slopes around them. In the flatlands they engineered irrigation canals for the maximum number of crops possible in the area. Working without metal plows or beasts of burden (such as horses or oxen), the Aztecs used sharp sticks to dig in the soft soil. They used human waste as fertilizer, collecting it regularly

from the city's public "bathrooms," which were set on canoes in the canals for easy transportation.

Farming was done by the common workers. Although they did not own their own land, the land they worked was owned by their *calpulli*, and families were given plots for their use. Each *calpulli* was required to give crops or labor to the empire. The farming goods might be used to feed the huge armies or to fund public projects, such as building of temples, irrigation canals, and causeways. All farmers were expected to serve in the Aztec army as well.

Trade

In its peak years, Tenochtitlán was fabulously wealthy with goods from all around Mesoamerica. Its extensive market system made it the hub of a huge long-distance trading network. By the fifteenth century, the city supported a large population of artisans who created and sold fine cloths, pot-

Aztecs building a *chinampa*, or "floating garden."
© *Gianni Dagli Orti/Corbis.*

Copy of a manuscript showing Aztec farmers cultivating fields. *The Library of Congress.*

tery, baskets, jewelry, feather weavings, and tools. Like farmers, the craftspeople operated in *calpultin*—such as a feather workers' *calpulli* or a house servants' *calpulli*.

These specialist *calpultin* paid their tribute to the government in the form of a tax on their sales. The raw materials the craftspeople needed for their work were generally brought in by the *pochteca* and were available for sale at Tenochtitlán's busy markets. Some of the crafts they made were sold in the city, while others were carried out by the *pochteca* to distant lands and traded for more raw materials. Although there was no coined or printed money, the Aztecs used cacao beans (beans that grow on an evergreen tree from which cocoa, chocolate, and cocoa butter are made), cloth, and salt as mediums of exchange. The trade system and the huge markets of Tenochtitlán operated independently of the government and were highly profitable. Industrious craftspeople and laborers who hired out their services could become wealthy.

The last days

Although they did not directly rule the fifteen million people of their vast empire, the Aztecs brought about some widespread changes. Their military muscle unified the many diverse peoples within their empire. The tremendous tribute payments the Aztecs imposed on these conquered peoples were certainly not agreeable to many of the conquered; yet, the outstanding Aztec trade network brought unexpected prosperity to some of the outlying regions. Aztec military dominance provided political stability as well. The major beneficiaries of the empire, though, were the people in the city of Tenochtitlán. The elite were not the only ones to benefit from the general prosperity of the times. The exchange of goods through trade and tribute payments created an unprecedented class of non-farming urban workers. By the time the Spanish arrived in 1519, according to Clendinnen, "most of the city's commoners lived by an urban trade: as sandal makers, fuel sellers, potters, mat weavers, carriers, or any of the multitude of services required in a busy metropolis." Many commoners, who in previous times would have toiled at the same work without hope for anything better, faced a very different world in which wealth and opportunity were within reach of a much larger portion of the population.

For More Information

Books

Clendinnen, Inga. *Aztecs: An Interpretation*. Cambridge, UK: Cambridge University Press, 1991.

Coe, Michael D. *Mexico: From the Olmecs to the Aztecs,* 4th ed. London and New York: Thames and Hudson, 1994.

Hull, Robert. *The Aztecs*. Austin, TX: Steck-Vaughn, 1998.

Meyer, Michael C., and William L. Sherman. *The Course of Mexican History,* 5th ed. New York and Oxford: Oxford University Press, 1995.

Thomas, Hugh. *Conquest: Montezuma, Cortés, and the Fall of Old Mexico.* New York: Simon & Schuster, 1993.

Wood, Tim. *The Aztecs*. New York: Viking, 1992.

Web Sites

"Aztec." *E-Museum @ Minnesota State University, Mankato.* http://www.mnsu.edu/emuseum/cultural/mesoamerica/aztec.html (accessed on October 18, 2004).

The Aztecs. http://www.elbalero.gob.mx/kids/history/html/conquista/aztecas.html (accessed on October 18, 2004).

Hooker, Richard. "Civilizations in America: The Mexica/Aztecs." *World Civilizations, Washington State University.* http://www.wsu.edu/~dee/CIVAMRCA/AZTECS.HTM (accessed on October 18, 2004).

Aztec Religion, Culture, and Daily Life

27

The Spanish conquistadores (conquerors) arriving in Tenochtitlán (pronounced tay-notch-teet-LAHN) in 1521 marveled at the extremely refined and artistic culture they found there. Many claimed that the capital city of the Aztecs surpassed the cities of Europe in architecture, engineering, and the arts. The city's laws were sophisticated and there was little crime. Its markets were orderly and its streets were clean, fragrant, and brightly painted. The Spaniards' first sights, walking down the streets of Tenochtitlán, might have led them to believe they had discovered a serenely peaceful civilization. During the battle for the conquest of the city, however, the Spaniards witnessed some of their fellow soldiers, who had been captured by the Aztec soldiers, being sacrificed to the gods. They looked on as the hearts were torn out of the living bodies of their comrades. Though the Spanish were responsible for burning at the stake those people who did not conform to their religious beliefs during the Spanish Inquisition (1478–34), the sight of these human sacrifices filled the soldiers with utter fear and horror. The two sides of the Aztecs these first Spaniards in Mesoamerica witnessed—the great capacity for beauty, logic,

Words to Know

Amerindian: An indigenous, or native, person from North or South America. The term "Amerindian" is used in place of the terms "American Indian" or "Native American" in these volumes, as the term "Native American" is often associated with the United States and the term "Indian" is offensive to some people.

Aviary: A building where birds are housed.

Calpulli: (The word means "big house"; the plural form is *calpultin.*) Social units consisting of groups of families who were either related in some way or had lived among each other over the generations. *Calpultin* formed the basic social unit for farmers, craftspeople, and merchants. The precise way they worked is not known.

Codex: A handmade book written on a long strip of bark paper and folded into accordion-like pages.

Deify: Place in a godlike position; treat as a god.

Empire: A vast, complex political unit extending across political boundaries and dominated by one central power, which generally takes control of the economy, government, and culture in communities throughout its territory.

Glyph: A figure (often carved into stone or wood) used as a symbol to represent words, ideas, or sounds.

Nahuatl: The language spoken by the Aztecs and many other groups in the Valley of Mexico.

Pantheon: All of the gods that a particular group of people worship.

Ritual: A formal act performed the same way each time, usually used as a means of religious worship by a particular group.

Scribe: Someone hired to write down the language, to copy a manuscript, or record a spoken passage.

Vigesimal: Based on the number twenty (as a numeric system).

and order and the violent culture based on war and "feeding" the gods with the blood of sacrifice victims—were difficult for them to reconcile. Though almost all societies have practiced human sacrifice in their past and many continue to have brutal violence in the present, grasping both of these two contrasting sides of the great Aztec civilization is difficult even today.

Religion

The early Aztecs who wandered the Valley of Mexico before 1325 probably had a much simpler world view than

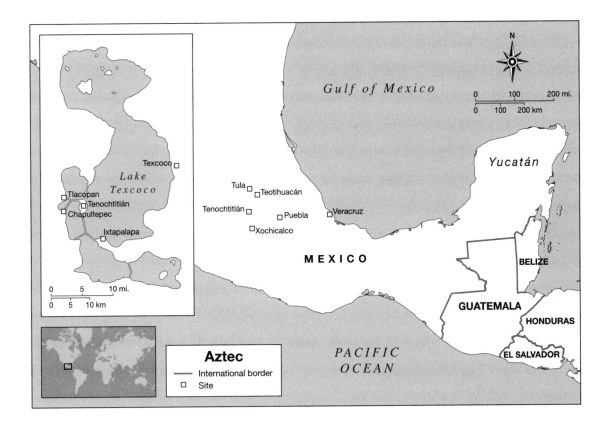

Map showing the sites of the ancient Aztec civilization in Mesoamerica. *Map by XNR Productions. The Gale Group.*

that of their empire-ruling descendents. (An empire is a vast, complex political unit extending across political boundaries and dominated by one central power, which generally takes control of the economy, government, and culture in communities throughout its territory.) During their travels they learned about the gods of the different peoples living in the valley and, over time, added them to their own pantheon (all of the gods in their religion). Awed by the traditions and the ruins of the valley's ancient cities, they also incorporated much of the region's history and mythology (a collection of myths—traditional, often imaginary stories about ancestors, heroes, or supernatural beings that usually make an attempt to explain a belief, practice, or natural phenomenon).

The Aztecs came to believe that Teotihuacán (pronounced TAY-uh-tee-wah-KAHN) was the birthplace of their gods and the Toltecs (pronounced TOHL-tecks) were the chosen people of the gods. It was not long before the Aztecs cast themselves as the descendants of the Toltecs and the new chosen rulers of the valley. While the Aztecs adopted traditions and practices from other people, they still maintained many of their own traditions as they adapted to their new home. Their supreme god Huitzilopochtli (pronounced hweets-ee-loh-PAWCH-tlee), for example, joined the gods of the valley and eventually earned top status as the sun and warrior god of the Aztec empire.

The Aztec pantheon

There were hundreds of gods in the Aztec pantheon. They all embodied the principles of a world view that began with a creator god named Ometeotl, "the dual god," who was both male and female. Ometeotl resided above the stars and planets on the uppermost layer of the spirit world. There were thirteen layers of the heavens in the Aztec cosmos, with nine levels of the underworld as well. Residing in the lowest of these was Ometeotl's dark counterpart (another version of the god, with characteristics exactly the opposite of the heavenly god). Though neither god was considered "bad" or "good," the heavenly Ometeotl was associated with creation, light, and day, while the underworld Ometeotl was associated with death, darkness, and night.

The Aztec pantheon originated when Ometeotl's male and female aspects gave birth to the gods of the four cardinal directions (east, west, north, and south). These gods were Black Tezcatlipoca of the north, or "Smoking Mirror," the powerful god of war, night, and sorcery; White Tezcatlipoca of the west, or Quetzalcoatl (pronounced kates-ahl-koh-AH-tul), the feathered serpent, who was the god of life and holiness; Red Tezcatlipoca of the east, also called Xipe Totec or "god of flayed flesh," the god of spring and birth; and Blue Tezcatlipoca of the south, or Huitzilopochtli, the "blue hummingbird" and warrior god of the sun.

In the Aztec spiritual world, nature itself was deified (made into gods). The Aztecs considered rain, wind, thunder, and sun actual gods in themselves, not just forces represented by gods. Mountains, rivers, lakes, trees, and rocks were sacred and had spirits. But besides the deified natural world they also had gods that represented the forces of nature, like Tlaloc (pronounced TLAH-lock), the rain god, and Coatlicue, the earth goddess. There were also gods associated with most of the elements of human behavior—gods of sleep, filth, and drinking, for example—as well as gods associated with the stars, planets, and all natural phenomena. In their pantheon there was room for many representations of the spirit world.

The world of the Fifth Sun

The Aztecs believed there had been four worlds prior to the current world. Each of the former worlds had been completely destroyed by a major catastrophe. With each destruction, the world's sun was extinguished and there was nothing left but darkness. These destructions were due to an ongoing struggle between the dark and warlike Black Tezcatlipoca and holy and peaceful Quetzalcoatl. The Aztecs believed that in each new world, one or the other of these two gods dominated. Neither was considered better than the other.

The Aztecs honored many gods that represented the forces of nature. This statue is of Ehecatl, the god of wind. © *Gianni Dagli Orti/Corbis.*

Each time the world and its sun were destroyed, all of the gods of the Aztec pantheon created a new world with a new sun. After the fourth world had been destroyed by floods, the gods met at the ancient city of Teotihuacán (see Chapter 18 for more information) to make plans for a fifth world. There, they chose two gods—one rich and the other poor and sickly—to sacrifice themselves so the world would be renewed.

When it came time for the gods to sacrifice themselves, the rich god froze. The poor and sickly god, though, jumped straight into the sacrificial fire. Not wanting to be outdone, the rich god finally jumped into the fire as well. The rest of the gods waited after the two sacrifices, but nothing happened. At last, all the gods, one by one, threw themselves into the fire. After all the gods had sacrificed themselves, the new sun arose and the new world of the Fifth Sun had begun. Because the gods had sacrificed themselves for human beings, the Aztecs believed it was the duty of humans to repay the gods by sacrificing themselves.

The world of the Fifth Sun was believed to be the final world—when it ended there would never be another. Human beings would disappear forever, and time itself would stop. The Aztecs believed the Fifth Sun would eventually be destroyed by earthquakes. Many of their religious practices, particularly human sacrifice, were their attempt to delay this final worldwide destruction. Though they looked to the gods for help, the Aztecs firmly believed that natural forces would eventually destroy them.

The Aztecs followed a complex calendar system (see Science below) to help stage the correct rituals (formal acts performed the same way each time) at the right times to delay the destructive forces of nature and the inevitable end of the world. The basic Aztec system of measuring time combined use of the sacred and solar calendars. Every 52 years all possible combinations of both sacred and solar day-names and numbers had been used, and the cycles would start over. Each period of 52 years was called a "bundle of years" and could be viewed as similar to current centuries. At the end of each bundle, there was a 12-day period before the next one started. These were days that were similar to leap years. By the modern solar calendar, it takes 365.2422 days for Earth to orbit the sun. If there were no leap year, after 100 years the modern calendar would be 24 days ahead of the seasons. Similarly, by the Aztec calendar systems, at the end of each "bundle of years" there was a 12-day period to align the calendar with the seasons.

It was believed that in these 12-day periods the world would be destroyed if the sacrifices and other rituals were not performed. As the end of each bundle approached, Aztecs were filled with dread, fearing that, on the last night of the bundle, the sun might fail to rise. On this night they followed a long ritual called the New Fire Ceremony. As evening approached, the Aztec people in every home broke all their dishes. Every fire in every house, workshop, and temple was put out. On a mountaintop in the Valley of Mexico the priests began an all-night prayer for the sun to rise. In homes throughout the valley, the Aztec people sat awake, praying.

Even children were not allowed to sleep through this night, or else evil spirits might invade their bodies.

All awaited to see if the sun would appear. When it arose, cries of joy and thankfulness filled the whole region. On the mountaintop, a human being was sacrificed to show gratitude to the gods. A fire was lit, and torches taken from this new fire were used to light all other fires. For the Aztecs, it was the beginning of a new century, and the fire gave them hope of survival for another fifty-two-year bundle. The last New Fire Ceremony before the Spanish conquest was in 1507.

The cult of Huitzilopochtli

The chief god of the Aztecs was Huitzilopochtli, their god of war and sun, who was said to have led them, in the form of a hummingbird, to Tenochtitlán. In Nahuatl (pronounced NAH-wah-tul), his name is a combination of *huitzilin,* or hummingbird, and *opochtli,* which means "left." The Aztecs believed the south was the left side of the earth, so Huitzilopochtli was the hummingbird from the south. In most Aztec art, Huitzilopochtli appears either as a hummingbird or as a blue human with a headdress made of hummingbird feathers.

Many scholars believe Huitzilopochtli may not have been part of the pantheon of Mesoamerican gods until the Aztecs wandered into the Valley of Mexico sometime in the twelfth century. Some have speculated there was an Aztec leader named Huitzilopochtli who was deified by his people after his death. In the early days of settlement in Tenochtitlán, Huitzilopochtli was not the primary god of the Aztecs. When the emperor Itzcoatl (pronounced eetz-coe-WAH-tul; ruled 1427–1440) and his powerful adviser Tlacaelel came into power in 1427, however, they raised the god to the highest position in the pantheon. Worship of Huitzilopochtli became the hallmark (distinguishing characteristic) of Aztec spirituality, and conquered cities and states were forced to worship him. With this elevation of Huitzilopochtli, there was a tremendous increase in the number of human sacrifices in the empire.

In one creation story, Huitzilopochtli was the son of the earth goddess Coatlicue. Coatlicue was made pregnant by a ball of feathers that dropped from the sky. Her children did

Illustration of Huitzilopochtli, the god of the sun and war, and the primary god of the Aztecs. *The Art Archive/National Archives Mexico/Mireille Vautier.*

not believe feathers had caused their mother's pregnancy. Ashamed of her behavior, they decided to kill her. As they approached her, a fully armed (and grown up, according to some versions) Huitzilopochtli sprang from Coatlicue's womb and immediately cut off the head of his sister, Coyolxauhqui. He then tossed her head into the air, and it rose as the moon. Huitzilopochtli became the sun.

As the sun god, Huitzilopochtli was reborn every morning to make his mighty trip across the heavens. At night, he was the warrior god, who descended into the underworld to battle death and darkness so he might return to be born and rise again the next morning. The Aztecs believed the only food that could nourish Huitzilopochtli's heroic daily journey was the beating hearts of sacrificed warriors.

Human sacrifice

Human sacrifice was practiced to some extent by all of the ancient civilizations of Mesoamerica. Most historians believe that before the era of the Aztec empire began in 1427, it was practiced only on a small scale in Tenochtitlán. In one form of the early Aztec practice, a victim was picked from among the top noble warriors a year before the sacrifice was to take place. During the year the young warrior assumed the role of one of the gods. He was given the best of everything, living in a luxurious house with attractive women, fine clothes, and delicious foods. He was honored and worshiped and attended as if he were a god. On the day of his sacrifice, he would dress as a god and walk bravely but sadly to the stone upon which he was to be sacrificed with great ceremony. The Aztec priests gave him final instructions to bring their messages to the gods. He was then killed and his heart cut out by a priest.

Stone representation of the Aztec goddess Coatlicue. *The Library of Congress.*

The Aztecs viewed their world as a network of potentially bad and destructive forces. The world was a place where things could, and often did, go terribly wrong. Their experiences with nature may have led them to this belief. The Valley of Mexico is the site of volcanic mountains and has experienced many earthquakes. The lakes in the valley dried up at times and flooded at others. Frosts at the wrong times could destroy all crops.

In the year of 1 Rabbit (1454) the Aztecs learned this lesson only too well when a great famine began, set off by untimely rain and floods mixed with frosts. For three years in a row the crops of the valley were ruined and there was little to eat. Many people died. In desperation, the nobles and priests kept increasing their human sacrifice ceremonies. By the third year of the famine they were practicing mass sacrifices on a frequent basis, sometimes with hundreds of victims. When the famine finally ended and healthy crops appeared in the valley, the Aztec priests and rulers believed the sacrifices were responsible for restoring prosperity to the valley. From then on, the Aztec practice of human sacrifice took

An Aztec sacrificial stone, upon which human offerings to the gods were often made. *The Library of Congress.*

on very large-scale proportions. The exact number of victims per year is still a matter of debate.

In 1487, when the Aztec empire celebrated the completion of the great temple to Huitzilopochtli, thousands of prisoners were brought in to be sacrificed as a dedication to the new building. There were so many victims they formed lines running miles down the four city streets, each of them awaiting his time to die on the temple steps. Some estimate hundreds of thousands of victims were sacrificed in this four-day celebration, but most historians believe about twenty thousand victims died in Tenochtitlán during those four days.

This particular celebration was exceptional and it is estimated that for more common events, fifty or sixty sacrifice victims were usually required. As the number of sacrifices rose, there was less ceremony for individual victims, but many still believed it was a great honor to be sacrificed. Aztecs prepared their male children to die in battle or by sacrifice from the time they were born. Sacrifice victims were believed to have their own special section of heaven or, alternatively, they were reborn as hummingbirds and spent the rest of eternity drinking the nectar of fragrant flowers.

Still, the practice inflicted terrible pain and suffering. The sacrifices were not limited to noble warriors—slaves became common victims and women and children were often sacrificed as well, sometimes in nightmarish circumstances. In the most common form of sacrifice, the victim was laid out upon a stone block, with four men holding his or her hands and feet down. A highly trained priest with a very sharp obsidian knife quickly cut open the chest, reached under the ribcage, and pulled out the still-beating heart. The heart was then either burned or smeared on a small statue of a particular god. The victim's head was cut off and mounted on a *tzompantli,* a rack to display sacrificial heads.

The body of a sacrifice victim was thrown down the temple stairs, or sometimes cut up and eaten by the nobles. In some cases, the skin was removed and worn by a priest. Huitzilopochtli was not the only god who required human sacrifices, and the grisly sacrifice rituals to the various gods took a number of different forms. It is important to remember that the Aztecs' view of death was very different than twentieth-century views. Nevertheless, from modern standpoints, the practice of human sacrifice was a horrible one. The mass sacrifices were considered repulsive to many people of the Aztec empire at the time as well.

Science

The Aztec number system, like many other Mesoamerican systems, was vigesimal—based on the number twenty. Most people believe the Mesoamericans chose the base of twenty because it was the number of fingers and toes they had to count with. The primary number system of the modern-day world is decimal—based on ten. In Maya (pronounced MY-uh) mathematics, numbers larger than 20 were written in powers of 20, just as modern numbers are written in powers of 10.

To write their numbers, the Aztecs generally used a system of dots and glyphs. Numbers up to the numeral 20 were

The sacred *tonalpohualli,* an Aztec calendar with a 260-day year. *The Library of Congress.*

represented by sequences of dots standing for numbers (9 dots, for example, stood for the number 9). For numbers above 20, they used glyphs representing multiples of 20. The number 20 was represented by a flag, 400 by a feather, and the number 8,000 was represented by a bag of incense (a substance, such as wood, that omits a pleasant odor when burned). Sometimes the Aztecs used the older bar and dot system, in which a bar had a value of five and a dot the value of one. Three bars and a dot, for example, would have a value of 16.

The calendar system

Religion and science were probably a single concept in the Aztec world, and their complex, three-calendar system is an example of the way they used science to understand and attempt to manipulate the world of the gods. One calendar, the sacred *tonalpohualli* (pronounced toe-nah-poe-WHAHL-lee), had a 260-day year. The days of the year were made up from a combination of 20 day-names, such as Flint Knife, Rain, Flower, Crocodile, and Wind, and the numerals 1 through 13. Using every combination of the 13 numbers with the 20 day-names in a specific sequence created 260 days of the year. Each of the days was associated with a god and with various traits. If a child was born on day considered unlucky, for example, it was assumed his or her life would be unlucky. The sacred calendar was used by the Aztec priests for seeing into the future and choosing lucky days for weddings, wars, and other important events.

A second Aztec calendar, the *xihuitl* (pronounced shee-WHEE-tul) or solar calendar, was used to measure the agricultural seasons and was more like the Gregorian calendar (the calendar used by contemporary society). It had a 360-day year with eighteen 20-day months. A five-day period at year's end, to finish out the 365-day solar year, was thought to be a very unlucky time. The Aztecs also used a third calendar that marked the rise of Venus, or the Morning Star, every 584 days.

Arts

The modern concept of art as a form of individual expression would not have made much sense to most Aztec artists, particularly those in the visual arts—painting, sculpture, and metalworking. For most Aztec artists—with the exception of Aztec poets—their works were not meant to express feelings or thoughts, nor were they meant to be beautiful or pleasing to view. Art was almost entirely in the service of Aztec religion.

Since the Aztec common people could not read, art was the central means of conveying the ideas and stories of the spirit world and communicating religious truths to them. Of the visual arts, many scholars believe the Aztecs excelled most at sculpture. Sculptures of the gods were necessary for worship. These statues, often made in the detailed image of one of the gods, existed in every Aztec home. There were thousands in temples and in other public places. Drawing on religious themes, some of the sculptures of the gods and events in the spirit world were utterly terrifying or brutal. Most were made from limestone, which was abundant in the area. Other sculptures were done in basalt (a fine-grained, dark gray rock used for building). Some were tiny, and of course, others towered over the city streets.

The Aztecs were highly skilled at working with features, especially the highly prized bright-green feathers of the quetzal bird. From these they created headdresses, cloaks, and elaborate ceremonial costumes. In Tenochtitlán there was a very large aviary (building where birds are housed), in which thousands of birds were kept and their feathers gathered regularly. Highly skilled workers wove the feathers into intricate costume pieces. Since most of the feathers have long since decomposed, only pictures and carvings of these elaborate feather creations are left. The Aztecs also excelled at painting and weaving baskets, most of which disintegrated.

Although much Aztec art did not survive over the years, the Aztecs did leave behind some exquisite jewelry. They treasured the green gemstone called jade above any other material, including gold. Jade was called *chalchiuitl* (pronounced chahl-CHWEE-tul), or "precious stone." The Aztecs also fashioned fine metalwork. It is said they brought in metalworkers from distant lands to make fine gold jewelry in Tenochtitlán.

The Aztecs had many festivals throughout the year, and music and dance were an important part of religious rituals. Music, like the other arts, was meant to please the gods rather than the listener. Aztecs learned as children how to dance and play musical instruments, and at the festivals, everyone participated in special dances enacting religious stories or themes. Sometimes there were hundreds of dancers performing the intricate steps. The music was played by a group, many using *huehuetls* (pronounced whay-WHAY-tuls), drums made from logs. Other percussion instruments included gongs, rattles, and bells. Conch shells sounded like trumpets, and whistles and flutes were made out of bones or bamboo.

Language and writing

The Aztecs spoke a version of the language called Nahuatl. Nahuatl belongs to the Uto-Aztecan family of Amerindian languages (languages of the indigenous, or native peoples from North or South America), which also includes the languages of the Shoshone, Comanche, Pima, and To-

hono O'ohdam tribes in the present-day United States. When the Aztecs arrived in the Valley of Mexico, there were already many Nahuatl-speaking groups. There were also people who spoke other languages, such as Otomi, Tarascan, and Totonac.

In the twenty-first century about 1.5 million people in Mexico speak Nahuatl; it is the most widely spoken native language. Though almost all Mexicans speak Spanish, more than five million Mexicans use an Amerindian language in daily life. Besides Nahuatl, those languages include Mayan, Mixtec, Otomi, Tarascan, and Zapotec.

When the Aztecs arrived in the Valley of Mexico, there were already forms of Mesoamerican writing in the area, which they adopted along with other elements of the culture. The Aztec form of writing entailed making pictures as symbols or glyphs, which represented a word or idea. Most of their glyphs were actually illustrations of the word they meant to convey. For example, the glyph for war was a pic-

The Aztec form of writing involves glyphs, pictures or symbols that represent a word or idea, such as the ones shown in this Aztec manuscript. © *Historical Picture Archive/Corbis.*

Painting depicting Aztec scribes at work. © *Gianni Dagli Orti/Corbis.*

ture of a war club and shield. The glyph for tree was the picture of a tree. The Aztecs had some glyphs representing sounds or syllables, and these could be put together to form the name of a place. They also had a few glyphs that were not illustrations, but stood for ideas or words. The Aztec writing system never reproduced the full spoken language like that of the Maya.

The Aztecs generally did their writing in books called codices (plural of codex). Inside a codex was a very long sheet of paper that had been folded in an accordion-like fashion. The paper was usually made from the bark of fig trees, which was treated with lime and then pounded into a pulp. The pulp was then flattened into thin sheets of paper. Huge quantities of paper were often required as tribute payments from conquered lands in the empire. Strips of paper, sometimes 30 feet (9 meters) long, were glued to wooden book covers. The pages of the codex were marked off by lines and then folded like a fan. The writing and pictures covering both sides of each page were read from the top to the bottom.

Common people in the Aztec empire were not taught how to read or write in school. Most reading and writing in Tenochtitlán and other cities was done by professional scribes (people whose function was to write the language) who were highly skilled in drawing and interpreting the glyphs. When they used glyphs to write on a page, the scribes did not arrange them in the order the reader would read them, but in patterns that would have significance only to a professional reader.

For keeping records and recording the movements of the stars, this writing system functioned fairly well. For telling the history or stories of the empire, however, the system relied on the memory of the person telling the story, as in the old method of relaying oral traditions (passing information or stories by spoken word from generation to generation). The person reading the page would already have committed its contents to memory, but he was able to use the glyphs and pictures to jog his memory as he related the page's meaning.

The Aztec rulers relied heavily on their writing system to manage their empire. The system was extremely useful as a means to record numbers, dates, places, names of people, and many other concepts. Scribes recorded the collection of taxes and the legal proceedings of the Aztec courts. The social units called *calpulli*, groups of families who shared land, kept track of their holdings with land titles and maps. The *pochteca* (merchants) recorded their sales and profits. The Aztec priests relied heavily on books in their observations of the stars and calendar systems. Each temple had a full library of codices with astronomical observations and notes about the movements of the planets and stars.

Nahuatl literature

Sadly, all of the codices of the Aztec world perished. The oldest were lost long before the Spanish conquest. In 1430 Emperor Itzcoatl demanded the burning of all books in his realm, probably so that he could rewrite history to include a more heroic Aztec background. Then, almost one hundred years later in 1528, Spanish missionaries (people, usually working for a religious organization, who try to convert others, usually in a foreign land, to their religion) piled up all the Aztec codices they could find and burned them in the Texcoco marketplace. Any hidden books that survived the book burnings apparently decomposed over the years.

All knowledge of Nahuatl literature relied on the memories of the Aztec people after the Spanish conquest. Some Aztec priests worked in secret to reproduce their books, but many of the reproduced codices or written recordings were the collaborative projects of Spanish missionaries and Aztec elders (people who have authority because of their age and experience).

Poetry

The magnificent poetry and songs of the Aztecs, some of the supreme cultural artistic achievements of their era, were fading from memory in the turbulent years of the mid-sixteenth century. Still, some of the Aztec elders remembered them very clearly. Fortunately, a few of the early Spanish missionaries attempted to learn as much about the Aztec culture as possible and began to interview the Aztec priests and elders. Some of the missionaries wrote down what the Aztec elders told them about their culture, while others directed the Aztec elders to write down their memories, including what they remembered of poems and literature, themselves. Because there was not a system to write the spoken Nahuatl language, the elders were taught to use the Spanish alphabet and its sounds to write down the Nahuatl language. Although these records of Aztec literature may have picked up some of the interpretations of the missionaries, without them, most Aztec literature would have been lost forever.

Prior to the conquest, poetry was abundant in Aztec life and central to their culture. Poetry was easily learned, since poems and songs were repeated many times at festivals and ceremonies over years and generations. Groups of people chanted together while they danced, or they would sing the poems in a rhythm, as songs. Many poems were directed to the gods and were a central part of Aztec worship. Other poems were more practical; some presented rules for living a moral life, with parents reciting the rules of social conduct to their children. These poems were passed down through the generations.

The Aztecs had an extensive tradition of lyric poetry that expressed the thoughts and feelings of individual thinkers. Many questioned the meaning of life and the fragile existence of human beings. Some of the poems are highly philosophical and at the same time present their ideas in powerful images. These were called "flower and song," with the flower as a metaphor (a word used to compare two dissimilar things) for art and poetry.

Scholars have noted that the poetry of some nobility in the last decades of the empire indicated they had begun questioning the violence of their culture. Some poetry reflected a desire for a more peaceful and gentler world where mass human sacrifice was not a common event. Many of the poems that survived were collected in *Cantares mexicanos* (Mexican Songs), made up of ninety-one songs gathered for recording by a group of *tlamatinime* (men of words, or the poets and philosophers of the Aztecs) between 1560 and 1580 under the direction of a Spanish missionary. Another collection made at the same time and in a similar manner was called *Romances de los señores de Nueva España* (Romances of the Lords of New Spain).

By far the best known of the many Aztec poets was the king of Texcoco, Nezahualcoyotl (pronounced ne-za-hwahl-coy-OH-tul; 1403–1473). Renowned as a great ruler, scientist, and legal scholar, Nezahualcoyotl is still best remembered for the beauty and wisdom of his poetry. Miguel León-Portilla (1926–), a Mexican historian and anthropologist considered the world's top authority on Aztec literature, listed some of the most pervasive themes of Nezahualcoyotl's poetry in his book *Fifteen Poets of the Aztec World*. According to León-Portilla, Nezahualcoyotl wrote of "time and the fugacity [lasting only a short time] of all that exists; the inevitability of death ... the beyond and the region of the 'fleshless'; the meaning of 'flower and song' [art]; [and] the possibility of glimpsing something about the Inventor of Himself [God]." Like many artists both past and present, Nezahualcoyotl viewed his artistic endeavors as a way to comprehend life and the gods themselves. His poetry reflected his belief that while human beings die, the art that comes from deep within the heart endures: "My flowers will not come to an end/My songs will not come to an end...." Nezahualcoyotl says in one of his poems.

Daily life

The Aztecs believed in living orderly, disciplined lives. Their oral literature is full of rules and guidelines of good conduct. Their streets were clean, children were well-behaved, they bathed every day, and there was no drunkenness or adultery. People were expected to conform to a strict code of behavior, and the punishments were very severe if they failed.

Marriage and family

Although the Aztec nobility often had many wives, the Aztec common people were monogamous (had only one spouse). Most Aztec men married by the age of twenty; women usually married at the age of sixteen. The marriages were between people from the same *calpulli,* or group of families living among each other in the same district, and they were usually arranged. Priests were often enlisted to find the correct calendar day for a wedding, one to bring good luck to the couple.

Wedding ceremonies, which took place at night with great festivities, were taken seriously. As part of the ceremony, the bride's shirt or dress was tied to her new husband's cloak, indicating the union. Divorce was available if things did not work out, but as in modern times, it was a legal matter. Either partner could apply to the courts and explain his or her complaint to a judge who could end the marriage. If the divorced couple had children, the mother got custody of the girls and the father got custody of the boys. Prior to marriage, each partner listed his or her belongings, so there would be no confusion in case of divorce. Women had significant legal rights, including the right to own property, although many historians note that in practice, women were usually not treated as equals.

After the wedding, the couple lived with the husband's family for a time and then their families built them a house. If

Aztec manuscript depicting scenes from everyday life. © *Bettmann/Corbis.*

they were farmers, both the man and the woman would tend to the fields, but the woman had a larger role in maintaining the home, preparing food, and raising children. Women in almost all Aztec homes spent a significant portion of their time weaving cloth. Women also worked making crafts.

Bearing children was a very important part of an Aztec woman's life. If a woman died in childbirth, the Aztecs believed there was a very special section of heaven for her, just as they believed there was a special section of heaven for warriors who died in combat.

Growing up

Aztec parents did not treat their girls the same way they treated their boys. Michael D. Coe, in his book *Mexico: From the Olmecs to the Aztecs* (1994), noted that even at birth newborn girls and boys received different treatment. The girl was cherished for the comfort she provided and for her beauty. Her fate was to live in her home, and her role was practical and earthly. The male child, on the other hand, was told upon birth "that the house in which he was born was not a true home, but just a resting place, for he was a warrior," whose mission it was to "give the sun the blood of enemies to drink." Boys were considered warriors from the moment they were born.

As one might expect in a rigidly disciplined society, Aztec parents were very strict with their children, demanding them to be obedient, do their share of work from a very early age, stay clean, and show good manners and behavior. The punishments for children who misbehaved were extremely harsh. One method was to hold the child directly over a fire of burning chili peppers so the smoke would sting their eyes and burn their noses and throats. Sometimes the children were whipped with sticks. Parents also expected their children to learn to remain stone-faced when unhappy or in pain.

Prior to going to school, children were trained skills they would need. Mothers and other women of the *calpulli* taught girls weaving and household skills. If they were farmers, fathers taught their sons to work the fields and to hunt and fish. Craftspeople passed their skills onto their children as well. If a child was born to a metalworker, he or she would become a metalworker in Aztec society, unless special circumstances arose.

The Aztecs had schools for everyone—not just the children of nobles, and not just boys. All children started school at least by the age of fifteen. Children of nobles went to the *calmecac,* a seminary or religious school run by priests. In these schools, boys and girls were separated. Boys studied mathematics, the calendar, law, and astrology, and learned to chant the songs and stories of Aztec history and religion. Girls learned mainly about religion and often spent their hours in silent meditation.

If a male student graduating from the *calmecac* wished to become a priest, he would go on to an upper-level school in which priests trained him further. Most male graduates of the *calmecac* spent time in the military as officers. If they did their military duties well, they might go on to become judges or government officials. Sometimes the son of a family of commoners was allowed to attend the *calmecac* if he was notably intelligent or disciplined.

The children of commoners went to free schools called *telpochcalli,* or "houses of youth." The girls were separated from the boys and trained in singing, dancing, and religion. The primary training for the boys was in the skills of war, though many learned trades as well. The boys were toughened up through hard work and extremely strict discipline. Some hired themselves out as assistants to army officers going off to battle to learn more about being a soldier. For commoners, there was no better way to rise up the social ladder than by excelling at war.

Houses

The houses of nobles were usually adobe (sun-baked bricks of mud) or made from stone. They were often rectangular and built around a courtyard that featured flower gardens and pools or fountains. Flowers were prized by the Aztecs, and colorful and fragrant blossoms could be found adorning most houses and public paths. Inside the homes of nobles there were many rooms: rooms for dining, sleeping, cooking, receiving guests, and housing the servants. The interiors of the houses were divided by walls; cloth mats were hung in the doorways for privacy. Most of the houses of nobles had steam rooms similar to modern saunas.

The houses of common workers were much smaller and usually made from either adobe or cane (woody grass stems or reeds) with a thatched roof. In Tenochtitlán the houses of common people were found at the outskirts of the city. They generally had only one or two rooms, with a steam room outside. There was only one door and no windows, and the house was probably smoky from the pine torches used to light it. For beds, the Aztecs used woven mats, and there was little other furniture. The houses, whether adobe or cane, were painted and kept very clean.

Food

As elsewhere in Mesoamerica, maize (corn) was the main staple of the Aztec diet, particularly when it was ground into flour and made into cakes, or tortillas, which were consumed in great quantities. Ground maize was also the main ingredient of *atole,* a corn porridge. Maize flour was placed in cornhusks with other ingredients and baked to make tamales. Other common foods were beans, chilies, squash, melons, and a grain called amaranth.

Commoners often supplemented their diets with insects, frogs, and other small creatures that added protein. Otherwise the Aztec diet had little meat in it, though occasionally hunters would bring in deer or rabbits. The only animals raised by the Aztecs to be eaten were dogs, and dog meat was usually only eaten on special occasions. While the common workers tended to eat many forms of maize, with beans and vegetables on the side, the nobles had a much more varied diet with meat and fish. The nobility were also privileged enough to drink chocolate made from cacao beans, which was considered a delicacy. Most commoners drank water.

The Aztecs made a potent alcoholic beverage from cactus called *pulque* (pronounced PUHL-kay). In theory, Aztecs could only legally drink *pulque* at ceremonies and special celebrations because drunkenness was a crime. The exception was for the elderly, who were allowed to drink as much as they wanted. The first time one was caught drunk the punishment was usually some form of public humilia-

tion, such a having one's hair cut off. But the second time, the punishment was death.

Clothing and adornment

Aztecs were modest people who did not approve of public nudity, which was commonplace among some tribes around them. Aztec nobles generally dressed in fine cotton adorned with designs made from gold or feathers. The men wore a cotton loincloth, with a cloak and sandals. Male commoners usually just wore loincloths; female commoners wore simple, loose dresses. Commoners made their own clothes from maguey (an agave, a plant with spiny leaves) fibers.

The Aztecs liked to adorn themselves in a variety of ways. Among the commoners, tattoos and stained teeth were considered attractive. Some women dyed their skin to be more yellow. Both sexes wore plenty of jewelry.

Law and order

The Aztecs valued law and order very highly and had an advanced and detailed legal system, which protected their property and safety. The poet-king of Texcoco, King Nezahualcoyotl, created a code of laws that would become standard throughout the empire.

In the Aztec system, the emperor appointed a *cihuacoatl*, an independent judge, for every major city in the empire. The judge had the authority to rule on all of his city's cases, whether civil, such as lawsuits and divorces, or criminal cases. What the judge ordered was law; not even the emperor could change the sentences issued by the judge. The judge also oversaw the administrators who collected taxes in his city. If a lawsuit or criminal case proved to be very difficult, it might be passed to a council of judges in Texcoco, which had the most advanced legal system.

In the Aztec courts, people were expected to behave in an orderly and dignified way. There were no lawyers to represent people, so they represented themselves. The court clerk kept record of the proceedings using Aztec glyphs and illustrations. These records were highly accurate.

Codices clearly spelled out Aztec laws, which were quite harsh. Many crimes were punishable by death, including drunkenness, adultery, and stealing. Aztec nobles received much harsher sentences for breaking laws and standards of conduct than commoners since they were expected to set an example. The laws dictated that all people do their jobs well and honestly. Tax collectors who embezzled (stole money), musicians whose instruments were out of tune, and priests who led immoral lives were all subject to the death penalty. Even the judges were held to the highest standards; if a judge gave favored treatment to a noble over a commoner, it was punishable by death. In many cases, a commoner might only have received a public whipping for the same kind of offense.

Medicine

The Aztecs believed illness came from the spirit world. Sickness was believed to originate in an unlucky calendar day or in the ever-changing temperament of a god. A healer's first treatment plan for a sick patient was likely to be prayer and possibly the sacrifice of an animal or another offering to the gods.

Over the years, the Aztecs had studied the power of plants to heal and had found hundreds of herbal remedies—some still in use today. Healers knew how to set broken bones and performed some form of brain surgery. While Aztecs did not try to cure diseases, believing they were sent by the gods and could not be cured by humans, they did try to alleviate pain and symptoms of disease.

For More Information

Books

Clendinnen, Inga. *Aztecs: An Interpretation.* Cambridge, UK: Cambridge University Press, 1991.

Coe, Michael D. *Mexico: From the Olmecs to the Aztecs,* 4th ed. London and New York: Thames and Hudson, 1994.

León-Portilla, Miguel. *Fifteen Poets of the Aztec World.* Norman: University of Oklahoma Press, 1992.

Meyer, Michael C., and William L. Sherman. *The Course of Mexican History,* 5th ed. New York and Oxford: Oxford University Press, 1995.

Web Sites

"Aztec Books, Documents, and Writing." *Azteca.com.* http://www.azteca.net/aztec/nahuatl/writing.html (accessed on October 6, 2004).

Hooker, Richard. "Civilizations in America: The Mexica/Aztecs." *World Civilizations, Washington State University.* http://www.wsu.edu/~dee/CIVAMRCA/AZTECS.HTM (accessed on October 18, 2004).

The Conquest of the Aztecs

28

In its two hundred years of existence, the Aztec city of Tenochtitlán (pronounced tay-notch-teet-LAHN) rose out of a rough swampland settlement to become one of the largest and most magnificent cities of its time in the world. In 1325, when the Aztecs settled Tenochtitlán, they had been an egalitarian (everyone had an equal say in political, social, and economic decision making, and no one was considered the leader) and nomadic (roaming) society. As they built their rough houses on the swampy island in Lake Texcoco, they were barely able to feed themselves. By the beginning of the sixteenth century, however, the vast Aztec empire (a vast, complex political unit extending across political boundaries and dominated by one central power, which generally takes control of the economy, government, and culture in communities throughout its territory) encompassed all of what is present-day central and southern Mexico extending all the way down into Guatemala, including the Mexican states of Puebla, Hidalgo, Mexico, Morelos, most of Veracruz, Guerrero, and Oaxaca (pronounced wah-HAH-kah), and parts of Chiapas. The estimated population of the empire was about fifteen million people. The em-

Words to Know

Amerindian: An indigenous, or native, person from North or South America. The term "Amerindian" is used in place of the terms "American Indian" or "Native American" in these volumes, as the term "Native American" is often associated with the United States and the term "Indian" is offensive to some people.

Baptism: A Christian ritual celebrating an individual joining a church, in which sprinkling holy water or dunking signifies his or her spiritual cleansing and rebirth.

Chronicler: A person who writes down a record of historical events, arranged in the order of occurrence.

Creole: A person of European descent who is born in the Americas; in this chapter, a Spaniard who is born in Mexico.

Egalitarian: A society or government in which everyone has an equal say in political, social, and economic decisions and no individual or group is considered the leader.

Empire: A vast, complex political unit extending across political boundaries and dominated by one central power, which generally takes control of the economy, government, and culture in communities throughout its territory.

Encomienda: A grant to Spanish conquistadores giving them privilege to collect tribute from Amerindians in a particular region. The *encomendero* (grant holder) had the responsibility to train Amerindians in Christianity and Spanish, and to protect them from invasion. Most *encomenderos*, however, treated the Amerindians under their grants like slaves, forcing them into inhuman labor conditions often resulting in the collapse or death of the workers.

Hierarchy: The ranking of a group of people according to their social, economic, or political position.

Mestizo: A person having mixed ancestry, specifically European and Amerindian.

Missionary: A person, usually working for a religious organization, who tries to convert people, usually in a foreign land, to his or her religion.

Nomadic: Roaming from place to place without a fixed home.

Peninsulares: People living in Mexico who were born in Spain.

Smallpox: A severe contagious viral disease spread by particles emitted from the mouth when an infected person speaks, coughs, or sneezes.

Tribute: A payment to a nation or its ruler, usually made by people from a conquered territory as a sign that they surrender to the imposed rule; payment could be made in goods or labor or both.

---

pire was wealthy, and the Aztec armies were strong. Then came the first sightings of ships with bearded, fair-skinned men aboard, and the Aztec empire entered its final years.

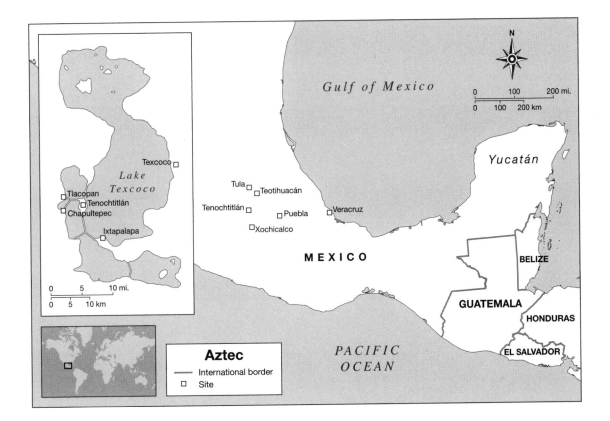

Map showing the sites of the ancient Aztec civilization in Mesoamerica. *Map by XNR Productions. The Gale Group.*

The reign of Montezuma II, 1502 to 1520

Montezuma II (pronounced mohk-the-ZOO-mah; the name is more correctly spelled Motecuhzoma Xocoyótzin, meaning Montezuma the Younger; c. 1480–1520) became emperor in Tenochtitlán in 1502. By this time, the empire was well established. Tributes—payments made on a regular basis in goods or labor by the people the Aztecs had conquered—flowed into the capital city of Tenochtitlán, making it a place of incredible wealth, at least for some of its people. Products from all over Mesoamerica abounded in the city's huge markets, which swarmed with tens of thousands of people, both locals and traders from distant lands.

Impressive pyramids graced the skies, echoing the shape of the mountains surrounding the city. Gold, silver, and jade objects lined the niches in every wall of the grand palaces and homes of the nobles. The city was adorned with exquisite

Montezuma II, emperor of the Aztec empire when the Spanish arrived in Tenochtitlán.
© Bettmann/Corbis.

art, and fragrant flowers bloomed in its beautifully kept gardens. Bright-colored birds and exotic animals entertained pedestrians passing by the perfectly maintained public grounds and palace courtyards. The nobility lived in luxury, attended by large staffs of servants, living in large homes with the finest food and clothing.

The new emperor exhibited a mixture of strong qualities. Montezuma II's education taught him to excel as both warrior and priest. He was, by most accounts, a good student with a keen understanding of Mexican history and was prone to scholarly or philosophical pursuits. He had trained for the priesthood, had a very successful career as a military general, and also served as the chief priest of the empire before he was chosen to succeed Emperor Ahuitzotl (pronounced ah-weet-ZOH-tul; ruled c. 1486–1502) upon the latter's death.

During the first seven years of Montezuma II's reign, the emperor led his warriors in successful battles at the furthest reaches of the empire, even as far away as present-day Nicaragua. In 1509 Montezuma II apparently decided to give up leading his warriors in battle. According to accounts of the Spanish chroniclers (people who wrote down their accounts of history), the emperor was overwhelmed with a sense of impending disaster and wished to devote himself to worshipping the gods.

The return of Quetzalcoatl

One day a messenger brought Montezuma II a picture, drawn by an eyewitness, of strange occurrences on the eastern coast. The picture showed three white temples built atop three canoes floating on the ocean. This picture was probably the first report to reach Tenochtitlán about the Spanish fleets, which had been sailing off the Mexican coast on expeditions. More reports of the strange people in large ships continued to arrive over the next few years. Most historians estimate that Montezuma II knew about the arrival of the Spanish in the Caribbean by at least 1513.

As Montezuma II pondered the meaning of the arrival of the intruders, a series of omens (signs of upcoming events interpreted as either good or evil) heightened his sense of doom. He consulted priests, magicians, and oracles (people, usually priests or priestesses, through whom the gods are believed to speak), as well as many of the nobility of Tenochtitlán and other cities around Lake Texcoco. Montezuma II was said to have been utterly ruthless in seeking answers about what it all meant, killing many of the people he consulted.

One factor in Montezuma II's apparent nervousness was shared among the Aztec people. Mesoamerican mythology (traditional, often imaginary stories dealing with ancestors, heroes, or supernatural beings, and usually making an attempt to explain a belief, practice, or natural phenomenon) had long foretold that in the year 1 Reed, or 1519 by the current calendar, a bearded and fair-skinned Quetzalcoatl (pronounced kates-ahl-koh-AH-tul), the creator god of the Toltecs, would return from the east to take over the Aztec world. Quetzalcoatl was a holy and benevolent (kind) god and, according to some of the ancient legends (stories handed down from earlier times, often believed to be historically true), one of the few gods who did not approve of human sacrifice. The legends of Quetzalcoatl varied greatly, however; clearly Montezuma II did not know what to expect of this god.

Quetzalcoatl was regarded as a father to humankind—in one legend he traveled deep into the underworld and retrieved the bones of dead human beings. By spilling his own blood on the bones, he brought humans back to life. In Toltec legend, Quetzalcoatl and the god of darkness, Tezcatlipoca (pronounced tez-caht-lee-POE-cah), had at some time in the past entered into a terrible battle for power. In the time of the Toltec civilization, Tezcatlipoca had won the struggle. Quetzalcoatl is said to have sailed away from the Toltecs on a raft made of serpents after his defeat, promising to return in the year 1 Reed (see Chapter 24 for more information). The promise was not forgotten by the Aztecs as the year swiftly approached.

The Conquistadores

Hernán Cortés and the men who joined him in the expedition to "explore" Mexico were not professional navigators and explorers. They were not soldiers of the Spanish military, nor did they work for the Spanish or provincial New World (the Americas) governments. The expedition was financed privately, and the men who joined it were carpenters, blacksmiths, doctors, and others. Cortés himself was a notary (someone who is authorized to witness signatures and certify documents) by trade.

Although the Cuban governor gave them permission to explore and trade along the coast of Mexico, Cortés and his crew had much more than exploring in mind, as crewmember Bernal Díaz (del Castillo; pronounced cah-STEE-yoe; c. 1492–1584) expressed in his memoirs, *The Conquest of New Spain* (written in 1568; first published in 1632 as *Historia verdadera de la conquista de Nueva España*): "We came here to serve God and the king, and also to get rich." At one point in their endeavors in Tenochtitlán, Cortés and his crew were pursued as criminals by the Spanish authorities in Cuba for overstepping their authority. This put them in conflict with their own government as well as the powerful Aztec nation.

Men who would take such risks in an unknown country were certainly daring adventurers, but they were not necessarily law-abiding, responsible, or remotely concerned with the welfare of others. In those days, according to Anna Lanyon in *Malinche's Conquest* (1999), the word *conquistador* did not exist. The Spanish coined the word in an effort to describe these adventurers in the New World.

The conquistadores, in their quest for the gold and riches of the New World, had proved a powerful force. Their efforts, legal or not, were responsible for the con-

The arrival of the Spanish

Two years after Montezuma II assumed the Aztec throne, Hernán Cortés (1485-1547), a young law student from a poor but noble Spanish family, gave up his studies and shipped out to the Caribbean island of Hispaniola. He settled for a time at the first permanent Spanish New World settlement, Santo Domingo, which had been founded by Bartholomeo Columbus, brother of Christopher, in 1496. In 1511 Cortés accompanied Spanish soldier and administrator Diego Velázquez (1465–1524) in his conquest of Cuba.

Velázquez became Cuba's governor, and Cortés worked for him in Cuba. In 1518 Velázquez appointed Cortés

quest of Mexico and for the region becoming a province of Spain. In return for their efforts, the conquistadores wanted riches. They looted the treasures of the Amerindian cities wherever they could, but few came away with enough to provide for a lifetime of ease. Adhering to old traditions, the Spanish government reluctantly granted the conquistadores *encomiendas* as rewards for their service to the country. An *encomienda* was a grant giving them the right to collect tribute from the Amerindians who lived in the region they oversaw.

In theory, the Spanish conquistadores were to teach Christianity and European ways in exchange for the tribute. In practice, however, many conquistadores put the natives to work in a system similar to slavery that led to horrible abuses of the workers.

Many of the conquistadores did very well for themselves in New Spain with the sweat and labor of the natives. Cortés, for example, became very wealthy from looting the treasures of the cities he attacked. Although he did not rise in political power as he had hoped, he settled in Mexico into the life of a wealthy *encomendero* (grant holder). He collected tribute from the Amerindians in his *encomienda* in the form of gold dust, textiles, maize (corn), poultry, and other goods.

Cortés used forced labor to pan for gold and mine for silver. Cortés also raised a large number of cattle and hogs, as well as grew grain, fruits, and vegetables on large diversified estates called *haciendas,* also with the labor of Amerindians. He had become very wealthy by these means by 1528, and by the time of his death in 1547 he was still receiving large amounts of goods and money annually in *encomienda* tribute payments.

to head an expedition to explore the newly discovered Mexican coast. This was the third attempt to explore the Mexican coast—the first two expeditions were failures due to resistance of the Amerindians (indigenous, or native, persons from North or South America). Cortés had heard stories of a magnificent and very wealthy kingdom set on an island in a lake in Mexico. His interest in heading up an expedition was not for the sake of exploration; he wanted to conquer and rule the new territory and get rich in the process.

The crew

The Cortés expedition consisting of eleven ships and about 550 soldiers set off for Mexico near the end of the year in 1518. One of the soldiers on board was Bernal Díaz (c. 1492–1584), who would write the account of the Spanish conquest most often used by historians in the twenty-first century (*The Conquest of New Spain*). There were also sixteen horses on board, the first to come to the Americas. The ships reached the Yucatán coast in February 1519. As they traveled along the coast to Tabasco, the Spaniards made contact with the Mayas (pronounced MY-uhs) of the region. Early in their travels, the members of the expedition had encountered a fellow Spaniard, Geronimo de Aguilar, who had washed up on the Mexican shores after a shipwreck in 1511. He had been living with the Maya ever since and knew their language. Gratefully joining the expedition, Aguilar served as a translator.

In March the Spanish fleet arrived in the Maya city of Potonchan in Tabasco. As soon as the Spaniards came ashore, the Maya attacked them, but the Spanish won the battle. The Maya nobles then offered the Spaniards many gifts of surrender, including twenty young women. One of these was later baptized Doña Marina, but she has come to be known to many as Malinche (c. 1501–1550).

Malinche spoke two languages, Mayan and Nahuatl (pronounced NAH-wa-tul). Cortés soon realized that since she could translate Nahuatl to Mayan, and Aguilar could then translate Malinche's Mayan into Spanish for him, he was well equipped to converse with the Nahuatl-speaking Aztecs at Tenochtitlán, the island kingdom he was seeking. During the next couple of years Malinche was an able translator, quickly learning the Spanish language. She gained a great deal of respect among the conquistadores for her courage and intelligence. She also became Cortés's mistress and bore his son.

Aztecs and Spaniards make contact

From a Nahuatl-speaking city in Veracruz—one of many cities within the Aztec empire—Cortés sent word to Montezuma II that he wanted to meet with him in Tenochtitlán. Montezuma II had been informed of the Spanish expedition's movements for some time, even getting pictures of their ships. Uncertain if this was an enemy or the god Quetzalcoatl, Montezuma II stalled for time, sending many valuable gifts of jade (a green gemstone), cloth, and gold to Cortés along with regrets that he was too ill to make the journey.

Montezuma II had by this time heard many reports of these strangers. He was especially disturbed to hear about their weapons, which seemed to the Amerindian observers to spew fire. Worse yet were the horses, bigger than any animal the Aztecs had ever seen. Montezuma II called together a council to decide how to proceed. While many recommended gathering a full Aztec army to destroy the small Spanish force before they came to the city, others recommended treating Cortés as an honored ambassador (diplomatic official who represents a government or a society) from a great king. Montezuma II remained conflicted. Throughout Cortés's travels toward Tenochtitlán, the emperor continued to send messengers with gifts, hoping he could persuade Cortés not to come to the capital.

Cortés founded a settlement in Veracruz and then continued on with his explorations by land. The Spaniards found friends among the Totonac people at Cempoala (pronounced sem-pwahl-AH) in central Veracruz. The Totonacs were tired of paying tribute to Tenochtitlán and were happy to tell Cortés the route to the city and to describe its great wealth. Cortés shrewdly caused a conflict between the Totonacs and the Aztecs by urging the Totonacs to arrest the Aztec tribute collectors who arrived shortly after he did. He then released the two collectors so they could go back to Montezuma II and report the bad behavior of the Totonacs.

Fearing reprisal, the Totonacs felt they had no other choice but to attack Tenochtitlán before Montezuma decided to attack them. Cortés continued to anger other provinces of the empire as he continued in his travels, gathering allies for the Spanish and making enemies for Montezuma II.

The expedition arrived at the city of Tlaxcala in south-central Mexico in September 1519. The Tlaxcalans were bitter enemies of the Aztecs, but they met the Spaniards in a fierce battle, perhaps believing the Spanish had allied themselves with Montezuma II. After the battle the Tlaxcalans had a change of heart and committed themselves to fighting with the Spanish against Tenochtitlán. This was an important factor in the Spanish conquest, which may well have failed without the alliance of the fierce Tlaxcalans.

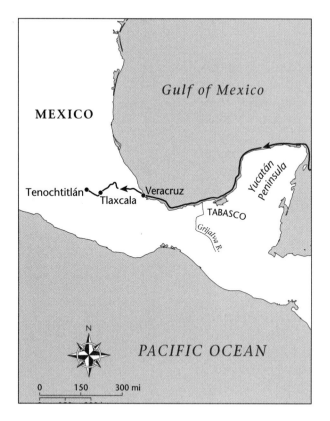

Map showing Hernán Cortés's route through Mesoamerica towards Tenochtitlán. *Map by XNR Productions. The Gale Group.*

When Cortés left Tlaxcala to continue his march to Tenochtitlán, he had one thousand Tlaxcalan allies with him.

Montezuma II's ambassadors asked Cortés to visit the important religious center of Cholula, so the Spaniards camped out there. While they stayed in the city they began to fear an attack. Malinche, in talking to a local woman, learned their fears were justified; the nobles of the city had arranged for a huge army to surround and kill the Spaniards. Cortés led an attack on the Cholulans instead, which turned into a violent massacre of Cholulan men, women, and children.

Back at Tenochtitlán, Montezuma II heard the news of the Cholula massacre with great dread. The Spaniards were only 60 miles (96.5 kilometers) away. Montezuma II finally made a decision. He invited Cortés and his men to be his guests in Tenochtitlán. The emperor could have mustered a huge army at any time and stopped their approach. His reasons for not doing so may have come from a lingering belief that Cortés was in fact the god Quetzalcoatl, or he may have felt safe in bringing them into the city because his army still greatly outnumbered the Spanish and their allies.

Cortés enters Tenochtitlán

On November 8, 1519, Cortés marched along the longest causeway (a road built over the water; there were three causeways, each over a mile long, leading from the shores of Lake Texcoco to the city) leading into Tenochtitlán. He and his crew were spellbound by the splendor of the city. Cortés described it in a letter to the Spanish king, Charles V (1500–1558; ruled 1516–56), remarking on the great markets, commerce, shops, and very wide and clean streets. He was amazed by the agricultural abundance and variety of goods, and he admitted his confusion that a non-Christian and such a "barbarous" people could live such a civilized existence.

The people of Tenochtitlán and the other cities around Lake Texcoco watched as the strangers approached the city, entering by one of the causeways. In the city, Montezuma II was waiting for them. At the time he was between forty and fifty years old (sources differ on his birth date). He was described as a very courteous and dignified man, of slender build and average height. He wore his dark hair long. Díaz witnessed the meeting between Cortés and Montezuma II, and wrote of the event in his book *The Conquest of New Spain* as follows:

> When we came near to Mexico, at a place where there were some other small towers, the Great Montezuma descended from his litter [an enclosed platform with a couch or bench carried on long poles], and these other great Caciques [leaders] supported him beneath a marvelously rich canopy of green feathers, decorated with gold work, silver, pearls, and chalchihuites [various green precious stones, mainly jade], which hung from a sort of border. It was a marvelous sight. The Great Montezuma was magnificently clad, in their fashion, and wore sandals of a kind for which their name is cactli, the soles of which are of gold and the upper parts ornamented with precious stones…. There were four other great Caciques who carried the canopy above their heads, and many more lords who walked before the great Montezuma, sweeping the ground on which he was to tread, and laying down cloaks so that his feet should not touch the earth. Not one of these chieftains dared to look him in the face. All kept their eyes lowered most reverently except those four lords, his nephews, who were supporting him.

Cortés and Montezuma II exchanged necklaces. According to some of the chroniclers, Montezuma II addressed Cortés as Quetzalcoatl and welcomed him home.

A copy of a letter from Hernán Cortés to King Charles V of Spain, 1542, describing his encounter with Aztec civilization. *The Library of Congress.*

The capture and death of Montezuma II

Cortés told Montezuma II that the Spanish king wanted to make Catholic Christians of the Aztecs. Montezu-

Hernán Cortés and his crew enter Tenochtitlán and are greeted by the emperor, Montezuma II. *The Library of Congress.*

ma II listened politely and presented gifts to Cortés, and then provided them with lodging. The Spaniards, free to roam Tenochtitlán, stared in amazement at what they saw, thinking, as Díaz put it, they must be dreaming.

Although they were treated well, Cortés disliked being surrounded by Aztec warriors. In an utterly bold and daring move, he took the emperor captive. By most accounts, Montezuma II submitted without a struggle and went so far as to calm his people, asking them not to rise up against the Spaniards. If this is true, his motives remain a mystery. Although Montezuma II was in custody, he was allowed to go about his business more or less as usual.

In the midst of the drama in Tenochtitlán, Cortés was forced to leave the city to go back to Veracruz. Velázquez had sent more than one thousand Spanish soldiers to arrest him for going beyond his authority in Mexico (he had only been given the task of exploration and

minor trading; certainly not establishing settlements and taking over kingdoms). After a skirmish with the new arrivals, Cortés persuaded many of the soldiers to join his expedition, promising them the opportunity to share in the vast wealth of Tenochtitlán when it had been conquered. He made his way back to Tenochtitlán with more men than he had arrived with.

About 140 of Cortés's men remained in Tenochtitlán, attending the kidnapped emperor. They were surrounded by thousands of increasingly hostile Aztecs, and it is likely they panicked. As the Aztecs began to celebrate a feast in honor of their god Huitzilopochtli (pronounced hweets-ee-loh-PAWCH-tlee), Cortés's lieutenant, Pedro de Alvarado (d. 1541), ordered an attack on them. Two hundred unarmed nobles were brutally murdered. The Aztecs were furious, and Montezuma II appears to have saved the soldiers from immediate death with his influence. Nonetheless, when Cortés returned, the Aztecs began to attack.

Montezuma II being taken prisoner by Spanish conquistadores. *The Library of Congress.*

The Toll of Epidemics on the Native Populations of Mexico

Though violence and warfare claimed many Amerindian lives in the conquest of Tenochtitlán, nothing killed as many of the native peoples as disease. The Europeans brought several deadly diseases with them, but most devastating were smallpox (a severe contagious viral disease spread by particles emitted from the mouth when an infected person speaks, coughs, or sneezes) and measles. The first epidemic of smallpox in Mexico began in 1519 when the Cuban expedition sent to arrest Hernán Cortés landed at Veracruz. One of the soldiers aboard was infected with smallpox. Although he could not have known it, his presence in the New World was probably the most significant factor in the conquistadores' defeat of the Aztecs at Tenochtitlán.

The epidemic that hit the Aztecs after their first battle with Cortés was remembered in the accounts of one of the survivors and appears in Miguel León-Portilla's book, *Broken Spears* (1992). The elder (people who have authority because of their age and experience) describes what he calls "a great plague":

> Sores erupted on our faces, our breasts, our bellies; we were covered with agonizing sores from head to foot. The illness was so dreadful that no one could walk or move. The sick were so utterly helpless that they could only lie on their beds like corpses, unable to move their limbs or even their heads. They could not lie face down or roll from one side to the other. If they did move their bodies, they screamed with pain. A great many died from this plague, and many others died of hunger. They could not get up to search for food,

In the ensuing battle, Montezuma II was killed, though no one knows how he actually died. The Spanish said he stood upon a wall to try to talk his people out of attacking the Spaniards. In the chaos, a stone thrown blindly by one of the people accidentally hit him in the head and killed him. Other accounts suggest the Aztec people were fed up with Montezuma II's failure to defend them and killed him on purpose. Many believe it was actually Cortés who had Montezuma II killed. The truth will probably never be known.

On June 30, 1520, a night the Spanish called "La noche triste," Cortés knew his crew could no longer hold out against the increasing attacks of the Aztecs. He ordered his men—some thirteen hundred Spaniards and well over two thousand Tlaxcalans—to secretly prepare to leave. As darkness fell they slipped out and raced toward the causeway. An Aztec guard sounded the alarm, and the Aztecs attacked the

and everyone else was too sick to care for them, so they starved to death in their beds.

Such was the state of the population when Cortés and his one hundred thousand Amerindian allies returned to attack Tenochtitlán. Díaz noted that when the Spanish attacked Tenochtitlán: "all the houses and stockades in the lake were full of heads and corpses. It was the same in the streets and courts ... we could not walk without treading on the bodies and heads of dead Indians. Indeed, the stench was so bad that no one could endure it."

In 1519 there were an estimated 11 million Amerindians in the region of Central Mexico according to the censuses of the Spanish priests. By 1540 the population had dropped by about one-half to about 6.4 million. By the end of the century there were only about 2.5 million Amerindians in the same area, and in 1650 there were only 1.5 million. Other factors contributed to the terrible depopulation (decrease in population), particularly the harsh treatment of Amerindian laborers, but the major cause of death was disease—smallpox and the measles.

The effect of these epidemics on the morale of the Aztecs at Tenochtitlán must have been profound. In *Viruses, Plagues and History* (1998), Michael Oldstone comments: "The havoc wrought by smallpox also brought a morbid state of mind to the Aztecs. The only interpretation open to them ... was that they were being punished by angry gods."

fleeing Spaniards and their allies with full force. Many of the Spaniards were unable to escape because they were so heavily weighed down by the gold and silver they had looted from the city. The Aztecs, who usually tried not to kill their enemies in war so they would have sacrifice victims afterward, fought with an unusual intent to kill. More than 450 Spaniards and one thousand Tlaxcalans were killed or sacrificed that night.

A new king in Tenochtitlán

With Montezuma II dead and the Spanish gone, the Aztecs celebrated their victory. They elected a new emperor, Montezuma II's brother Cuitláhuac. They prepared for an all-out war, determined that if the Spanish struck again, they would attack without moderation.

Sadly, no preparations could have strengthened the Aztecs against the assault of smallpox. Smallpox and the other contagious diseases the Spanish brought with them were new to the Americas. The Amerindians had no resistance to the germs. When smallpox struck, the population of Tenochtitlán was destroyed by the disease. Smallpox took the life of the new emperor, Cuitláhuac, who was replaced during the siege by the last Aztec emperor, Cuauhtémoc.

The fall of Tenochtitlán

After their disastrous flight from Tenochtitlán in July, Cortés and his troops returned to Tlaxcala where they were given refuge as they healed from their wounds and regained strength. Cortés seems to have never doubted his path; he spent the next couple of months preparing for another attack. He contacted and made allies of many different Amerindian groups, in some cases by promising them a share in the loot and an end to the Aztec's reign.

In other cases Cortés resorted to threatening punishment if the native peoples did not join his forces. The fierce Tlaxcalans were determined to destroy Tenochtitlán and were highly persuasive in scaring other groups into joining the Spaniards. One by one, the subjects of the Aztec empire stopped paying tribute to Tenochtitlán.

Since Lake Texcoco provided protection for the island city, Cortés had thirteen boats built for the next attack. These were carried by thousands of Amerindian allies to Lake Texcoco in pieces and then assembled. When they were ready to make a renewed attack on Tenochtitlán, Cortés and his crew numbered about nine hundred Spaniards and as many as one hundred thousand Amerindian warriors. They settled for a time on the shores of the lake, among people who had only recently been loyal to the empire. In May 1521 the conquistadores made their attack.

Cortés had devised a plan of attack in which his forces bore down on the city of Tenochtitlán from every possible entryway—his fleet of ships came in by water and thousands of warriors marched down each of the three causeways leading into the city. Though the Spanish had superior

weapons and some horses, the Aztecs resisted the invasion fiercely, giving little ground.

Spanish soldiers were unable to use their cannons effectively because of the city's tall temples, so they used them to level as many buildings as possible then set fire to the rest. The Spanish also set up a blockade, so no food or water could reach the island from the mainland. Many Aztecs died of starvation or dysentery (an intestinal ailment with diarrhea), and the warriors were weakened. The Aztec warriors, nevertheless, fought on, showing remarkable bravery under terrible circumstances. Slowly the Spanish took possession of more and more of their city.

The siege of Tenochtitlán lasted for nearly three months. The surrender took place on August 13, 1521, when there was no hope left for the Aztecs. Their last elected emperor, Cuauhtémoc, was either captured by the Spanish or surrendered to them, depending on the source. He is remem-

Illustration showing Spanish soldiers and Aztec warriors battling for control of Tenochtitlán. © *Corbis.*

bered as a brave warrior and a symbol of strength to the be-sieged people. In some accounts of his surrender, he is said to have grabbed Cortés's dagger (knife) and pleaded to be killed since he could no longer defend his city or his people.

Cortés treated Cuauhtémoc with dignity at the time, but he later had the leader tortured, hoping to force him to reveal the location of more Aztec treasures. Cuauhtémoc gave him no information and was hanged in 1523. After the Aztecs surrendered, the Tlaxcalans, still bent on revenge, slaughtered many defenseless people.

"Broken Spears," one of several Aztec poems recalled by the survivors of the siege and recorded in Spanish in 1528 (published in translation in Miguel León-Portilla's *The Broken Spears: The Aztec Account of the Conquest of Mexico*), captured the grief and despair of the defeated Aztecs at Tenochtitlán. Notably, the poem laments the death of the great city as if the violence had been done to the walls rather than the people who built them: "The houses are roofless now, and their walls/are red with blood." The poem goes on to depict the gruesome mutilation of the city and the frustration of a war-rior society that could not protect what was held most sacred:

> We have pounded our hands in despair
> against the adobe walls,
> for our inheritance, our city, is lost and dead.
> The shields of our warriors were its defense,
> but they could not save it.

The aftermath

Cortés ordered that a new city be built right on top of the ruins of Tenochtitlán. Mexico City, like Tenochtitlán, was a magnificent city, built by the tremendous labor of tens of thousands of Amerindians working for the Spanish. In Tenochtitlán and the surrounding cities, wherever the Span-ish found an Aztec temple, they built a Roman Catholic church right on top of it or, if this was not possible, right be-side it. In the twenty-first century, in the heart of Mexico City, people are still finding the ruins of ancient Aztec mon-uments underneath the early buildings of the Spanish.

The Aztec empire ceased to exist on August 13, 1521. Although it would take the Spanish many more years to bring all of Mexico under its control, the fall of Tenochtitlán, as the capital of the huge Aztec empire, meant most of the vast empire's people immediately fell under the rule of the Spaniards. The peoples of the empire survived, though their numbers diminished greatly over the next century.

The Spanish were ruthless in killing Aztec priests, who they believed practiced an evil form of black magic. These feelings were strong among those who witnessed some of the soldiers being sacrificed. Of the nobles and warriors who survived the conquest, some managed to escape from Tenochtitlán and disappeared into distant regions of Mexico. The common people had little choice but to remain where they were.

The nobles who remained in Tenochtitlán were treated well by the Spanish as long as they accepted the Christian religion. The missionaries worked with them, teaching them Spanish and even how to raise and breed the animals (cows, sheep, and pigs) being brought into Mexico. These converted nobles then helped the missionaries (people, usually working for a religious organization, who try to convert people, usually in a foreign land, to his or her religion) convert others to their new religion and culture. The increasing numbers of missionaries who arrived in Mexico were very enthusiastic about their work, and immediately began baptizing the Amerindians.

Baptisms are a Christian ritual to celebrate a person joining the church. The sprinkling of or dunking in water signifies the baptized person's spiritual cleansing and rebirth as a Christian. Hundreds of thousands of Amerindians were baptized during the first decades of the new Spanish colony. Soon most of the Nahuatl-speaking people in the empire had adopted the Roman Catholic religion, some just for show, but others embracing it with sincerity.

The missionaries burned all the codices (Aztec books) they could find and eliminated lingering aspects of Aztec culture in their efforts to convert the population. Some Aztecs clung to their own gods, worshiping in private. This private worship kept parts of their religion alive, and it continues among some groups to the present day.

The Spanish king and many of the Catholic missionaries wished to set up a fair and humane government in their new colony in Mesoamerica where the natives could prosper in their new life, but this was not to be. After the conquistadores had defeated the Aztecs at Tenochtitlán, they felt they deserved more wealth and prestige than what they had already stolen from the Aztec cities. The Spanish government reluctantly agreed to the *encomienda* system, in which the conquistadores were paid tribute by the Amerindians of their regions.

According to the government, the *encomendero,* or grant holder, was responsible for training the Amerindians in Christianity and Spanish and for providing protection. The Amerindians, in turn, were to pay tribute to the conquistador. The system, however, never worked in this way and most Amerindians were slaves. When the Spanish found silver mines in Mexico, the *encomenderos* forced the natives to do the mining under terrible conditions. Over the years, some missionaries and the Spanish crown tried to reform the *encomienda* system for the sake of the natives, but little was ever done.

Many Amerindian groups who lived in remote rural parts of Mexico were able to rule themselves, without much interference from the Spanish. In the cities of Mexico, however, the Spanish were in control. Since many of the conquistadores had come over without wives, they often took partners from among the Amerindian women and raised families with them.

The mixing of Spanish and Amerindian blood prompted a new class system in Mexico. At the top of the social hierarchy (ranking of a group of people according to their social, economic, or political position) were the *peninsulares,* people who had been born in Spain. Under the *peninsulares* were the *creoles,* Spaniards who had been born in Mexico. Next were the *mestizos,* people of mixed Spanish and Amerindian ancestry, which were by far the largest group. At the bottom of the social ladder were the Amerindians, who worked the mines or served as laborers on the growing *haciendas,* or ranches owned by the *peninsulares* and *creoles.* Soon, African slaves were brought into Mexico to provide additional labor. In time, they too would intermarry, and their offspring would become *mestizos.*

The descendents

Experts estimate there are about 1.5 million descendants of the Aztec empire living in Mexico in the twenty-first century. Some speak only Spanish, some speak only Nahuatl, and others speak both languages fluently. The Nahuatl spoken in the twenty-first century has been heavily influenced by Spanish, and Spanish has also been influenced by Nahuatl. Many of the customs and arts found in present-day Mexico are also a cross between native and Spanish cultures.

A good example of the blend of Aztec and Spanish cultures is the celebration of the Days of the Dead (in Spanish, "Los días de los muertos") beginning on October 31 and running through November 2 every year. Days of the Dead traditions go back to the Aztec belief that death was just one phase of a long cycle of life; not an ending but a transition. Each autumn, they and other native people celebrated two feasts for the departed: one for children and one for adults. After the Spanish missionaries arrived, the traditional Aztec

Mexican women celebrating the Days of the Dead, a festival blending Aztec and Spanish cultures.
© *Charles & Josette Lenars/Corbis.*

two-day feast came to be carried out on All Saints Day and All Souls Day. Many of the Aztec deities were supplanted with Catholic saints. The holiday that evolved is a combination of native and Spanish customs.

In Mexico, the Days of the Dead are a time to rejoice. On October 31, a family goes to the market to buy food, candles, incense, and flowers. They buy, among other things, sugar *calaveras* ("skulls"), sweet breads, and *pan de muertos*—loaves of bread decorated with bones—and a type of marigold called *zenpasuchitl*. At home, the families prepare *ofrendas*, altars filled with offerings of food, candles, and flowers for the departed in their families.

Families go to cemeteries and adorn the graves of their loved ones. After dark, solemnity reigns. Many people remain at the cemetery throughout the night. The overall emotion of the two days—of welcoming the dead—is happiness. Parades run through towns with coffins carrying the "dead" (who sit up and smile and accept the oranges tossed to them). Toys and trinkets abound and bakeries are filled with holiday food. The dead are seen by the living as playful and happy beings who want to be entertained, feasted, and cherished. The holiday celebrates the life of the ancestors, not their passing.

For More Information

Books

Clendinnen, Inga. *Aztecs: An Interpretation*. Cambridge, UK: Cambridge University Press, 1991.

Coe, Michael D. *Mexico: From the Olmecs to the Aztecs,* 4th ed. London and New York: Thames and Hudson, 1994.

Díaz, Bernal. *The Conquest of New Spain*. Translated by J.M. Cohen. London and New York: Penguin Books, 1963.

Lanyon, Anna. *Malinche's Conquest*. New South Wales, Australia: Allen & Unwin, 1999.

León-Portilla, Miguel, ed. *The Broken Spears: The Aztec Account of the Conquest of Mexico*. Translated from Nahuatl into Spanish by Angel Maria Garibay K; English translation by Lysander Kemp. Boston: Beacon Press, 1992.

León-Portilla, Miguel. *Fifteen Poets of the Aztec World*. Norman: University of Oklahoma Press, 1992.

Meyer, Michael C., and William L. Sherman. *The Course of Mexican History,* 5th ed. New York and Oxford: Oxford University Press, 1995.

Oldstone, Michael B.A. *Viruses, Plagues, and History.* New York: Oxford University Press, 1998.

Thomas, Hugh. *Conquest: Montezuma, Cortés, and the Fall of Old Mexico.* New York: Simon & Schuster, 1993.

Web Sites

"Aztec." *E-Museum @ Minnesota State University, Mankato.* http://www.mnsu.edu/emuseum/cultural/mesoamerica/aztec.html (accessed on October 18, 2004).

"The Conquest of the Aztecs." *WebChron/North Park University Chicago* http://campus.northpark.edu/history/WebChron/Americas/Cortes.html (accessed on October 18, 2004).

Where to Learn More

Books

Adams, Richard E. W. *Ancient Civilizations of the New World.* Boulder, CO: Westview Press, 1997.

Adovasio, J. M., with Jake Page. *The First Americans: In Pursuit of Archaeology's Greatest Mystery.* New York: Random House, 2002.

Betanzos, Juan de. *Narrative of the Incas.* Translated by Roland Hamilton. Austin: University of Texas Press, 1996.

Burger, Richard L. *Chavín and the Origins of Andean Civilization.* London and New York: Thames and Hudson, 1992.

Clendinnen, Inga. *Aztecs: An Interpretation.* Cambridge, UK: Cambridge University Press, 1991.

Coe, Michael D. *Mexico: From the Olmecs to the Aztecs,* fourth ed. New York: Thames and Hudson, 1994.

Coe, Michael D., and Mark Van Stone. *Reading the Maya Glyphs.* London and New York: Thames and Hudson, 2001.

Coe, Michael, Dean Snow, and Elizabeth Benson. *Atlas of Ancient America.* New York: Facts on File, 1986.

Davies, Nigel. *The Ancient Kingdoms of Peru.* London: Penguin, 1997.

Dewar, Elaine. *Bones: Discovering the First Americans.* New York: Carroll and Graf, 2001.

Díaz, Bernal (del Castillo). *The Conquest of New Spain.* Translated by J. M. Cohen. London and New York: Penguin Books, 1963.

Fagan, Brian. *Kingdoms of Gold, Kingdoms of Jade: The Americas Before Columbus.* London and New York: Thames and Hudson, 1991.

Gallenkamp, Charles. *Maya: The Riddle and Rediscovery of a Lost Civilization,* third ed. New York: Viking, 1985.

Galvin, Irene Flum. *The Ancient Maya.* New York: Benchmark Books, 1997.

Henderson, John S. *The World of the Ancient Maya,* second edition. Ithaca and London: Cornell University Press, 1997.

Hull, Robert. *The Aztecs.* Austin, TX: Steck-Vaughn, 1998.

Incas: Lords of Gold and Glory. Editors of Time-Life Books. Alexandria, VA: Time-Life Books, 1992.

Katz, Friedrich. *The Ancient American Civilizations.* London: Phoenix Press, 2000.

Lanyon, Anna. *Malinche's Conquest.* New South Wales, Australia: Allen & Unwin, 1999.

León-Portilla, Miguel, ed. *The Broken Spears: The Aztec Account of the Conquest of Mexico.* Translated from Nahuatl into Spanish by Angel Maria Garibay K. English translation by Lysander Kemp. Boston: Beacon Press, 1992.

León-Portilla, Miguel. *Fifteen Poets of the Aztec World.* Norman: University of Oklahoma Press, 1992.

The Magnificent Maya. Editors of Time-Life Books. Alexandria, VA: 1993.

Malpass, Michael A. *Daily Life in the Inca Empire.* Westport, CT: Greenwood Press, 1996.

Meyer, Carolyn. *The Mystery of the Ancient Maya,* revised edition. New York: Margaret K. McElderry Books, 1995.

Meyer, Michael C., and William L. Sherman. *The Course of Mexican History,* fifth ed. New York and Oxford: Oxford University Press, 1995.

Morris, Craig, and Adriana Von Hagen. *The Inka Empire: And Its Andean Origins.* New York: Abbeville Press, 1993.

Morris, Craig, and Adriana Von Hagen. *The Cities of the Ancient Andes.* New York: Thames and Hudson, 1998.

Moseley, Michael E. *The Incas and Their Ancestors: The Archaeology of Peru.* London and New York: Thames and Hudson, 1992.

Montgomery, John. *Tikal: An Illustrated History.* New York: Hippocrene Books, 2001.

Newsome, Elizabeth A. *Trees of Paradise and Pillars of the World: The Serial Stela Cycle of "18-Rabbit-God K," King of Copan.* Austin: University of Texas Press, 2001.

Sabloff, Jeremy A. *The Cities of Ancient Mexico: Reconstructing a Lost World,* revised edition. New York and London: Thames and Hudson, 1997.

Schele, Linda, and Mary Miller. *The Blood of Kings: Dynasty and Ritual in Maya Art.* New York: W.W. Norton, 1986.

Schobinger, Juan. *The First Americans.* Grand Rapids, MI: William B. Eerdmans Publishing Company, 1994.

Stirling, Stuart. *The Last Conquistador: Manso Serra de Leguizamón and the Conquest of the Incas.* Phoenix Mill, Stroud, Gloucestershire, UK: Sutton Publishing, 1999.

Thomas, Hugh. *Conquest: Montezuma, Cortés, and the Fall of Old Mexico.* New York: Simon & Schuster, 1993.

Wood, Tim. *The Aztecs.* New York: Viking, 1992.

Periodicals

McClintock, Jack. "The Nasca Lines Solution." *Discover,* December 2000.

Morell, Virginia. "Empires Across the Andes." *National Geographic,* June 2002.

Wade, Nicholas, and John Noble Wilford. "New World Ancestors Lose 12,000 Years." *New York Times*, July 25, 2003.

Wright, Karen. "First Americans (Origins of Man)." *Discover.* February 1999.

Web Sites

"Aztec Books, Documents, and Writing," *Azteca.com.* Available at http://www.azteca.net/aztec/nahuatl/writing.html (accessed December 8, 2004).

Begley, Sharon, and Andrew Murr. "The First Americans." *Newsweek,* April 26, 1999. Available at http://www.abotech.com/Articles/firstamericans.htm (accessed December 8, 2004).

Dillehay, Tom. "Tracking the First Americans." *Nature,* Vol. 425, September 4, 2003. Available at http://www.nature.com (accessed December 8, 2004).

Donnan, Christopher B. "Iconography of the Moche: Unraveling the Mystery of the Warrior–Priest." *National Geographic,* Vol. 174, No. 4, October 1988, pp. 551–55. Available at

http://muweb.millersville.edu/~columbus/data/art/DONNAN01.ART (accessed December 8, 2004).

"Early Archaeology in the Maya Lowlands." University of California. Available at http://id-archserve.ucsb.edu/Anth3/Courseware/History/Maya.html (accessed December 8, 2004).

"Early Maya Murals at San Bartolo, Guatemala." Peabody Museum of Archaeology and Ethnology. Available at http://www.peabody.harvard.edu/SanBartolo.htm (accessed December 8, 2004).

Ebersole, Rene S. "What Lies Beneath: Discovery of a Maya Palace in Guatemala, and Insights into the Maya Civilization around Cancuen." *Current Science,* November 17, 2000. Available at http://www.findarti

cles.com/p/articles/mi_m0BFU/is_6_86/ai_67326281 (accessed December 8, 2004).

Hooker, Richard. "Civilizations in America." *World Civilizations, Washington State University.* Available at http://www.wsu.edu/~dee/CIVAMRCA/MAYAS.HTM (accessed December 8, 2004).

"The Lost Pyramids of Caral." *BBC: Science and Nature: TV and Radio Follow-Up.* January 31, 2002. Available at http://www.bbc.co.uk/science/horizon/2001/caraltrans.shtml (accessed December 8, 2004).

Lovgren, Stefan. "Masks, Other Finds Suggest Early Maya Flourished." *National Geographic News,* May 5, 2004. Available at http://news.nationalgeographic.com/news/2004/05/0504_040505_mayamasks.html (accessed December 8, 2004).

Lovgren, Stefan. "Who Were the First Americans?" *National Geographic,* September 3, 2003. Available at http://www.nationalgeographic.com (accessed December 8, 2004).

Marcus, Joyce. "First Dates: The Maya Calendar and Writing System Were Not the Only Ones in Mesoamerica—or Even the Earliest." *Natural History,* April 1991, pp. 22–25. Available at http://muweb.millersville.edu/~columbus/data/ant/MARCUS01.ANT (accessed December 8, 2004.

Maya Civilization. Canadian Museum of Civilization Corporation. "Maya Calendars" available at http://www.civilization.ca/civil/maya/mmc06eng.html (accessed August 17, 2004). "Maya Writing and Hieroglyphics" available at http://www.civilization.ca/civil/maya/mmc04eng.html (accessed December 8, 2004).

"The Olmec." *Mesoweb: An Exploration of Mesoamerican Cultures.* Available at http://www.mesoweb.com/olmec/ (accessed December 8, 2004.)

Pringle, Heather. "Temples of Doom." *Discover,* March, 1999. Available at http://www.findarticles.com/cf_dls/m1511/3_20/54359911/p6/article.jhtml?term= (accessed December 8, 2004.)

Parsell, D. L. "Oldest Intact Maya Mural Found in Guatemala." *National Geographic News,* March 22, 2002. Available at http://news.nationalgeographic.com/news/2002/03/0312_0314_mayamurals.html (accessed December 8, 2004).

Ross, John F. "First City in the New World? Peru's Caral Suggests Civilization Emerged in the Americas 1,000 Years Earlier Than Experts Believed." *Smithsonian.* August 2002. Available at http://www.smithsonianmag.si.edu/smithsonian/issues02/aug02/caral.html (accessed December 8, 2004.)

Rostworowski, Maria. "The Incas." Available at http://incas.perucultural.org.pe/english/hissurg4.htm (accessed December 8, 2004.)

Schuster, Angela M. H. "New Tomb at Teotihuacan." *Archaeology, Online Features.* December 4, 1998. Available at http://www.archaeology.org/online/features/mexico/ (accessed December 8, 2004).

Williams, Patrick Ryan, Michael E. Moseley, and Donna J. Nash. "Empires of the Andes." *Scientific American: Discovering Archaeology,* March/April 2000. Available at www.aymara.org/biblio/baul.html (accessed December 8, 2004).

Index

Italic indicates volume number; illustrations are marked by (ill.).

Armies. *See* Military forces
Arrow Knights, *2:* 493
Art
  Aztec, *2:* 512 (ill.), 513–20, 515 (ill.)
  Chavín, *1:* 70–72, 71 (ill.)
  Inca, *1:* 210–16, 213 (ill.)
  kingdom of Chimor, *1:* 144, 144 (ill.), 147 (ill.), 148–49, 149 (ill.), 151–52, 210
  Maya, *2:* 352, 362, 391, 396–404, 397 (ill.), 399 (ill.)
  Moche, *1:* 87, 99–102, 100 (ill.), 101 (ill.)
  Olmec, *2:* 285–86, 292–93, 293 (ill.)
  Sumerian, *1:* 9
  Teotihuacán, *2:* 329–31, 330 (ill.)
  Tiwanaku, *1:* 118 (ill.), 119–20
  Toltec, *2:* 444, 454–55, 455 (ill.)
  Wari, *1:* 133–34, 134 (ill.)
  Zapotec, *2:* 310, 311 (ill.)
Artifacts, *1:* 2, 20, 94; *2:* 262, 277, 316, 334, 438
Artisans
  Aztec, *2:* 497–98, 513–14
  Cancuen, *2:* 417, 419
  Inca, *1:* 196, 224
  kingdom of Chimor, *1:* 148–49
  Teotihuacán, *2:* 320, 326–27
Asian migrants, *1:* 28–31, 32
Aspero, Peru, *1:* 46–47
Astronomers, *2:* 392
Astronomical observatories
  defined, *1:* 76; *2:* 348
  Maya, *2:* 354, 367, 412
  Nazca, *1:* 81
  Zapotec, *2:* 305–6, 308 (ill.), 312
Astronomy
  defined, *2:* 316
  Inca, *1:* 219–20
  Maya, *2:* 349, 411–13
  Olmec, *2:* 296
Atahuallpa
  death of, *1:* 250–51, 252 (ill.)
  Huáscar and, *1:* 176–77, 246, 246 (ill.)
  Huayna Capac and, *1:* 243
  Pizarro and, *1:* 9–10, 248–51, 251 (ill.)
  rule of, *1:* 171, 182
  wife of, *1:* 168

Atlantes, 2: 438, 443, 450 (ill.), 455
Atlatls, 2: 455, 495
Atole, 2: 524
Audiencias, 1: 141
Authoritarian governments, *1:* 122
Aveni, Anthony, *1:* 84
Avenue of the Dead, *2:* 318–19
Aviary, *2:* 502
Axayácatl, *2:* 485
Axe bearers, *2:* 385
Axes, jade, *2:* 351
Ayacucho Valley, Peru, *1:* 123–24, 128
Ayar Anca, *1:* 170
Ayar Cachi, *1:* 170, 171
Ayar Manco. *See* Manco Capac
Ayar Uchu, *1:* 170
Ayllu
  daily life in, *1:* 225–26
  defined, *1:* 36, 106, 156, 180, 200, 222
  development of, *1:* 55
  Inca, *1:* 171, 185, 203–4, 225–26
  present day, *1:* 258
  Tiwanaku, *1:* 115–16
  worship, *1:* 203–4
Aymara people, *1:* 107, 116, 117
Aymoray, *1:* 207
Ayni, 1: 116, 188, 258
Azángaro, Peru, *1:* 124 (ill.), 126
Azcapotzalco, Mexico, *2:* 471, 481, 484
Aztecs
  agriculture, *2:* 461–62, 496–97, 498 (ill.)
  architecture, *2:* 463, 464, 464 (ill.), 523–24
  art, *2:* 512 (ill.), 513–20, 515 (ill.)
  background of, *2:* 467–70
  class system, *2:* 488–92
  creation myths, *2:* 324–25
  daily life, *2:* 520–27, 521 (ill.)
  descendents of, *2:* 549–50, 549 (ill.)
  development of, *2:* 272
  economy, *2:* 477–79, 481, 483–85, 487, 495–99
  empire building, *2:* 471–73, 480–86, 529–30
  epidemics and, *2:* 542–43

Cacao beans, *2:* 420 (ill.), 431 (ill.)
 chocolate from, *2:* 422, 430–31
 defined, *2:* 416, 478
 as money, *2:* 498
Cactus beverage, *2:* 447, 524–25
Cactus, San Pedro, *1:* 70
Cahuachi, Peru, *1:* 76–77
Caiman imagery, *1:* 69; *2:* 292
Cajamarca, Peru, *1:* 158 (ill.), 174, 249–51
Calakmul, Guatemala, *2:* 357, 385
Calculators. *See Quipu*
Calendar Round system, *2:* 307, 312
Calendars. *See also* Sacred calendars; Solar calendars
 Aztec, *2:* 506, 512–13
 Calendar Round system, *2:* 307, 312
 52-year cycle, *2:* 377–78, 410, 506
 Inca, *1:* 219–20
 Long Count, *2:* 283–84, 294, 410–11
 Maya, *2:* 354, 377–78, 406–11, 409 (ill.)
 Nazca line drawings as, *1:* 82
 Olmec, *2:* 283–84, 294, 296, 306
 Teotihuacán, *2:* 331
 two-calendar systems, *2:* 283–84, 294, 296, 306
 Zapotec, *2:* 306–7, 312
Callanca, 1: 156
Calmecac, 2: 463, 493–94, 523
Calpullec, 2: 491
Calpulli, 2: 478, 491, 495, 498, 502, 517
Camelids, *1:* 36, 42–43. *See also* Alpaca; Llamas
Canals, *1:* 61, 110–11. *See also* Irrigation
 Aztec, *2:* 461–62, 464
 kingdom of Chimor, *1:* 152
 Maya, *2:* 424–25
Canatares mexicanos, 2: 519
Cancuen, Guatemala, *2:* 416–19, 418 (ill.)
Capac Raymi, *1:* 207–8
Capac Yupanqui, *1:* 170 (ill.), 171
Captives. *See* Prisoners of war
Caracol, *2:* 367
Caral, Peru, *1:* 49–54, 51 (ill.)

Caravanserai, *1:* 138
Casma Valley, Peru, *1:* 143, 144
Castedo, Leopold, *2:* 490
Castillo, *1:* 64–65
Cat imagery. *See* Feline imagery
Catherwood, Frederick, *2:* 334–38, 340, 345, 362, 364
Cauac Sky, *2:* 399
Caucasoid features, *1:* 29, 31
Cave paintings, *1:* 42
Caves, *2:* 324, 377
Cempoala, Mexico, *2:* 537
Cenotes, *2:* 348, 365, 368, 416, 424
Central Acropolis, *2:* 355
Ceque, 1: 200
Ceramics. *See* Pottery
Ceremonial centers. *See also* specific sites
 vs. cities, *1:* 48
 defined, *1:* 2, 36, 60, 76, 88; *2:* 262, 277, 300, 316, 348
 early Andean, *1:* 35–36
Cerro Baúl, Peru, *1:* 126–27, 127 (ill.), 135
Cerro Blanco, Peru, *1:* 89–92, 96, 102
Cerro Sechín, Peru, *1:* 56, 56 (ill.)
Cerro Victoria, Peru, *1:* 165
Chac, *2:* 375
Chacmool, 2: 438, 443, 455, 455 (ill.)
Chalcatzingo, Mexico, *2:* 284–85
Chan Bahlum, *2:* 359, 361
Chan Chan, Peru, *1:* 137, 139–42, 151 (ill.)
 architecture, *1:* 140–42, 140 (ill.), 141 (ill.)
 Inca defeat of, *1:* 152–53
 kingdom of Chimor and, *1:* 143, 147
 location of, *1:* 139 (ill.)
Chancas, *1:* 172–73, 179, 190
Charisma, *2:* 372
Charles V, *2:* 538, 539 (ill.)
Chasqui, 1: 180, 192, 193 (ill.)
Chavín culture, *1:* 11, 59–73
 architecture, *1:* 64–65, 64 (ill.), 65 (ill.)
 arts and sciences, *1:* 70–72, 71 (ill.)
 decline of, *1:* 72
 economy, *1:* 67–69
 government, *1:* 67

Nazca, *1:* 79
nomads and, *1:* 1
Spanish, *2:* 548
Tiwanaku, *1:* 114–15
Valley of Mexico, *2:* 466
Zapotec, *2:* 306–9
Grains, *1:* 4, 6, 233–34
Grant holders, *2:* 548
Gray, Martin, *2:* 366
Great Ball Court, *2:* 367, 368
Great Festival, *1:* 207–8
Great Ice Age, *1:* 22–23, 22 (ill.), 42
Great Plaza, *2:* 305, 355, 355 (ill.)
Great Pyramid, *2:* 354
Great Speaker, *2:* 488
Grolier Codex, *2:* 401
Group of the Thousand Columns, *2:* 367
Guanaco, *1:* 37, 42, 43, 106
Guano, *1:* 99
Guidon, Niede, *1:* 27
Guilds, *1:* 149

H

Haab. See Solar calendars
Haas, Jonathan, *1:* 54
Hairstyles, *2:* 430
Hallucinogenic drugs
    Chavín and, *1:* 70
    defined, *1:* 61, 122; *2:* 277, 372
    Maya and, *2:* 378
    Olmec and, *2:* 289–90
    Wari and, *1:* 132
Hanan, 1: 156
Harpies, *2:* 292
Harqubus, *1:* 242
Harvest Mountain Lord, *2:* 295
Head sculptures, *2:* 276, 280, 281 (ill.), 282, 292
Head shape, *2:* 432
Health. *See* Medicine
Heartland, *2:* 277
Heaven, *2:* 375–80
Herbs, *1:* 218, 219 (ill.); *2:* 527
Hero Twins, *2:* 376–77, 383
Heyerdahl, Thor, *1:* 143
Hierarchy, *1:* 180, 222; *2:* 478, 530. *See also* Class system
Hieroglyphic Staircase, *2:* 359–60, 362, 364, 399–400

Highlands, *2:* 334
Hispaniola, *1:* 244
Historia del Nuevo Mundo (Cobo), *1:* 168
Historical art, *2:* 397
History of the Incas (Sarmiento de Gamboa), *1:* 168
History of the New World (Cobo), *1:* 168
Honey, *2:* 420
Hooker, Richard, *2:* 340
Horses, *1:* 249; *2:* 263–64, 537
Hostages, *1:* 189
House of Phalli, *2:* 366
House of the Deer, *2:* 365
Houses
    Aztec, *2:* 464
    Inca, *1:* 231–33, 231 (ill.)
    Maya, *2:* 427–28, 428 (ill.)
    Teotihuacán, *2:* 321–22
Huaca. See also Shrines
    Cuzco, *1:* 159–65
    defined, *1:* 37, 88, 156
    priests and, *1:* 206
    worship, *1:* 203–4
Huaca de La Luna, *1:* 89–92, 91 (ill.), 96, 98–99
Huaca de Los Idios, *1:* 46–47
Huaca de Los Sacrificios, *1:* 46–47
Huaca del Sol, *1:* 89–92, 90 (ill.), 96
Huaca Fortaleza, Peru, *1:* 102–3
Huaca Prieta, Peru, *1:* 46
Huaca Rajada, Peru, *1:* 94–95
Huantsán Mountain, Peru, *1:* 70
Huánuco Pampa, Peru, *1:* 158 (ill.), 161–62
Huaqueros, 1: 94
Huari culture. *See* Wari culture
Huarpa people, *1:* 128
Huáscar, *1:* 171, 176, 182, 245–46
Huayna Capac, *1:* 175 (ill.)
    death of, *1:* 176, 244–45
    mummy of, *1:* 239–40
    Pachacutec and, *1:* 173
    rule of, *1:* 171, 175–76, 182, 242–45
Huehuetls, 2: 514
Huejotzingo, Mexico, *2:* 474
Huemac, *2:* 449, 455–56
Huey tlatoanis, 2: 472, 484
Huitzilhuitl, *2:* 484
Huitzilopochtli, *2:* 504, 508 (ill.)
    conquered people and, *2:* 483

Manchán, Peru, *1:* 139 (ill.), 143
Manco Capac, *1:* 167, 167 (ill.), 170–71, 170 (ill.), 201
Manco Inca, *1:* 171, 251–54
Mangrove swamps, *1:* 40–41
Manhood ceremony. *See* Puberty ceremony
Mani, Mexico, *2:* 343
Manly Heart. *See* Tlacaelel
Mano, 2: 429
Marcus, Joyce, *2:* 312
Marketplace, *2:* 320, 327, 463, 498
Marriage
    Aztec, *2:* 520–22
    Inca, *1:* 182, 194, 206, 229–31, 237
    Maya, *2:* 425–26, 427
Masks, *2:* 330 (ill.), 331, 349–51, 360
Mass human sacrifice
    Aztec, *2:* 473–74, 473 (ill.)
    defined, *2:* 438, 458
    Toltec, *2:* 444, 454
Mass production, *1:* 224
Maya, *1:* 13–14; *2:* 333–46
    agriculture, *2:* 422–25
    Ahaw kings, *2:* 380–85
    architecture, *2:* 349, 354–57, 355 (ill.), 359–62, 359 (ill.), 360 (ill.), 364–67, 366 (ill.), 367 (ill.), 398
    art, *2:* 352, 362, 391, 396–404, 397 (ill.), 399 (ill.)
    astronomy, *2:* 349, 411–13
    Aztec and, *2:* 483
    calendars, *2:* 356, 377–78, 406–11
    cities, *2:* 333, 334–38, 347–70, 349 (ill.), 381–82, 425
    class system, *2:* 384–86, 385 (ill.), 388, 421
    Classic era, *2:* 341, 353–65, 383–85, 398, 401, 420
    codex, *2:* 343–44, 344 (ill.), 400–1
    creation myths, *2:* 352
    daily life, *2:* 415–16, 425–30, 434 (ill.)
    dates of, *2:* 339–41
    decline of, *2:* 347–70, 386, 387–89
    description of, *2:* 338–39
    economy, *2:* 415–25

    entertainment, *2:* 431–33
    government, *2:* 371–89, 430–31
    Lacandón, *2:* 435
    languages, *2:* 338–39
    location of, *2:* 339–40, 339 (ill.), 349 (ill.), 393 (ill.), 417 (ill.)
    nobles, *2:* 382, 384–86
    number systems, *2:* 404–6
    population density, *2:* 425
    post-Classic era, *2:* 341, 365–68, 401, 420–21
    pre-Classic era, *2:* 341, 349–53
    rebellion against, *2:* 386, 388
    rediscovery of, *2:* 334–38
    religion, *2:* 371–89
    rise of, *2:* 271–72, 347–70
    Spanish chronicles of, *1:* 16–17
    Spanish conquest of, *1:* 14; *2:* 342, 368–69
    survival of, *2:* 433–35
    universe, *2:* 375–80
    writing systems, *1:* 16; *2:* 271, 341–44, 342 (ill.), 345, 391–96
Mayapán, Mexico, *2:* 333, 365, 368, 388
Mayta Capac, *1:* 170 (ill.), 171
McEwan, Gordon, *1:* 125–26, 133
Meadowcroft Rockshelter, Pennsylvania, *1:* 26, 33
Measles, *2:* 369, 542–43
Meat, *1:* 233; *2:* 425, 524
Medicine
    Aztec, *2:* 526–27
    Inca, *1:* 216, 218–19
Memorization, *1:* 214
Mercenary soldiers, *2:* 458, 469, 471, 478
Merchants, *2:* 490–91
Mérida, Mexico, *2:* 369
Mesoamericans, early. *See* Early Mesoamericans
Mesopotamia, *1:* 5, 6, 9
Mestizo, 1: 242; *2:* 530, 548
Metalwork
    Aztec, *2:* 514
    Chavín, *1:* 71, 71 (ill.)
    Inca, *1:* 210, 228
    kingdom of Chimor, *1:* 144, 144 (ill.), 147 (ill.), 148–49, 149 (ill.), 152, 210
    Moche, *1:* 99–101, 101 (ill.)
    Toltec, *2:* 451
    Wari, *1:* 134

Metate, 2: 429
Mexico, *1:* 244; *2:* 548. *See also*
    Valley of Mexico
Mexico City, Mexico, *1:* 12; *2:*
    546
Meyer, Michael C., *2:* 444, 490
Middle class, *1:* 6, 51
Middle pre-Classic era, *2:* 268
Migrations
    Bering Land Bridge, *1:* 23–25,
        24 (ill.), 32
    First Americans, *1:* 19–34
    Paleoamerican, *1:* 28–31
    Paleo-Indian, *1:* 30
    seaworthy boats and, *1:* 27–28
Military forces. *See also* Warfare
    Aztec, *2:* 468–69, 471–73,
        477–78, 492–95, 494 (ill.),
        499
    development of, *1:* 7
    Inca, *1:* 190–91
    Maya, *2:* 430–31
    mercenary, *2:* 458, 469, 471,
        478
    Teotihuacán, *2:* 325, 329–30
    Toltec, *2:* 448–50
    Wari, *1:* 129
Miller, Mary, *2:* 382
Milpa, 2: 416, 423–25
Minchancaman, *1:* 145, 153
Mines, *1:* 228, 257
Missionaries
    Atahuallpa and, *1:* 249–50
    as chroniclers, *1:* 168
    codex and, *2:* 401
    defined, *1:* 157; *2:* 530
    Maya and, *2:* 342–44, 433–34
Mit'a, 1: 186 (ill.), 187–88, 191
    agriculture and, *1:* 194
    ayllu and, *1:* 116, 188
    defined, *1:* 181, 222
    requirements of, *1:* 187–88,
        227–28, 230
Mitima, 1: 181, 189, 243
Mixcoatl, *2:* 446
Mixe-Zoquean language, *2:* 293
Mixtec, *2:* 313
Moche culture, *1:* 87–103
    architecture, *1:* 89–92, 90 (ill.),
        91 (ill.)
    art and sciences, *1:* 87 (ill.),
        99–102, 100 (ill.), 101 (ill.)
    decline of, *1:* 102–3
    economy, *1:* 99

government and religion, *1:*
    96–99
history, *1:* 92–96
human sacrifice rituals, *1:*
    97–99, 98 (ill.)
important sites, *1:* 89–92
kingdom of Chimor and, *1:*
    143
location of, *1:* 88–92, 89 (ill.)
religion, *1:* 96–99
Mochica culture. *See* Moche cul-
    ture
Moctezuma. *See* Montezuma I
Monarchy, *2:* 480. *See also* Rulers
Mongoloid features, *1:* 28–29
Monogamy, *1:* 194, 222; *2:* 426.
    See also Marriage
Monte Albán, Mexico, *2:* 299,
    303–6
    astronomical observatory, *2:*
        305–6, 308 (ill.), 312
    decline of, *2:* 312–13
    government and economy, *2:*
        306–9
    history of, *2:* 303–6
    location of, *2:* 301, 302 (ill.)
    stone carvings, *2:* 310, 310 (ill.)
    trade with, *2:* 287
Monte Verde, Chile, *1:* 25–26, 27,
    39–40
Montejo, Francisco de, *2:* 369
Montezuma I, *2:* 472–73, 485
Montezuma II, *2:* 532 (ill.)
    capture of, *2:* 539–41, 541 (ill.)
    Cortés, Hernán and, *2:* 448,
        454, 536–43
    death of, *2:* 542
    rule of, *1:* 15; *2:* 474, 485,
        531–33
Montezuma Ikhuicamina. *See*
    Montezuma I
Monumental architecture, *1:* 2–3,
    5–6, 37, 45–48, 48 (ill.), 61
Moon Goddess, *1:* 202; *2:* 373
Moquegua Valley, Peru, *1:* 108,
    126
Morris, Craig, *1:* 67
Moseley, Michael, *1:* 128, 185
Motecuhzoma Xocoyótzin. *See*
    Montezuma II
Moundbuilders, *2:* 452–53
Mummies
    Chincorro, *1:* 41
    defined, *1:* 181, 200

S

T

art and science, *1:* 133–34, 134 (ill.)
decline of, *1:* 134–35
economy, *1:* 130–32
festivals, *1:* 131, 236
government, *1:* 129–30
history, *1:* 128–29
Inca and, *1:* 122–23, 135
location of, *1:* 123–24, 124 (ill.)
Nazca and, *1:* 85
religion, *1:* 132–33
Tiwanaku and, *1:* 105–6, 121, 127–28, 132, 135
Warrior cults, *2:* 443, 449–50, 451, 455, 468, 492
Warrior gods, *2:* 504
Warrior priests, *1:* 95, 95 (ill.), 97
Warriors. *See* Military forces; Warfare
Water sources
  Aztec, *2:* 465
  kingdom of Chimor, *1:* 152–53
  Maya, *2:* 365
  Moche, *1:* 93
  Nazca line drawings and, *1:* 82–84
  Wari, *1:* 128–29
Weapons, *2:* 495
Weaving, *1:* 102, 212–13, 230, 237, 259. *See also* Textiles
Welfare state, *1:* 181, 196
Were-jaguar, *2:* 290, 292
Wheel, *1:* 6
White clay, *2:* 285
White Tezcatlipoca. *See* Quetzalcoatl
Williams, Patrick Ryan, *1:* 131
Wind God (Ehecatl), *2:* 463, 505 (ill.)
Women
  Aztec, *2:* 520, 522
  chosen, *1:* 206–7, 207 (ill.), 208 (ill.), 212
  labor obligations of, *1:* 228, 230
  Maya, *2:* 427, 428–29
  Sapa Inca and, *1:* 182–83
Wool, *1:* 43, 118, 259
Working class
  Aztec, *2:* 491, 494, 497, 499, 523–25
  Caral, *1:* 51
  children of, *1:* 230–31; *2:* 523
  clothing, *1:* 235–36
  daily life of, *1:* 225–36

development of, *1:* 6, 7
festivals for, *1:* 236
food, *1:* 233–35
houses, *1:* 231–33, 231 (ill.); *2:* 427–28, 428 (ill.)
Inca, *1:* 192–94, 196, 203–4, 221, 225–36
labor obligations of, *1:* 227–28
marriage, *1:* 229–31
Maya, *2:* 386, 421, 433–34
Olmec, *2:* 289
Workshops, *2:* 417
World Tree, *2:* 376–77, 382, 400
Wright Codex, *2:* 402
Writing systems. *See also* Glyphs
  Aztec, *2:* 514–20, 515 (ill.)
  development of, *1:* 6
  Maya, *1:* 16; *2:* 271, 341–44, 342 (ill.), 345, 391–96
  Olmec, *2:* 283–84, 293–96, 295 (ill.), 296 (ill.)
  Sumerian, *1:* 9
  Teotihuacán, *2:* 331
  Zapotec, *2:* 303, 310–12

X

Xbalanque, *2:* 376–77
Xi. *See* Olmec culture
Xibalbá, *2:* 375–80
Xihuitl, *2:* 513
Xipe Totec, *2:* 309, 342
Xochicalco, *2:* 445
Xocoatl, *2:* 422, 430–31
Xoloti, *2:* 451

Y

Yahuar Huaca, *1:* 170 (ill.), 171
Yampellec, *1:* 146
Yanaconas, *1:* 222, 228–29
Yax Cha'aktel Xok, *2:* 357
Yax Eb' Xook, *2:* 357
Yax Pasah, *2:* 364–65
Yaxchilan, *2:* 405
Yucatán peninsula, *2:* 335, 341 (ill.)
Yucatec languages, *2:* 344
Yucatecs, *2:* 434
Yum Kaax, *2:* 375
Yupanque, Angelina, *1:* 168

Z

Zacan, 2: 429
Zapotecs, 2: 299–313
    architecture, 2: 304–6, 304 (ill.)
    art, 2: 310, 311 (ill.)
    decline of, 2: 312–13
    glyphs, 2: 271
    government and economy, 2: 306–9

history of, 1: 13; 2: 267, 301–6
location of, 2: 301, 302 (ill.)
Olmec and, 2: 300
religion, 2: 309–10
science, 2: 312
writing and language, 2: 303, 310–12
Zero, 2: 406
Ziegler, Gary, 1: 165
Ziggurat, 1: 3, 9